FILM MUSIC ANALYSIS

Since the establishment of film music studies, there has been a steady growth of serious analytical work on the film music repertoire. *Film Music Analysis: Studying the Score* offers the first collection of essays dedicated to the close investigation of musical structure and meaning in film music. Showcasing scholarship from a diverse and distinguished group of music theorists and musicologists, this book presents the many ways to inspect the inner workings of film music in a manner that is exciting and accessible to anyone curious about this music, regardless of their background in film or music theory.

Each chapter takes as its focus one music-theoretical parameter and explores how that concept can be used to analyze and interpret film music. Covering theoretical concepts that range from familiar categories such as leitmotif and pitch structure to more cutting-edge ideas such as timbral associativity, topic theory, and metrical states, the book provides a toolkit with which to explore this captivatingly varied repertoire. With example analyses drawn from classic and contemporary films, *Film Music Analysis: Studying the Score* is a valuable teaching tool and an indispensable addition to the library of any lover of film and music.

Frank Lehman is Associate Professor of Music at Tufts University, Massachusetts, USA.

Routledge Music and Screen Media Series
Series Editor: Neil Lerner

The **Routledge Music and Screen Media Series** offers edited collections of original essays on music in particular genres of cinema, television, video games and new media. These edited essay collections are written for an interdisciplinary audience of students and scholars of music and film and media studies.

Music in the Role-Playing Game
Heroes & Harmonies
Edited by William Gibbons and Steven Reale

The Soundtrack Album
Listening to Media
Edited by Paul N. Reinsch and Laurel Westrup

Music in Action Film
Sounds Like Action!
Edited by James Buhler and Mark Durrand

Music in Twin Peaks
Listen to the Sounds
Edited by Reba Wissner and Katherine Reed

Women's Music for the Screen
Diverse Narratives in Sound
Edited by Felicity Wilcox

Music in Star Trek
Sound, Utopia, and the Future
Edited by Jessica Getman, Brooke McCorkle Okazaki and Evan Ware

Film Music Analysis
Studying the Score
Edited by Frank Lehman

For more information about this series, please visit: www.routledge.com/Routledge-Music-and-Screen-Media-Series/book-series/RMSM

FILM MUSIC ANALYSIS

Studying the Score

Edited by Frank Lehman

NEW YORK AND LONDON

Designed cover image: © INSAGO / Shutterstock

First published 2024
by Routledge
605 Third Avenue, New York, NY 10158

and by Routledge
4 Park Square, Milton Park, Abingdon, Oxon, OX14 4RN

Routledge is an imprint of the Taylor & Francis Group, an informa business

© 2024 Taylor & Francis

The right of Frank Lehman to be identified as the author of the editorial material, and of the authors for their individual chapters, has been asserted in accordance with sections 77 and 78 of the Copyright, Designs and Patents Act 1988.

All rights reserved. No part of this book may be reprinted or reproduced or utilised in any form or by any electronic, mechanical, or other means, now known or hereafter invented, including photocopying and recording, or in any information storage or retrieval system, without permission in writing from the publishers.

Trademark notice: Product or corporate names may be trademarks or registered trademarks, and are used only for identification and explanation without intent to infringe.

ISBN: 978-0-367-43077-1 (hbk)
ISBN: 978-0-367-43076-4 (pbk)
ISBN: 978-1-003-00117-1 (ebk)

DOI: 10.4324/9781003001171

Typeset in Sabon
by Deanta Global Publishing Services, Chennai, India

CONTENTS

Foreword vii
Introduction: Film and Music, Theory and Analysis ix
Frank Lehman

1 Timbre in Film Music: Making Magic through Tone Color 1
  Chelsea Oden

2 'The click is your friend': Film Scores and Tempo Analysis 20
  Rebecca M. Doran Eaton

3 Tracking Progressions of Heroic Chord Progressions in
  Recent Popular Screen Media 46
  Scott Murphy

4 John Williams's *Star Wars* Themes: Good vs. Evil
  Conflicts as a Structural Principle for Leitmotifs 63
  Mark Richards

5 Topic Theory and Film: Coming of Age in 1994's and
  2019's *Little Women* 87
  Janet Bourne

6 A Matter of Time: Reality and Fantasy through
  Metrical Analysis in Contemporary Hollywood Film 110
  Andrew S. Powell

7	Film Music and Dialogic Form *Charity Lofthouse*	134
8	Tonal Analysis of the Integrated Soundtrack: Music, Sound, and Dialogue in *Baby Driver* *Táhirih Motazedian*	156
9	Analyzing Musical Metamorphoses: Thematic Transformation in Shirley Walker's *Batman* *Frank Lehman*	173
10	Post-Tonal Theory and Hollywood Scores: Three Analytical Vignettes *Erik Heine*	202
11	Attuning Serialism: David Shire's Scores for *The Taking of Pelham One Two Three*, *2010: The Year We Made Contact*, and *Zodiac* *Juan Chattah*	225
12	Romance and the Two Poles of Underscore *James Buhler*	248
List of Contributors		277
Index		280

FOREWORD

While the scholarly conversations about music in film and visual media have been expanding prodigiously since the last quarter of the twentieth century, a need remains for focused, specialized studies of particular films as they relate more broadly to genres. This series includes scholars from across the disciplines of music and film and media studies, of specialists in both the audible as well as the visual, who share the goal of broadening and deepening these scholarly dialogues about music in particular genres of cinema, television, videogames, and new media. Claiming a chronological arc from the birth of cinema in the 1890s to the most recent releases, the *Music and Screen Media* Series offers collections of original essays written for an interdisciplinary audience of students and scholars of music, film, and media studies in general, and interdisciplinary humanists who give strong attention to music. Driving the study of music here is the underlying assumption that music together with screen media (understood broadly, to accommodate rapidly developing new technologies) participates in important ways in the creation of meaning and that including music in an analysis opens up the possibility for interpretations that remain invisible when only using the eye.

The series was designed with the goal of providing a thematically unified group of supplemental essays in a single volume that can be assigned in a variety of undergraduate and graduate courses (including courses in film studies, in film music, and other interdisciplinary topics). We look forward to adding future volumes addressing emerging technologies and reflecting the growth of the academic study of screen media. Rather than attempting an exhaustive history or unified theory, these studies—persuasive explications supported by textual and contextual evidence—will pose questions of musical style, strategies of rhetoric, and critical cultural analysis, as they help us to see, to hear, and ultimately to understand these texts in new ways.

Neil Lerner
Series Editor

INTRODUCTION

Film and Music, Theory and Analysis

Frank Lehman

It has become something of a truism among musicologists that for as long as there has been film, there has been film music. From the stock anthologies that pianists and organists depended on during the silent era, to the symphonic scores and later pop-song compilations that dominated mid-century cinema, to the stylistic eclecticism and timbral experimentalism one hears at the movies today, there appears to be something genuinely indispensable about music to the function of the moving image.

This same indispensability cannot be said, however, for the *analysis* of film music. Prior to the solidification of the field of film music studies in the late 1980s and 1990s, rigorous and technically oriented analysis was isolated and sporadic. Exceptional examples of systematic study—essays by Hans Keller and Lawrence Morton in the 1940s, for example, or a swell of Bernard Herrmann studies in the 1970s and 1980s—provided penetrating insight into the workings of film music and were not afraid to dig deep into technicalities of thematic structure, pitch design, and other such matters that required some music-theoretical expertise to appreciate.[1] But at the time, these contributions did not have a well-developed scholarly discourse from which to draw—nor contribute. Indeed, it was only decades after the formation of music theory as an autonomous discipline in North America that music for any commercial and popular genre would even occur to most academics as worthy of close inspection, much less the basis of a scholarly field.

The reticence to engage with film music at a highly analytical level involves a number of complex historical and aesthetic factors that do not warrant full rehearsal here. Suffice it to say, a movie soundtrack is a tough sell when what one was used to studying (and is professionally *validated* for studying) is closer to Bernd Zimmerman than Hans Zimmer. Despite manifold stylistic linkages to concert music, film composition was considered in the twentieth century at best an adjunct to the Western classical canon—the repertoire at which academic music theory was aimed—and at worst, a perfect negative image of what classical music was supposed to be: Populist instead of high-brow, functional rather than autonomous, conservative rather than path-breaking. And, to be fair to reluctant theorists having been trained on absolute music, a film score is indeed typically a subordinated element of a larger text ('music *for* film'), in a manner even more radical than other genres that were themselves already viewed with some analytical suspicion, like ballet and opera.[2] Add to this the repertoire's ostensible imperative for emotional directness, broad accessibility, and textual legibility, and it becomes explicable why some notable critics would find this style to obviate complex analytical work in the first place. There nevertheless seems something that is, if not completely wrongheaded, at least profoundly premature, in the arguments presented by Theodor Adorno and Hanns Eisler in their jointly-written manifesto *Composing for the Films*. Throughout this brilliant but frustrating and tendentious study, Adorno and Eisler go out of their way to critique the impulse to over-complicate the study of film music by recruiting conceptual apparatuses designed for more 'difficult' aesthetic objects. To employ the tools of High Culture analysis and criticism to describe movie music is for Adorno and Eisler to use 'heavy artillery to shoot sparrows.'[3]

Thankfully for students of music and multimedia, Adorno and Eisler's injunctions are honored almost entirely in the breach today. The intellectual prejudices and bad habits that sanctioned years of analytical neglect of film music are largely gone from the current academic landscape, thanks in no small part to an outpouring of seminal texts on the history, aesthetics, and ideology of music and moving image.[4] One could cite any number of cultural shifts that facilitated this reversal of attitude: The spread across the humanities of popular-culture studies, the growth of parallel creative disciplines like commercial composition and arranging, and the waning power of hierarchical models of musical worth. I like to think that much of this energy and interest in film music comes simply from a belated recognition that this music is really rich and exciting and complex—and that lots of people care deeply about it.

Since the establishment of film musicology, there has been a steady increase in theoretical and analytical work on this repertoire. In the English-speaking world, film scores made their way into the canon of acceptable objects of music-theoretical study tentatively at first. A real measure of academic legitimacy is the occurrence of special issues of general music theory journals dedicated to film, as was the case with two issues of *Indiana Theory Review* in the 1990s and, more recently, *Music Analysis* in the late 2010s.[5] By the time an official 'Film Music and Multimedia' interest group was founded by the Society for Music Theory in 2013, it was clear that film music analysis—as practiced and promulgated by self-identified music theorists—had attained disciplinary stability as a vigorous and firmly established field of inquiry. Interest in film music analysis is high, as evidenced by a flood of recent conferences, monographs, and articles, not to mention many popular offerings in the spirit of 'public musicology,' many of which are cited throughout this present volume.[6]

With a sizable number of both established and fresh-faced music theorists now focused on the systematic study of film music, it is a natural time to consolidate the discourse. *Film Music Analysis: Studying the Score* aims to achieve just this, gathering some of the field's most important voices together to show the very best in advanced music-theoretical and analytical approaches to film music. *Studying the Score* is not meant to be an exercise in inward-looking technicality-for-technicality's-sake, however. A central objective of this volume is to present the many ways in which one can inspect the inner workings of film music in a way that is **accessible** and **exciting** to anyone curious about this repertoire, regardless of their prior music or film theoretical training. Rather than fall back on conceptual and theoretical tools designed for other (generally Western classical) styles, readers will have models of film music analyzed *on their own terms*. When those pre-established tools are invoked, such as *Formenlehre* or tone-row analysis, it is always with the intrinsic limitations and affordances of film in mind.

So, while the authors make no excuses for their use of high-powered theoretical 'artillery'—indeed, its unashamed and frankly overdue deployment is celebrated within these pages!—we do not envision there being only one type of ideal reader. The essays within are written such that they may speak to many audiences: The undergraduate taking a film music appreciation course, the composer looking to explore new expressive resources, or the general music fan who simply wishes to see film music investigated in new and novel ways.

Producing a study that serves both as an authoritative and discipline-fortifying text *and* a user-friendly guide to novices and experts alike poses a special challenge. To ensure both aims are met, *Studying the Score* is organized in a unique and highly deliberate way. Rather than centering on a single genre (as many prior entries in this series have done), nor base individual chapters around case studies of a single filmic text, this book proceeds **parametrically**. Each author chose a specific music-theoretical parameter, and their chapters explore the parameter as a potential analytical focal point, with all the challenges and interpretive opportunities it offers.

These parameters cover a range of the most basic dimensions of structure and meaning in all music. The chapters begin with Chelsea Oden's essay, on tone color in the *Harry Potter* franchise, setting the bewilderingly under-acknowledged parameter of **timbre** where it belongs, right at the beginning of any and all considerations of film musical form and meaning. Rebecca M. Doran Eaton's examination of **tempo** follows, bringing a degree of rigor and hermeneutic depth to a topic similarly unsung but of absolute centrality to the effect of music in multimedia. Rounding off this initial trio of chapters on the 'big three' parameters of musical structure and meaning is Scott Murphy's essay on **tonal harmony**, in which a robust new system for describing and tracking harmonic progressions is offered, with a particularly common 'Heroic' chord succession in contemporary film forming his primary case study.

In his essay on musical **theme**, Mark Richards builds on his previous work on film-thematic archetypes in the pursuit of a sensitive and synthetic overview of the variegated leitmotifs of the *Star Wars* series. Janet Bourne tackles a unit of similar semantic richness, the musical **topic**, extending this critical semiotic category familiar to scholars of eighteenth-century instrumental music to the realm of contemporary cinema, where it is shown to be a remarkably apt analytical device. Topics are also a concern for Andrew S. Powell in his examination of the conjunction of stylistic topoi with musical **meter**, one of the most active and exciting areas in contemporary music theory research, yet whose expressive value has until recently seldom been appreciated in film.

The next three chapters deal with comparatively larger units of musical meaning and deploy and adapt devices originally devised for classical music. Charity Lofthouse brings **form** to the forefront of film score analysis. One of the most highly developed of music-theoretical subdisciplines for Western art music, *Formenlehre* is tricky to apply to a repertoire where immediate dramatic need frequently trumps long-range musical organization, but as Lofthouse demonstrates, we do film scores a great injustice by ignoring the possibility for meticulous formal organization. Táhirih Motazedian offers an ambitious rehabilitation of the parameter of **key** in film music, demonstrating convincingly that, far from a musical epiphenomenon, careful choices regarding key areas, in the right filmic hands, can produce magnificently subtle and impactful scores, much more than the sum of their tonal parts. Rounding off this section of old-fashioned tools in new contexts, Frank Lehman considers the category of **thematic transformation**, a vaunted category among theorists of nineteenth-century opera and programmatic music, but valuable to film and television too, where its innately narratival qualities can more than support but *power* storytelling in a visual medium.

The final three chapters consider musical idiom as itself a parameter worthy of focused analysis. Erik Heine, noting the prevalence of **post-tonal** styles in contemporary scoring, offers a diverse toolkit with which to approach the varied manifestations of music that does not quite adhere to a traditional conception of key or centricity; he advocates for a methodological eclecticism that helps itself to techniques as diverse as neo-Riemannian theory, pitch-class sets, and good old-fashioned Roman numerals, always applied what the music *itself* is telling us in mind. Further delving into the heady waters of atonality is Juan Chattah's essay on **serialism**. While hardly a common technique in contemporary cinema, if it ever was, Chattah's analysis of selected scores by David Shire demonstrates what great film music analysis should be: Rigorous but not dry, interpretively-minded, and backed up by a deep feeling for a composer's personal idiolect, as well as what audiences can hear—and can be encouraged, with gentle guiding, to hear. Rounding off the collection is James Buhler's philosophically-minded treatment of dramatic **underscore** as a locus of complex and sometimes contradictory, but always productive, poles of meaning and affect. His highly original treatment of films like *Now Voyager* and *Casablanca*—scores that are firmly within the 'film music canon' in terms of prior attention and appreciation—is a fitting conclusion to this volume in its synthesis of long-studied texts and cutting-edge analytical and conceptual perspectives.

Notes

The editor wishes to thank the many people involved in bringing *Film Music Analysis: Studying the Score* to fruition: Series Editor Neil Lerner, Managing Editor at Routledge Genevieve Aoki, Editorial Assistant Neha Peri, and Senior Project Manager at Deanta Rachel Cook. Profoundest thanks goes to Erin K Maher for preparing this book's index, and the eleven brilliant contributors whose patience, diligence, creativity, and enthusiasm made preparing this volume a true pleasure.

1 See, for example, Hans Keller, *Film Music and Beyond: Writings on Music and the Screen, 1946–59* (ed. Christopher Wintle, London: Plumbago Books and Arts, 2006); and Lawrence Morton's contributions to *Hollywood Quarterly* in the 1940s (e.g., 'The Music of *Objective Burma*,' *Hollywood Quarterly* 1.4, 1946: 378–395). For an overview of the many important foundational studies of Bernard Herrmann's music from analysts including Fred Steiner, Roy Prendergast, and Graham Bruce, see David Neumeyer, 'Film Music and Music Theory: On the Intersection of Two Traditions' in *Music in the Mirror* (eds. Andreas Giger and Thomas J. Mathiesen, Lincoln: University of Nebraska Press, 2002).

2 This is to say nothing of the difficulty in accessing the musical 'text' itself, if it even exists in a stable form. Analysts used to having nicely notated and definitive scores at their fingertips often face frustration with the difficulty in obtaining such seemingly indispensable resource when it comes to film soundtracks. Indeed, it is a distinct point of pride that every analysis, every example, in this volume comes solely from meticulously prepared transcriptions by each chapter's author.

3 Adorno and Eisler, *Composing for the Films* (London: Continuum, [1947] 2007: 107). The context for this phrase is as part of a polemical critique of Sergei Eisenstein's analysis of Prokofiev's score to his own film *Alexander Nevsky* in *The Film Sense* (trans. Jay Leyda, San Diego: Harcourt Brace & Company, [1942] 1975: 157–216). Eisenstein's reading of the cue 'Battle on the Ice' recruits elaborate visual metaphors and intricate diagrams to explain the score's interaction with visual motifs and contribution to the scene's build up of tension. Adorno and Eisler criticize Eisenstein for overloading his analytic metaphors and reading the audio-visual interface too literally. Yet Eisenstein's surprisingly nuanced and self-reflexive interpretation of the score deserves more credit; certainly, it was written with admirable analytical zeal, and repays the close filmic reader of *Nevsky*. See also Nicholas Cook (*Analysing Musical Multimedia*, Oxford: Oxford University Press, 1998: 61–67) for a more deeply theorized, if still critical perspective on Eisenstein's analysis. See also Andrew S. Powell's chapter in this volume.

4 Among the best representatives of this outpouring are Mervyn Cooke, *A History of Film Music* (Cambridge: Cambridge University Press, 2008); Michel Chion, *Audiovision* (trans. Claudia Gorbman, New York: Columbia University Press, 1994); Kathryn Kalinak, *Settling the Score: Music and the Classic Hollywood Score* (London: University of Wisconsin Press, 1992); and the foundational Claudia Gorbman, *Unheard Melodies: Narrative Film Music* (Bloomington: University of Indiana Press, 1987).

5 See *Indiana Theory Review* Vols. 11 (1990) and 19 (1998) and *Music Analysis* Vol. 37.1 (2018).

6 A short and by no means exhaustive list of significant large-scale screen music-theoretical studies to come out of the past 15 years include: Scott Murphy, 'An Eightfold Taxonomy of Harmonic Progressions and Its Application to Triads Related by Major Third and Their Significance in Recent Screen Music,' *Journal of Music Theory* 67.1 (2023: 141–169); Daniel Obluda, 'Topics in Hollywood Scores: Using Topic Theory to Expand on Recent Neo-Riemannian Analyses of Film Music' (PhD diss., University of Colorado Boulder, 2021); Chelsea Oden, 'There is a Body in the Sound: Timbre and Embodiment in the Overlap of Film, Music, and Dance' (PhD diss., University of Oregon, 2021); Steven Rahn, 'Beyond the Leitmotif: Musical Narration in the Post-Classical Film Score' (PhD diss., University of Texas at Austin, 2021); James Buhler, *Theories of the Soundtrack* (New York: Oxford University Press, 2018); Emilio Audissino, *Film/Music Analysis: A Film Studies Approach* (Switzerland: Palgrave MacMillan, 2017); Frank Lehman, *Hollywood Harmony: Musical Wonder and the Sound of Cinema* (New York: Oxford University Press, 2018); Táhirih Motazedian, 'To Key or Not To Key: Tonal Design in Film Music' (PhD diss., Yale University, 2016); Mark Richards, 'Film Music Themes: Analysis and Corpus Study,' *Music Theory Online* 22.1 (2016); David Neumeyer, *Meaning and Interpretation in Music for Cinema* (Bloomington: University of Indiana Press, 2015); and Ronald Rodman, *Tuning In: American Narrative Television Music* (New York: Oxford University Press).

1
TIMBRE IN FILM MUSIC
Making Magic through Tone Color

Chelsea Oden

What Is Timbre?

In a famous scene from *Harry Potter and the Deathly Hallows, Part 2* (2011) [41:46–43:22], Professor McGonagall (Maggie Smith) waves her wand at stone soldiers lofted in the walls of Hogwarts castle. '*Piertotum Locomotor!*' she incants. The soldiers come to life, crash to the ground, rise, and march forward to defend Hogwarts in its final battle. McGonagall's spell summons more than living stone: It also summons an orchestra. Composed and conducted by Alexandre Desplat, and orchestrated by Jean-Pascal Beintus, Bill Newlin, Conrad Pope, Nan Schwartz, and Clifford J. Tasner, the cue's warm, midrange strings propel the soldiers forward. The strings infuse this moment with a beautifully empathetic sense of the epic—they are sinewy, communal, and steadfast, the sounds of muscle, togetherness, and a singular purpose. Even with the same poetic melody—a downward stepwise falter that recovers and leaps upward—other musical tone colors would have changed the heart of this moment. Were the strings replaced with piano, McGonagall's spell and the fate of Hogwarts would feel colder, distant, and perhaps tragic. A brass choir might have colored the scene with a more militaristic tone, drawing attention to the ritual of the battle more than the creatures enlisted into it. A kazoo would have ripped the film's fabric entirely.[1] This chapter is about musical tone color, or *timbre*, and how it creates meaning in a film.

For those outside the world of music scholarship, *timbre* may be an unfamiliar term, even though its impacts are some of the most immediate. When we as music scholars talk about timbre, we are referring to the quality of a musical sound. Timbre is what makes an acoustic guitar sound

DOI: 10.4324/9781003001171-1

different from a marimba, what makes your voice sound distinct from mine. *If timbre is such a foundational characteristic of musical sound,* you might be wondering, *then why haven't I heard more about it?* The reason, simply put, is that timbre is hard to talk about. Imagine, for example, that I have never heard a clarinet and you are tasked with describing its sound to me. Maybe you turn to the Vienna Symphonic Library's description of the sound characteristics of the B♭ clarinet for assistance:

> *Rich, mellow, warm, gentle, melodic, vocal, round, lustrous, brilliant, bright, dark, menacing, dramatic, explosive, incisive, shrill, reedy, pale, lively.*[2]

Though vivid, the various adjectives could just as easily describe the sound of an oboe, English horn, or bassoon as that of a clarinet. Cross-modally, they reference luminance (lustrous, brilliant, bright, dark, pale), temperature (warm), shape (round), movement (explosive, incisive, gentle, lively), demeanor (mellow, menacing, dramatic), taste (rich), and mode of production (vocal, reedy).[3] Only 'shrill' and 'melodic' are really words about sound. And at that, 'shrill' draws on onomatopoeia (the use of a word that sounds like what it means), while 'melodic' suggests, instead, notions of pitch and rhythm. Despite the evocative description, it is doubtful that I would be able to know the sound of a clarinet based on description alone.

The absence of consistent language to describe timbre is the result of what musicologist Cornelia Fales has called the 'paradox of timbre.'[4] Fales writes: 'To the general listener, [...] pitch and loudness are things a sound does, timbre is what a sound is.'[5] In other words, we tend to think of sounds in terms of the physical objects that produce them. The sound of a clarinet *is* a clarinet. The sound of your voice *is* your voice.

Fales' 'timbral paradox' also tells us that we do not hear sounds 'as they are.' She argues that we interpret sound through a process called 'perceptualization.' Perceptualization is the way our brain explains timbre to us. Unlike a spectrograph, which can collect relatively unmediated sonic data, our perception of timbre is largely shaped by our own experiences. Perceptualization involves, to borrow from Megan Lavengood, 'culture, identity, and other sociological and non-acoustic components' as our brain and body decide which sonic information is important, what it means, and how we feel about it.[6]

In Western music scholarship, the timbral paradox—that we perceive sound in terms of objects and that our perception of sound is subjective—has resulted in the tendency to focus on pitch, relegating timbre to the status of a secondary parameter.[7] Despite the challenge of talking about timbre, an increasing number of music scholars are addressing timbre centrally in their work. As the next section shows, timbre scholarship does not merely seek to fill in a gap but to understand more deeply what is perhaps the most fundamental element of music.

Why Is Timbre Important?

Zachary Wallmark and Roger Kendall have argued that timbre is powerful, in part, because it has encyclopedic meaning. They write:

> Timbre [...] [provides] access to an encyclopedic range of non-timbral associations. A *warm* sound implicitly references all other kinds of experiences of *warmness*: the warm cat on your lap, the warm light seeping into your room on a spring morning, the warm laugh of your son. When we describe timbre, we're often describing other kinds of experiences that resemble in certain nonobjective ways the dynamics of what we hear. [...] The notorious 'problem' of talking about timbre may, in fact, be its greatest asset.[8]

In other words, timbre is full of meaning. It is literally *meaningful*. Three of the most striking ways timbre is meaningful are through its physical relationship with our environment, through its relationship with our bodies, and through its relationship with our cultural experiences. These three ways of meaning are inextricably linked—timbre is objectively physical *and* subjectively perceived at once.

Timbre is deeply connected with the spatial and material aspects of our physical environment.[9] Through timbre, we can tell the size of an object, its location relative to us, if it is moving or still, the materials it's made of, and perhaps even its construction and shape.[10] We can tell if we are listening in a large space or a small one, in an echoey space or a dry one, in a crowded space or an empty one. We can tell if we are listening through walls, water, an old radio, a megaphone, or, a mask. In film music, this aspect of timbre is crucial. Film constantly relies on sound to give us a visceral sense of the physics displayed on screen, and musical timbre can expand this physics meaningfully.[11]

Consider, for example, how timbre manipulates the feeling of physical space in 'The Steward of Gondor,' a famous scene from *The Lord of the Rings: The Return of the King* (2003) [1:09:30–1:10:50].[12] The hobbit Pippin (Billy Boyd) sings 'Edge of Night' for Denethor (John Noble), the unsound steward of Gondor's throne. Denethor has just ordered his own son, Faramir (David Wenham), into the throes of a needless and hopeless battle. In the following transcription of Pippin's lyrics, the text shading reflects the resonance of Pippin's voice. The lighter-colored text corresponds with a drier vocal tone while increasingly dark text corresponds with an increasingly resonant tone color:

Home is behind, the world ahead.
And there are many paths to tread.
Through shadow, to the edge of night.
Until the stars are alight.

Mist and shadow,
Cloud and shade.
All shall fade.
All shall... fade.

Pippin's voice begins intimately—it sounds as though it has been recorded in a small room with a closely placed microphone. Over the course of his song, his voice becomes more resonant. It is the sound of an invisible, expanding space. I *feel* the physical opening of the world Pippin describes, its many 'paths' swirling in resonance around me. Pippin's voice contrasts deeply with cuts to Denethor's violent, close-mic'ed eating. This sonically represents Denethor as the true perpetrator of violence while the battlefield is shrouded in Pippin's mournful, spacious prayer. As an orc raises his bow to draw the battle's first arrow, dry, tensely rising strings emerge in the underscore. In tandem with the orcish weapon's tensioning bowstring, the orchestral strings grow thicker, louder, and more dissonant. The dry strings cannot physically emanate from the same space as Pippin's reverberant utterance: Pippin's song is from a world of hope, the orc's arrow from a world of death. Over the rising strings, Pippin sings, 'All shall fade, all shall...' The release of arrows interrupts the strings and Pippin's voice. The camera cuts to red juices dripping down Denethor's chin and his unnervingly close-mic'ed chewing. Pippin's final 'fade' is no longer resonant. Not only do I feel the sudden collapse of the invisible resonant space, but I also *feel* that a single, irreversible 'path' has been chosen. In this example, the invisible physics that is visceral in the timbre of Pippin's voice conveys a hopeful and tragic prayer against the violently doomed battle.

The spatiality of timbre discussed above is powerful because I feel it in my body. Music theorist Arnie Cox describes embodiment as the 'bodily processing of musical sounds.'[13] He argues that part of the way humans make meaning of music, including its timbre, is through a kind of physical empathy. His mimetic hypothesis holds that as we listen to music, we imagine not only the physical properties of the thing producing the sound but also what it would be like *to be* the sound.[14] This means that timbre in film music does more than represent physics: It physically immerses us.

As film scholar Vivian Sobchack observes, discussing the crucial role of embodiment in the cinematic experience, 'our fingers, our skin and nose and lips and tongue and stomach and all the other parts of us understand what we see in the film experience.'[15] Resonating sympathetically with Sobchack, music theorist Juan Chattah writes about embodiment in film music specifically:

> It is primarily through embodiment [...] that music functions phenomenologically within a film. Embodiment mediates signification, enabling the music to guide the audience's attention toward particular visual events, [...] to trigger a myriad of bodily states, and ultimately to present a unique perspective on the discourse of characters and cinematic narrative.[16]

When Pippin sings 'Edge of Night,' for instance, I hear in his solo voice the experience of singing alone. My body tells me that the expanding reverberance in Pippin's vocal timbre is not merely spaciousness but also emptiness—a space without other bodies. Likewise, the strings that build to the first arrow's release beckon my body to hold its breath, to strain its muscles, to *feel* the continuing tension of the bowstring, even as the image cuts away from it.

Finally, timbre is important because it has cultural meaning.[17] In the sound world of Harry Potter, for instance, part of what makes Hogwarts castle feel old is the use of historical English instrumentation. Consider the 'Double Trouble' choral performance from *Harry Potter and the Prisoner of Azkaban* (2004) [23:52], composed and conducted by John Williams who set the text from Shakespeare's *Macbeth*, and sung by the London Oratory School Schola. The combination of nearly basso continuo-style bassoon and harpsichord, large, resonant drum, and commentating recorder all point to Baroque-era stylistic traits. Maddy Shaw Roberts, writing for *Classic FM*, described the musical aesthetic as 'straight out of an early Purcell opera.'[18] Jamie Lynn Webster discusses a similar timbral reference in *Harry Potter and the Chamber of Secrets* (2002) [1:17:17] when headless horsemen ghosts crash through Hogwarts' ornate windows to the sound of English Renaissance crumhorns, shawms, and sackbuts. Describing this cue, which was composed and performed by the early-music ensemble The Dufay Collective, Webster writes:

> [T]he viewer hears an ensemble of reeds, horns, and percussion instruments playing a tune akin to Renaissance dance music which refers to the notion of medieval pageantry at Hogwarts. [...] This example seems more like source music than the Renaissance tune used for Nearly-Headless Nick in the second film because the specialized instruments stand apart more from the conventional orchestral timbres.[19]

These culturally, historically, and stylistically situated timbres, in other words, help us to hear Hogwarts as a centuries-old, European castle.

In sum, musical timbre in film is powerful because we experience it through our knowledge of physical laws, through our own bodies, and through cultural lenses. For several reasons, a useful case study to explore these facets more deeply is spells performed in the Harry Potter film series. First, because timbre is deeply connected with physical experience and magic is concerned with warping physical reality, the musical timbres tasked with sonifying these specific magical acts can teach us about embodiment and imagination, about physically believable renderings of the physically impossible. Additionally, as an integral part of the Harry Potter universe, the musical timbre of spells can reveal the mechanics of magic itself (*Where does magic come from? What does magic do?*) as well as what it means to perform magic (*Is magic a curious, awe-inspiring thing? Is it a tool? A weapon? Does it have consequences?*). This in turn has implications about the potential impact of musical timbre in narrative films beyond the Harry Potter universe.

More broadly, the music of the Harry Potter film series is attractive because of its historical and cultural context. It traversed the decade from 2001 to 2011, a period that saw an increase in timbrally-motivated atmospheric and minimalist film scores. En route, it amassed $7.7 billion in box offices worldwide with its final entry, *Harry Potter and the Deathly Hallows – Part 2*, becoming the third-highest-grossing film in the world at the time.[20] The franchise includes the voices of dozens of individual creative artists: Composers (John Williams, Patrick Doyle, Nicholas Hooper, and Alexandre Desplat); orchestrators (including Conrad Pope, Eddie Karam, Patrick Doyle, James Shearman, Lawrence Ashmore, John Bell, Alastair King, Julian Kershaw, Geoff Alexander, Simon Whiteside, Bradley Miles, Jeff Atmajian, Daryl Griffith, Jean-Pascal Beintus, Alexandre Desplat, Nan Schwartz, Richard Stewart, Clifford J. Tasner, and Bill Newlin); sound designers (including Randy Thom, Eddy Joseph, Dennis Leonard, Richard Beggs, David Evans, and James Mather); and directors (Chris Columbus, Alfonso Cuarón, Mike Newell, and David Yates)—all of whom, in some way, negotiated what the sound world had been and what it could be. In a way, spells in Harry Potter represent a multifaceted, decade-long conversation about musical meaning in film.

Defining a Semiotic Approach to Timbre in Film Music

Because film music carries such meaningful and complex associations, some film music theorists have turned to semiotics as a powerful analytical tool.[21] Semiotics is the study of signs—that is, ways we communicate meaning. This chapter will use a stripped-down version of semiotics as developed by Charles Sanders Peirce to look specifically at timbre in film music. Three types of signs from Peircean semiotics help us to understand three basic ways musical timbres create meaning in film: Index, icon, and symbol.

An *index* is a type of sign that indicates a cause–effect relationship. A musical timbre is *indexical* of anything that seems to produce it. For example, in *Harry Potter and the Sorcerer's Stone* (2001) [1:50:22–1:50:51], the central trio—Harry (Daniel Radcliffe), Ron (Rupert Grint), and Hermione (Emma Watson)—confront Hagrid (Robbie Coltrane) playing John Williams's 'Hedwig's Theme' on a recorder while sitting on the steps of his hut. Because we perceive Hagrid as causing the recorder sound, the recorder's timbre is indexical of Hagrid's playing.

An *icon* is a type of sign that resembles what it signifies. During a transition scene in *Harry Potter and the Prisoner of Azkaban* [28:48], for example, we hear a fluttering flute solo underscore the flight of a bluebird that meets its end in the branches of the Whomping Willow. The flute's timbre is iconic of the fluttering bird: The speediness and virtuosic nature of the solo map onto the unpredictable but fluid twists and turns of the bird's flight, its airiness is like the breeze through which the bird flits, and the small instrument it indexes (the flute) is small in body like the bird. The flute's timbre is not the literal sound of the bird's flight (index) but instead *resembles* the bird's flight, acting as an icon.

A *symbol* is a type of sign whose meaning is arbitrary and relies on a pre-defined cultural context rather than a directly discernible material (indexical) or metaphorical (iconic) linkage with the signified. In *Harry Potter and the Sorcerer's Stone* when Harry's wand chooses him, for instance, wordless choral voices haunt the scene [28:00], symbolizing the workings of fate. Cultural knowledge of the context within the Harry Potter world contributes to reading this moment as fateful—this wand connects Harry with the dark wizard Voldemort, whom he is destined to fight to the death. Choral voices also popularly signal the workings of fate in other fantasy media. John Williams' aptly named cue 'Duel of the Fates' for the deadly, epic lightsaber battle in *Star Wars: Episode I – The Phantom Menace* (1999), is an exemplar of this convention. The choral voices in Harry's first wand scene thus symbolize fate by relying on knowledge of both the Harry Potter universe and fantasy film score tropes more broadly.

Harry's first wand scene further shows how index, icon, and symbol can deepen one another. First, the choral voices' fateful symbolism is enriched by an indexical relationship: The host of voices may very well emanate from the wand itself. As we learn later in the series, a wand keeps a record of every spell it has cast, in a way containing the voices of its previous users. Second, the wordlessness of the chorus has iconic implications: The voices are *like* a mythic presence narrating and guiding the course of events from a mysterious realm. Through these many layers of meaning, Harry's first wand scene foreshadows fate both metaphorically and viscerally.

TABLE 1.1 Three semiotic categories

Sign type	How it signifies	Example
Index	Caused or produced by something	Recorder timbre is produced by Hagrid playing recorder
Icon	Resembles, mimics, or imitates something	Flute timbres mimic bluebird flying into Whomping Willow
Symbol	Relies on cultural system or context	Choral timbres symbolize fate when Harry gets his wand

In sum, a timbre functions as an index when it refers to something that produces it; an icon when it resembles, mimics, or imitates something; and a symbol when its meaning relies on a cultural system or context. These three definitions are summarized in the Table 1.1.

Each of these sign-types connects with a concept in film music theory *and* with a question about magic in the Harry Potter universe. First, we will see that musical timbre and index relate to the film theory concept of diegesis. This will connect with the question: *What are the physical origins of magic?* Second, we will see that musical timbre and icon relate to the technique of mickey-mousing—highly literal-minded, closely synchronized scoring—as it pertains to embodiment. Timbre's iconic meanings will connect with the question: *What are the physical qualities of magic?* Finally, we will see that musical timbre and symbol relate to theories of *leit-timbre* (the association of a timbre with a character, place, or idea), topic theory, and broader narrative symbolism while connecting with the question: *What does it mean to perform magic?*

The Physical Origins of Magic: Index and the Diegetic Boundary

Magic shortcuts our reality to produce physically impossible events. The diegetic boundary suggests a fundamental physics of its own sort in the sound space of film. *Diegetic* sounds occur within the story world and can in principle be heard by the characters: For example, when Professor Lupin (David Thewlis) puts on music for his students to confront the Boggart in *Harry Potter and the Prisoner of Azkaban* [0:42:50]. *Non-diegetic* sounds occur outside of the story world and cannot be heard by the characters. In the 'Change of Seasons' sequence from the first film, for example, Harry walks through a snowy courtyard with Hedwig on his arm [1:36:36] but does not literally hear the lyrical music that accompanies their walk.[22] We, the audience, can hear it, but Harry and Hedwig cannot.

Because the diegetic boundary marks which musical sounds are physically real to characters, and because magic plays with physical reality, the question of music's role in magical physics is especially curious. Timbre, as an indicator of a sound's physicality, is central to this curiosity. Together, musical timbre, the diegetic boundary, and index offer answers to the questions: *What does magic sound like?* and *Where does magic come from?*

In the case of casting spells, musical timbre often breaks the diegetic boundary to serve as the sound of magic. For example, consider the spell *Immobulus*, cast by Hermione in *Harry Potter and the Chamber of Secrets* to sedate a fiendish horde of pixies wreaking havoc in the Defense Against the Dark Arts classroom [0:36:33–0:37:56]. When Hermione yells '*Immobulus*!' and her wand ignites with an explosive sound effect, the music sounds in the non-diegetic realm, inaudible to the characters. But then, the spell's magical effect—a sudden, somewhat icy stillness—materializes as a musical sound. Hermione summons harp glissandi, sustained upper register strings, and a softly shimmering bell-tree—almost like wind chimes—to her world to freeze the pixies. In crossing the diegetic boundary into the perceptible realm of the characters, musical timbre acts as an index of magic.

See Example 1.1 and Figure 1.1 for a visualization of this timbral spell. Because musical sounds break into the characters' world *to be the sound of magic*, we can theorize that music and magic emanate from the same

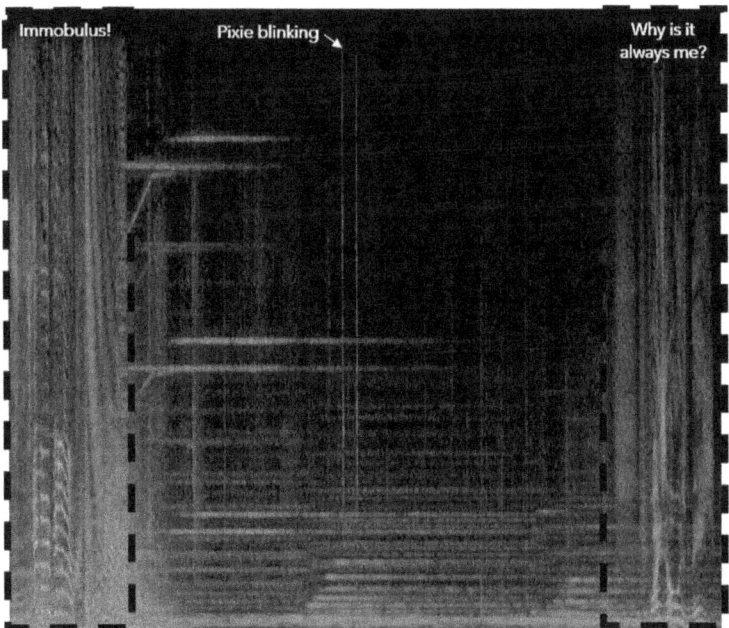

FIGURE 1.1 Annotated spectrogram of *Immobulus*.

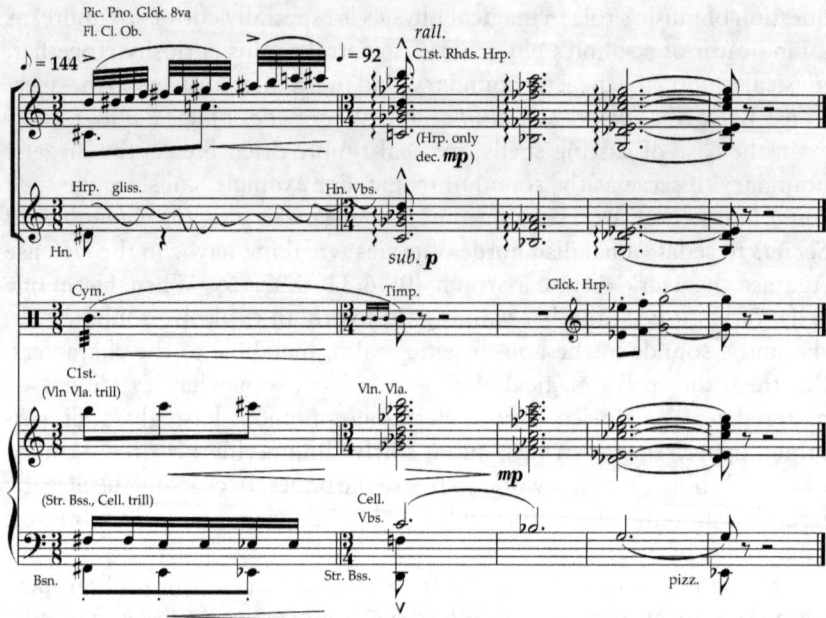

EXAMPLE 1.1 Williams, *Harry Potter and the Chamber of Secrets*, 'Flying Pixies,' underscoring *Immobulus* (author's transcription).

narrative *and physical* space—a space just beyond the everyday reach of the characters (Example 1.1).

The physically transformative impact of music as the sound of magic resonates with Robynn Stilwell's theorization of the diegetic boundary as a fantastical gap.

She writes:

> The border crossing is not so much an event as a process, not simply a crossing, or even passing through distinct intermediary states, but a trajectory, a vector, a gesture. It unfolds through time, like film, like music.[23]

Musical spell sounds in the Harry Potter films are the embodiment of the fantastic physics Stilwell describes. Proposing a related model of non-diegetic music as a supernatural force peering into the diegesis, Kevin Donnelly notes:

> This notion of the paranormal is particularly suited to describing and conceptualizing non-diegetic music in film, which has an origin outside the diegetic world of the film it inhabits[.][24]

Underscores exist within films as a spectral presence, a celestial voice of God, seemingly appearing from nowhere, almost as if from heaven itself.[25]

Magic and its musical sound do indeed 'seemingly [appear] from nowhere.' Donnelly goes on to argue that non-diegetic music can be conceptualized as a demon that possesses and controls both the characters and the audience. Though there are instances of literal spiritual possession in the cinematic Potterverse, performed spells point to different physical rules about magic.[26] Rather than possessing characters of their own free will, musical magic tends to act like a conscious well of energy that the characters channel and guide. Parallel to the wand-wielding wizard is the conductor waving a baton before an orchestra. When musical magic arrests characters, it is usually at someone's bidding.[27]

Qualities of Spells: Icon and Embodiment

Both music and magic invite us to use imagination. Timbre scholar Isabella van Elferen describes the relationship between music and magic in popular fantasy media this way:

> Fantasy is a curiously musical genre. [...] Music suggests the possibility of another reality: a world or universe more beautiful, more harmonic, more brilliant than ours. The simple fact of its sound makes music lift the veil of the supernatural, [...] making audible a fragment of that other world by traversing the timespace from then and there to here and now. It is because of its otherworldly origins that music is often described in fantasy literature as sounding like 'nothing ever heard before.'[28]

Because musical and magical sound are, in part, acts of imagination, we can believe that musical sound *is* the sound of magic (index) and at the same time recognize that musical sound *resembles* magic (icon), acting as a best guess at magic's mystery. The way in which music resembles the physical qualities of magic is nicely illustrated with one of the most widely recognized spells of the Harry Potter series: *Expecto Patronum*, an enchantment used to repel soul-sucking creatures called Dementors that feed on despair. Also called the Patronus Charm, it creates a bright white shield that sometimes coalesces into a protective guardian figure. *Expecto Patronum* is advanced magic, usually requiring years of training to produce as it relies on the caster's ability to focus on a deeply happy memory.

As seen in Table 1.2, almost every instance of the charm involves a warm, pulsating sound effect overlaid with a sustained chorus and intermittent or melodic brass. The video essayist and multimedia editor Evan

TABLE 1.2 All instances of the Patronus Charm

Patronus #	Film and timestamp	Description
Patronus 1	*Prisoner of Azkaban* [0:22:17]	Lupin casts the spell wordlessly. • Shield only, no guardian figure • Preceded by brass and flute • Underscored by voices, warm sound effect
Patronus 2	*Prisoner of Azkaban* [1:08:48]	Harry attempts to cast the spell and fails. • No guardian figure or shield • Predicting brass leads into Lily's scream • No voices or warm sound effect
Patronus 3	*Prisoner of Azkaban* [1:10:12]	Harry first casts the spell against a Boggart. • Shield only, no guardian figure • Preceded by flute • Underscored by voices, warm sound effect • Triumphant brass concludes the spell
Patronus 4	*Prisoner of Azkaban* [1:43:15]	Harry attempts to save himself and Sirius and fails. • White shield briefly sustains then collapses • Predicting brass • No voices, only sound effect
Patronus 5	*Prisoner of Azkaban* [1:44:11]	The spell saves Harry and Sirius, caster unknown. • No audible incantation • Guardian figure, then shield • Harp, voices, warm sound effect, intermittent brass, chimes
Patronus 6	*Prisoner of Azkaban* [2:01:01]	Harry casts the spell to save himself and Sirius. • Shield and guardian figure • Predicting brass • Underscored by voices, warm sound effect, and lyrical French horn
Patronus 7	*Order of the Phoenix* [0:04:08]	Harry casts the spell to save himself and Dudley. • Shield and guardian figure • Underscored by voices, warm sound effect, low brass, and low timpani
Patronus 8	*Deathly Hallows P. 2* [1:06:44]	Aberforth casts the spell wordlessly during the Battle of Hogwarts. • Pulsating cylinder of light rings, no shield or guardian figure • Underscored by warm sound effect and Desplat's 'Statues' cue—strings and brass

Puschak, using the handle Nerdwriter, describes the Patronus Charm as being 'built out of voices, a chorus of angels that fits with that heavenly projection of your soul without fear.'[29] Puschak centralizes choral voices as the essence of *Expecto Patronum*. The voices are highly effective as this specific magical sound. Indexically, I know that to produce a controlled, sustained, and resonant vocal tone (like the ones I hear in the spell), my body must be in a safe and stable place. This timbre is the result of taking a breath and supporting it uninterrupted by violence. Resembling the spell's peaceful and powerful impact, the timbre functions as an icon, its impact enabled by and deepened through bodily self-knowledge.

The hovering, luminous choral voices are likewise iconic of the enchantment's luminous white shield. Several scholars have written about the relationship between sound quality and metaphors of luminance. Zachary Wallmark and Roger Kendall, for instance, have discussed the prevalence of the SOUND IS LIGHT conceptual metaphor in psychological timbre research of the past four decades.[30] (See also Rebecca Eaton's contribution to this volume for other film-musically pertinent conceptual metaphors.) Wallmark and Kendall show that luminance is among the most common categories of timbre description shared across multiple languages.[31] I would argue that the luminance of the voices in *Expecto Patronum* differs from many of the ways scholars tend to talk about timbral brightness. The voices are not piercing, nasal, shrill, narrow, or abrasive, as descriptions of 'bright' timbres often suggest. Instead, they are individually clear, resonant, and open, expanding into their environment just like the light of the spell's white shield. Collectively, they amass in a shimmer of harmonically dense seconds that make for a full, rich, thick, encompassing sort of brightness— as full-bodied and powerful as the luminous stag at the shield's center.

The first time we experience the Patronus Charm in the Harry Potter films (Patronus 1 in Table 1.2), it is cast wordlessly by an expert, Professor Lupin. He drives away a Dementor whose presence is most unwelcome in the train cabin he shares with Hermione, Ron, and Harry. As the white shield emanates from Professor Lupin's wand, the luminous soprano voices are joined by a low, warm pulsating sound effect. The sound effect is grounding, linear, and smooth, in spite of its fluctuations. In combination with the luminous voices and the spell's white shield, it truly feels as though I am pushing something—an impending darkness—gradually and gracefully away from me. Though Professor Lupin quickly expels the Dementor, Harry nonetheless falls victim to its dark effects. In quick succession, the choral voices in the soundtrack begin to fade and are overlaid by the distant voice of Harry's late mother, Lily, crying, 'Harry!' Simultaneously the camera zooms in towards Harry's wide pupil until the screen is completely black. Lily's voice then blends with a crescendoing train whistle that, alongside Hermione's concerned questioning, stirs Harry back to consciousness.

In contrast to Patronus 1, Harry's first successful attempt (Patronus 3 in Table 1.2) is clearly that of a novice. Under Professor Lupin's guidance, Harry practices the spell against a Dementor imitation (a Boggart). Far from seamless, a pause follows Harry's incantation before the emergence of the white shield, illustrating the effort involved in channeling the spell. The moment the shield appears, the luminous voices and warm sound effects also materialize. In this particular cast, we hear lower voices colliding roughly and somewhat eerily with Harry's labored breaths. Uneasy strings arch back and forth between A♭4 and D♭5. The oscillating strings feel like a body trying to hold two places at once, mirroring Harry's effort to sustain the spell and repel the Boggart.

The film's final Patronus Charm is especially striking because Harry experiences it twice: Once as he is saved by it (Patronus 5 in Table 1.2) and again as he casts it from the future (Patronus 6 in Table 1.2). Though Patronus 5 and 6 are theoretically the same instance of the spell, their musical timbres express two unique perspectives. Patronus 5 is mysterious. It has no incantation and instead begins as the fully-formed guardian figure taking the shape of a white stag, which catches Harry's eye through the horde of Dementors as he leans hopelessly over his dying godfather, Sirius [1:44:11]. When Harry sees the stag, we do not hear the warm sound effect or the luminous voices. Instead, a harp underscores the image, its timbre sinewy yet effervescent with a tactile attack and ethereal decay and release [1:44:13]. The timbre suggests Harry is contemplating the apparition, and perhaps whether it is real. As the camera zooms in on the luminous stag, tubular bell chimes hint at the plot's play with time, and a white shield begins to flicker out from the stag's chest [1:44:20]. Choral voices crescendo as the shield expands, joined by the warm sound effect. Brass intermittently punctuates the soundscape as Dementors flee from the charm. As the spell fades, so do the sound effects and voices.

The final time Harry casts *Expecto Patronum* in the third film (Patronus 6 in Table 1.2) is the most musically lush [2:01:06]. Immediately following Harry's dramatic incantation, the luminous soprano voices enter the soundscape [2:01:09]. Before the emergence of the white shield and warm sound effect, we hear only the soprano voices and Harry's breath. For this second and a half, the world feels like all it contains is light and breath, despite the absence of the white light on screen. When the low, warm sound effect and bright white shield emanate from Harry's wand, the spell feels all the fuller and more vibrant, as though foretold by the soprano voices [2:01:11]. The white shield continues to expand, repelling Dementors, and flickering into the corporeal form of Harry's Patronus: A stag (the same as his late father's). As the spell swells, a warm and lyrical French horn glides through the 'Window to the Past' theme [2:01:20]. In contrast to the low, rough voices audible in the background of Harry's first Patronus Charm (Patronus 3), and to the mysterious chimes and intermittent brass of Patronus 5, the additional musical timbres in this climactic cast are as sustained and hopeful as the luminous soprano voices that consistently define the spell.

What It Means to Perform Magic: Symbolizing Awe, Utility, and Consequences

In one of the most impactful transformations over the course of the series, musical sound—or its absence—symbolizes the evolving significance of magic-making, as characters mature, plots thicken, and wizardly knowledge expands. A fourth instance of Harry casting *Expecto Patronum* illustrates this change. At the beginning of the fifth film, *Harry Potter and the Order of the Phoenix* (2005), the protagonist and his non-magical cousin Dudley (Harry Melling) find themselves as the targets of two Dementors that have strayed far from their usual range [0:03:26]. In stark contrast to the musically lush and extensive Patronus that Harry performs near the end of the third film, this charm is brisk and reactive. Its brevity—both sonically and visually—reflects its use as a tool, rather than its magical wonder. Further, Harry directs the spell with the control of a now-expert sorcerer. He casts it toward one Dementor, then launches the spell at the other in the opposite direction. Unlike the one-size-fits-all, wide-angle shield of *Harry Potter and the Prisoner of Azkaban*'s final Patronus Charm, this spell cast shows that Harry now possesses the expertise to direct and redirect the spell at specific targets.

This trend, towards an unceremonious, purely practical sort of magic-use, is true of the films more broadly. In the early films, the timbres of spells are more sustained, their musicality more prominently emphasized. They symbolize the curiosity and awe of first learning magic. As political tensions escalate and the characters gain a more technical knowledge of sorcery—and its consequences—spell timbres become increasingly reflective of magic's utility and its larger impact, for good or ill.

Exemplary of how spells lose their musical sounds later in the series is the Room of Requirement montage from the fifth film [0:58:44–1:03:37]. During this montage, Dumbledore's Army (a secret student group formed in response to the Ministry's increasingly restrictive interference at Hogwarts) gathers in the Room of Requirement and under Harry's direction practices a variety of defensive spells. The montage cuts between the students' practice and the efforts of Dolores Umbridge (Imelda Staunton) and Argus Filch (David Bradley) to disband Dumbledore's Army. The montage is backed by a comedic orchestral underscore, but the sequence's several spells are notably stripped of musical sounds. The decoupling of music and witchcraft at such a critical moment in the students' educational journey shows that magic's usefulness replaces awe as the students mature. The increasing number of fight sequences as the plot culminates reinforces this new meaning of wizardry—that it is a tool or a weapon more than a fantastical mystery.

As characters are exposed to more complicated magic with more serious consequences, musical timbres increasingly speak to spells' symbolism. Consider, in the sixth film, when Harry casts *Sectumsempra* against Draco Malfoy (Tom Felton) without knowing the incantation's gruesome effect [1:38:48–1:39:37]. The sound that issues from Harry's wand as he yells 'Sectumsempra!' is electrical—like small, sparking wires—and airy—like the forceful gust generated by a fast, direct (and invisible) object. Malfoy cries out as his body thuds to the floor of the flooded bathroom. In the absence of distinctively musical timbres, Harry's breath, the leaking water, and Malfoy's labored whimpers are the most prominent sounds. As Harry walks slowly towards the point where Malfoy fell out of the frame, the sound of his footsteps is notably absent. The sound design seems to reflect Harry's fear of approaching Malfoy to see the damage he has done. As Malfoy's body becomes visible, a soft, high, string harmonic evokes physiological shock.[32] A low rumbling bass enters like dread boiling in the pit of my stomach. As Harry gets closer to Malfoy's body, mournful midrange strings join him, moving slowly, as though attentive to the severity of harm Harry has caused Malfoy. In part because the strings are sinewy—like a muscle-bound body—and in part because they are in a range comfortably accessible to the human voice, they sound strikingly empathetic. In this musical sound, I hear the consequences of Harry's spell: The mortal peril of a very real human body.

A final, powerful example of musical timbre symbolizing what it means to perform magic is the scene described at the opening of this chapter, when Professor Minerva McGonagall casts *Piertotum Locomotor* in the last film. As McGonagall walks to the castle's entrance alongside Molly Weasley (Julie Walters) and Professor Filius Flitwick (Warwick Davis), we hear gradually descending midrange (E♭4–B♭4) strings supporting a fateful tubular bell. The bell's ringing is iconic of large cathedral bells marking the time of day, and here symbolizes 'the final hour.' Pausing midway down the stairs to Hogwarts' doors, Flitwick confirms the fateful significance of the occasion. 'You do realize we can't keep out You-Know-Who indefinitely,' he says. The camera cuts to frame the three wizards from the doors of Hogwarts, looking out to the bridge by which the dark wizard Voldemort (Ralph Fiennes) will presumably approach. McGonagall responds, 'That doesn't mean we can't delay him.' The camera cuts back to face the three wizards with McGonagall at the center. A sustaining, warm, midrange (G4–B♭4) solo trumpet enters as the chime ceases and McGonagall continues, 'And his name is *Voldemort*, Filius. You might as well use it. He's going to try to kill you either way.' The trumpet timbre recalls the 'Taps' bugle call performed by solo trumpeters at military funerals and, in referencing this somber ritual, predicts death.

The single trumpet lingers as the camera cuts back to framing the three wizards from behind, looking out from the steps of Hogwarts at the path of their impending doom. A harshly articulated, low, militaristic drum rings out as McGonagall turns sharply towards Hogwarts to face the camera with her wand extended. The lone trumpet and the dissipating rumble of the low drum seem to hold their breath as McGonagall incants, '*Piertotum Locomotor!*' The first stone soldier crashes to the ground, and we hear the onset of a simple, full-bodied melody in midrange (B♭3 to F4) strings. The melody falters poetically down and then rises, as emboldened as the stone statues yet as vulnerable as the mortal wizards casting protective enchantments over Hogwarts. Bringing stone to life and stirring empathetic strings, McGonagall's spell is more than a weapon of defense. It symbolizes, viscerally, a uniting act of faith and courage against forces far greater than any one of the characters alone.

Conclusion

The musical timbres of spells in the Harry Potter film franchise illustrate powers of musical timbre that are at work in films beyond the boundary of the fantasy genre. Index, icon, and symbol, as stripped-down tools from Peircean semiotics, give us ways to talk about timbre's power. When I hear the theremin in *The Day the Earth Stood Still* (1951), for instance, its eeriness is created in part by an indexical relationship: I envision the musician passing their hands through an invisible electromagnetic field to produce a sound that seems to materialize from nowhere. Its eeriness is also produced through an iconic relationship: The theremin's timbre is uncannily similar to a human voice. And through my modern cultural lens, the theremin timbre is also symbolic, referencing its use in many other film media to accompany supernatural encounters. Likewise, the 'coyote whistle' in *The Good, The Bad, and the Ugly* (1966) evokes the Western's setting. Its airiness is indexical of ocarinas and flutes—instruments whose airy timbres invite me to recall the feeling of wind across a vast desert. The 'coyote whistle' is also iconic of the desert-dwelling coyote's call. And through my cultural knowledge of 'the coyote whistle' in other film media, it symbolizes a culminating showdown. As a final example, the infamous horn BRAAAM from *Inception* (2010) is epic and haunting, in part because it is the sound of something massive. Its timbre is also unnerving because it resembles the sound of a large warning horn. Yet after its frequent use in subsequent film media, it has also been used symbolically in parody. In short, timbre in film music is powerful because it connects us to physical sources, to likenesses, and to evolving cultural conversations.

To close, I'd like to reflect on defining timbre as difference: Timbre is what makes a kazoo sound different from a piano. Film music shows us, instead, that timbre is substance: It has physically immersive meaning, it ignites our imaginations by referencing familiar sounds, and it draws deeply on cultural knowledge. To pull so many dimensions together, one might say of timbre what Dumbledore said of music: That it is indeed a magic beyond all feats of wizardry.

Notes

1 This kind of thought experiment is closely related to what Claudia Gorbman calls the *commutation test*. See *Unheard Melodies: Narrative Film Music* (Bloomington: Indiana University Press, 1987), 18. Likewise, Philip Tagg calls this kind of thought experiment *hypothetical substitution* (HS). See 'Analyzing Popular Music: Theory, Method and Practice,' *Popular Music* 2 (1982): 37–67.
2 'Clarinet (Bb),' *Vienna Symphonic Library*, www.vsl.co.at/en/Clarinet_in_Bb/Sound_Characteristics, accessed December 15, 2020.
3 See Lindsey Reymore and David Huron, 'Using auditory imagery tasks to map the cognitive linguistic dimensions of musical instrument timbre qualia,' *Psychomusicology: Music, Mind, and Brain* 30.33 (2020): 124–144; Zachary Wallmark and Roger A. Kendall, 'Describing Sound: The Cognitive Linguistics of Timbre,' in Emily Dolan and Alexander Rehding (eds.), *The Oxford Handbook of Timbre* (New York: Oxford University Press, 2018), 578–608; and Zachary Wallmark, 'A corpus analysis of timbre semantics in orchestration treatises,' *Psychology of Music* 47.4 (2019): 585–605.
4 Cornelia Fales, 'The Paradox of Timbre,' *Ethnomusicology* 46.1 (2002): 56–95.
5 Ibid., 58.
6 Megan Lavengood, 'A New Approach to the Analysis of Timbre,' PhD diss. (The City University of New York, 2017), 4.
7 Leonard Meyer, *Style and Music: Theory, History, and Ideology* (Chicago: University of Chicago Press, 1989).
8 Wallmark and Kendall, 'Describing Sound,' 25.
9 See Robert A. Butler, 'The relative influence of pitch and timbre on the apparent location of sound in the median sagittal plane,' *Perception and Psychoacoustics* 14.2 (1973): 255–258; and Timothy Morton, 'Ecology without Nature,' accessed July 7, 2021.
10 Butler, ibid.
11 See Danijela Kulezic-Wilson, *The Musicality of Narrative Film* (New York: Palgrave MacMillan, 2015), 73–92.
12 For further context, see Melinda Eschenfelder's close thematic analysis of this scene in 'Musical Narratives: Thematic Combination and Alignment in Fantasy and Superhero Films,' MA thesis (University of Oregon, 2019).
13 Arnie Cox, *Music and Embodied Cognition: Listening, Moving, Feeling, and Thinking* (Bloomington: Indiana University Press, 2016), 4.
14 Ibid. See principles 1, 3–6, and 11 on pp. 14–15.
15 Vivian Sobchack, 'What My Fingers Knew: The Cinesthetic Subject, or, Vision in the Flesh,' in *Carnal Thoughts, Embodiment and Moving Image Culture* (Berkeley: University of California Press, 2004), 93.

16 Juan Chattah, 'Film Music as Embodiment,' in Maarten Coëgnarts and Peter Kravanja (eds.), *Embodied Cognition and Cinema* (Leuven: Leuven University Press, 2015), 81.
17 See especially Andrew Sutherland, 'The Developing Timbre Palette of Film Music: The Emergence of World Instruments for Non-ethnographic Association,' *The International Journal of Arts Theory and History* 13.2 (June 2018): 28–29.
18 Maddy Shaw Roberts, 'Harry Potter soundtrack: "Hedwig's Theme" and everything you need to know about the film franchise's magical score,' *Classic FM*, September 8, 2020, www.classicfm.com/discover-music/periods-genres/film-tv/harry-potter-soundtrack-hedwig-theme-john-williams/.
19 Jamie Lynn Webster, 'The Music of Harry Potter: Continuity and Change in the First Five Films,' PhD diss. (University of Oregon, 2009), 208.
20 See 'Worldwide Grosses,' *Box Office Mojo,* October 11, 2011, https://web.archive.org/web/20111031012438/http://www.boxofficemojo.com/alltime/world/.
21 See Juan Chattah, 'Semiotics, Pragmatics, and Metaphor in Film Music Analysis,' PhD diss. (Florida State University, 2006), and Alex Michael Newton, 'Semiotics of Music, Semiotics of Sound, and Film: Toward a Theory of Acousticons,' PhD diss. (University of Texas at Austin, 2015).
22 See Frank Lehman's transcription of this sequence in 'Hollywood Cadences: Music and the Structure of Cinematic Expectation,' *Music Theory Online* 19.4 (December 2013).
23 Robynn J. Stilwell, 'The Fantastical Gap between Diegetic and Nondiegetic,' in Daniel Goldmark, Lawrence Kramer, and Richard Leppert (eds.), *Beyond the Soundtrack: Representing Music in Cinema* (Berkeley: University of California Press, 2007), 184–185. See also choreographer Paul Harris' discussion of the *gesture* of spell casts in the final four films: Alyssa Tieman, 'Exclusive Interview: Paul Harris Shares His Journey to Creating the Wand Choreography of "Harry Potter,"' *Fan Fest*, August 17, 2019, https://fanfest.com/exclusive-interview-paul-harris-wand-choreographer/.
24 Kevin Donnelly, *The Spectre of Sound: Music in Film and Television* (London: British Film Institute, 2005), 19.
25 Ibid., 41.
26 Consider Trelawney's prophecy in *Harry Potter and the Prisoner of Azkaban* (1:21:23), Harry speaking Parseltongue in *Harry Potter and the Chamber of Secrets* (1:08:23), or Voldemort speaking through Harry in *Harry Potter and the Order of the Phoenix* (1:37:37).
27 For more examples of spells with musical sound effects, see Chelsea Oden, 'Fantastic Timbres and Where To Find Them' in 'There is a Body in the Sound: Timbre and Embodiment in the Overlap of Film, Music, and Dance,' PhD diss. (University of Oregon, June 2021), 74–99.
28 Isabella van Elferen. 'Fantasy Music: Epic Soundtracks, Magical Instruments, Musical Metaphysics,' *Journal of the Fantastic Art* 24.2 (2013): 4.
29 Nerdwriter1, 'Harry Potter: What Magic Sounds Like,' YouTube, November 15, 2018, video, 4:24 to 4:32, www.youtube.com/watch?v=bJvOqXdsEp8.
30 Wallmark and Kendall, 'Describing Sound.'
31 Ibid. See also Asterios Zacharakis et al, 'An Interlanguage Study of Musical Timbre Semantic Dimensions and Their Acoustic Correlates,' *Music Perception: An Interdisciplinary Journal* 31 (2014): 339–358; Lindsey Reymore, 'Empirical approaches to timbre semantics as foundation for musical analysis,' PhD diss. (Ohio State University, 2020).
32 Danijela Kulezic-Wilson, 'The Music of Film Silence,' *Music and the Moving Image* 2.3 (Fall 2009): 1–10.

2
'THE CLICK IS YOUR FRIEND'
Film Scores and Tempo Analysis

Rebecca M. Doran Eaton

Tracking Tempo

Ask any film music aficionado—musicologist or not—to describe the main themes of *Star Wars* and *The Good, the Bad, and the Ugly*, and chances are they will not respond with, 'Well, they both move at a moderate tempo, with *Star Wars* at 100 beats per minute (BPM) and *The Good, the Bad, and the Ugly* clocking in at 108.' Instead, they might recount Williams's cue as showcasing a bold and brassily orchestrated melody, replete with perfect fourth and fifth intervals and some triplet rhythms—all characteristics of the *hero* and *fanfare* musical topic. (Here and elsewhere, the initial mention of a specific topic will be indicated by italicized text.) Morricone's score will likely draw reflections on its idiosyncratic instrumentation including bass ocarina, soprano recorder, electric guitar, and wordless male chorus. (On topics and timbre and film analysis, see chapters by Bourne and Oden respectively.)

While catchy themes such as the one blared at the beginning of *Star Wars* and distinctive timbres such as the tumbleweed whistle of *The Good, the Bad, and the Ugly* remain the most consciously conspicuous components of film scores, tempo forces an unconscious, immediate, visceral reaction. Tempo—the speed of music, or the rate at which the beats of music occur—affects both body and cognition. Following a 2000 study from Lang et al. which showed that a faster video cutting rate—quicker visual tempo—elevates physiological and cognitive arousal, Carpentier and Potter performed a similar experiment in 2007 that discovered faster *musical* tempo similarly affects the autonomic

DOI: 10.4324/9781003001171-2

nervous system.[1] Both video game and film composers understand this intuitively and exploit this tight linkage of tempo and excitement to heart-pounding effect: *Accelerandi* and brisk music highlight running-out game timers and film chase scenes alike.[2] And while empirical research demonstrates that musical speed shifts affect arousal, it also suggests that tempo affects audio-viewers' higher-level perceptions, including the interpretation of on-screen emotion. For instance, Cohen's 1994 animation experiments found that bouncing balls with higher pitch and faster tempo were appraised as happier.[3] So despite seeming quotidian or insignificant, tempo directly and often decisively influences psychophysiological response.

Filmmakers, at least, grasp this well. Musical speed emerges as a crucial consideration during film music's spotting, composing, recording, and editing processes. During a spotting session, the director, composer, and music editor decide where music should go in a film, precisely how long the musical cue should last, the cue's musical characteristics, and if there are any required sync (or hit) points—places where the music should emphasize or synchronize with on-screen events. But before notating any pitches, Richard Davis explains, 'the tempo of the music must be established before writing can begin.'[4] Henry Mancini agrees: 'Arriving at the proper tempo is all-important to the success of the music. Having to slow down or speed up to reach a sync point is not acceptable for the professional film composer.'[5] Recognizing musical tempo as fundamental scoring infrastructure, how-to manuals for multimedia composers, including *On the Track*, *Complete Guide to Film Scoring*, *Advanced Techniques for Film Scoring*, and *Music Composition for Film and Television*, detail how to select an appropriate one.[6] The composer may utilize some tool—a calculator, a click book, Auricle, Frans Absil's Film Tempo Calculation Tool website, or the 'Find Tempo' function in a DAW such as Digital Performer—to identify the ideal speed so that music can best align with required hit points. Once ready for recording, conductors and session musicians customarily wear headphones emitting a frames-per-beat click track, guaranteeing that the live performance matches the meticulously selected tempi. In rare cases, conductors choose 'free timing' rather than a click track. In such circumstances, the pacing of music is still carefully controlled, though with a bit more human freedom between hit points; conductors rely on 'punch and streamer' visuals overlaid on a projected film to indicate approaching required sync points and adjust their batons accordingly.[7] Contributing an entire additional layer of tempo manipulation, editors ensure during postproduction that musical and visual moments properly align.[8]

Given the palpable effects of musical speed on both the compositional and psychological-receptive dimensions of film, tempo analysis serves as an essential component of a film music theorist's toolbox, particularly when it comes to more meaning-oriented hermeneutic or topical analyses. Empirical research in music cognition on tempo's effect on arousal and emotional valence supports claims of musical-speed-related audiovisual meaning and clarifies why certain film musical topics correlate with particular tempi. Considering the vital importance of tempo to the film scoring and editing process, analysis of musical speed also reveals traces of the multimedia production process, a fascinating type of performance practice in its own right. Careful investigation of tempo and its interaction with film cuts and synchronization points elucidates directorial and editorial preferences and sheds light on film grammar or structure. It shows, quite literally, how the film is put together. This chapter aims to demonstrate the utility of tempo analysis to topical, hermeneutic, and performance practice-based readings of movie music. Before diving into theory, however, it will serve to delve into practical how-to problems and pitfalls peculiar to film music tempo analysis.

Deriving Film Music Tempo

Unfortunately, tempo research suffers from the same roadblock that bedevils most film music analysis: One must transcribe it from the film itself. Scores and recordings prove tempting shortcuts that may lead one astray. While archives hold some older scores, non-archival printed scores for the cues in question may be unavailable, vague, or incorrect, particularly if sourced cheaply or from unsanctioned internet sources. Scores available for purchase regularly display terms such as *Allegro* or *Moderato*, ranges not precise enough for study.[9] Beats-per-minute markings, when indicated, often display only the numbers preset on pendulum mechanical metronomes—including 72, 80, 88, 96, 104, 112, and 120— oversimplifications rather than the true speed of the cue as it appears in the film. Film composers do not constrain themselves to these settings and deploy odd tempi such as 83, 114, or 130 to hit synchronization points. Nor can we take concert renderings as necessarily reflecting original in-film timings. Michel Worek's 2001 concert band arrangement of cues from *A Beautiful Mind* includes MM (metronome marking), and while the beats-per-minute setting for 'A Kaleidoscope of Mathematics' accurately matches the film's MM 144, the arrangement indicates MM 152 for 'Playing a Game of Go'—22 beats faster than the in-film score metronome marking of 130. Even internet-hosted film clips may be as unreliable as sources for tempo as sheet music. Aiming to circumvent copyright protection algorithms, some uploaders to sites including YouTube run multimedia through pitch or tempo-shifting software, rendering them inaccurate and thus unusable for tempo—and sometimes pitch!—analysis. Commercially available soundtrack audio recordings, given that they sometimes feature re-recorded suites with pitch and tempo alterations rather than being taken directly from the film, are susceptible to similar issues.

While scholars must analyze the music within the film itself rather than rely upon sheet music, soundtrack recordings, or YouTube film clips, the transcription of tempo remains simpler than that of pitch. Instead of transcribing entire musical structures, one simply taps with the beat. David Temperley notes that most students are able to complete this activity in agreement.[10] Empirical research confirms that humans are accurate beat-finders, particularly when faced with tempi between 110 and 120 BPM, though Martens notes that some listeners tap at different metrical levels.[11] Given the ease of tactus tapping, tempo analysis serves as an accessible entry point for the film music theory neophyte. It remains fairly simple to do, requires easily available and often free tools, and can lead to valuable scholarly contributions—all while requiring less jargon and insider disciplinary knowledge when compared to musical topics or transformational theory, to name two established analytical methodologies.

A number of digital tools are available that translate taps into numerical data for analysis. Smartphone apps like 'The Metronome' by Soundbrenner can convert touchscreen finger tattoos into metronome markings. While a straightforward option for music at *lento* through *moderato* speeds, this app's accuracy deteriorates with *presto* tempi due to touchscreen and processor latency issues. Several websites also offer free tempo tap-to-BPM tools, including getsongbpm.com and the bare-bones BPM tool on www.all8.com. For rapid musical speeds, these options outperform touchscreen apps, as the spacebar taps they involve avoid touchscreen latency issues. DAWs such as Logic Pro X, Cubase, and Studio One, or audio analysis programs such as the free and open-source Sonic Visualizer, are to a certain extent able to automate the process, though the output of their automatic tempo-detection tools require thoughtful refinement with film scores if they are to produce dependable results. Some tempo-detection software seems to operate on algorithms similar to Lakoff/Johnson and Temperley's cognitive preference rules and, as a result, has a tendency to overestimate tempo when confronted with frequent regular subdivisions such as straight sixteenth notes.[12] Böck and Davies note that computer-based tempo detection works best on drum-driven music such as rock and EDM—decidedly not the norm for either classical music or much film music. For that reason, pop music-based soundtracks and scores from companies like Remote Control Productions with a predilection for drum loops might be suited to these tools.[13] However, even the most refined automated methods fail when the dialogue or sound effects laid over the music confound waveform or spectrographic beat detection.[14] All of the above options function adequately when conductors use a click track and the cue does not contain *accelerandi* or *ritardandi*. DAWs with user-adjustable tempo maps and Sonic Visualizer serve as better choices for analyzing free-timing conductors or cues with numerous speed fluctuations. For optimal outcomes in all cases, a little human discretion is advised.

Discretion is also advised when picking which metrical layer to tap and analyze. Tempo traditionally marks the *tactus*, or the most salient felt pulse of a given musical passage, in BPM. This metrical layer functions fine for most film score analyses. But there are some kinds of music that benefit from a measurement of a lower, faster, subtactus layer. 'Pulse pattern minimalism' as Robert Fink calls it—minimalist music with a steady pulse and repeated rhythmic patterns—often features a lower metrical level of continuous equally-divided subdivisions, as does much 'hurry' music from Remote Control Studios.[15] Given these quick notes' seemingly interminable flow, any drastic rate change in their progress becomes marked, even if BPM remains the same; listeners attend to such differences. Rather than measuring pulse pattern-minimalist music solely in BPM, it behooves the analyst to incorporate a system that measures the articulation rate of these continuous subdivisions. Following Peter Martens, I label this subdivision layer as fastest consistent pulse (*FCP*) and measure its speed per minute as fastest consistent pulse per minute or *FCPPM*.[16] Having both of these tempo metrics proves profitable in the analysis of musical meaning, particularly in terms of characterizing musical topics. A piece with a BPM of 96 and an FCPPM of 192 feels quite different from a passage with a BPM of 84 and an FCPPM of 336.

Tempo and Topic

One rationale for careful analysis of tempi is to identify and differentiate between the use of musical topics in film. Theorists define a number of musical topics partly in terms of their tempo. For Clive McClelland, tempo serves as a primary differentiator between the *ombra* (slow or moderate) and *tempesta* (fast) topoi, signifiers of unrest originating in the eighteenth century that otherwise share a similar musical profile: Surprise elements, tremolo figures, and minor keys.[17] In the realm of film scores, James Buhler and David Neumeyer observe that the *love theme* topic tends to fall on the 'slow side of moderate (often *andante*, roughly or just a bit slower than the average resting heartbeat rate),' while the 'hurry' or *agitato* topic, underscoring chase and action scenes, proceeds briskly.[18]

Buhler and Neumeyer's reference to heart rate suggests another point of contact with psychophysiological research. While many musical topics—film or otherwise—may be purely conventional, based on an arbitrary sign/signifier relationship imposed solely through culture, the embodied effects of tempo on arousal and emotion drive the association of particular topics with specific musical speeds. The love theme's *andante* relaxes the viewer into tender sentimentality, while the hurry's *vivace* or *presto* raises the audio-viewer's pulse in tandem with arousing action on screen. In some of the only film music research mentioning tempo in more than passing detail, Juan Chattah remarks that 'action movies frequently use the TEMPO IS SPEED OF PHYSICAL MOVEMENT conceptual metaphor' and that a quick tempo 'activates sensory-motor simulations triggered at the reflexive level; the viewers not only perceive but also physically simulate the increasing velocity and aggressiveness.'[19]

Chattah's linkage between musical speed and embodied human movement also plays out, although through a different conceptual metaphor, with scores deploying minimalist techniques.[20] In my own research on minimalism in film, I found tempo analysis instrumental in arriving at a definition of the *minimalist mathematical genius* topic (MGT), particularly in distinction with other types of repetitive film scoring styles. In the following sections, I will demonstrate two different ways in which tempo helps construct this topic in the hands of different composers, either as *the* indispensable musical parameter in the MGT or one among many. Specifically, I will show that: 1) Tempo is the sole musically salient feature differentiating the MGT from other film music of minimalist composer Philip Glass; and 2) tempo is but one element among others—timbre, texture, and tessitura included—that distinguishes the minimalist math topic in Hans Zimmer's output from action/chase-sequence scoring techniques.

In the 2014 article 'Marking Minimalism: Minimal Music as a Sign of Machines and Mathematics in Multimedia,' I established that minimalist techniques have become associated with portrayals of rationality.[21] As primarily a musicological study, this article only briefly touched upon musical characteristics leading to this signification, so this research continued with a theoretical analysis of seven tokens of this film musical topic, all from different composers, ranging from blockbusters to documentaries, to cartoons. Through this comparative analysis, I defined the characteristics of the MGT (or minimalist genius topic).[22] Example 2.1 presents an invented musical passage that highlights the customary features of the MGT.

As shown in Example 2.1, the MGT is usually situated in a minor key, with little to no chromaticism or dissonance. A derivative of the tension ostinato or *agitato*, it features an average of 333 continuous articulations per minute (FCPPM) in the C4 octave register, usually produced by piano arpeggios or block chords. While Chattah tied the rapidity of action

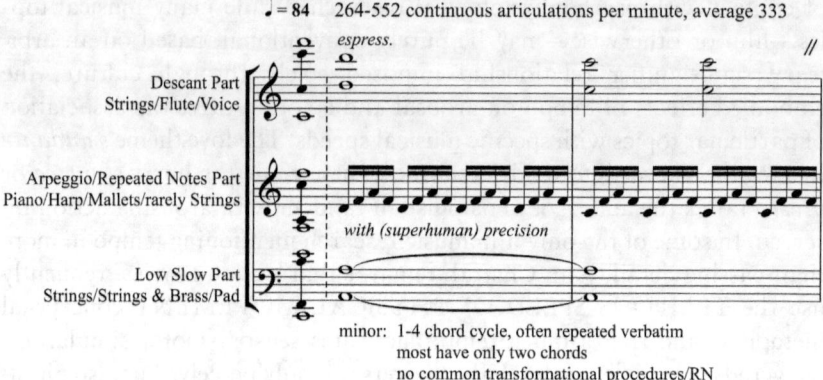

EXAMPLE 2.1 Characteristics of the minimalist mathematical genius topic (MGT).

movie cues to a TEMPO IS SPEED OF PHYSICAL MOVEMENT metaphor, here the energetic speed qualifies as what Chattah terms a qualitative iconic metaphor: SPEED OF MUSICAL ARTICULATION IS SPEED OF COGNITION.[23] The nimble arpeggio, according to this metaphorical relationship, is taken to be analogous to the inhumanly quick mental machinery of a genius. Layered over the rapid repetitions of the prototypical MGT floats a soaring *espressivo* descant, and a slow string bed sometimes thickens the texture an octave below. The fifth scale degree is often emphasized metrically or registrally, lending the topic a sense of expectation—some kind of never-ending cadential 6/4. Many examples of the MGT share a longer-range formal feature: A eureka moment accompanied by musical *durchbruch* (breakthrough)—either musical cessation or dramatic change—represented schematically in Example 2.1 by a caesura.

Besides the obligatory presence of a relentlessly repetitive musical texture, the tempo element of the MGT serves as its primary distinguishing characteristic. Several film cues by the well-known minimalist composer Philip Glass bear some of the hallmarks of the MGT but lack the requisite impression of brisk surface tempo. While it does not underscore a math genius at work, 'Escape!' from *The Hours*, a portion of which is reproduced in reduction in Example 2.2, shares multiple features with the MGT.[24] The A minor passage pictured contains a low repeating arpeggio piano part, an octave-higher *espressivo* string descant, an occasional octave-lower slow string line, and an emphasis on the fifth scale degree. Besides an only slightly lower than average arpeggio tessitura, tempo remains the only noticeable difference between 'Escape!' and the

MGT: The MGT features a 264–552 FCPPM, while 'Escape!' features only 192 for the majority of the piece.²⁵ This much slower metrical layer is sufficient to disqualify the cue as an instance of the MGT. More generally, whether or not a style topic is instantiated depends less on what is being accompanied immediately and more on a combination of structural features (of which tempo is decisive) and the degree of topical markedness in the wider stylistic context of a given text—or its lack, as in the thoroughly minimalist, and thus unmarked, backdrop of Glass's score to *The Hours*.

While the tempo of 'Escape!' remains the only salient structural (as opposed to dramatic) characteristic distinguishing it from the MGT, a number of features separate the MGT from other types of repetitive style topics, including the electronic-heavy and faster version of what Frank Lehman calls the *cathartic ostinato* film music of Hans Zimmer. I will call this louder, faster, more synthetic subset of the cathartic ostinato the **amplified agitato**.²⁶ Like the MGT, the amplified agitato likely derives from the hurry topic, has a similar tempo range, and skews minor. Both topics regularly accompany scenes with scant dialogue—likely because their rapid articulations interfere with dialogue clarity or, relatedly, that scenes without the normal attentional hook of dialogue still require interest and energy—and both are built from the accumulation of small, repeated motifs, stratified into midrange rhythmic, upper-range melodic, and the occasional slower, lower-range punctuative bass layer. But the similarities largely end there. In terms of timbre, textural density, and register, the MGT and amplified agitato are quite dissimilar, and produce wildly different affects that suit the scenes they underscore: The MGT aurally dramatizes the internal event of intense cognition, while the amplified agitato often accompanies chase or other action scenes.

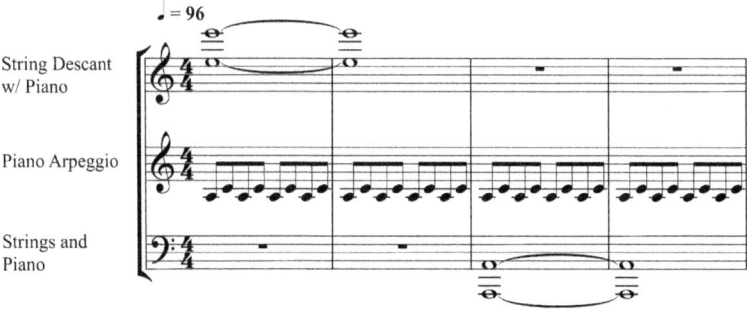

EXAMPLE 2.2   Glass, *The Hours*, 'Escape!' mm. 9–12 (all examples transcribed by author).

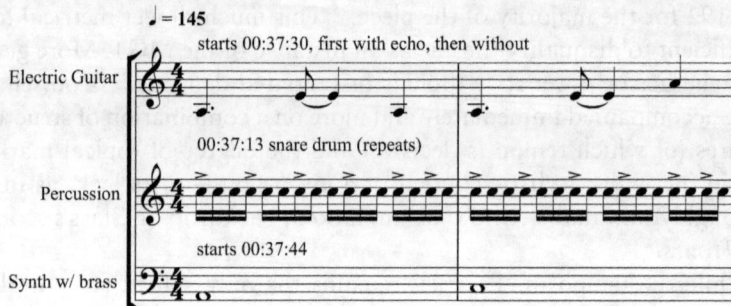

EXAMPLE 2.3   Zimmer, *Inception*, 'Mombasa,' first two measures of each of the three layers that occur in 0:37:13–0:37:50.

Timbre functions as the most obvious distinction between the MGT and the amplified agitato. The MGT calls for lighter acoustic instruments, usually piano and strings or flute, with the rare electric guitar or synth pad. Zimmer's work leans heavily on drums, electric guitar, and brass, and sports electronic reinforcement, if not an ensemble entirely consisting of sampled or synthetic instruments. While both types of cues often begin with the rhythmic layer, then add the more melodic, then the lower layer, the MGT generally avoids thickening that three-layer texture except through metric division modulation. The cathartic ostinato tends to thicken the texture through the addition of more instruments in multiple octaves upon each new iteration to build tension. In films including *Inception* and the Christopher Nolan-directed *Batman* films (composed with James Newton Howard), the cathartic ostinato also tends to be an octave lower than the MGT, more syncopated, and in chase scenes, more dissonant. Tempo-wise, however, the MGT and cathartic ostinato share a similar range, though the amplified agitato sub-topic may sprint even faster. Zimmer and Newton Howard's 'Tumbler Chase' from *Batman Begins* features continuous 16th notes at MM 102 for 408 articulations per minute, while Zimmer's 'Mombasa' from *Inception*, depicted in Example 2.3, races at MM 145 for 580 continuous articulations per minute, exceeding existing examples of the MGT.

Tempo and Hermeneutic Readings

In addition to helping differentiate, and indeed *define* some musical topics, tempo provides an intriguing ancillary focal point when performing hermeneutic analysis. In what follows, I demonstrate how tempo-centered analysis of tokens of the MGT supports harmonically-oriented hermeneutic readings—or can suggest alternative avenues of interpretation—with *A Beautiful Mind* serving as a case study. *A Beautiful Mind* (2001) stands as one of the first major Hollywood movies to signify math or science cognition with minimalist-inflected cues.[27] The biopic, directed by Ron Howard, stars Russell Crowe as John Nash, the Nobel-prize-winning mathematician. The movie loosely traces his life, from his arrival at Princeton as a graduate student, through struggles with paranoid schizophrenia, up to a final act dramatizing the resumption of mathematical practice and winning the Nobel.

James Horner's score for *A Beautiful Mind* features many cues whose continuous piano articulations clearly reference minimalist techniques, accompanying Nash as he attempts to solve problems, often while writing or speaking numbers. The repeated conjunction of this style of music with acts of mathematical brilliance links them, and the association is further solidified before and after the film narrative proper, during the title and end credit music. Table 2.1 lists these MGT cues with their timing and tempo.[28]

In 'Transformational Analysis and the Representation of Genius in Film Music,' Lehman presents a close reading of three MGT-bearing cues from *A Beautiful Mind*: 'A Kaleidoscope of Mathematics,' 'Playing a Game of Go,' and 'Cracking the Russian Codes.' In emphasizing the tonal trajectory of these densely chromatic sequences, Lehman omits BPM indications in the text or in musical examples, and leaves questions of tempo aside, except in the loosely defined sense of *harmonic* rhythm:

> Horner's 'genius music' in *A Beautiful Mind* bears a consistently triadic surface with little variation of texture beyond minimalist chordal figurations. The textural uniformity, along with a fast harmonic rhythm for long spans of score, focuses the listener's attention away from the triads themselves, and squarely onto their interactions.[29]

It is those chordal interactions, as analyzed through neo-Riemannian transformations, that serve as the basis for Lehman's hermeneutic readings. In what follows below, I briefly present his findings and demonstrate how tempo analysis may: 1) Enhance or nuance his NRT readings; 2) suggest cues worth investigating that are not discussed within the confines of Lehman's study; and 3) reveal interpretative pathways unavailable to a purely harmonic analytical perspective.

TABLE 2.1 Minimalist genius topic (MGT) cues in Horner, *A Beautiful Mind*

Cue (only portions with continuous piano articulations)	Time	Tactus BPM (beats per minute) *and* Meter	FCPPM (fastest consistent pulses per minute)
1a. Kaleidoscope of Mathematics	0:00:00–0:01:19	144 (simple triple)	288
1b. Kaleidoscope of Mathematics	0:01:19–0:01:30	144 (compound duple/quadruple)	432
2. Playing a Game of Go	0:10:04–0:10:54	130 (simple quadruple)	260
3a. Barroom Breakthrough	0:20:09–0:20:44	102–108 then 72 (simple triple metric modulation to comp. duple)	216
3b. Barroom Breakthrough	0:20:45–0:21:00	72 (still comp. duple; twice as many articulations)	432
4. Creating Governing Dynamics	0:21:34–0:21:37	114 (compound duple/quadruple, with many BPM switches)	342
5a. Cracking the Russian Codes	0:25:34–0:26:02	Starts 94 (comp. quadruple), continuous accel. to next part	276+ (continuous accel.)
5b. Cracking the Russian Codes	0:26:02–0:26:58	120 (comp. triple)	360
6. Newspaper Codes	0:45:01–0:46:04	122, gradual slowing to 114 (simple quad)	244 slows to 228
7. Leaving for Work	1:54:42–1:55:38	83 (simple triple)	166
8. Final Credits	2:11:38–2:13:12	64 (or 128), varies (simple quadruple)	256 (varies slightly, free-timed?)

Tempo's Additive Properties: Tempo Analysis Enhances or Nuances Harmonic Readings

Lehman reads Horner's title cue, 'A Kaleidoscope of Mathematics,' as following an epiphany narrative. The opening and closing key of D minor he associates with 'occupying both the initiation of a problem and the arrival at its solution.' The 'relations around A♭ that present it in variance to D minor' represent swift thinking. The connection of that nagging A♭ with the minor dominant of D minor, A minor, through the triadic transformation **SLIDE**, suggests mental breakthrough.[30]

Lehman's focus on triadic interactions as primary bearers of meaning makes sense in light of the repetitious minimalist techniques in play in Horner's music. With timbral, textural, and arpeggio repetitions far exceeding four times, these cues exemplify what David Lidov terms 'textural repetition.' According to Lidov, the repeated musical content 'cancels out its own claim on our attention and thereby refers our focus elsewhere, to another voice or to a changing aspect'—in the case of this cue, the contextually more dynamic parameter of harmony.[31] But while 'Kaleidoscope' and the other genius cues might indeed contain 'little variation of texture,' they do not have *none*. Both 'Kaleidoscope' and 'Barroom Breakthrough' feature an abrupt metric modulation. This disruption—given its formal location—enhances Lehman's epiphanic interpretation.

'Kaleidoscope' begins in D minor in simple triple meter at 144 BPM, with an FCPPM of 288. Lehman's tonal associative reading ties 'mathematical epiphany' to the chromatic neighbor motions of A♭ major/A minor and 'solution' to the return of the opening key of D minor in m. 66 [0:01:19]. I completely concur that the breakthrough occurs here and that harmonic evidence supports it; however, visual and tempo clues do not merely reinforce this interpretation. They are essential to its effect. First, m. 66 marks the appearance of the title card: Seeing the words 'A Beautiful Mind' while hearing the dominant function to tonic resolution of A♭/A to D minor cements the connection of this musical process to a literal textual assertion of exceptional cognitive prowess. Second, this tonal resolution coincides precisely with a dramatic metric division modulation.[32] While 'Kaleidoscope' retains the underlying 144 BPM at this formal juncture, it upshifts to 432 FCPPM. This temporal modulation from *prestissimo* to something almost like acoustic speedcore synchronizes with both the title card and the return to D minor. According to empirical tempo research including that of Richard Parncutt, articulations above 300 per minute might 'sound rhythmic' to humans but are never considered the tactus.[33] An FCPPM of 288 reaches the upper bounds of what might be tapped, but 432 goes beyond even the software/hardware capabilities of a touchscreen metronome app. Recall Chattah's conceptual metaphor: SPEED OF MUSICAL ARTICULATION IS SPEED OF COGNITION. With this division modulation in 'Kaleidoscope,' the film declares the arrival of an intellect beyond merely human.

Tempo analysis further supports and nuances Lehman's reading of 'Playing a Game of Go,' which he presents as conveying a harmonic win/loss narrative. The cue progresses logically, like the board game it underscores, through a repeatedly iterated **LR-L-S** triadic sequence until an uncharacteristic **HEXPOLE** operation aborts its cyclic progress at the moment Nash loses to his Princeton grad-student opponent.[34] This harmonic disruption synchronizes with an abrupt cessation of the cue's 260 FCPPM and the corresponding disappearance of continuous piano pulses [0:10:54]. This moment of rhythmic negation, in which the entire metrical level that had been providing a sense of the rapid tempo of Nash's thought vanishes, cements the impression that the score signifies a *failure* of intellect. All here—even tempo—is lost. But measuring the FCPPM does more here than support a win/loss harmonic reading. It suggests that the film's titular ingenious mind has not yet arrived at its full power; the game could not have been won. 'Kaleidoscope' opens with a 288 FCPPM that recalibrates to 432 at the moment of solution. 'Go' flows at 260 FCPPM, a slower tempo than 'Kaleidoscope' even begins. This brain, the score is telling us, is not yet operating at full speed. 'Playing a Game of Go' avoids metric division modulation and avoids FCPPM change; this mind—and the music—fails to grasp the breakthrough the prelude of 'Kaleidoscope' promises.

Lehman claims that, at least harmonically, 'Cracking the Russian Codes' does. Where 'Playing a Game of Go' begins a chromatic cycle that is disrupted when Nash loses to a grad school nemesis, 'Codes' accompanies a confident now-professor Nash as he deciphers codes for the military; it completes 'the full cycling of the **LR-LS** sequence through its twinned whole-tone scales' at 0:26:41. 'Codes' thus pursues a different goal-directed process than the chromatic rapprochement of chromatic dominants and returns to the home key posited for 'Kaleidoscope.'[35] Lehman claims that 'Without the climactic [cycle-completing] harmonic event and its accumulated associations… the moment of Nash's epiphany would be ambiguous, left undetermined by visuals.' Indeed, unlike 'Kaleidoscope' or 'Go,' tempo change does not accompany epiphanic events in 'Codes' and does not neatly align with the tonal-associationist reading. At the moment of harmonic breakthrough/solution, there is no FCPPM change; rather, the fastest consistent pulse shifts gesturally from repeated block chords to sweeping arpeggios. The tempo/metrical change that *does* occur in 'Codes' marks not a solution but a different moment of cognition, earlier, at the moment when Nash—and the camera—begins to focus. 'Codes' opens at 00:25:34 with a string FCPPM of 276, close to the original 'Kaleidoscope' 288. The camera repeatedly spins around Nash, accompanied by continuous accelerando, as the general describes the problem. The FCPPM reaches its peak, 360, with a cut to a zoom-in on Nash as the piano begins repeated block chords (00:26:01), and there it remains.

Extrapolate Tempo Correlations: Tempo Suggests Cues Worth Investigating

In *A Beautiful Mind*, we have thus seen examples of both careful correlation and conspicuous non-alignment of harmonic and tempo-based musical parameters in constructing the mathematical genius topic. And it is in such cases of misalignment where tempo analysis comes into its own, not simply synergistically supporting pitch-based readings but proclaiming things pitch cannot. It may also advance moments that otherwise might be missed.

When one begins with a harmonic analytical lens, of course the most arresting chordal movements become the focus. In 'Transformational Analysis and the Representation of Genius in Film Music,' Lehman identifies ten 'genius music' cues, analyzing three in detail: 'Kaleidoscope,' 'Go,' and 'Codes.' This narrowed scope allows for detail, and 'Go' and 'Codes' move through similar harmonic pathways to 'Kaleidoscope,' lending a natural fit. Besides placing 'Barroom Breakthrough' in a chart of 'genius music cues,' the article bypasses this music, perhaps because only it omits the distinctively Hornerian neo-Riemannian **SLIDE** transformation that Lehman so associates with 'Kaleidoscope' and the other genius music cues.

But what happens if an analyst starts with musical speed? After an initial tempo analysis (see Table 2.1), 'Barroom Breakthrough' stands out as worthy of investigation, emerging as the only cue approaching the *prestissimo* FCPPM that marked the breakthrough moment in 'Kaleidoscope.' The second half of 'Kaleidoscope' and 'Barroom' reach *exactly* 432 FCPPM, surpassing even the 360 FCPPM of 'Cracking the Russian Codes.' And further inspection of the tonal and tempo content of 'Barroom Breakthrough' reveals an even closer connection to 'Kaleidoscope' beyond their shared FCPPM, a link that suggests this cue marks the true arrival of the *A Beautiful Mind* promised in the title music (see Example 2.4).

Up to this point in the film, doctoral student Nash blusters but fails to complete original work. He and his graduate cohort relax in a bar when a blonde woman and her friends enter, and the men immediately begin to argue about approaching the women. Nash's rival quotes a proposition of economist Adam Smith, and after pondering its application, Nash smirks and says 'Adam Smith needs revision' (m. 4). Then, accompanied by the

EXAMPLE 2.4 Horner, *A Beautiful Mind*, 'Barroom Breakthrough' reduction. The x-noteheads mark the rhythm of the FCPPM. Breath markings locate the start of dialogue lines, with the first few words of the phrase indicated above the breath mark. The visuals that go with the music are located above the score and dialogue.

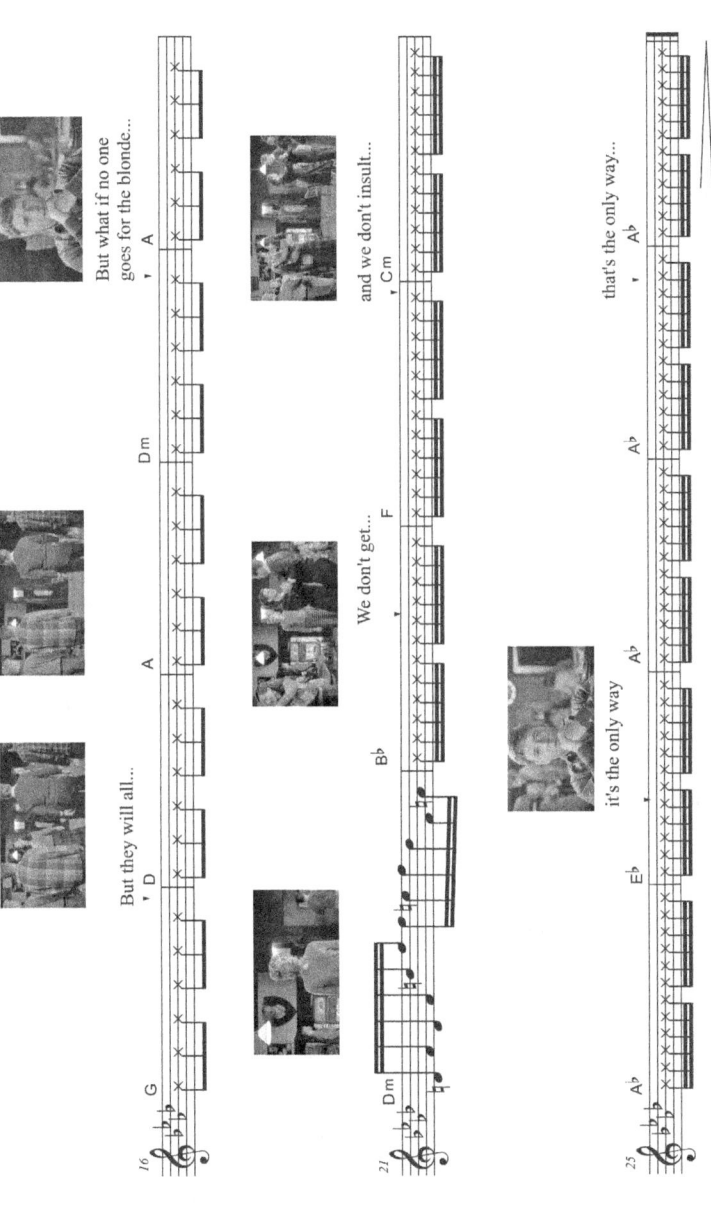

EXAMPLE 2.4 Continued

cue 'Barroom Breakthrough,' he excitedly proclaims the seed of his first novel mathematical proof.

'Barroom Breakthrough' opens in A♭ major, in simple triple time, with an FCPPM of 216. Charlotte Church's voice fades in, followed by a piano vamp as Nash proclaims his idea in a conditional statement: 'If we go for the blonde...' (m. 7). After completing the first part of his scenario, the next stage of his thought process, 'So then we go for her friends' (end of m. 14) is accompanied by a wavering of that triple meter through a touch of two-against-three rhythm, initially taken to be surface-level hemiola (m. 15). Immediately following the epiphany of Nash's second if/then statement, 'But what if no one goes for the blonde,' what sounded like hemiola is confirmed as a genuine metric modulation as the beat is further subdivided into sextuplets for a brisk 432 FCPPM in m. 21. This division modulation coincides with a tonal arrival on D minor, and synchronizes with the revelation of Nash's game-theoretic solution to the men's amorous impasse: 'We don't get in each other's way.' The music crossfades out on A♭ major to a diegetic jukebox as Nash completes his soliloquy.

'Barroom Breakthrough' bears a remarkable resemblance to 'Kaleidoscope.' First, both begin in simple triple meter. Second, both open with a tonic pedal point and scalar vamp that includes {$\hat{5}$-♭$\hat{6}$-♭$\hat{5}$} in its upper register (see the highest notes of mm. 3–6). Third, both cues contain a division modulation to 432 FCPPM following the moment of epiphany. Fourth, their keys mirror each other. Where 'Kaleidoscope' began in D minor, marked mental struggle toward a breakthrough with A♭ major, and then returned to D minor, 'Breakthrough' opens in A♭ major with the problem, marks the solution in D minor at m. 21, and then fades back to A♭ at the end before Nash runs to his room to type his theory.

If 'Codes' represented the fulfillment of the promise of the **LR•LS** cycle initiated in 'Kaleidoscope' and 'Go,' 'Barroom Breakthrough' realizes another kind of latent goal set up by that germinative cue: Reaching the promised superhuman cognitive speed of the title card, which is carried out with a comparable metric division modulation and interaction between the referential keys of D and A♭. Even though it omits the **SLIDE** transformation so typical of what Lehman dubs 'Horner space,' 'Breakthrough,' like 'Codes,' also completes a full NRT cycle,[36] one replacing S with N and **M**.[37] As the *Tonnetz* of Figure 2.1 demonstrates, after the initial A♭ pedal and vamp, 'Barroom Breakthrough' moves from A♭ up a semitone to A through **N•L•LR•M•L•LR•LR**. After arriving at A major, the cue rocks between D-min and A-maj triads (an **N** transformation). The sequence then repeats exactly starting at m. 20, identical to its predecessor except for a switch of the final **LR** to **RL** that

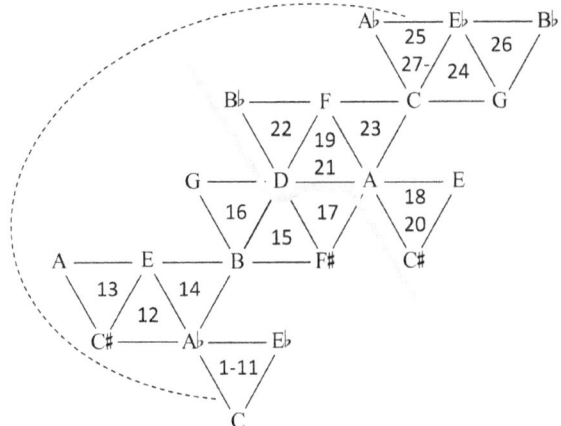

FIGURE 2.1 Horner, *A Beautiful Mind*, condensed *Tonnetz* analysis of 'Barroom Breakthrough.' Numbers represent measure numbers, the gray line demarcates where the chromatic sequence repeats, and the dotted line shows harmonic completion of the cycle.

allows the cue to have a complete run-through of the sequence while still ending with the loop-closing A♭ major triad already achieved two chords prior.[38]

In this case, tempo analysis indicated an identical FCPPM in 'Kaleidoscope of Mathematics' and 'Barroom Breakthrough.' The implied association of these cues prompted further study, revealing musical relationships that suggest that 'Barroom Breakthrough' accompanies the advent of the genius mind foreshadowed by the opening. Where, then, does this leave 'Cracking the Russian Codes'? The difference lies in the way tempo encodes not just relative activity but affect. Though the genius mind reached full speed and completed a problem cycle in 'Breakthrough,' 'Codes' musically depicts a less frenetic, more assured mind with its 360 FCPPM—a mind already having demonstrated its gift for superhumanly rapid thought (represented musically through tempo) and now showing its deep insight as well (represented through harmonic attainment). A darker interpretation, however, is also possible. Rather than suggest that 'Breakthrough' and 'Codes' separately fulfill both the tempo and harmonic promise respectively, one could read the coupling of these musical topics in 'Kaleidoscope' as an unattainable, illusory ideal. The brilliance of the 432 FCPPM and the assurance of the inevitability of the **SLIDE** transformation's culmination cannot coincide; Nash's circumstances prevent perfection of his potential.

Inequivalent Variables: Tempo Implies Meanings Tonal Analysis Cannot

Deploying the qualitative iconic metaphor SPEED OF MUSICAL EVENTS IS SPEED OF COGNITION allows the analyst of *A Beautiful Mind* to make additional connections between the state of the main character's mind and his musical accompaniment. Both 'Newspaper Codes' and 'Leaving for Work' prove excellent examples of how tempo as analytical focus can suggest interpretations unavailable to or difficult to support with strictly tonal readings.

'Newspaper Codes' accompanies Nash as he, circled by newsprint clippings, sees white-light letters emerge just as numbers did in 'Cracking the Russian Codes.' While the music still slides along chromatic progressions introduced back in 'Kaleidoscope,' a novel sound of rumbling, ponderous strings replaces Charlotte Church's vocal muse in this unsettling variant of Horner's mathematical genius topic. The score's low tessitura and descending minor thirds lend an ominous air, but it is a tempo that most clearly indicates Nash's decline: The cue begins with a 244 FCPPM, slower than any other 'genius music' heard so far save the onset of 'Barroom Breakthrough.' Rather than achieving epiphany through a division modulation, this cue contains the only genius music *ritardando* of the film, slowing down to 228 FCPPM, a veridical surprise.[39] After several prior genius cues employing click-track-steady tempi and division modulations to dramatically quicker FCPPM, this lag disconcerts.

After an hour of film following 'Newspaper Codes' focusing on Nash's mental illness—and thus omitting minimalist genius music—its perpetual piano chords reappear when he returns to problem-solving with 'Leaving for Work.' This cue's drastically slower but continuous FCPPM of 160 combines with the mathematician's plodding pace and deliberate scrawls to reinforce a mind, now steady, in autumn.

Parsing Performance Practice

In addition to its utility for meaning-driven interpretive approaches, tempo analysis is also an indispensable tool for shedding light on both film music conducting/recording and audiovisual editing practices. Is a cue free-timed or recorded with a click track? Pitch analysis proves unsurprisingly ineffectual at answering that question, but software that reveals precise details of waveform and spectral content such as Sonic Visualizer may begin to address this issue. The level of variability, or fluctuation in BPM or FCPPM from beat to beat, in a Sonic Visualizer tempo graph, may support a claim that studio musicians recorded a cue with a click

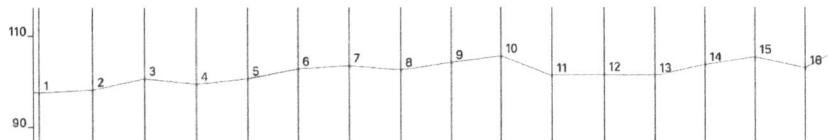

FIGURE 2.2 Horner, *A Beautiful Mind*, 'Barroom Breakthrough' tempo change in 16 beats starting at 0:20:14.

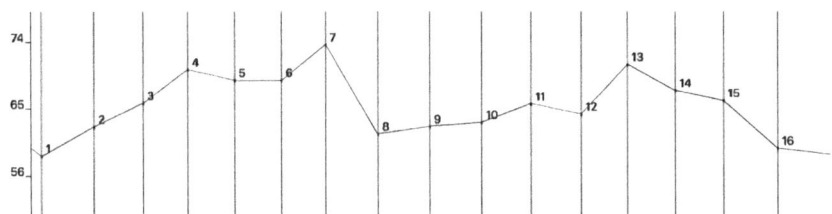

FIGURE 2.3 Horner, *A Beautiful Mind*, end credits at the MGT, tempo of 16 beats starting at 2:11:38.

track or that the conductor used a more flexible method such as punches and streamers. In an era where electronic music has become commonplace—and, with better sampling, sometimes difficult to identify by ear as computer-based—near-zero tempo variability may also indicate synthetic scores.

Figures 2.2 and 2.3 display tempo change graphs created with Sonic Visualizer for 'Barroom Breakthrough' (starting at 20:14) and the MGT section of the end credits of *A Beautiful Mind* (starting at 2:11:38). The numbers on the far-left y-axis indicate a beats-per-minute tempo scale, and the numbers 1–16 and the vertical lines adjacent to them mark the first 16 beats of these segments. The height of the beat numbers and the horizontal line show the change in tempo since the previous beat. As is clear from Figure 2.2, 'Barroom Breakthrough' shows minimal tempo variation from beat to beat. Figure 2.3, on the other hand, demonstrates more fluctuation in the BPM of the MGT in the end credits, with a pronounced tempo stretch near phrase endings (see #7–8 and #15–16). These graphs suggest the recording of 'Barroom Breakthrough' utilized a click track while omitting it for at least this segment of the end credits of *A Beautiful Mind*. This makes sense, as end credits sequences have few (if any) hit points and thus aren't subject to the same micro-controlled editorial and time constraints as the main body of the film.

While tempo graphs might be marshaled as evidence that cues were recorded more freely or with click tracks, musicologists more interested in larger trends could follow José Antonio Bowen in using such diagrams to demonstrate how performance practice has changed over time.[40] Rather than modeling how one particular piece's performance has sped up over decades, researchers can indicate how particular composers, directors, or even particular types of scenes or film genres are more likely to have either flexible or strictly regimented tempi—and how that may have changed throughout film history.

A theorist might also devise a tempo graph of an entire scene or even film to reveal more global audiovisual editing strategies. A number of computer scientists including Brett Adams have developed techniques to extract 'film tempo,' i.e., the cutting rhythm and amount of camera and/or visual movement within a shot.[41] While some researchers including Anan Liu have included audio tempo as a partial determinant of film tempo, most scholarship in this area remains insensitive to the structural contributions of the music track; music theorists might therefore fruitfully deploy techniques developed by Adams and Liu in conjunction with musical tempo graphs to interrogate how tempo on the soundtrack intersects with visual tempo, creating a modern analysis similar in spirit but finer-grained than Sergei Eisenstein's *Alexander Nevsky* sequence diagrams.[42]

While visual and musical tempo may—or may not—line up, another kind of film alignment, synchronization, remains the primary reason a composer and/or director may have selected a musical tempo in the first place. Given that composers from Mancini to Davis precompositionally determine a cue's tempo so as to enable easy hitting of selected synch points, analyzing moments of clear audiovisual synchronization can provide a window into why a particular tempo was chosen.

Consider again 'Barroom Breakthrough': Why does this instance of the MGT feature an FCPPM of 216 doubling to 432? As the film dramatizes the schizophrenic symptom of apophenia—the seeing of connections or patterns where none exist—it is tempting to proclaim this tempo an inside joke by Horner. New Age conspiracy theorists allege the number 432 permeates all, from the frequency of the universe to Pythagoras and Mozart's tuning systems.[43] But, as Lehman warns in his article on *A Beautiful Mind*, one must be judicious with musico-theoretical pattern finding.

A less contrived explanation is revealed through analysis of points of synchronization: Horner chose FCPPMs of 216 and 432 because those rates allow for precisely aligned hit points at both the measure and phrase level (see Example 2.4). The cue sneaks in, without any overt synchronization, under a medium close-up shot of Nash. A visual cut with synchronized dialogue—but still not music—first occurs halfway through m. 5, when Nash's rival says, 'What are you talking about?'

After this line, Horner avoids committing Mancini's dreaded sin of arbitrarily altering tempo in order to reach a sync point—but he does drop a beat in m. 6, with a measure of 2/4 in the overall 3/4 environment. Other MGTs in the film, including 'Kaleidoscope,' drop beats, so this is not a particularly sharp violation of contextual expectations. The slightly unexpected metrical change, however, does add extra intensity to the first musical synchronization of the cue: At m. 7, beat 1 aligns with a cut back to a medium close-up shot of Nash. Another tight hit point follows exactly four bars later, at the start of the next phrase, when m. 11.1 (read: Measure 11, beat 1) aligns with the completion of a fade-in zoom-in to a medium shot of the blonde woman. The arrival at the next measure, 12.1, syncs with an overhead shot of the blonde. The line 'So then we go for her friends' and a return to the medium shot of the blonde loosely syncs with m. 15.1. 'But they will all give us the cold shoulder' and the appearance of the blonde's friends aligns in loose sync with m. 17.1, while m. 18.1 matches perfectly with a special effects shot of the blonde's friends disappearing.[44]

Horner's specific tempo decision allows for musico-visual synchronization of three phrases (at m. 7, m. 11, and m.15) and two pairs of consecutive measures (mm. 11–12 and mm. 17–18) down to the millisecond. No other tempi, except further doubled ones, would afford these particular hit points. Given the close synchronization of this scene and its music, it seems reasonable to surmise that 'Kaleidoscope'—which likewise features a 432 FCPPM but needs not hit any sync points beyond the title card—either borrowed its tempo from 'Barroom Breakthrough' or that 'Barroom Breakthrough' was cut to 'Kaleidoscope' (or a temp track with an identical tempo).

Conclusion

In Hans Zimmer's MasterClass, he declares, 'The only thing that's my friend is the metronome because it's just there. It's steady. It's reliable... If it's in the grid, you're already a step ahead. Just put up a click and listen to the click, and look at the picture.'[45] Fred Karlin and Rayburn Wright's scoring manual *On the Track* devotes multiple chapters to finding film timings. Film composers find tempo fundamental. For whatever reason—whether lack of fashionable tools such as *Tonnetz*, few citable precedents, or the seemingly facile fiber of tempo—film musicologists and theorists regularly forget musical speed in favor of harmonic, orchestrational, and thematic points of focus. For concert-music analysis, that makes sense: Of all musical parameters, tempo is the one where performers are given the most freedom. How do you analyze something as variable as '*Allegro*'?

But filmmaking practice changes the calculus. As soon as score is locked to picture, tempo is no longer a variable. It becomes a discrete measurable quantity—integers!—that theorists can compare and use to design appealing and revealing diagrams. From supporting harmonic readings to illuminating audiovisual editing and performance practices, to suggesting interpretive pathways unavailable to purely pitch-based perspectives, film score tempo analysis provides a hitherto untapped reservoir of potential. As Zimmer quips, 'The click is your friend.'[46]

Notes

1 See Annie Lang, Shuhua Zhou, Nancy Schwartz, Paul D. Bolls, and Robert F. Potter, 'The Effects of Edits on Arousal, Attention and Memory for Television Messages: When an Edit Is an Edit Can an Edit Be Too Much?' *Journal of Broadcasting & Electronic Media* 44.1 (2000): 94–109; and Francesca R. Dillman Carpentier and Robert F. Potter, 'Effects of Music on Physiological Arousal: Explorations into Tempo and Genre,' *Media Psychology* 10.3 (2007): 339–363. These effects were shown to be applicable to the classical and swing genres, not, strangely, for rock. See also Gabriela Husain, William Forde Thompson, and E. Glenn Schellenberg, 'Effects of Musical Tempo and Mode on Arousal, Mood, and Spatial Abilities,' *Music Perception* 20.2 (December 1, 2002): 151–171, and Marjolein D. van der Zwaag, Joyce H.D.M. Westerink, and Egon L. van den Broek, 'Emotional and Psychophysiological Responses to Tempo, Mode, and Percussiveness,' *Musicae Scientiae* 15.2 (July 1, 2011): 250–269.
2 See Michael Sweet, *Writing Interactive Music for Video Games: A Composer's Guide*, 1st ed. (Upper Saddle River, NJ: Addison-Wesley Professional, 2014), 213; Zach Whalen, 'Play Along—an Approach to Videogame Music,' *Game Studies* 4 (Nov 2004), http://gamestudies.org/0401/whalen; and Karen Collins, *Game Sound: An Introduction to the History, Theory, and Practice of Video Game Music and Sound Design* (Cambridge: MIT Press, 2008), 148.
3 See Valerie J. Bolivar, Annabel J. Cohen, and John C. Fentress, 'Semantic and Formal Congruency in Music and Motion Pictures: Effects on the Interpretation of Visual Action,' *Psychomusicology: A Journal of Research in Music Cognition* 13.1–2 (1994): 28–59.
4 Richard Davis, *Complete Guide to Film Scoring: The Art and Business of Writing Music for Movies and TV* (Boston: Berklee Press, 1999): 154.
5 Henry Mancini, *Case History of a Film Score: 'The Thorn Birds'* (New York: Northridge Music Company, 2004), 19.
6 Fred Karlin and Rayburn Wright, *On the Track: A Guide to Contemporary Film Scoring* (Abingdon: Routledge, 2013); Davis *Complete Guide to Film Scoring*, 154; Earle Hagen, *Advanced Techniques for Film Scoring: A Complete Text* (Los Angeles: Alfred Publishing Company, Inc., 1990); and Lalo Schifrin, *Music Composition for Film and Television* (Boston, MA: Berklee Press, 2011).
7 John Williams is recognized as a free-timing conductor. After tempo tapping with several Williams cues, this author agrees this seems to be the case— Williams's music regularly contains more tempo variation when compared to, for example, Horner's score for *A Beautiful Mind*. See Karlin and Wright,

On the Track, 112; see also Tim Davies, 'Conducting Part 4,' deBreved: The Tim Davies Orchestration Blog, March 13, 2013, www.timusic.net/debreved/conducting-part-4/.

8 See Karlin and Wright, *On the Track*; Frans Absil, 'BPM Calculator for Fixed Tempo Film and Video Game Music Cues: Film Music Tempo Calculation Tool—Version 3.1,' accessed December 18, 2020, www.fransabsil.nl/htm/eventhit.htm; and Davies, 'Conducting Part 4.'

9 Encouragingly, the small but increasing number of study scores from outlets like Omni Music Publishing do indeed include precise metronome markings.

10 David Temperley, *The Cognition of Basic Musical Structures* (Cambridge, MA: The MIT Press, 2004), 23–24.

11 Peter A. Martens, 'The Ambiguous Tactus: Tempo, Subdivision Benefit, And Three Listener Strategies,' *Music Perception* 28. 5 (June 1, 2011): 436. See also Birgitta Burger, Marc R. Thompson, Geoff Luck, Suvi H. Saarikallio, and Petri Toiviainen, 'Hunting for the Beat in the Body: On Period and Phase Locking in Music-Induced Movement,' *Frontiers in Human Neuroscience* 8 (November 7, 2014).

12 ISMIR (the International Society for Music Information Retrieval) created metrics for the accuracy of tempo estimation algorithms. One metric, AAC_2, allows for 'octave errors' of tempo detection by 2, 3, 1/2, and 1/3, essentially still counting it correct if the tempo measurement indicates the wrong metrical level. See Hendrik Schreiber, Julián Urbano, and Meinard Müller, 'Music Tempo Estimation: Are We Done Yet?' *Transactions of the International Society for Music Information Retrieval* 3.1 (August 24, 2020): 111–125; Konstantinos Trochidis and Leontios Hadjileontiadis, 'Tempo Induction from Music Recordings Using Ensemble Empirical Mode Decomposition Analysis,' *Computer Music Journal* 35 (December 1, 2011): 83–97; and Aggelos Pikrakis and S. Theodoridis, 'An Application of Empirical Mode Decomposition On Tempo Induction From Music Recordings,' in *Proceedings of the 8th International Conference on Music Information Retrieval*, ISMIR (Vienna, 2007), 301–304.

13 Sebastian Böck and Matthew E. P. Davies, 'Deconstruct, Analyse, Reconstruct: How to improve Tempo, Beat, and Downbeat Estimation,' in *Proceedings of the 21st International Society for Music Information Retrieval Conference* (Montréal: Canada, 2020), 575.

14 None of the automated tempo detection tools worked on a cue I analyze in this essay, 'Barroom Breakthrough,' from *A Beautiful Mind*, likely because the frequent irregular word onsets created spikes that interfered with the regularity of the quicker metrical level of the cue. In some cases, particularly if the dialogue is panned to the center, it might be possible to use Audacity to remove dialogue or vocals before using automated tempo detection.

15 Robert Fink, *Repeating Ourselves: American Minimalism as Cultural Practice* (Berkeley: University of California Press, 2005), 20.

16 Martens, 'The Ambiguous Tactus,' 436.

17 Clive McClelland, 'Ombra and Tempesta,' in Danuta Mirka (ed.), *The Oxford Handbook of Topic Theory* (Oxford University Press, 2014), 282. On the subject of the *ombra* topic in film music, see also William Rosar, 'The Penumbra of Wagner's Ombra in Two Science Fiction Films: *The Thing from Another World* and *The Day the Earth Stood Still*,' in Jeongwon Joe and Sander L. Gilman (eds.), *Wagner and Cinema* (Bloomington: University of Indiana Press, 2010), 152–166.

18 James Buhler and David Neumeyer, *Hearing the Movies: Music and Sound in Film History*, 2nd ed., (New York, New York: Oxford University Press, 2015), 124–133.
19 Juan Chattah, 'Film Music as Embodiment,' in Maarten Coëgnarts and Peter Kravanja (eds.), *Embodied Cognition and Cinema* (Leuven: Leuven University Press, 2015), 83.
20 All the works I discuss could properly be called 'postminimalist,' but I follow the tradition of most popular press writers and film critics and use the blanket term 'minimalism' to discuss post-1980 film scores.
21 Rebecca M. Doran Eaton, 'Marking Minimalism: Minimal Music as a Sign of Machines and Mathematics in Multimedia,' *Music and the Moving Image* 7.1 (2014): 3–23.
22 Eaton, 'Multivariable Minimalism: Differentiating the Characteristics of Music for Mathematicians,' Paper presented at the *Sixth International Conference on Music & Minimalism*, Nief-Norf Summer Festival, UT-Knoxville, Knoxville, TN, United States (June 24, 2017); Eaton, 'Multivariable Minimalism: Differentiating the Characteristics of Music for Mathematicians,' Lightning Talk presented at the Film and Multimedia Interest Group, *Society for Music Theory Conference*, Vancouver, Canada, November 4, 2016.
23 A qualitative iconic metaphor is when there is some kind of linear correlation between a musical quality and the visual and/or idea it underscores; for instance, a descending musical glissando could accompany a falling character on screen. Some qualitative iconic metaphors—like the falling character one—are called 'mickey-mousing' in the realm of screen music composition. See Chattah, 'Semiotics, Pragmatics, and Metaphor in Film Music Analysis,' PhD diss. (Florida State University, 2006), 29–40, http://purl.flvc.org/fsu/fd/FSU_migr_etd-3874.
24 'Escape!' (2003) sounds more similar to the MGT than its 1988 and 1989 versions, the piano/flute 'Prologue' from *A Thin Blue Line* and the solo piano 'Metamorphosis II,' due to its instrumentation with rich strings in the descant.
25 There are a few measures of triplet 16th notes, but they comprise a small portion of the middle of the work. Those triplets at MM 96 create 576 continuous repeated articulations per minute for a brief moment.
26 Frank Lehman, 'Manufacturing the Epic Score: Hans Zimmer and the Sounds of Significance,' in Stephen C. Meyer (ed.), *Music in Epic Film: Listening to Spectacle*, Routledge Music and Screen Media Series (Abingdon: Routledge, 2016), 27–55.
27 For more on films and other media that link mathematicians with minimalist music, including precursors to *A Beautiful Mind*, see Eaton, 'Marking Minimalism.'
28 Lehman gives a similar list in his treatment of *A Beautiful Mind* but includes several cues as 'genius music' that I do not. To be instances of the minimalist genius topic as defined here, I require continuous steady repeated articulations. Lehman's inclusion of cues is primarily based on thematic and/or harmonic content, not what I consider the most perceptually relevant parameters: Minimalist texture and repetition, specifically in this score continuous repeating piano. Frank Lehman, 'Transformational Analysis and the Representation of Genius in Film Music,' *Music Theory Spectrum* 35.1 (2013): 1–22.
29 Lehman, 'Transformational Analysis,' 10.
30 Lehman, 'Transformational Analysis,' 15–16.
31 David Lidov, *Is Language a Music?: Writings on Musical Form and Signification* (Indiana University Press, 2005), 35.

32 I borrow the term 'division modulation' from Jose Garza. Garza, 'Adapt and Prevail: New Applications of Rhythmic and Metric Analysis in Contemporary Metal Music,' PhD diss. (Florida State University, 2017), 91, http://purl.flvc.org/fsu/fd/FSU_FALL2017_Garza_fsu_0071E_14184.
33 Richard Parncutt, 'A Perceptual Model of Pulse Salience and Metrical Accent in Musical Rhythms,' *Music Perception* 11.4 (1994): 409–464.
34 Lehman, 'Transformational Analysis,' 16–17.
35 Ibid.,18.
36 This is a somewhat loose application of the idea of an NRT cycle: It is not an exact iteration of a single transformational cell but more of a mix-and-match. When examining Example 2.6, however, it is clear that the cue takes the same kind of path through pitch space twice, akin to traversing the exact same instruction set—with one minor alteration that ends up having the same effect downstream—and ends up where it started in pitch space.
37 The neo-Riemannian operator M I borrow from Lehman, 'Transformational Analysis,' 3.
38 Measure 20 also marks Nash's second if/then pair in the dialogue and immediately precedes the metric division modulation. Thus, his second conditional statement aligns perfectly with the second musical traverse through the same transformational pattern.
39 See David Brian Huron, *Sweet Anticipation: Music and the Psychology of Expectation* (MIT Press, 2008), 269.
40 José Antonio Bowen, 'Tempo, Duration, and Flexibility: Techniques in the Analysis of Performance.' *Journal of Musicological Research* 16.2 (January 1, 1996): 111–156; José A. Bowen, 'Finding the Music in Musicology: Performance History in Musical Works,' in Nicholas Cook and Mark Everist (eds.), *Rethinking Music* (Oxford: Oxford University Press, 1999), 424–451.
41 Brett Adams, Chitra Dorai, and Svetha Venkatesh, 'Formulating Film Tempo,' in Chitra Dorai and Svetha Venkatesh (eds.), *Media Computing: Computational Media Aesthetics*, The Springer International Series in Video Computing (Boston, MA: Springer US, 2002), 57–84.
42 Anan Liu, Jintao Li, Yongdong Zhang, Sheng Tang, Yan Song, and Zhaoxuan Yang, 'An Innovative Model of Tempo and Its Application in Action Scene Detection for Movie Analysis,' in *Proceedings of the IEEE Workshop on Applications of Computer Vision (WACV)*, v. 1, Copper Mountain, CO, US.
43 See, for example Assaf Dar Sagol, 'Music Theory: 432 Hz Tuning—Separating Fact from Fiction,' Ask Audio, 27 Feb 2016, http://ask.audio/articles/music-theory-432-hz-tuning-separating-fact-from-fiction.
44 See Catrin Watts for more on tight versus loose sync points. Catrin Angharad Watts, 'Popular Music and Audiovisual Editing in Contemporary Action Films,' PhD diss. (University of Texas at Austin, 2018).
45 Hans Zimmer, 'Tempo,' MasterClass, January 2017, www.masterclass.com/classes/hans-zimmer-teaches-film-scoring/chapters/tempo.
46 In the 'Tempo' chapter of his MasterClass, Zimmer reiterates the importance of tempo over pitch, continuing, 'The click is your friend. It's reliable. It's the only thing I can rely on. The notes are lying to me. I am lying to me, going yes, today you're going to write a great tune. Well, that's bullshit.'

3

TRACKING PROGRESSIONS OF HEROIC CHORD PROGRESSIONS IN RECENT POPULAR SCREEN MEDIA

Scott Murphy

Example 3.1 provides a reduced transcription of Alan Silvestri's 'Avengers theme' as first heard [1:51:54] within the Marvel Cinematic Universe (MCU) toward the end of the 2012 superhero film *The Avengers*. Its first phrase (mm. 1–8) accompanies a welcome success for 'Earth's Mightiest Heroes' after some setbacks during the movie's climactic battle in New York, and the repetition of this phrase (mm. 9–15) accompanies the film's iconic 360-degree shot of the six champions finally assembled.

Many aspects of this music exude heroism and grandeur, such as its loud and high brass, its rising perfect fifths, its broad consonant triads, and, according to recent scholarship, particular successions of these triads. The music theorist Erik Heine has observed how the progression of two major triads a minor third apart 'has accumulated a heroic narrative connotation through its repeated use over time in similar filmic scenarios.'[1] He calls this progression both 'Hero' and, more technically, M3, since both triads are major (M) and a minor third spans three semitones (3). Heine offers seven, mostly late-twentieth-century, examples of films that associate M3 with heroism, from John Williams's 'Rebel Fanfare' in *Star Wars Episode IV: A New Hope* (1977) to James Newton Howard's 'The Hand of Fate' in *Signs* (2002).

On the one hand, Silvestri's *Avengers* theme from ten years later well belongs to this set of examples as supporting evidence for M3's affinity with heroism in film music, as this theme places major triads rooted on C and A temporally adjacent to one another, and a minor third separates the pitches A and C. In fact, no other pair of triads appears more often as an adjacency in this theme: The five M3s, annotated in Example 3.1, suffuse the theme

DOI: 10.4324/9781003001171-3

EXAMPLE 3.1 Silvestri, *The Avengers*, 1:51:54–1:52:25 (all examples transcribed by author).

with a harmonic progression that, as Heine's 'Hero,' taps into expressive affiliations amassed over previous decades. On the other hand, Silvestri's *Avengers* theme, when cast alongside Heine's seven examples, is in a smaller class by itself. The music notated in Example 3.1 unequivocally projects a tonic of E: This pitch serves as the root of the first and last chords and the pitch of the first and last melodic notes. The theme's tonality of E situates its M3's major chords with roots of A and C as subdominant (IV) and submediant (VI), respectively. None of Heine's examples tonally situates its M3 this clearly as such. This does not surprise. Only in the twenty-first century does this more precise kind of M3—the compound of IV and VI—begin to corner the blockbuster cinematic market as a progression signifying heroism, courtesy of not only the MCU but also other franchises as well.

This chapter provides a selective history of this progression's rise to prominence, focusing on the Marvel, DC, and James Bond franchises, and speculates about its dramatic passage among studios and its mutation into variants.[2] After this section, I conclude by hypothesizing how only this more precise kind of M3 closely but also covertly follows from another seemingly dissimilar harmonic progression associated with heroism in the movies, particularly before the rise of this more precise kind of M3. However, before embarking on these parts, I wish to put into play a nomenclature that dispenses with labels like 'more precise kind of M3,' reveals shortcomings in Roman numerals, and offers different degrees of precision useful in teasing out different threads of this historical account as well as nuances of associational meaning.

Labels

Heine's M3 label is independent not only of the progression's clear tonal orientation, if there is one, but also of the temporal order of the two triads. My earlier claim about the more precise signification of cinematic heroism by an IV-VI adjacency departs from the former while it appears to conform to the latter. However, attending to the chord's chronological arrangement permits finer distinctions in describing this convention. Most notably, if either an isolated juxtaposition of IV and VI or an oscillation between IV and VI accompanies heroism in mainstream film, the VI appears first in a great majority of cases.[3] Example 3.1's mm. 6–7, and mm. 2–4 (and 10–12), respectively, exemplify both of these stylistic generalizations. Therefore, when designating a common chord-progression accompaniment of twenty-first-century on-screen heroism, the time-dependent label of VI→IV is primary and most specific, the time-independent label of VI←→IV is secondary and less specific, and Heine's time- and tonality-independent of M3 is tertiary and even less specific.

Yet, in spite of the prevalence of Roman numerals when naming tonally situated triads in musical discourse, Heine's kind of label better represents its signified than VI→IV and VI←→IV represent theirs, for at least two reasons. First, Roman numerals use a diatonic scale as its basis of measurement, whereas many of the distinctions among harmonic progressions and their extra-musical associations innovated or perpetuated within screen media are best gauged using the chromatic scale. To illustrate: The aforementioned 'more precise kind of M3' has remarkably formed an alliance with cinematic heroes of the last two decades regardless of whether the tonic harmony is major or minor (or neither). (The four notated examples in this chapter encapsulate this freedom: Two, including Example 3.1, are in the minor mode, and the other two are in the major mode.) Such a switch complicates consistent diatonic labeling, since the chords represented by unmodified Roman numerals traditionally derive their exact position from the diatonic scale whose mode matches that of the tonic triad. For instance, if Example 3.1's E-minor tonic triads are swapped for E major, the label of VI→IV for mm. 2–3 must become the different label of ♭VI→IV; otherwise, E: VI→IV could signify C♯M→AM, a categorically contrasting sound that Heine calls M4 or 'Magic.' However, the chromatic scale accommodates this modal substitution: The root of the typically first chord in the heroic progression remains eight semitones above the tonic pitch, like C is eight semitones above E in Example 3.1.

Second, imagine exchanging Example 3.1's E-minor tonic triads with major or minor tonic triads rooted on D or A. Heine's M3 theory holds that this ersatz music is also heroic broadly speaking, and I assert that it would be less quintessentially heroic for films of the past couple of decades. Both views are important. However, any new labels of Example 3.1's M3s based on Roman numerals to which these changes of tonality would give rise, such as ♭III→I or ♭VII→V, belie the sliding scale formed between these views, as the 'M3-ness' shared between these progressions is completely absent in their labels.

Therefore, to more accurately describe a range of harmonic-progression signifiers in film music, I recommend a 'MnM' labeling system that affords and standardizes various means of description that the previous discussion has shown to be of particular use. Figure 3.1 provides a schematic diagram of a label within this system. Foremost, this system indicates how the progression it labels can be transformed without altering its designated identity. For example, an M3 progression remains labeled as such after both a retrogradation of its two chords and a change of key, but a VI→IV progression endures neither without a change of label. Therefore, the label equivalent to M3 would include rightmost subscripts of both R (for retrogradation) and K (for key change), and a label equivalent to VI→IV would have neither subscript, putting the null character (Ø) in their place to underscore their absence. Using one of the four possible combinations of R and K within this scope (Ø, R, K, or RK) as rightmost subscripts immediately conveys to the reader in what specific way a label generalizes classes of harmonic progression. Additionally, this system embraces chromatic measurement, foregrounding the distance in semitones between the roots of the two chords, and, if applicable, the distance in semitones between the progression and the tonic pitch. Lastly, two single characters—M for major, and m for minor—indicate the quality

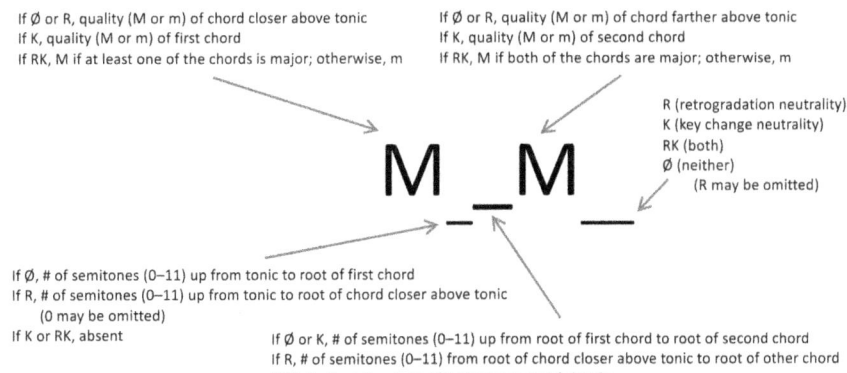

FIGURE 3.1 Anatomy of an MnM label.

of each of the two triads in the progression; unlike Heine's system, this allows the triads to be of different types.[4]

For example, E: CM→AM can be labeled as a $M_8 9 M_\emptyset$. The rightmost $\emptyset$ as subscript symbolizes the dismissal of both retrogradation and key change as label-preserving transformations, which results in the most precise type of label within this scope. The first and second Ms represent the qualities of the chronologically first and second triads, respectively. The subscripted 8 represents the number of semitones up from the tonic pitch of E to the first triad's root of C, and the 9 represents the number of semitones up from the first triad's root of C to the second triad's root of A. $M_8 9 M_\emptyset$ is equivalent to the 'more precise kind of M3' as more loosely described earlier.

Furthermore, E: CM→AM can also be labeled as a $M_5 3 M_R$. The rightmost R as subscript symbolizes the analyst's acceptance of retrogradation, but not key change, as a label-preserving transformation, which results in a less precise type of label within this scope, because $M_5 3 M_R$ also applies to E: AM→CM. The method of calculation of the numerical characters adjusts to this labeling type as spelled out in Figure 3.1. E: CM→AM can also be labeled as $M9M_K$; when any change of key (K) preserves the label, a subscript as second character is not necessary. Lastly (at least within this scope), E: CM→AM can also be labeled as a $M3M_{RK}$, which is synonymous with Heine's M3.

Although my less wieldy label of $M3M_{RK}$ is three characters longer than Heine's more nimble M3, the parametric orthography of the system to which this label belongs easily adapts to new situations and other category types, and facilitates quick and gradated comparisons with other similarly constructed labels. Some of these label-enabled comparisons take place within a hierarchical taxonomy, like the binomial nomenclature of biological classification, in which word accrual—the *canis familiaris* species is a subset of the *canis* genus—makes clear the inclusional relationship. For one example, I can easily recognize $M3M_K$ as one subclass of $M3M_{RK}$, and acknowledging $M9M_K$ as $M3M_{RK}$'s other subclass only requires recognizing that 3 and 9 sum to 12. For another example, I can easily recognize $M_5 3 M_\emptyset$ as one subclass of $M_5 3 M_R$; acknowledging $M_8 9 M_\emptyset$ as $M_5 3 M_R$'s other subclass only requires recognizing that, for each label, the two numbers of one label sum modulo 12 to the subscript of the other (8+9 $\cong$ 5, 5+3 $\cong$ 8). But this comparative system also transcends hierarchy to become a network of overlapping classes. Using both the M3s from Example 3.1 as concrete stand-ins and the tonal shifts imagined earlier, Figure 3.2 provides a portion of this network relevant to the historical discussion to follow.

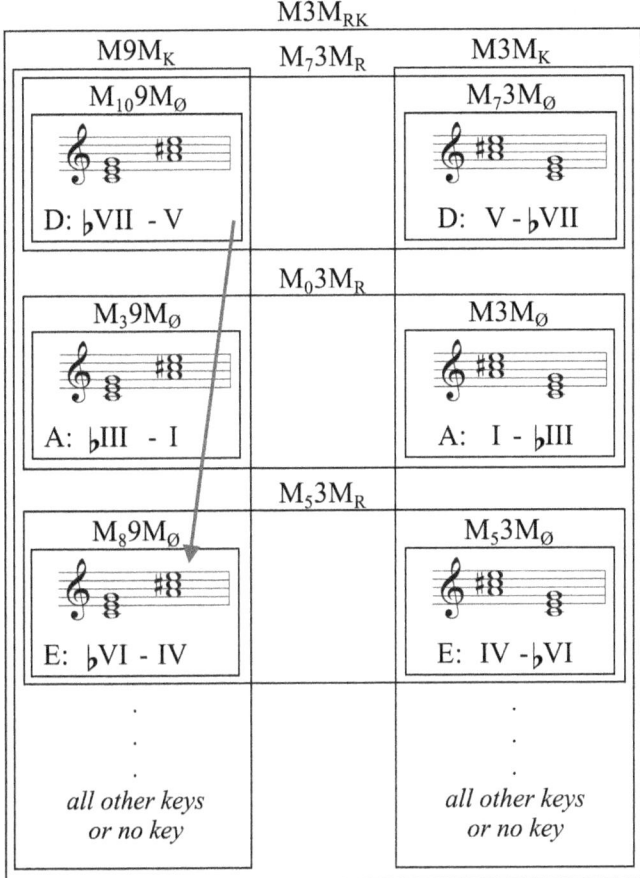

FIGURE 3.2 Different forms of MnM harmonic-progression categorization and their interrelationships.

Timeline

In what ways has $M_8 9 M_\emptyset$ been associated with heroism in screen media before and after its appearance in *The Avengers*? In short, the ample prevalence and considerable popular exposure of this specific affiliation—dozens upon dozens of examples—from the last two to three decades is unmatched in any other genre or during any other era to my knowledge. However, there exist both isolated precedents of this specific case, as well as more numerous precedents of progressions connected to $M_8 9 M_\emptyset$ to some degree within the relational network that Figure 3.2 shows in part. I will briefly address the latter type of precedent first, before engaging the former.

Earlier I observed that among Heine's corpus of $M3M_{RK}$ examples, none is clearly $M_{8}9M_{\emptyset}$ or even the more general $M_{5}3M_{R}$. Furthermore, the majority of $M3M_{RK}$s in his catalog belong to $M3M_{K}$ rather than $M_{8}9M_{\emptyset}$'s superclass of $M9M_{K}$, which means that, even setting key aside, the order in which Silvestri arranges his heroic triads in *The Avengers* theme breaks from any trend that might be inferred from Heine's sample. However, Frank Lehman has established that $M9M_{K}$, realized in the form of $M_{10}9M_{\emptyset}$ rather than $M_{8}9M_{\emptyset}$, serves as a half cadence for themes in multiple big-screen Westerns starting around 1960.[5] Perhaps, as indicated with the arrow in Figure 3.2, the $M_{10}9M_{\emptyset}$ of twentieth-century cowboy heroics migrated two perfect fifths lower within tonal space and to an earlier position within the phrase to become the $M_{8}9M_{\emptyset}$ of twenty-first-century superhuman heroics, while staying within the $M9M_{K}$ corridor.[6]

Moviegoers can hear $M_{8}9M_{\emptyset}$ sporadically accompanying heroism in movie theaters before the MCU begins in 2008. It gradually emerges from a powerful four-chord loop soon after Andy bravely escapes from a brutal prison [2:00:02] in *The Shawshank Redemption* (1994, Thomas Newman).[7] $M_{8}9M_{\emptyset}$ forms the second half of a four-chord loop (i→II7→VI→IV), used throughout *V for Vendetta* (2005) for heroic moments [e.g., 1:10:51], that the composer Dario Marianelli calls 'Freedom Chords.'[8] In *United 93* (2006, John Powell), when terrorists first learn that the hijacked passengers are possibly planning an attack on them [1:28:51], $M_{8}9M_{\emptyset}$ appears twice in succession. It also appears twice in succession [1:35:57] at the climactic end of Remy's heroic preparation of the titular dish for his food critic nemesis in *Ratatouille* (2007, Michael Giacchino).

With the exception of *V for Vendetta*, a comic-book adaptation, none of these uses is thematized, and all four occur in the second half of the movie, avoiding involvement in the upfront branding that becomes more frequent as $M_{8}9M_{\emptyset}$ moves into the next decade. One good example of $M_{8}9M_{\emptyset}$'s gradual promotion to marquee prominence is in the James Bond franchise. Although the 'James Bond Theme,' a collaboration of Monty Norman and John Barry, has appeared in all of the Bond films since the beginning with *Dr. No* (1962), its famous $\hat{5}$-♭$\hat{6}$-♮$\hat{6}$ line has been deliberately harmonized with $M_{8}9M_{\emptyset}$ only relatively recently. When he took over scoring the series in 1997, David Arnold demonstrated the potential of this reharmonization for a brief moment when Bond enjoys the aftermath of a small success (*Tomorrow Never Dies* (1997), 40:35) but otherwise followed standard procedure until *Casino Royale* (2006) and its strapping new actor Daniel Craig. The movie's title song 'You Know My Name,' co-written by Arnold and its singer Chris Cornell, features $M_{8}9M_{\emptyset}$ at the end of the instrumental intro and the beginning of the chorus, putting $\hat{5}$-♭$\hat{6}$-♮$\hat{6}$ squarely in the vocal part. Arnold also uses $M_{8}9M_{\emptyset}$ for a moment when Bond, in his iconic tuxedo, admires himself in the mirror [1:08:36], further tying the new harmonies with the new Bond. Although $M_8 9M_\emptyset$ still appears sporadically during the narratives of subsequent Bond movies (*Quantum of Solace* (2008, Arnold), 48:14; *Skyfall* (2012, Thomas Newman), 33:15), it has also maintained its top billing not only through its use in verses and chorus of Adele's title song for *Skyfall* but even in a position earlier in the film when it accompanies the Columbia studio logo at the outset of *Spectre* (2015, Newman). In *No Time to Die* (2021), $M_8 9M_\emptyset$ accompanies both the logo and Billie Eilish's title song. Other spy-based screen products picked up on this new harmonization, as in the pilot episode for *Chuck* (2007, Tim Jones, 4:38), and Matthew Margeson's and Henry Jackman's pervasive main theme for the *Kingsman* trilogy (2014, 2017, 2021).

A gradual shift of $M_8 9M_\emptyset$ toward a larger share of the franchise's commercial identity well describes the first half of the MCU's first 12 years. In the first movie, *Iron Man* (2008, Ramin Djawadi), $M_8 9M_\emptyset$ adjoins a geography- and character-establishing shot of Tony Stark's coastal Malibu home [9:28] and the heroic rescue of a chuteless ejected pilot [1:24:03]. The music for the comic ending of the title character's maiden flight [1:04:34] incorporates the $M_5 3M_\emptyset$ variant. These moments, like Stark's display of cocky bravado at the end [16:51] of a congressional hearing in *Iron Man 2* (2010, John Debney), or a matching Malibu establishing shot [4:59] in *Iron Man 3* (2013, Brian Tyler), insinuate $M_8 9M_\emptyset$ into a (super)heroic identity while sidestepping overt thematization. Such $M_8 9M_\emptyset$-based thematization accompanies not the title characters in other early MCU movies—*The Incredible Hulk* (2008), *Thor* (2011), or *Captain America: The First Avenger* (2011)—but with their initial assembly in *The Avengers* and its main theme of Example 3.1. Silvestri's theme lives at the musical heart of the MCU, accentuating its most visually and narratologically apotheotic moments, such as *The Avengers: Age of Ultron* (2015) at 1:56:09, *The Avengers: Infinity War* (2018) at 1:45:30, and *The Avengers: Endgame* (2019) at 2:18:33.

However, both the MCU and its claim to $M_8 9M_\emptyset$ faced competition in 2013. On April 16 of this year, DC Comics released the final trailer for the first movie in their own planned cinematic universe: The Superman reboot *Man of Steel*, scheduled for theatrical release two months later. Snippets of the original music for a movie—in contrast to its visuals, story, and celebrity—typically cannot adorn its advanced advertisements, as music is usually one of the last components to be added in post-production. However, the final trailer for *Man of Steel* shared with fans a theme by composer Hans Zimmer (Example 3.2) that would appear in the film as the main character tests his limits and learns to fly [49:33]. This theme dominates the three-minute trailer, and $M_8 9M_\emptyset$ specifically and $M_5 3M_R$ more generally dominate the theme's most vigorous portions, potentially siphoning its associations from Silvestri's *Avengers*

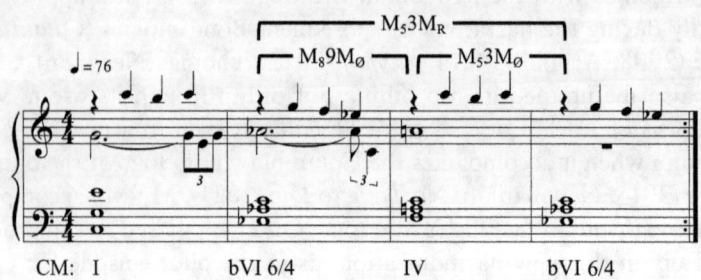

EXAMPLE 3.2   Zimmer, *Man of Steel,* 'Flight' theme.

theme released the year before and fast-tracking a front-and-center thematic position for $M_8 9M_\emptyset$ in the DC Extended Universe (DCEU).

Yet later the same year, Marvel expanded $M_8 9M_\emptyset$'s brand within its own territory by establishing consistent music for the Marvel Studios logo. Composer Brian Tyler had already provided the score for *Iron Man 3* earlier in 2013, including a new theme highlighting $M_8 9M_\emptyset$. His 'Marvel Fanfare,' provided in Example 3.3, first accompanies Marvel's logo for *Thor: The Dark World*, released on November 8, 2013, and for three more Marvel movies to follow. Although the linear content differs from Marvel's previous $M_8 9M_\emptyset$-based themes and even changes a bit in some of the subsequent logos, each fanfare has $M_8 9M_\emptyset$ at its core. Producer Kevin Feige cites Disney's acquisition of Marvel Studios as the reason for the logo's new look and sound, but, at the time, I could not help but hear Marvel (re)gain a sonic-signifying upper hand in its rivalry with the DCEU.[9]

The years 2012–13 and Marvel's logo music also represent the high-water mark for $M_8 9M_\emptyset$, because the $M_5 3M_\emptyset$ variant that reverses $M_8 9M_\emptyset$'s two chords, but still preserves the more generic superheroic $M_5 3M_R$ as distinct from, say, the cowboy's $M_7 3M_R$, becomes more commonplace afterward in the screen products of both the DCEU and the MCU. Curiously, a preference for $M_5 3M_\emptyset$ over $M_8 9M_\emptyset$ as heroic had already begun in Blake Neely's music for the first season (2014) of *The Flash* [e.g., E4, 31:19; E6, 34:52]. For DC *Man of Steel* sequels, the first time that the $M_8 9M_\emptyset$ of Zimmer's 'Flight' theme refers to Superman is in the character's absence: After Superman's death at the end of *Batman vs. Superman: Dawn of Justice* (2016, Hans Zimmer and Junkie XL), Martha Kent gives Lois Lane a package with a wedding ring from Clark [2:16:45, Ultimate Edition]. DC instead turns to the $M_5 3M_\emptyset$ variant for assembling its superheroic pantheon, whether it is furtively teasing its potential in the mid-credits scene [1:55:17] following *Suicide Squad* (2016, Steven Price) or the shot of all five of its main characters in a line

EXAMPLE 3.3 Tyler, First Marvel Fanfare.

ready for the final battle [1:31:03] in Joss Whedon's cut of *Justice League* (2017, Danny Elfman), although Junkie XL returned to $M_8 9M_\emptyset$ to represent heroism for Zach Synder's longer 2021 cut of the film, such as for the appearance of J'onn J'onzz [2:20:07]. Both $M_5 3M_\emptyset$ and its continuation into an oscillating $M_5 3M_R$ join Diana Prince as she tests her limits by preternaturally jumping over a chasm to reach a tower with powerful weapons [33:56] in *Wonder Woman* (2017, Rupert Gregson-Williams). DC returns to the prototypical $M_8 9M_\emptyset$ only two years later for *Shazam!* (2019, Benjamin Wallfisch), most notably when the title character transforms his siblings into superheroes during the final battle [1:45:38].

After 2013, Marvel tweaked the formula for its MCU movies, moving toward more comedic fare and lesser-known characters, and its composers correspondingly tweaked the $M_8 9M_\emptyset$ formula in a variety of ways. One of those ways, like DC, was to use the $M_5 3M_\emptyset$ permutation of $M_8 9M_\emptyset$, as in Tyler Bates's main theme for *Guardians of the Galaxy* (2014), first heard as the title characters culminate their first heroic scene as a team [41:09], and 'Guardians Inferno,' the 70s-spoof song written by Bates and director James Gunn that starts the end credits [2:12:07] in *Guardians of the Galaxy Vol. 2* (2017). Christophe Beck's main theme for *Ant-Man* (2015) not only uses the $M_5 3M_\emptyset$ variant but also shifts it from its typical position at a theme's beginning to its end, substantially displacing both chords' $\hat{1}$ with a longer $\hat{7}$ before it. For episodic spin-offs, $M_5 3M_\emptyset$ appears in both Christopher Lennertz's main title and end credits for *Agent Carter* (2015–2016), and for references to heroism [e.g., E1, 41:39; E2, 42:06] in Laura Karpman's underscoring of *Ms. Marvel* (2022). By contrast, a heroic theme by Marco Beltrami and Philip Glass that recurs throughout the reboot of Marvel's *Fantastic Four* (2015)—the first appearance is at 11:05—begins with the standard $M_8 9M_\emptyset$, but this film was produced by 20th Century Fox outside of the MCU.

Within the MCU, $M_8 9M_\emptyset$ takes a step back after 2013 in other ways besides thematized permutation. The progression surfaces for quieter non-thematic moments that adumbrate heroism instead of broadcasting it. Examples include adding a dash of 'all in a (hero's) day's work' to the story (*Agents of S.H.I.E.L.D*, 2016, S4, E1, Bear McCreary, 5:29; *Jessica Jones*, 2015, S1, E1, Sean Callery, 48:07), refracting heroism through the sweet imagination of a superhero's young daughter (*Ant-Man*, 2015, 17:41; *Ant-Man and the Wasp*, 2018, Beck, 1:09:09), or foreshadowing how the inhibited title character will later become the 'best version of' herself (*Captain Marvel*, Pinar Toprak, 4:28). When Michael Giacchino penned a new Marvel fanfare to open *Doctor Strange* (2016) and subsequent MCU movies, he pushed $M_8 9M_\emptyset$ to near the end, and reduced it to one-third its duration. He further replaced the opening progression with a different $M3M_{RK}$—$M_0 3M_R$—a progression which had not been this overtly branded since Howard Shore's 'Fellowship theme' from the *Lord of the Rings* cinematic trilogy (2001, 2002, 2003).

Giacchino's manipulation of $M_8 9M_\emptyset$ for his main theme to *Spider-Man: Homecoming* (2017) resourcefully accords with the title character, the youngest in MCU's roster and an Avengers aspirant. In the first four measures of his main theme, reduced in Example 3.4, Giacchino wedges apart the two chords of $M_8 9M_\emptyset$, driving a tonic harmony in between

EXAMPLE 3.4 Giacchino, *Spider-Man: Homecoming*, main theme.

them.[10] This interpolation slightly enfeebles $M_89M_\emptyset$'s expression of heroism, which relates well to the story of a hero-in-training. In the theme's next four measures, VI and IV finally do appear back-to-back, achieving $M_89M_\emptyset$ status and creating a simple but effective attainment narrative that mirrors that of the main character. At the movie's end, Tony Stark offers Peter Parker a new suit and Avengers membership, but Peter turns both down, only to have the new suit show up in his apartment bedroom. In each of these two scenes [1:59:50, 2:02:32], both four-measure units are clearly audible.

During this time period, $M_89M_\emptyset$ and its variants underline heroism in other screen products apart from the MCU or DCEU based on comic-book heroes. It appears a couple of times in Marvel's X-Men franchise, such as the $M_53M_\emptyset$ when Erik Lehnsherr superhumanly lifts an enemy submarine out of the water in *X-Men: First Class* (2011, Henry Jackman, 1:41:38) and when a $M_89M_\emptyset$ helps Mystique proclaim to a group of young recruits at the end of *X-Men: Apocalypse* (2016, John Ottman): 'You're not students anymore… you're X-Men' [2:13:21]. As Peter Parker heroically rescues Miles Morales from falling to his death [21:51] in *Spider-Man: Into the Spider-Verse* (2018), Daniel Pemberton inserts an $M_89M_\emptyset$. Brian Tyler uses $M_89M_\emptyset$ a few times to underscore heroism in *Teenage Mutant Ninja Turtles* (2014), such as when April O'Neil recounts the story of a mysterious vigilante fighting injustice [9:07]. Michael Corcoran's main theme that plays during the opening and ending titles and credits for Nickelodeon's comic-book-like superhero comedy TV show *Henry Danger* (2014–20) ends with an $M_89M_\emptyset$.

Diachrony

What makes an association between M_53M_R in general, and $M_89M_\emptyset$ in particular, and heroism appropriate? One way music theorists, after likewise laying out an abundance of examples, have answered questions like this is to marshal technical analyses of the progression to assert a significant degree of non-arbitrariness in its multimedial affiliation. The two-part form of this research method follows the model set by Richard Cohn in his 2004 archaeology of the uncanny hexatonic-pole (H) harmonic progression in pre-1950 art music.[11] I adopted this model for subsequent film music studies of the major tritone progression in outer space and of the 'loss gesture.'[12]

The present study, however, affords an opportunity for an alternate type of reasoning. Using words coined by the Swiss semiologist Ferdinand de Saussure, I call this type of reasoning 'diachronic,' because it is analogous to how, over time, a newer word can substitute for, and perhaps supplant to some extent, an older word in its signifying role.[13] In 2019, I presented a theory for why the Slide (S) harmonic progression, rather than the H progression, accompanies uncanniness in post-2000 screen narratives. Instead of mustering a new analysis of the S progression, I showed how Cohn's structural analysis of the H progression also applies specifically to S in a broader context and then proposed that the suitability of H's signification of uncanniness revealed by this analysis could likewise be transferred to that of S.

As I have argued, one of the most salient and important chord progressions signifying heroism in movies and movie trailers starting around 2000 is some transposition of the (often looped) progression Am→FM→CM→GM, what I called aFCG for short.[14] In some ways, aFCG and $M_8 9M_\emptyset$ are interchangeable, especially proven by the DCEU on a couple of occasions. In 2012, Warner Bros Pictures released the first trailer of *Man of Steel*, which features the end of Howard Shore's 'Bridge of Khazad Dum' music from *Lord of the Rings: The Fellowship of the Ring* (2001) and its attendant aFCG. As mentioned above, the last trailer for *Man of Steel* previewed Zimmer's newly composed 'Flight' theme from Example 3.2, whose $M_8 9M_\emptyset$ served an epic-inducing purpose identical to the aFCG of the first trailer. This interchangeability came full circle in *Wonder Woman 1984* (2020) as the title character learns how to fly [1:58:58] in a manner that parallels Superman's $M_8 9M_\emptyset$-accompanied scene from *Man of Steel*, but lending aural support is not music from Hans Zimmer, but John Murphy's 'Adagio in D Minor' from *Sunshine* (2007) and *Kick-Ass* (2010), a theme inundated with aFCG. But in other ways, one can plausibly hear $M_8 9M_\emptyset$ as taking over some of aFCG's signifying market share. The choice of music for movie trailers in the second decade of the twenty-first century indicates one facet of this takeover. Figure 3.3 graphs the specific year in which 51 post-2012 trailers, all employing either $M_8 9M_\emptyset$ or aFCG, were released. Evidently, aFCG has gradually become less frequent, whereas $M_8 9M_\emptyset$ appears to be gaining more of a foothold, especially recently.

My diachronic interpretation is laid out in the two parallel columns that comprise Table 3.1. The left column furnishes a simplified version of my previously published argument for a similarity between one structure of aFCG and one structure of heroics, and the right column lays out a similarity between $M_8 9M_\emptyset$ and the same structure of heroics with language that corresponds closely, although not exactly, with the language of the aFCG-generating column, essentially treating relative-key relations

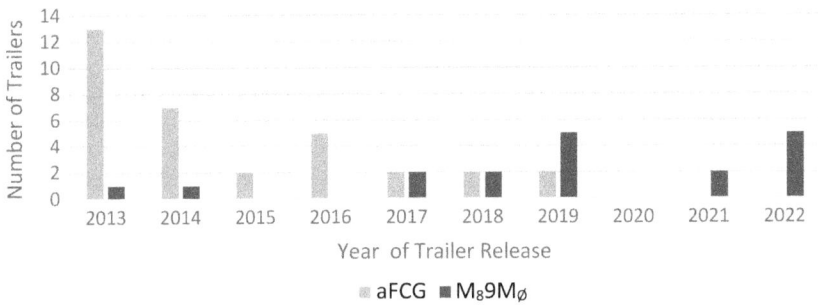

FIGURE 3.3 Chart of use of $M_89M_\varnothing$ or aFCG in 51 movie trailers.

and parallel-key relations as duals of one another. To maximize the correspondence, the outcome of the right column is necessarily more than just M_53M_R: It is M_53M_R plus a proximal major or minor tonic triad. It is this tonic triad that defines the nearby $M9M_K$ or $M3M_K$ as a $M_89M_\varnothing$ or $M_53M_\varnothing$, respectively, and whose presence, both in the notated examples and in all of the other cited instances, has been tacitly but vitally with us for this entire chapter.

Five, ten, or twenty years from now, $M_89M_\varnothing$ and on-screen heroism will likely progress away from one another as signifier and signified. However, having in mind an arrangement like Table 3.1 can help both composers and listeners alike anticipate where these signs might turn up next. Think of Figure 3.2 as an acreage divided into plots: Two MnM_Ks ($M3M_K$ and $M9M_K$), 12 M_n3M_Rs, and 24 $M_n3M_\varnothing$s and $M_n9M_\varnothing$s. When a signifying convention turns into cliché, depleting one part of the field, some in the moving-image industry leave it fallow and move the crop. But it is not unusual to move it to an adjoining part of the field, especially if it has not been tilled much, or for a while, or at all. As exercises in recognizing these incremental shifts, I recommend asking in what ways the harmonic progressions in Jeff Russo's main theme for *Star Trek: Discovery* (2017–) and Theodore Shapiro's music for the climactic downfall of the villain [1:40:37] in *Bombshell* (2019) are $M_89M_\varnothing$-adjacent and thus still heroic in some strategic fashion.

Yet some tracts of ground are naturally more fertile than others. As conventions of musical multimedia settle in, critics may bemoan the banality, but these consistencies supply scholars of music and humanity with a teeming array of information about how individuals and societies relate tone to life—even if mimetic—and how those relations might progress over time, reflecting, or even guiding, how we progress too.

TABLE 3.1 Diachronic interpretation of aFCG and $M_5 3M_R$-type progressions

aFCG	$M_5 3M_R$ ($M_8 9M_\varnothing$ or $M_5 3M_\varnothing$)
A diatonic collection, such as CDEFGAB, offers to the listener a sonic residence, which is distinct from the 11 other possible diatonic-collections-as-residences, to metaphorically call home. Within this diatonic home are exactly six consonant triads: Three major (C, F, G) and three minor (a, d, e). However, only two of them—one major and one minor—are the tonic triads of Western music's privileged modes of ionian and aeolian: C and a.	A single pitch class, such as E, offers to the listener a sonic residence, which is distinct from the 11 other possible pitch-classes-as-residences, to metaphorically call home. This pitch-class home is within exactly six consonant triads: Three major (A, C, E) and three minor (a, c♭, e).[a] However, only two of them—one major and one minor—use this home pitch class as their root, which privileges them as tonic triads: E and e.
These modes, as keys, share what is commonly described as a relative-key relationship: Same key signature, but different tonic pitch. The presence of both tonic triads can be interpreted as designed to bring these two modes into direct major-minor opposition, which suitably matches a Manichean conflict between light and dark—or success and failure, or good and evil—at the heart of archetypal heroism.	These triads, as expanded to keys, share what is commonly described as a parallel-key relationship: Same tonic pitch, but different key signature. The freedom of the tonic triad to appear in either mode can be interpreted as designed to bring these two modes into implicit major-minor opposition, which suitably matches a Manichean conflict between light and dark—or success and failure, or good and evil—at the heart of archetypal heroism.
Crucial to this opposition is the selection of two other triads that are both within, and fully complete, the home diatonic collection, thereby giving rise to the two tonics in the first place. The two triads of F and G do this: FAC + GBD + either tonic = CDEFGAB. Although other pairs of triads also do so, this pair is the only pair in which both triads are major, imparting a generally positive affect to the hero grappling with this conflict.	Crucial to this opposition is the selection of two other triads that both include the home pitch class and straddle the two modes, thereby giving rise to the two modes in the first place. The two triads of A and C do this: A is in E major, and C is in E minor. Although other pairs of triads also do so, this pair is the only pair in which both triads are major, imparting a generally positive affect to the hero grappling with this conflict.

(*Continued*)

TABLE 3.1 (Continued)

$aFCG$	$M_5 3M_R$ ($M_8 9M_\emptyset$ or $M_5 3M_\emptyset$)
The progression should therefore consist of both tonic chords—a and C—placed in formally marked positions such as beginnings or at metrically strong moments. The progression should also consist of the second selected pair of chords: F and G. The inclusion of one of both of the remaining triads—d or e—should be understood as a departure from the archetypal heroic signifier.	The progression should therefore consist of either tonic chord—e or E—placed in a formally marked position such as a beginning or at a metrically strong moment. The progression should also consist of the second selected pair of chords: A and C. The inclusion of one of both of the remaining triads—c♭ or a—should be understood as a departure from the archetypal heroic signifier.

[a] Richard Cohn calls the group of six triads that share a single pitch class a 'neighborhood.' Cohn, *Audacious Euphony*, 113.

Notes

1 Erik Heine, 'Chromatic Mediants and Narrative Context in Film,' *Music Analysis* 37.1 (2018): 103–133.
2 This chapter cites 34 of the 106 popular English-language movies or television programs first released between 2005 and 2022 in which I hear (♭)VI–IV distinctly accompany a heroic character or situation, or brand the media product as a heroic genre, at least once.
3 I am aware of 28—far fewer than the 106 referred to in the previous note—popular English-language movies or television programs first released between 2005 and 2022 in which a IV–(♭)VI, not immediately preceded by a (♭)VI–IV as it is in Example 1, assumes the signifying role cited in the previous note. Of these 28, 10 are cited in this chapter, and 12 of these 28 also overlap with the aforementioned 106. Claims like this are distilled from notes that I have taken on the music for over 1200 films and television programs that are mostly popular, mostly recent, and mostly in the English language.
4 This approach is a four-fold expansion of my tonal-triadic progression classes, which exercises a form of equivalence that uses retrogradation, but not key change, as a label-preserving transformation. See Scott Murphy, 'Transformational Theory and the Analysis of Film Music,' in David Neumeyer (ed.), *Oxford Handbook of Film Music Studies* (Oxford: Oxford University Press, 2014): 471–499. The scope laid out in this chapter is broadened two-fold in more recent publications by including inversion as a label-preserving transformation; this larger scope fully subsumes a form of harmonic-progression labeling called 'neo-Riemannian theory.' See Scott Murphy, 'S as a Latter-Day H: Mortally Liminal SLIDES in Recent Popular Film and Television,' *Theory and Practice* 44 (2019): 165–194 and 'An Eightfold Taxonomy of Harmonic Progressions, and Its Application to Triads Related by Major Third and Their Significance in Recent Screen Music,' *Journal of Music Theory* 67.1 (2023): 141–170. On neo-Riemannian theory, see Richard Cohn, *Audacious Euphony: Chromaticism and the Triad's Second Nature* (New York: Oxford University

Press, 2012) and Frank Lehman, *Hollywood Harmony: Musical Wonder and the Sound of Cinema* (New York: Oxford University Press, 2018).
5 Frank Lehman, 'Hollywood Cadences: Music and the Structure of Cinematic Expectation,' *Music Theory Online* 19.4 (2013), www.mtosmt.org/issues/mto.13.19.4/mto.13.19.4.lehman.html.
6 This tonal transposition down by two perfect fifths is as far as one can transpose $M_{10}9M_\varnothing$, by perfect fifths in either direction, before involving a major triad unavailable within either the tonic major or tonic natural minor scale. This suggests that, in seeking a signifier with broad appeal, this migration avoided more chromatic climates.
7 The time in parentheses indicates the moment in the film of the first $M3M_{RK}$, whether as $M_89M_\varnothing$, $M_53M_\varnothing$, or otherwise.
8 Lindsay Coleman, 'Dario Marianelli Interview,' in Lindsay Coleman and Joakim Tillman (eds.), *Contemporary Film Music: Investigating Cinema Narratives and Composition* (London: Palgrave Macmillan, 2017), 149.
9 See James Buhler, 'Branding the Franchise: Music, Opening Credits, and the (Corporate) Myth of Origin,' in Stephen C. Meyer (ed.), *Music in Epic Film: Listening to Spectacle* (New York: Routledge, 2017), 18.
10 In *The Avengers* (1:41:58), Silvestri creates a similar wedge as Tony Stark reclaims his Iron Man suit while falling from the top of a tall building, a musical and visual presentiment of the music of Example 1 and the solidarity it accompanies ten minutes later in the movie.
11 Richard Cohn, 'Uncanny Resemblances: Tonal Signification in the Freudian Age,' *Journal of the American Musicological Society* 57.2 (2004): 285–323.
12 Scott Murphy, 'The Major Tritone Progression in Recent Hollywood Science Fiction Films,' *Music Theory Online* 13.2 (2006), www.mtosmt.org/issues/mto.06.12.2/mto.06.12.2.murphy.html; and 'Scoring Loss in Some Recent Popular Film and Television,' *Music Theory Spectrum* 36.2 (2014): 295–314.
13 Ferdinand de Saussure, *Course in General Linguistics* [*Cours de linguistique Générale*], trans. Wade Baskin (New York: The Philosophical Society 1916[1959]): 140ff.
14 Scott Murphy, 'A Pop Music Progression in Recent Popular Movies and Movie Trailers,' *Music, Sound, and the Moving Image* 8.2 (2014): 141–163.

4

JOHN WILLIAMS'S *STAR WARS* THEMES

Good vs. Evil Conflicts as a Structural Principle for Leitmotifs

Mark Richards

Given the predominance of themes as leitmotifs in film, there has been proportionately little scholarship focusing on their internal structure, yet analysis of such structures has yielded insights into various aspects of film scoring and filmmaking in general. This type of analysis has demonstrated, for example, how major cultural and technological shifts in filmmaking are reflected in the thematic structures of main themes. It has also shown how Bernard Herrmann reversed Hollywood norms for theme-writing in scoring one of history's most revered films, Alfred Hitchcock's *Vertigo* (1958). Similarly, it has revealed one of the ways in which John Williams hones his leitmotifs for fantasy-based associations through the use of variation in a theme's internal structure.[1]

In this chapter, I wish to explore another kind of insight that can be drawn from the analysis of a theme's internal structure: How consistent approaches to thematic structuring can clarify and indeed highlight narrative details not just in a single film but across an entire film series. There is perhaps no better example of this in film history than John Williams and his scores for the nine films of the *Star Wars* 'Skywalker saga' (1977–2019), for which his leitmotifs are form-fitted to the narrative. Several recent studies have begun to examine just how this fit is achieved through a variety of musical facets such as harmony, orchestration, musical topic, and dramaturgy.[2] Here, however, I build on my previous work on thematic structure in film music, arguing that, in each of his nine *Star Wars* scores, Williams fashions the form of new leitmotifs for good or evil to consistently emphasize their respective movie's core conflict.[3] This relationship

DOI: 10.4324/9781003001171-4

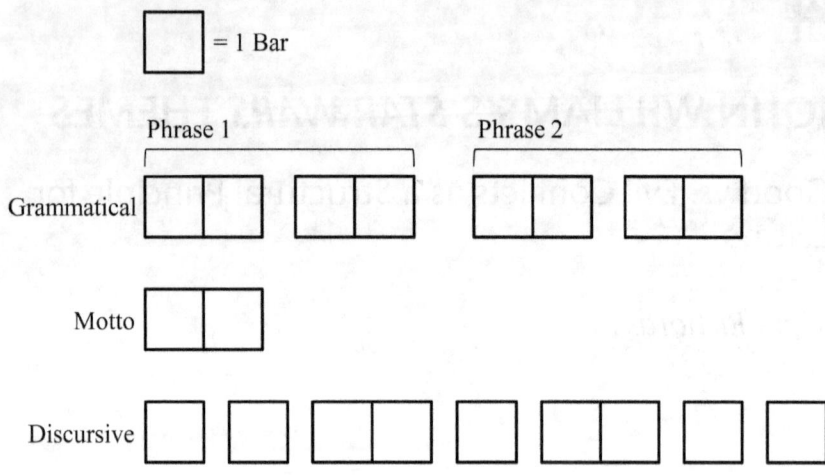

FIGURE 4.1 Theme categories in film music.

demonstrates Williams's acumen in comprehending the narrative heart of a film and translating it into purely musical terms.

Thematic structures in film generally fall into one of three broad categories (see Figure 4.1). For Williams—and for most of Hollywood's history—the most common form is that which is based on eight-bar models with two phrases.[4] These phrases constitute a kind of statement and response, or beginning and ending, and so form a complete thought, much like a grammatical sentence. For this reason, I call these *grammatical themes*. The second category contains themes that are shorter, usually only one to six bars in total, and lacking a balancing second half. Because of their brevity, I call these *motto themes*. The third and final category includes themes that are eight bars or more in length but divided into something other than the two-phrase model of grammatical themes. These *discursive themes* have a more unpredictable quality, usually running beyond the standard eight-bar length for grammatical themes.

These categories of thematic structure reinforce the main conflict in each *Star Wars* film that Williams scored by drawing on a relatively simple musical attribute: Length. It is not, however, the lengths of themes *per se* that emphasize the conflict but rather the relative difference in the lengths of themes for good versus themes for evil. And each theme category has certain advantages over the others for film scoring.

Because grammatical themes are substantial musical structures of around eight bars and have a two-phrase statement-and-response construction that is easily discerned by listeners, they attain a prominent musical presence in film. This prominence lends these themes more importance, as they highlight their narrative association more than a shorter motto theme can. This greater importance is what I will call the theme's *dramatic weight*. Unlike either the motto theme or the much longer discursive theme, grammatical themes convey a sense of completeness through the statement-and-response relationship of their two phrases. In this way, grammatical themes can tell a miniature story and are thereby able to provide a rich musical characterization of their associated ideas in the narrative, rendering them an ideal melodic structure for a film's main characters, places, and things. Williams facilitates the immediate audibility and accessibility of the statement-response relationship by ensuring that whatever motives occur at the start of phrase two are closely related to those introduced in phrase one. By far, the two grammatical theme structures that Williams relies on most in *Star Wars* films are those in which the initial idea returns at the start of the second four-bar phrase (what is called a *period*) and those in which the first two bars of the second phrase vary the two-bar idea ending the first phrase (what is called a *clause*).[5] While grammatical themes in underscore are usually stated in an abbreviated form, we understand these truncated statements to represent the full theme, something like a short form of a name.[6] We are, after all, encouraged to remember full statements of leitmotifs that are grammatical themes as they generally occur with an important onscreen event: Either the introduction of the associated idea or an audiovisual foregrounding of it.

Motto themes generally carry far less dramatic weight than grammatical themes due to their shorter full length and consequently briefer amount of time with each statement, along with their inability to present complete statement-response-type structures. This contrast can represent good versus evil in general or primary versus secondary plot devices and threats more specifically. Mottos are also ideal for action scenes, where the fast pace of events and editing more easily accommodates short musical statements than more extensive themes with multiple phrases.

Discursive themes, with their multi-part construction and long length, score entire scenes or relatively large portions of them. As a result, while they can emphasize their associated narrative ideas more than grammatical themes, that they express a single association for a relatively long time renders them unwieldy for most scenes. Yet, compared to their grammatical counterparts, discursive themes are more loosely structured and can be treated as a series of motto themes strung together, each of which may be repeated several times before moving on to another. Thus, in terms of their immediate expressive state, discursive themes can be made to readily flow with an extended and changing film sequence. When they do, the sustained focus on a single leitmotif lends hefty dramatic weight to the sequence—a tactic Williams deploys to great effect in the *Star Wars* prequels (Episodes I–III), specifically in climactic fight scenes where good prevails.

Leitmotifs are, of course, not the only way that good and evil are musically portrayed in the *Star Wars* films. Emotionally charged underscore and incidental motifs also contribute to the expression of each film's two moral sides. What distinguishes leitmotifs from these other factors, however, is their demand on the listener's conscious attention and memory. In this way, the current study strives to examine what is perhaps the most prominent form of musical expression in the *Star Wars* films.

The Three Strategies

In each of Williams's *Star Wars* scores, any new leitmotif for good is always written as a grammatical theme. What differentiates these scores in their approach to thematic structure is the form of any new leitmotifs for evil. Two key questions affect the construction of these leitmotifs:

- Is the main threat of the film a central villain in the manner of an evil mastermind, or is it divided among two or more villains in the manner of an evil organization?
- If there is a central villain, is that villain hidden from or exposed to the heroes?

Across the nine films, answers to these questions result in three different types of main threats:

1. Divided Threat   Episodes IV, VII, VIII
2. Central Hidden Villain   Episodes I, II, III
3. Central Exposed Villain   Episodes V, VI, IX

Fascinatingly, the nature of this threat, whether it is divided or centralized, hidden or exposed, also governs the way in which Williams distributes his new grammatical, motto, or discursive themes. I therefore call these types of threats *the three strategies* for Williams's thematic structures. Figure 4.2 shows the strategies schematically in relation to leitmotifs for good, evil, and action in the nine films. Parentheses indicate an element that is absent from at least one film of that strategy.

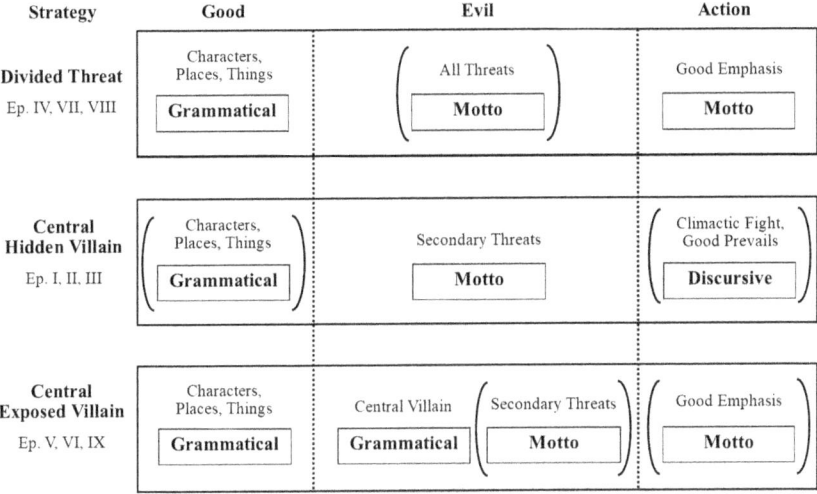

FIGURE 4.2 The three strategies for new leitmotifs for good and evil.

In the Divided Threat strategy, the evil deeds in the film have their source in two or more villains, positioning evil as the product of an organization (i.e., the Empire or First Order) rather than a single all-controlling villain. Williams reflects this setup in his scores by writing the new evil-oriented themes as mottos and sharply contrasting them with new, good-oriented grammatical themes. Thus, more dramatic weight is attached to the themes for good than the themes for evil. In action scenes where grammatical themes would be too unwieldy, motto leitmotifs for the heroes further bolster a good-over-evil perspective—for example, the use of the Rebel Fanfare in 'TIE Fighter Attack' from *A New Hope*.

The Central Hidden Villain strategy, which is specific to the three prequel films, aligns with the way in which Palpatine—the primary villain of the whole trilogy, first as Senator, then Chancellor, and finally Emperor—directs the evil actions of the other villains while concealing his own true identity. No new theme is given to Palpatine—he simply retains his grammatical Emperor theme from *Return of the Jedi*. Instead, the new evil-associated leitmotifs are assigned to secondary threats and are structured as mottos. The use of older material for Palpatine allows his music to be less prominent than the novel themes heard for the secondary threats. And at the same time, the new, short mottos grant the secondary threats less dramatic weight than the longer grammatical themes for the protagonists. In other words, while the mottos' novelty aptly diverts attention away from the true threat, their brevity actually keeps the secondary threats secondary. In these films, the most emphatic leitmotif is either purely for the good side (Across the Stars) or marks a climactic fight in which, even if it comes at a great cost, good does prevail (Duel of the Fates, Battle of the Heroes).

With the Central Exposed Villain strategy, a primary antagonist who is fully known to the heroes controls the evil actions in the film. This villain is presented as a particularly formidable foe, and the singularity of the resulting threat is reflected in the character's new theme, which is grammatical in construction. This theme structure serves as a musical foil to the heroes' themes, one of equivalent dramatic weight that musically reflects the strength of the villain at the conflict's core. Any leitmotifs for secondary villains in Central Exposed Villain films are written as motto themes, which set the primary villain's theme in high relief. As with the Divided Threat strategy, the good side may be musically reinforced in action scenes with motto themes, but the main feature of the Central Exposed Villain strategy is the balancing of thematic length between the new themes written for the good side and the central villain.

Each of these strategies will be more fully elaborated below as they are discussed in the context of each of the nine films of the *Star Wars* saga.

Defining the Leitmotifs

Not every theme is a leitmotif. As Frank Lehman clarifies, in order to be designated a leitmotif, a given theme in the *Star Wars* saga should adhere to four criteria:[7]

1) **Distinctiveness**—Musical idea has a clear and unique melody, without being wholly derived from or attached to another motif.
2) **Recurrence**—Musical idea is intentionally repeated in more than three discrete cues (including cut, replaced, or alternate/altered versions of a single cue).
3) **Variation**—Musical idea's repetitions are not exact.
4) **Intentionality**—Musical idea's repetitions are compositionally intentional, and do not require undue analytical detective work to notice.

Through these criteria, one obtains the list of leitmotifs given in Lehman's *Star Wars* thematic catalog, which includes entries from all nine of the Williams-scored films.[8]

As the present chapter is focused on new good and evil leitmotifs for each film, the list of relevant themes is somewhat shorter than Lehman's inventory and arrived at through a few other criteria. First, subsections of a theme, including introductions, accompaniments, and any B and C sections, are here considered a single theme in order to focus on the portions that allow classification of the leitmotif as grammatical, motto, or discursive.[9] Second, since this study focuses on themes that Williams composed as leitmotifs for the film at hand (according to the criteria set out here), themes that begin as incidental material but become leitmotifs through statements across subsequent films are excluded.[10] Third, a few themes are excluded as they are stated only a couple of times in the film they were written for and are also absent from the end credits suite, where Williams generally summarizes the main leitmotifs of each film.[11] Fourth, a few themes are more of a timbre or a collection of related ideas than a consistent theme in the melodic sense.[12] Fifth, variants of existing themes are also excluded.[13] Finally, two themes lack any sort of agency for good and evil in their respective films, and so are excluded.[14] When all the above criteria are taken into account, the resulting leitmotifs are as shown in Table 4.1, a list that will be a useful reference for the remainder of this chapter.

1. 'Divided Threat' Strategy

a) Episode IV: A New Hope

The three leitmotifs for good in 1977's *A New Hope* (Luke, Force, and Leia) are composed as grammatical themes, while the two for evil (Imperials, Death Star) are both mottos (see Example 4.1). With its more fully fleshed-out leitmotifs, the good side is musically more dramatically weighted than the evil side. The Rebel Fanfare, which is a motto theme, may seem to contradict this distinction, but as it is primarily a leitmotif for action sequences, it maintains an emphasis on the good side while also following the fast pacing of such scenes.

The Divided Threat strategy of good-grammatical and evil-motto themes in *A New Hope* captures the main thrust of the narrative with its generalized sense of good versus evil. In other words, at its core, the film's conflict does not revolve around a central villain but rather the Empire as a whole, as represented by Grand Moff Tarkin, Darth Vader, Stormtroopers, and other agents of the enemy. Although Tarkin outranks Vader, the two collaborate more or less as equals, carrying out each other's goals at different points in the plot. Through this mutual leadership, the source of the evil in this film is dispersed in the manner of an organization, rather than concentrated in the hands of a single all-powerful villain. Williams's hefty grammatical themes for good and more lightweight mottos for evil aptly sum up the broad nature of the film's good-versus-evil conflict.

TABLE 4.1 Theme categories of new leitmotifs for good or evil in each of Williams's *Star Wars* scores

Episode	Leitmotif	Good	Evil	Action	Grammatical	Motto	Discursive
4	Luke (Main Theme)	x			x		
4	Rebel Fanfare	x		x		x	
4	Force	x			x		
4	Leia	x			x		
4	Death Star		x				
4	Imperials		x			x	
5	Vader (Imperial March)		x		x	x	
5	Han and Leia	x			x		
5	Yoda	x			x		
5	Droids	x					
5	Boba Fett		x			x	
5	Cloud City	x			x		
6	Emperor		x		x		
6	Jabba		x		x		
6	Ewoks	x			x		
6	Luke and Leia	x			x	x	
1	Young Anakin	x			x	x	
1	Duel of the Fates	x		x			x
1	Droid March		x				
1	Darth Maul		x				
1	Jar-Jar	x			x		
1	Qui-Gon	x			x		
2	Across the Stars	x					
2	Conspiracy		x			x	
3	Battle of the Heroes	x		x			x

(Continued)

TABLE 4.1 (Continued)

Episode	Leitmotif	Good	Evil	Action	Grammatical	Motto	Discursive
3	General Grievous		x			x	
7	Kylo Ren A (Aggressive)		x			x	
7	Kylo Ren B (Hesitant)		x			x	
7	First Order		x			x	
7	Rey	x			x		
7	March of the Resistance	x			x		
7	Poe	x			x		
7	Finn/Pursuit	x		x		x	
8	Rose	x			x		
8	Luke in Exile (Theme)	x			x		
8	Luke in Exile (Fanfare)	x			x		
8	Desperation	x		x			
9	Friendship	x			x	x	
9	Victory	x			x		
9	Psalm of the Sith		x		x		
9	Knights of Ren		x			x	
9	Heroics (of Poe)	x		x		x	

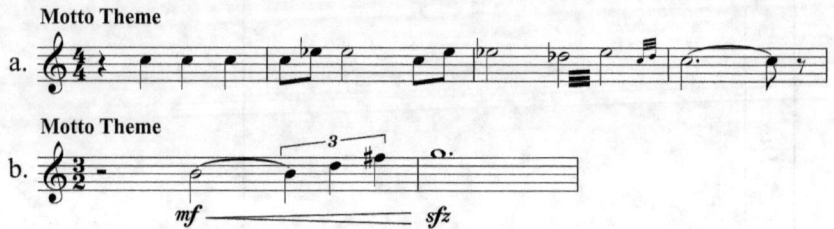

EXAMPLE 4.1 *A New Hope*, leitmotifs for evil: (a) Imperials; (b) Death Star (all examples transcribed by author).

b) Episode VII: The Force Awakens

Like *A New Hope*, the evil in *The Force Awakens* (2015) is diffusely spread across multiple characters, this time among the trio of Snoke, Kylo Ren, and General Hux. Again, although Snoke is the 'Supreme Leader' and issues commands to his subordinates, he also hears and adopts suggestions from Ren and Hux. This sharing of leadership responsibilities is indicative of the organizational rather than individual nature of the threat to the heroes of the film, the Resistance.

Characterizing this dynamic musically are Williams's three new leitmotifs for the good side (Rey, Poe, and March of the Resistance), three leitmotifs for the evil side (two for Kylo Ren and one for the First Order) (Example 4.2), and one good-oriented action leitmotif (Finn/Pursuit). That Ren receives two independent themes is surely a reflection of his substantial part in the narrative. What distinguishes his role in the film from that of, say, Vader in *The Empire Strikes Back* however is that Ren is an agent of evil in a larger network that consists of himself, Hux, and Snoke. In other

EXAMPLE 4.2 *The Force Awakens*, leitmotifs for evil: (a) Kylo Ren (aggressive); (b) Kylo Ren (hesitant); (c) First Order.

words, defeating Ren would not completely eliminate the evil acts that the Resistance suffers at the hands of the First Order.[15] In *The Empire Strikes Back*, by contrast, Vader is on a personal mission to find and capture Luke Skywalker. In other words, the main evil actions of the narrative originate with Vader rather than the Empire. The rich musical depiction of Ren contrasts with unexpectedly slight material for the First Order, whose theme in the film is not nearly as frequent nor as distinct in its association.[16]

The fact that the leitmotifs for the Resistance are all more substantial grammatical themes, and Ren's and the First Order's leitmotifs succinct mottos, mirrors the nature of the conflict between the two sides as whole entities, as in *A New Hope*, and not primarily between any individuals. And, like the heroic motto in *A New Hope*, the Finn/Pursuit theme accompanies the heroes in some of the action scenes. That Williams returned to the Divided Threat strategy for writing the new leitmotifs for good and evil in *The Force Awakens* is hardly surprising. The film is, after all, a soft remake of *A New Hope* that retains (among many other elements) an entire organization as its primary source of evil. And while the characterization of the villains in each of these two films is quite different (Tarkin and Vader are evil through and through while Ren feels inner conflict between the Dark and Light Sides), the dispersion of the evil actions across more than one evil authority is the same in both.

c) Episode VIII: The Last Jedi

The Last Jedi (2017) is unique in Williams's *Star Wars* scores in being the only one not to introduce at least one new leitmotif for the forces of evil. Whether this lack of a new evil theme was due to the unusually heavy reliance on a temp track, or for some other reason, *The Last Jedi* is the film of the sequel trilogy with the fewest new leitmotifs overall.[17] These new themes include two for Luke in his self-imposed exile, one for the new character of Rose, and one for the desperation of the Resistance in action scenes.

The Divided Threat strategy can still be understood as operative, even though the leitmotifs used for evil in the film are Ren's two themes from the previous film. Indeed, for most of the movie, the core conflict is as it was in *The Force Awakens*, with Snoke, Ren, and Hux still collectively running the First Order. About 70% of the way through *The Last Jedi*, however, Ren assassinates Snoke and declares himself Supreme Leader, though a power struggle arises thereafter between him and Hux. Only at the end of the film, as Ren enters the abandoned Resistance base alone, does Hux with a sneering look reluctantly accept Ren's leadership. Remarkably, Williams marks this moment of Ren's unchallenged authority by extending Ren's more aggressive leitmotif so that it now introduces the beginnings

Motto Theme - Extended to Near-Grammatical Length (6 bars)

EXAMPLE 4.3 *The Last Jedi*, new extended motto for Kylo Ren: 'Kylo Ren (aggressive).'

of a second half, and thus approaches the more substantial structure of a grammatical theme (Example 4.3).[18] The theme never reaches a full eight bars, however, leaving the elevation of his thematic structure—and indeed his status in the First Order—in question until the saga's next episode.

2. 'Central Hidden Villain' Strategy: The Prequel Trilogy

All three of the prequel films share a consistent approach to their core conflict. In each entry, Palpatine is the central villain, orchestrating from the shadows the conflicts faced by the protagonists, but his evil identity goes unknown to the heroes until halfway through the trilogy's final film. Furthermore, the evil actions in each film are mainly carried out by secondary villains who answer to Palpatine, or his Sith alter-ego, Darth Sidious. Williams's approach to his new themes in the prequel trilogy is likewise marked by a consistency in their type of structure, their differences reflecting finer details of each film's particular plot.

a) Episode I: The Phantom Menace

In *The Phantom Menace* (1999), new leitmotifs for good are assigned to Young Anakin, Jar-Jar, and Qui-Gon, all of which are grammatical. The new leitmotifs for evil are mottos and assigned to secondary threats: Darth Maul and the Droid Army (Example 4.4). At first glance, this may seem to amount to the Divided Threat strategy. But recall that, unlike the films with that strategy, the prequels *do* have a central villain, one who remains hidden, a true phantom menace, so to speak. While the retention of the old Emperor theme for Palpatine obviously promotes continuity between the trilogies, it also musically takes the spotlight off the character simply because his leitmotif is not novel as are those mentioned above. At the same time, the new evil-associated leitmotifs for Darth Maul and the

EXAMPLE 4.4 *The Phantom Menace*, new leitmotifs for evil: (a) Darth Maul; (b) Droid Army

Droid Army are motto themes, so their importance is diminished alongside the longer grammatical themes of the heroes.

Despite the addition of these new leitmotifs, it is the climactic saber fight between Maul, Qui-Gon, and Obi-Wan that garners the most notable new music in the film: Duel of the Fates, a theme that fits the discursive category with its extensive length and irregular structure (Example 4.5). As such, this leitmotif marks the three-way duel as leading to the most important victory in the film, even though the protagonists are unaware that the ultimate source of evil (Palpatine) has become a greater threat in rising to the position of Chancellor.[19] To sum up, then, Williams echoes the heart of the film's main conflict in the structure of his themes through the Central Hidden Villain strategy: The grammatical themes of the new good-associated leitmotifs, the motto themes of the new evil-associated leitmotifs, the discursive theme for the film's climactic good-prevailing saber battle, and the retention of the old

EXAMPLE 4.5 *The Phantom Menace*, climactic action leitmotif: Duel of the Fates.

Emperor theme for Palpatine. That is to say, in *The Phantom Menace*, good is musically heightened in importance over evil, while the primary villain is downplayed.

b) Episode II: Attack of the Clones

At its core, the conflict in *Attack of the Clones* (2002) involves Palpatine's deliberate escalation of tensions between the Republic and the Separatists in order to increase his political and military power. As in *The Phantom Menace*, Palpatine, as Darth Sidious, remains lurking in the shadows, the evil actions now being carried out by his apprentice, Count Dooku, and the Separatist leaders who conspire with him. Notably, the film's only new evil-oriented leitmotif is for this conspiracy (Example 4.6). As Obi-Wan follows the threads of the attempt on Padmé's life throughout the film, this theme is heard with many aspects of the conspiracy: We hear it accompany Zam the assassin, who tries to kill Obi-Wan; Count Dooku and the Separatist leaders as they plot; and even Palpatine himself as he feigns concern over Padmé's safety and, later on, is granted emergency powers to deal with the growing Separatist threat. The conspiracy theme therefore highlights the secretly-manufactured push of the two sides toward war for Palpatine's personal gain, without highlighting him as the villain responsible for this conflict. In other words, as in *The Phantom Menace*, the new evil theme is focused on the secondary threats from Palpatine's concealed evil, rather than the primary threat of Palpatine himself. Moreover, as this theme is a short motto, the Light Side is heightened in importance as in the other prequel films since the only new good-associated leitmotif in the film is the much more substantial Across the Stars grammatical theme for the forbidden love between Anakin and Padmé.

Like the other prequel films, *Attack of the Clones* contains a climactic saber fight at the film's conclusion, this time between Count Dooku, Obi-Wan, and Anakin, with Yoda joining the fray after the Count bests his two human opponents. This final fight differs from the others in the trilogy, however, in that good does not prevail over evil. Indeed, not only

EXAMPLE 4.6 *Attack of the Clones*, new leitmotif for evil: Conspiracy.

does Dooku defeat both Obi-Wan and Anakin, but he forces Yoda to be preoccupied long enough to escape. That this battle lacks an extensive leitmotif for evil-over-good allows the good-oriented Across the Stars to reign over the film as its most prominent leitmotif, especially as the theme is presented in grand fashion in the final frames of the film with Padmé and Anakin's wedding ceremony. Moreover, the only new evil-based leitmotif highlights the film's core conflict involving the Palpatine-created conspiracy.

c) Episode III: Revenge of the Sith

As in the previous two films, Palpatine is the central villain of *Revenge of the Sith* (2005). Although he is revealed to the heroes as Darth Sidious only halfway through, it was his long-hidden evil that created its central threats: The conversion of the democratic Republic into the dictatorship of the Empire, the assassination of the Jedi via the Clone Army, and Anakin's turn to the Dark Side. Williams's thematic structures remain associated with the Central Hidden Villain strategy throughout the film, reinforcing *Revenge of the Sith*'s tragic second half as a logical culmination of not just this particular episode but the entire prequel trilogy.

Also like the previous two films, the heroes pursue secondary villains thinking them to be primary villains, in this case Count Dooku and General Grievous, commander of the Droid army. Dooku is killed near the start of the film, leaving Grievous as the main antagonist. Grievous receives the only new evil-associated leitmotif, which is built as a motto theme (Example 4.7).

The most emphatic new leitmotif in the film—the only other major one Williams wrote, in fact—is Battle of the Heroes, which accompanies the climactic saber fight between Anakin and Obi-Wan.[20] Like Duel of the Fates, Battle of the Heroes is a discursive theme of substantial length and irregular structure, as is suitable for extended action sequences (Example 4.8). Recall that in *The Phantom Menace*, Duel of the Fates places dramatic emphasis on the battle with the secondary villain, leaving the

EXAMPLE 4.7   *Revenge of the Sith*, new leitmotif for evil: General Grievous.

Discursive Theme

Motto 1

Motto 2

EXAMPLE 4.8 *Revenge of the Sith*, climactic action leitmotif: Battle of the Heroes.

central villain to remain musically hidden in the shadows. Why have this new theme highlight a conflict that does not directly involve Palpatine, then, when the central villain is no longer hidden from the heroes?

Crucially, *Revenge of the Sith* is the only *Star Wars* film not to introduce new leitmotifs for the good side—a choice clearly rooted in the narrative's focus on the rise and triumph of evil. As the most emphatic new leitmotif, Battle of the Heroes draws attention to Obi-Wan's ultimate defeat of Anakin in the final duel. While the musical tone of this theme is clearly pained and tragic, that such an extensive and prominent leitmotif accompanies a battle in which good prevails preserves a fundamental good-over-evil orientation of *Star Wars* narratives even in the face of Anakin's tragic downfall. This orientation is emphasized on the large scale as well since, taken together, the Grievous motif with its short motto structure pales in importance next to the large discursive theme that is Battle of the Heroes.

3. 'Central Exposed Villain' strategy

a) Episode V: The Empire Strikes Back

One of the most drastic changes in *The Empire Strikes Back* (1980) over its predecessor, *A New Hope*, is in the nature of its central conflict. Whereas the Rebels in *A New Hope* battled the collective Empire as represented by Tarkin and Vader, in *The Empire Strikes Back*, they now try to escape from Vader specifically, who is on a personal quest to find Luke Skywalker. The film leaves no doubt that Vader is the central villain: Not only does he send out the probes at the start of the film, but he also searches the Hoth base himself, sends bounty hunters to track down the Millennium Falcon, and personally sets the trap for Luke on Bespin. Unlike the evil-associated leitmotifs of the other strategies, the

EXAMPLE 4.9   *The Empire Strikes Back*, new leitmotifs for evil: (a) Darth Vader; (b) Boba Fett.

new leitmotif for Vader in this film is grammatical and structured as a *developing clause* (Example 4.9a). With this melodic form, the Vader leitmotif parallels the broad grammatical themes of the new good-associated leitmotifs for Han and Leia's love, Yoda, and Cloud City, augmenting the already powerful musical portrayal of Vader as the film's main and basically only opponent. The only other good-oriented leitmotif, for the Droids, C-3PO and R2-D2, never sounds a closing idea to its would-be second phrase, so is exceptionally structured as a motto, perhaps due to these characters' comparatively minor role in the film.

A second new leitmotif for evil is assigned to the bounty hunter Boba Fett, and though at first it may seem to be an abbreviated grammatical theme in the form of a period, like the Droids leitmotif, it never sounds a full second phrase, so instead remains a shorter motto theme (Example 4.9b). By contrast, Vader's theme is a full-fledged grammatical theme with

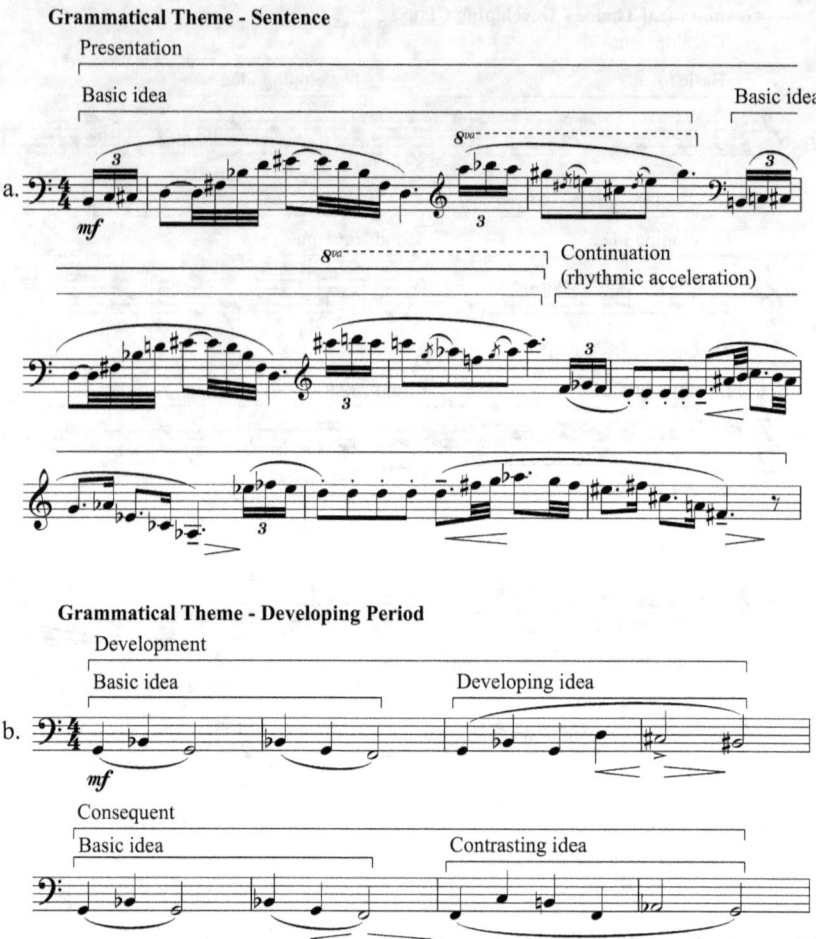

EXAMPLE 4.10 *Return of the Jedi*, new leitmotifs for evil: (a) Jabba the Hutt; (b) Emperor.

a second phrase that is repeated, as though to emphasize its imposing, authoritative quality.[21] Consequently, the leitmotif reigns supreme over Boba Fett's theme, just as the character himself does in the film. This, then, is the Central Exposed Villain strategy, which serves to highlight a single villain who is the evil mastermind behind the film's main conflict.

b) Episode VI: Return of the Jedi

The core conflict of *Return of the Jedi* (1983) falls into two parts, each of which revolves around a different central villain that is clearly evident to the heroes. The first part, encompassing nearly the first 40 minutes of the film, revolves around the crime lord Jabba the Hutt, whom the Rebels must defeat in order to rescue Han Solo. The second part centers on the Emperor, who plans to turn Luke to the Dark Side while simultaneously eliminating the Rebels with his new Death Star. Although Darth Vader may still seem to be a central villain, the film's conflict involves him carrying out the orders of his master rather than issuing his own as he did exclusively in *Empire*. This removal of Vader as central villain allows him to turn back to good and the film's main source of evil—the Emperor—to be physically vanquished, enacting an unequivocal good-over-evil finale to the trilogy.

Williams writes four new leitmotifs for the film. For the evil side, there are two new grammatical themes: One for Jabba the Hutt and one for the Emperor (Example 4.10). For the good side, there are two new grammatical themes as well: One for the Ewoks, and one for Luke and Leia. As in *The Empire Strikes Back*, the central villains wield considerable power over the heroes. Jabba captures and comes close to killing Luke and the band of Rebels before the tables turn, and the Emperor's meticulously planned trap nearly does away with our heroes as well. In comparison with the two new themes for good, then, Williams's two new ones for evil musically represent the magnitude of these villains' threats, which are the source of the film's conflict.

c) Episode IX: The Rise of Skywalker

By the end of *The Last Jedi*, Kylo Ren had emerged as the uncontested Supreme Leader of the First Order, General Hux having reluctantly accepted Ren's new position. But within the opening minutes of *The Rise of Skywalker* (2019), we learn that Palpatine, presumed dead since Episode VI, has returned and has been secretly in charge of the First Order all along. As in *Return of the Jedi*, Palpatine is the one who issues the orders, now to Ren and General Pryde, who leads the new fleet of planet-destroying Star Destroyers. Thus, there is no doubt that Palpatine is the central villain of the film—and one whose threat is fully exposed to the heroes as well, as an early scene with the Resistance informs us.

Williams's score contains two new evil-aligned leitmotifs: A grammatical theme called Psalm of the Sith (Example 4.11) and a motto for the Knights of Ren.[22] There are also two prominent new leitmotifs for the forces of good, both of which are grammatical: Friendship, for the main close-knit band of heroes; and Victory, for the Resistance's planning for and defeat of the First Order at the end of the film. Another leitmotif, Heroics, is a good-oriented action theme that highlights Poe's piloting skills.[23]

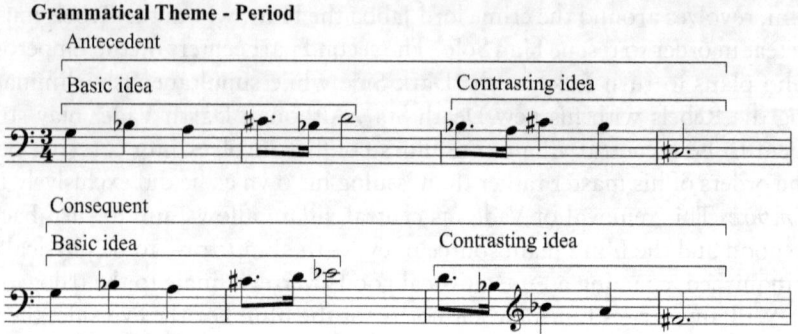

EXAMPLE 4.11   *The Rise of Skywalker*, new leitmotif for evil: Psalm of the Sith.

Palpatine retains his grammatical Emperor theme from *Return of the Jedi*, but the new, grammatical Psalm of the Sith serves as a kind of second leitmotif for him, not simply for his character but for his actions, influence, and surroundings. Although the original Emperor theme appears more frequently in *The Rise of Skywalker* than Psalm of the Sith, two of the latter theme's five appearances in the film proper fall at particularly key moments: When Ren reveals to Rey (and the audience) that she is Palpatine's granddaughter, and as one of Palpatine's new Star Destroyers demolishes the planet Kijimi on his orders. It also appears for both Ren's and Rey's journey to Exegol, the planet where Palpatine has been hiding. Strangely, Psalm of the Sith does not appear in its complete grammatical form in the final cut of the film but only in shorter forms that, in the context of the film proper, sound like mottos. The full theme does appear, however, in full in the end credits, where Williams tends to place important new leitmotifs from the film. Psalm of the Sith also appears in a cut portion of the written score accompanying the first scene with Palpatine, revealing the theme's complete structure and connection with Palpatine in its apparent first appearance near the start of the film.[24] It therefore seems clear that Williams intended the theme to appear in its complete grammatical form near the start of the film and to be associated with Palpatine, the principal villain of the film.

Assuming Psalm of the Sith was originally intended to have a larger role in *The Rise of Skywalker* than ultimately heard, then the other components of the Central Exposed Villain strategy become evident. Although the Knights of Ren theme is more aurally striking than Psalm of the Sith, the latter's placement at pivotal points in the film elevates it to a higher status. Following suit is the Knights of Ren's structure as a motto, which allows the lengthier, grammatical Psalm of the Sith to maintain its greater importance in depicting the evil of the film. Furthermore, this grammatical theme for the main villain musically poses a challenge to the film's new themes for good (Friendship and Victory) while a couple of the action scenes are weighted toward the good side with Poe's Heroics theme. For Kylo Ren's turn to the Light Side near the end of the film and the return to his original identity of Ben Solo, it was the director J.J. Abrams who requested that Williams use a variant of Kylo's theme (his 'aggressive' leitmotif) for the purpose.[25] The theme is therefore excluded from consideration since this study focuses on the themes devised by Williams himself.[26] Hence, despite a reworking of Williams's original cues for the film, the Central Exposed Villain strategy manages to shine through, reflecting the film's main conflict around Palpatine's re-emerged threat.

Conclusion

As we have seen, in each of his nine *Star Wars* scores, John Williams employs one of three different strategies for structuring new leitmotifs for good and evil: The Divided Threat, the Central Hidden Villain, and the Central Exposed Villain. These strategies display consistencies in shaping leitmotifs as the eight-bar-based grammatical theme, the shorter motto theme, or the longer, more irregular discursive theme. In each film, the particular strategy aligns with the structure of the core conflict between good and evil while also capturing key differences among some of the films. In these ways, the strategies demonstrate that Williams's ability to compose highly fitting leitmotifs is not limited to the content of the individual themes themselves but, at least in his *Star Wars* scores, includes consistently grouping them together by type of thematic structure, displaying a highly nuanced and appropriately tailored approach to theme-writing that has always been an essential part of the *Star Wars* saga.

Notes

1 See Mark Richards, 'Film Music Themes: Analysis and Corpus Study,' *Music Theory Online* 22.1 (2016), www.mtosmt.org/issues/mto.16.22.1/mto.16.22.1.richards.html; 'The Reversal of Hollywood Norms in Herrmann's Thematic Writing for *Vertigo*,' Presentation Given at Society for Music Theory, San Antonio, TX (November 2018); and 'The Use of Variation in John Williams' Film Music Themes,' in Emilio Audissino (ed.), *John Williams: Music for Films, Television and the Concert Stage* (Turnhout, Belgium: Brepols, 2018), 119–152.

2 See Emilio Audissino (ed.), *John Williams: Music for Films, Television and the Concert Stage* (Turnhout, Belgium: Brepols, 2018). Regarding themes specifically, the differentiation of music for good and evil in the first three films through the use of harmony is discussed in James Buhler, '*Star Wars*, Music, and Myth,' in James Buhler, Caryl Flinn, and David Neumeyer (eds.), *Music*

and *Cinema* (Hanover, NH: Wesleyan University Press, 2000), 33–57 (see esp. 44–49).

3 While the terms 'good' and 'evil' may appear to be simplistic when applied to warring sides in a narrative, the films of the *Star Wars* saga present morality in a decidedly straightforward fashion through such means as costumes, masks, vocal timbres, light saber colors, character names, and even defining the mystical religion-like Force in terms of 'light' and 'dark' sides.

4 For themes that contain multiple sections like a B section, C section, etc., the interpretation of that theme as grammatical is based on the A section, where an eight-bar model is evident.

5 The period is Williams's most favored structure for leitmotifs in all his film scores, as noted in Konstantinos Zacharopoulos, 'Musical Syntax in John Williams Film Music Themes,' in Lindsay Coleman and Joakim Tillman (eds.), *Contemporary Film Music: Investigating Cinema Narratives and Composition* (London: Palgrave Macmillan, 2017), 248.

6 See Justin London, 'Leitmotifs and Musical Reference in the Classical Film Score,' in James Buhler, Caryl Flinn, and David Neumeyer (eds.), *Music and Cinema* (Hanover, NH: Wesleyan University Press, 2000), 85–96.

7 Frank Lehman, 'Complete Catalogue of the Themes of *Star Wars*: A Guide to John Williams's Musical Universe,' revised and expanded, (Updated March 20, 2023), www.franklehman.com/starwars. See also Frank Lehman, 'The Themes of *Star Wars*: Catalogue and Commentary,' in Emilio Audissino (ed.), *John Williams: Music for Films, Television and the Concert Stage* (Turnhout, Belgium: Brepols, 2018), 153–190.

8 For other definitions of leitmotif in Williams's *Star Wars* scores, see the following: Matthew Bribitzer-Stull, *Understanding the Leitmotif: From Wagner to Hollywood Film Music* (Cambridge: Cambridge University Press, 2015), 274 and Chs. 1 and 7; and Chloé Huvet, 'D'Un nouvel espoir (1977) à La Revanche des Sith (2005): écriture musicale et traitement de la partition au sein du complexe audio-visuel dans la saga *Star Wars*,' PhD diss. (Université Bretagne Loire, 2017), 125–128.

9 This includes all the following themes and any subsections they contain: Main Theme, Imperial March, Han and Leia, Yoda, Cloud City, Ewoks, Duel of the Fates, Gloomy Courtship (which I hear as a C section of Across the Stars as it is used as such in the end credits), Across the Stars (Anakin and Padme), Battle of the Heroes, Kylo Ren C (which I hear as an introduction to either Kylo Ren A or B), Rey B (which I hear as introductory to Rey A), Rey C (which is an accompaniment figure to Rey A), March of the Resistance, and Rose (which has contrasting sections that went unused in the film). As explained below, I understand Jabba's theme as a single eight-bar theme, contrasting with the separate four-bar A and B sections presented in the catalog.

10 These themes include TIE Fighter Attack, Throne Room, Shmi, (Qui-Gon's) Funeral, and Jedi Steps.

11 This includes Jawas, It's a Trap!, Pastoral Courtship, Happy Landings (which has only a derived variant of the theme in a third statement), Kylo Ren C/First Order, and Pathos (which has two statements in one film, then other indirect recollections in later ones).

12 This includes Imperials (Ostinato 1 and 2), Dark Side (Basic Motif), Dark Side (Ostinato & Melody), Victory Fanfare, Revelations, Mystery, Descent (Dies Irae and Lament), Snoke, Tension, and Sith Artifacts (Wayfinder).

13 This includes Rey A Continued (Sweeping Variant and Alternate B-Phrase), which is a variant of Rey A, and Kylo Ren A (Redeemed Variant), which is a variant of Kylo Ren A (Aggressive).

14 These include Map and Sith Artifacts (Dagger), both of which are MacGuffins that motivate both good and evil characters rather than take part in the fight on a particular side.
15 As Lehman points out in 'Complete Catalogue' (33), the bass-line version of 'Kylo Ren C (Menacing)/First Order' (43a), which serves as an introduction to either of Kylo's themes, and the Extension version (43c) 'are closely related, perhaps derivatives of each other; both are based on a grasping four-note figure' that begins each version. Hence, the similarity in the level of threat of both Ren and the First Order is suggested not only by the motto structure of both but also by their similar motivic content.
16 While the First Order theme appears minimally in the film's final cut, an unused cue (1M3A R 'The First Order Approaches') shows it was to feature prominently near the start of the film as the First Order arrives on Jakku for an attack.
17 Director Rian Johnson has explained how his instructions to John Williams about the score for the film was communicated more with the temp track than with verbal discussions, and the temp track was almost entirely composed of Williams' own previous *Star Wars* music. See Rian Johnson, 'Episode 69: Rian Johnson on the Music of Star Wars & Other Movies,' Interview by Edith Bowman, *Soundtracking with Edith Bowman* (December 18 2017), http://audioboom.com/posts/6557819-episode-69-rian-johnson-on-the-music-of-star-wars-other-movies.
18 This theme is found in cue 9M85 'Finale Part I.' Lehman ('Complete Catalogue,' 32) notes that a different, partial, and traditional (i.e., grammatical) structure for Kylo Ren is also found in an unused cue from *The Force Awakens*, 2M17 'Kylo Ren,' in which Ren expresses guilt over feeling a pull to the Light Side of the Force while speaking to Vader's semi-melted helmet. Ren's theme here is his aggressive theme with a second phrase that begins like the first but ends differently, outlining an eight-bar grammatical theme (notated as four bars) in the form of a period. Since Ren is asking Vader to show him the power of the darkness, this expansion of Ren's aggressive theme might have suggested Ren's ambition to be as powerful as Vader, whose theme was of course a longer grammatical one as well rather than a motto.
19 The irony of the celebration ending the film is subtly suggested by the diegetic music, 'Augie's Municipal Band,' the main melody of which is a major-pentatonic reworking of the Emperor's theme.
20 Two other themes fall just short of being leitmotifs due to their appearance in only two cues: Lament (theme 37b in Lehman's *Catalogue*) and Happy Landings (theme 40).
21 For more on how Vader's theme musically expresses its association, see Mark Richards, 'John Williams Themes, Part 3 of 6: The Imperial March (Darth Vader's Theme),' *Film Music Notes* (March 16, 2013), http://filmmusicnotes.com/2013/03/16/john-williams-themes-part-3-of-6-the-imperial-march-darth-vaders-theme.
22 'Psalm of the Sith' is Williams's own preferred name for the theme referred to on the soundtrack album as 'Anthem of Evil.'
23 This theme is also heard when we first see Lando's face in the film, which is not associated with Poe's heroics. I consider this usage to be an instance of a freer use of leitmotif which Williams employs every so often, the use of Leia's theme for the death of Obi-Wan in *A New Hope* being the *locus classicus* in his *Star Wars* scores.
24 This earlier version of the cue is 1M8 'Approaching the Nursery,' which was originally titled 'Approaching the Emperor' in an even earlier version.

25 Instead of the twisted, evil-sounding opening figure of Ren's theme [$\hat{5}$-♮$\hat{4}$-$\hat{1}$], for Ben Solo we now hear a more human yet pathos-laden segment of a minor scale [$\hat{6}$-$\hat{5}$-$\hat{1}$].
26 See 'The Maestro's Finale,' digital-only bonus feature, *Star Wars, Episode IX: The Rise of Skywalker*, Walt Disney Pictures, 2020. In *Star Wars* films, when a theme is used to depict an old character in a new position or situation, Williams has always preferred to simply write a new theme. Examples include Vader's theme in *The Empire Strikes Back* instead of the Imperial Motif from *A New Hope*, Luke in Exile in *The Last Jedi* instead of Luke's theme, and Psalm of the Sith from *The Rise of Skywalker* instead of exclusively using the Emperor's theme.

5
TOPIC THEORY AND FILM
Coming of Age in 1994's and 2019's *Little Women*

Janet Bourne

The screen is black. Out of the silence, strains from a romantic accordion emerge, and we are transported to Paris. The following shot of the Eiffel Tower just confirms what we already knew. This isn't a specific movie, but at the same time, it's a million movies. Film studies scholar Claudia Gorbman writes that 'Any music bears cultural associations, and most of these associations have been further codified and exploited by the music industry' (1987).[1] These conventional figures have gone by many different names in film music scholarship, such as Gorbman's 'cultural codes' and Philip Tagg's 'musemes.'[2] Outside of academia, they might be called 'tropes' or even 'clichés.' In the discipline of music theory, they go by a special name—'topics'—and the well-developed discourse that surrounds them, topic theory, offers a promising framework that unifies the study of film semiotics and film structure.

Defining Topics

Topics are conventional musical signs with clear significations understood by most hearers due to being part of a musical referential code based on use and exposure.[3] They are musical clichés audiences know better than they realize: The aforementioned accordion providing a Parisian feel, the sultry solo saxophone signifying the *femme fatale*, the major march assuring the audience that the hero has arrived, and countless more. A topic has two components: Musical features and socio-cultural associations.[4] For example, the major march, with features of brass instrumentation and dotted rhythms, indicates soldiers or, in more recent film history, the

DOI: 10.4324/9781003001171-5

hero and all the associations audiences tie to heroic protagonists, such as bravery, courage, righteousness, and (problematically) masculinity. Topic theory originated with musicologist Leonard Ratner and his studies of eighteenth-century Western art music and was further expounded as part of a larger late-twentieth-century turn in music theory toward musical semiotics by scholars such as Kofi Agawu, Robert Hatten, Raymond Monelle, and Danuta Mirka.[5] While musicology has continued to focus on topics and their historical contexts largely within the sphere of eighteenth- and nineteenth-century Western art music, film music is starting to gain some much-deserved traction.[6]

It is no surprise that film composers use topics considering how efficiently they communicate meaning to an audience. Because topics become an auditory shorthand for certain associations or meanings, composers exploit them to communicate with their audiences. As film composer Dimitri Tiomkin admitted in 1951, 'I have used the "Indian music" [Native American topic] that everyone knows not because I am not resourceful enough to originate other music, but because it is a telegraphic code that audiences recognize.'[7] Because, for example, audiences hear the major march associated with the hero over and over across multiple films, they come to learn and internalize a semiotically stable component of musical discourse, a component with a conventional association—it becomes a topic. Easily implemented by composers and easily perceived by listeners, they create a musical vocabulary that filmmakers deploy for dramatic and communicative efficiency.

Topics often communicate information about the world in the film, such as locale, time period, emotion, and characters' ethnicity or sociocultural backgrounds, among other information.[8] Yet, topics can convey information beyond the film itself, revealing cultural ideologies of the system and social structure that created the film, such as power relations connected to gender, race, and age. For these reasons, topic theory is a singularly useful theoretical framework for analyzing these semiotically stable components of musical discourse and interpreting film music's expressive and referential powers.

Analyzing Topics

An analysis of topics occurs on two levels: Delimiting and interpreting. Subsequent sections of this chapter address each level, while I close with an analysis of what I call the **Childhood topic** within two film adaptations of *Little Women* from 1994 and 2019. In the 'delimiting' section, I briefly describe the origins of film musical topics in general and provide a short list of particularly well-utilized topics heard in this repertoire.

Then, I discuss how scholars theorize features and associations of a given topic as an abstract category, with those extrinsic associations typically understood through investigations of social and cultural history as Monelle suggests.[9] This abstract category resembles what Hatten calls a 'type,' an 'ideal or conceptual category defined by features or range of qualities.'[10] Afterward, I define the 'Childhood' topic, a newly described topic prevalent in film music. In the 'interpreting' section, I describe how topic theorists analyze the degree to which topics are realized within specific films and their hermeneutic implications.[11] Often, this involves analyzing tokens of a type, a token being a 'perceptible entity that embodies or manifests the features or qualities of the [more abstract] type.'[12] I present paths a scholar could take when interpreting how topics are used dramatically in a film. To demonstrate the power of this theoretical framework for analyzing music's expressive and referential powers, I conclude with an analysis of the contrasting *Little Women* scores, whose differential treatment of the Childhood topic marks a changing cultural stance toward the road from childhood to adulthood between 1994 and 2019.

Delimiting Topics

Film inherits many of its topics from Western art music, primarily nineteenth-century program music, incidental music, and opera.[13] Musicians like Erno Rapée, Hans Erdmann, and Giuseppe Becce solidified the practice of topical signification when they created catalogs of sheet music to accompany early cinema, like the *Motion Picture Moods for Pianists and Organists* (1924) and *Allgemeines Handbuch der Film-Musik* (1927).[14] In these catalogs, excerpts from the Western concert music repertory were sorted into affective or associational categories, such as 'love theme,' 'storm,' 'battle,' and so on.[15] These collections, with their clean semantic designations and wide dissemination, helped form the basis for topical practice in film, 'transcending the actual pieces catalogued' and helping 'delimit or confirm boundaries of topics, fitting newly composed music into them.'[16]

A list of film music topics would include those with a long history in Western art music—such as Pastoral—as well as those that likely originated within the medium—such as Italian Western. Agawu created a 'universe of topics,' a checklist of 27 topics heard in eighteenth-century Western art music.[17] In a similar vein, Tagg compiled a universe of topic-like patterns within popular culture and multimedia that he labeled 'feels,' a list that includes such items as pub song, slapstick comedy, seventies disco, and erotic tango, among others.[18] Creating a universe of topics is not my goal here. As Monelle has noted, lists of topics 'are probably of little use'; instead, topical analysis works better when we 'allow musical texts to suggest new topics as they arise.'[19] Nevertheless, a decidedly non-comprehensive list of a few especially robust filmic examples (see Table 5.1), along with references to studies in which they are examined, provides a useful starting point for scholars as they embark on topical analysis.

Scholars often sort out topics by cataloging clusters of features that span heterogeneous musical parameters. For example, Monelle and Hatten offer the following features for the Pastoral topic: Flute and oboe timbre, 6/8 or 12/8 meter, drone bass, pedal points, simple harmonies, major, slow harmonic rhythm, parallel thirds, subdominant emphasis, and 'simple lyricism.'[20] By definition, topics are perceptually salient in some way, usually because of one or more musical feature(s) that stand outside the standard musical language of a given text, be it a classical symphony or a blockbuster film. A challenge to topic theory has been delineating which features, and how many of them, are needed for a listener to identify a topic. Johanna Frymoyer suggests the analyst arrange features in a weighted hierarchy that declares certain features as essential (must be present to identify the topic), frequent (inessential but contribute to the topic's contextual salience), or stylistically particular or idiosyncratic (characteristics that appear in works of a particular style, composer, or compositional circle, so often stylistic sub-categories of the topic).[21] A similar approach would be to build a prototype (type) for the topic, which the listener uses to recognize examples (tokens) of that topic.[22] In the prototype model, while some features of the prototype are weighted (more important), no features are strictly necessary. One token could be a solo clarinet in 6/8, while another two flutes in parallel thirds in 4/4; both examples could be realizations of the Pastoral topic despite sharing no common features. For film music, one topical feature that tends to be weighted heavily relative to other genres is timbre.

In addition to recognizing features, theorists identify stable associations, or signifieds, when describing a topic. Mirka writes that topical signification extends on one hand 'to associations of styles and genres with affects, and on the other hand, to their associations with social contexts. For instance, dances raise associations with ballrooms and social status of dances; military marches with parades or battlefields.'[23] The Pastoral topic, for example, has a network of associations that includes historical or literary past, nature and country, nostalgia (real or imagined past), home, family and love, and female gender or femininity.[24] Yet, each associational node is also embedded in a broader web of significations; the Pastoral does

TABLE 5.1 Examples of film music topics

1. Pastoral[a]
2. Ombra[b]
3. Tempesta[c]
4. Soaring[d]
5. Genius[e]
6. Hymn[f]
7. Ethnicities/Place (Latin American, Middle Eastern, Scottish, Japanese, etc.)[g]
8. Pianto[h]
9. Fairy[i]
10. March (Military)[j]
11. Elegy[k]
12. Cowboy[l]
13. Waltz
14. Musical Genres (Rap, Rock, Jazz, etc.)
15. Femme Fatale[m]
16. Misterioso[n]
17. Twinkly Christmas
18. Childhood
19. Chorale[o]
20. Tango
21. Perpetual-Motion Etude[p]

[a] Janet Bourne, 'Hearing Film Music Topics Outside the Movie Theatre: Listening Cinematically to Pastorals,' in Carlo Cenciarelli (ed.), *Oxford Handbook of Cinematic Listening* (Oxford: Oxford University Press, 2021), 459–574; Neil Lerner, 'Copland's Music of Wide Open Spaces: Surveying the Pastoral Trope in Hollywood,' *Musical Quarterly* 85.3 (2001): 477–515; Anahid Kassabian, *Hearing Film: Tracking Identifications in Contemporary Hollywood Film Music* (New York: Routledge, 2001), 15–36.
[b] Clive McClelland, 'Of Gods and Monsters: Signification in Franz Waxman's Film Score Bride of Frankenstein,' *Journal of Film Music* 7.1 (2014): 5–19.
[c] McClelland, 'Of Gods and Monsters.'
[d] Sean Atkinson, 'Soaring Through the Sky: Topics and Tropes in Video Game Music,' *Music Theory Online* 25.2 (2019), https://mtosmt.org/issues/mto.19.25.2/mto.19.25.2.atkinson.html.
[e] Rebecca Doran Eaton, 'Marking Minimalism: Minimal Music as a Sign of Machines and Mathematics in Multimedia,' *Music and the Moving Image* 7.1 (2014): 3–23.
[f] Olga Sánchez-Kisielewska, 'The Hymn as a Musical Topic in the Age of Haydn, Mozart, and Beethoven,' Ph.D. diss. (Northwestern University, 2018).
[g] As an overview of some of these topics, see Brownrigg, 'Hearing Place: Film Music, Geography and Ethnicity.'
[h] Yayoi Uno Everett, 'Pianto as a Topical Signifier of Grief in Contemporary Operas by John Adams, Thomas Ades, and Kaija Saariaho,' in Esti Sheinberg and William P. Dougherty (eds.), *Routledge Handbook of Music Signification* (New York: Routledge, 2020).
[i] Dickensheets, 'The Topical Vocabulary of the Nineteenth Century,' 122.
[j] Monelle, *The Musical Topic*, 113–84.
[k] Todd Decker, *Hymns for the Fallen: Combat Movie Music and Sound after Vietnam* (Berkeley: University of California Press, 2017).

(Continued)

TABLE 5.1 (Continued)

l	Ronald Rodman, '"Coperettas," "Detecterns," and Space Operas: Music and Genre Hybridization in American Television,' in James Deaville (ed.), *Music in Television: Channels of Listening* (New York: Routledge, 2011), 43–49.
m	On 'Fallen Woman,' see Kathryn Kalinak, 'The Fallen Woman and the Virtuous Wife: Musical Stereotypes in the Informer, Gone with the Wind, and Laura,' *Film Reader 5* (1982): 76–82.
n	Plebuch, 'Mysteriosos Demystified: Topical Strategies within and beyond the Silent Cinema.'
o	Lehman describes what could be a Hans Zimmer-specific chorale that he labels the 'Consequential Chorale.' See Frank Lehman, 'Manufacturing the Epic Score: Hans Zimmer and the Sounds of Significance,' in Stephen Meyer (ed.), *Music in Epic Film: Listening to Spectacle* (New York: Routledge, 2017), 38–39.
p	David Neumeyer, *Meaning and Interpretation of Music in Cinema* (Bloomington: Indiana University Press, 2015), 187.

For studies on the topics in this table, see the following sources, listed in order of appearance in Table 5.1:

not just index 'home' or 'femininity' but also other emotions, concepts, and histories associated with these concepts within its cultural history.

After identifying a potential topic by noticing salient and oft-repeating musical material across multiple films via clusters of features, scholars can specify the associations with a potential film musical topic by analyzing imagery, character emotions, and narrative contexts in which the musical material coincides (salient musical material could be topics from Western art music imported to film music or originate in the medium of film music). This musical material can be solidified as a topic in Hollywood-style film scores in part by regularly occurring with conventionalized images and scenes. When audiences watch films, they learn to associate musical topics with images, narrative devices, and so on, and thus one topic accumulates a network of associations.

Case Study: The Childhood Topic

As an example of topical features and associations, I now discuss the 'Childhood' topic. With features that create a shimmery effect, film audiences associate this topic with children and childhood (Figure 5.1) due to its conventional appearance in film (Table 5.2). These features, which include high instrumentation and running eighth and sixteenth notes, accompanied children on screen as early as the 1920s, as many of them appear in pieces under Rapée's 'children' and 'music box' categories.[25]

A representative instance of the Childhood topic is the whimsical main theme for *Inside Out* (2015), with an eighth-note ostinato creating a consistent pulse underlying a syncopated, yet singable theme on a solo piano (Example 5.1).

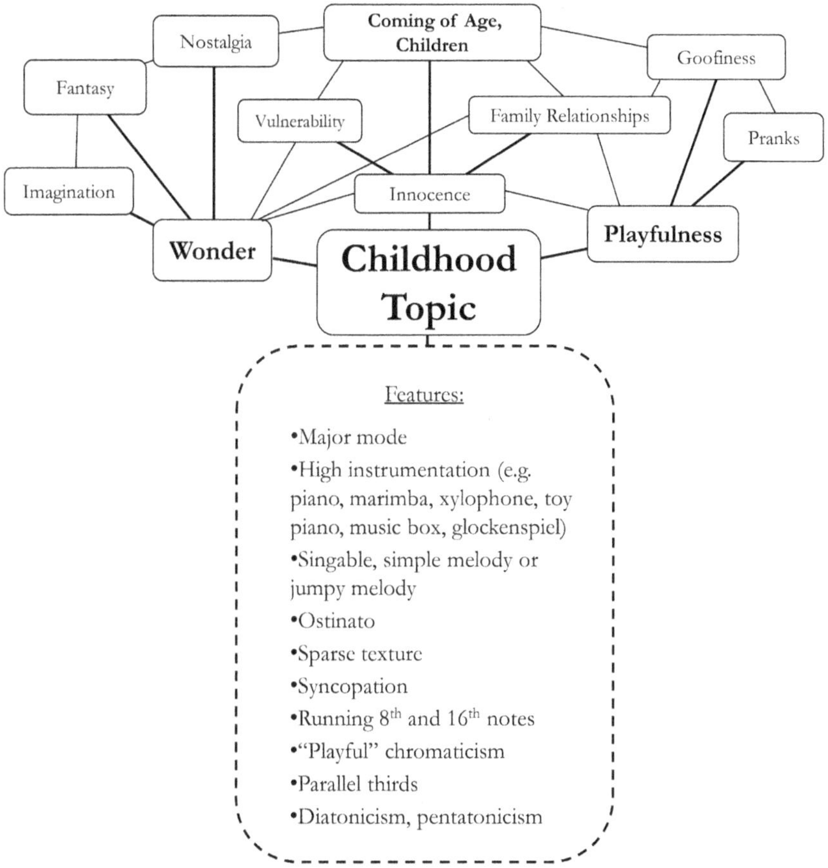

Topic Theory and Film   93

FIGURE 5.1   Features and network of associations for Childhood topic.

EXAMPLE 5.1   Giacchino, *Inside Out* (2015), excerpt from 'Bundle of Joy' (all examples transcribed by R. Hock.

TABLE 5.2 Small corpus of the Childhood topic in films from 1990–2020

Film	Track with Timestamp	Year	Composer
Edward Scissorhands	'Storytime,' 0:00–0:15	1990	Elfman
Hook	'Remembering Childhood,' 5:10–5:43	1991	Williams
Sandlot	'Main Title,' 0:25–0:50	1993	Newman
Little Women	'The Laurence Boy,' 0:00–0:12	1994	Newman
Babe	'Toreador / Mother & Son,' 0:40–1:00	1995	Westlake
A Little Princess	'The Miss Minchin School for Girls,' 0:00–0:50	1995	Doyle
Jack	'The Children's Crusade,' 1:58–2:13	1996	Kamen
James and the Giant Peach	'Lullaby,' 0:00–0:29	1996	Newman
Madeline	'Madeline's Theme,' 0:40–0:54	1998	Legrand
Stuart Little	'Adoption Day,' 0:45–0:52	1999	Silvestri
Chronicles of Narnia	'The Wardrobe,' 0:12–0:23	2005	Gregson-Williams
Sisterhood of the Traveling Pants 2	'Sisterhood,' 1:54–2:14	2008	Portman
Fantastic Mr. Fox	'Kristofferson's Theme,' 0:00–0:27	2009	Desplat
Jeff Who Lives at Home	Main Title, 0:00–1:30	2011	Andrews
The Book Thief	'Ilsa's Library,' 0:11–0:27	2013	Williams
Inside Out	'Bundle of Joy,' 0:00–0:10	2015	Giacchino
Star Wars: The Force Awakens	'Rey's Theme,' 0:14–0:25	2015	Williams
Gifted	'Mary's Theme,' 0:40–1:15	2017	Simonsen
Little Women	'The Letter,' 0:33–0:42	2019	Desplat
Onward	'Baby Legs,' 0:00–0:15	2020	Danna

Figure 5.1 also outlines an incomplete network of associations of the Childhood topic, which branch into two overarching ideas of child-like wonder and playfulness, either of which can connect to innocence and coming of age. These associations stem less from anyone's actual experience of young age than it does from how adults idealize and nostalgize childhood, with children viewed as 'powerless "others"' and themselves as 'gate-keepers' to innocence-destroying knowledge such as death, sexuality, and politics.[26] Appropriately, the audience first hears the main theme from *Inside Out* when introduced to the character Riley as a baby.

The Childhood topic frequently scores children on screen, although not always. It could appear when an adult character is (re)connected to childhood in some way, whether through affects related to childhood—such as wonder and fantasy—or reminders of inevitabilities of childhood—coming of age.[27] Or the adult could be recalling their childhood, as the grown-up Peter Pan does in *Hook* (1991), as the Childhood topic can be heard immediately after he says he ran away as a baby because, 'I was afraid, I didn't want to grow up,' and it underscores his recalling this unusual childhood. In *Jeff Who Lives at Home* (2011), the opening theme plays the Childhood topic with images of 30-year-old unemployed Jeff at the beginning of this coming-of-age story.

Interpreting Topics

An audience unconsciously perceives musical topics and then seeks an explanation for the topic in relation to a film's narrative structure.[28] Topic theory is not simply about 'appending style labels to musical moments,' but instead 'its hermeneutic elegance lies in its ability to explore the interplay of style [or meaning] *and* structure.'[29] Audiences use music to co-create narrative understanding in film along with image, dialog, and sound; in a suspenseful scene, for example, according to Kathryn Kalinak, music is not simply '*reinforcing* the suspense' but is 'part of the process that creates it.'[30] Topics lend themselves well to co-creating an emerging narrative structure since they communicate referential information so efficiently. Yet, topics are not merely neutral referential markers. They can also reveal deep ideological undercurrents regarding social and power structures, and so topic theory can be used if desired to interpret an ideological substrate of film.[31] As part of the hermeneutic process, an interpretive reading of a film, a topic theorist first analyzes how topics are invoked locally, in individual cues, and then how they are positioned globally, within the dramatic arc of a film as a whole. The following paragraphs briefly outline possibilities to consider embarking on this analytical course: 1) Stability and typicality; 2) troping; 3) leitmotifs and associative themes; 4) identification and relations; 5) audio-visual combinations; and 6) stereotypes and power relations.

1) *Stability and typicality of topic.* Topics are not always realized in an ideal or prototypical way and scholars have different ways of addressing how composers may modify a topic. Analyzing Western art music, Monelle suggests that topics occur in different forms. If a topic's features are intentionally distorted such as by seemingly unstable musical parameters—chromaticism instead of diatonicism, minor instead of major, changing meter—then this indicates a dysphoric form, which

is an unstable variant of a topic, often with 'corrupted' associations and negative connotations.[32] In *Little Women* (2019) for example, the audience hears a dysphoric Childhood topic when Amy March maliciously burns her sister Jo's novel (0:46:58). Normally heard in major mode, this realization of the topic was destabilized by a post-tonal context, while still maintaining high instrumentation, sparse texture, and simple melody, signifying a destructive deed and correspondingly corrupted sisterly relationship. A dysphoric Childhood topic—like in *Little Women* (2019)—would be an atypical token, more salient compared to prototypical tokens—like the theme for *Inside Out* (2015). An analyst can consider stability and/or typicality when reading a topic in a cue.

2) *Troping*.[33] Hatten defines 'troping' as the bringing together of two or more unrelated topics in close proximity (such as through simultaneous superimposition or successive juxtaposition) so as to 'spark an interpretation based on their interaction.'[34] Juan Chattah argues that musical troping is 'extremely valuable' in narrative film. Fusing 'two unrelated musical topics within a scene,' he observes, 'is generally motivated by a convergence of two distinct elements in the film's narrative.'[35] For example, *Jeff Who Lives at Home* (2011) is about Jeff, a 30-year-old unemployed stoner living in his mother's basement. The opening theme tropes the Childhood topic and a rock topic: A marimba plays repeating motifs in a high register with a guitar and drumset. This fusion of styles creates a musical representation of the character Jeff as a man-child—biologically an adult man (Rock topic) but culturally and psychologically still coming of age (Childhood topic). Therefore, troping can represent not only distinct elements of a narrative but also intersections of a character's identity.

3) *Leitmotif and associative themes*. A leitmotif is a musical theme that becomes identified with a situation, character, or idea in part due to repetition in a specific narrative text; it also develops over time as well as functions within a larger musical structure.[36] Most leitmotifs are capable of retaining their signifying powers amid transformations of topical context; the audiences can identify, say, a hero leitmotif irrespective of its local topical content, say being presented as a march, or in a Pastoral guise. In his analysis of the *Star Trek* episode 'Shore Leave,' for example, Ronald Rodman describes how a Don Juan leitmotif is heard clothed in a Renaissance topic. This musical material not only points the audience to the Don Juan character but also communicates that this character is of an antique time.[37] The *leitmotif*, therefore, reinforces a character, place, or idea in part via thematic repetition, while the topical *'clothing'* of that leitmotif provides content beyond denotation and into connotation.

One way a leitmotif can develop is by transforming from hosting one topic to another—a useful technique to communicate a change in character. In the *Lord of the Rings* trilogy, for example, the 'Sorrow of the Elves' goes from being presented through exotic, atmospheric fantasy topics early on into a rousing march when Elvish forces assist in the battle of Helm's Deep in *The Two Towers* (2002).[38] The topics that composers choose for their leitmotifs powerfully influence how audiences view that place, idea, or character.

4) *Identification and relations.* For a larger scale analysis, one could catalog which topics are used over the course of a film, how they relate to genre, narrative, or meta-narrative and to each other (I only discuss genre here, but see the *Little Women* analysis at the end of the chapter for discussions of narrative and meta-narrative). Some film genres become associated with certain collections of topics.[39] An audio-viewer sitting down for a Western film, for instance, might expect to hear Western cowboy topics (e.g., *The Good, the Bad, and the Ugly* main theme, *The Magnificent Seven* main theme, *Gunsmoke* theme), Native American topics (e.g., 'Indian music' from *Stagecoach*, 'Comanches' from *The Searchers*), Pastoral topics, and more.[40] Set in the *Star Wars* universe, Ludwig Göransson's theme for *The Mandalorian* uses a Western cowboy topic, which helps the audience connect the science fiction show to a space Western genre. A large-scale topical fingerprint creates an impression of a film. Topics that appear only once or twice are salient compared to others saturated throughout the film. In addition to identifying topics that appear, a scholar could consider topics that are noticeably absent. Carter Burwell's score for *True Grit* (2010) for example lacks many topics associated with the Western genre—big brassy themes, expansive orchestrations, galloping rhythms—relying instead on nineteenth-century Protestant hymns.

5) *Audio-visual combinations.* When a topic—along with its network of associations—combines with visuals, the topic does not only add clarifying associations but interprets the image and narrative, creating an emergent meaning, as described by film theorist Michel Chion's principle of added value.[41] Via Chion's principle of synchresis: By appearing at the same time, we forge a relationship between topics—what one hears—and imagery—what one sees—and figure out a way to combine them.[42] Because of added value and synchresis, the same scene underscored by different topics drastically alters our interpretation of that scene. While the topic colors how we perceive the image, similarly the image and narrative often suggest which nodes of the topic's network of associations we might activate. David Neumeyer analyzes how Bach's C Major Prelude, an example of the

Perpetual-motion etude topic, generates a broad range of effects in different visual contexts: 'In *Picnic at Hanging Rock*, the C Major Prelude is the European conflation of high art and cultural status but also a vehicle of escape; in *Thirty Two Short Films about Glenn Gould*, it is the peculiar combination of transcendence and subjectivity in recorded sound; in *Je vous salue, Marie*, it morphs from arpeggio prelude into murmuring of consciousness in the inner monologue of Marie; and in *Lola*, it likewise morphs, but now out of a dream of love.'[43]

6) *Stereotypes and power relations.* While composers use topics for their powers of significatory clarification, this can come at the risk of reinforcing destructive stereotypes and perpetuating harmfully unbalanced power relations, especially when it comes to racial and gender representation. Historically, film composers have often resorted to topics to score the racial other in stereotypical ways, too often to the effect of demonizing them.[44] For example, Gorbman has demonstrated how the musical topics employed to represent the Native American as Other varied and evolved during the 1930s through the 1950s in line with larger trends in political and cultural history.[45] A number of topics we have already encountered in this essay host gendered associations, including the military March (masculine) and the Pastoral (feminine); unsurprisingly, such topical differentiations have tended to limit and constrain the possibilities for the representation of women in a way they do not for men.[46] Music theorist James Buhler advocates for displacing 'the colonial structure, the regime of knowledge, that undergirds the stereotypical discourse and produce its social subjects.' For topics, this means 'proceeding not by identifying stereotypes and/or their dramatic function per se, but by analyzing their operation at the level of structure—both for how the work's structure requires and enables a particular stereotypical discourse as an ideological form and for how that ideological form serves to articulate the larger social structure in all its contradictoriness.'[47] In this way, topics reveal ideological undercurrents in social and power structures.

Case Study: The 1994 and 2019 Adaptations of *Little Women*

Considered the 'seminal classic novel of American girlhood,' Louisa May Alcott's 1868/1869 novel *Little Women* tells the story of four sisters—Jo, Meg, Beth, and Amy March—and their coming of age in New England during and immediately after the American Civil War.[48] In her introduction to the 1983 edition of the novel, Madelon Bedell claims that *Little Women* may be '*the* American female myth, its subject the primordial one of the passage from childhood, from girl to woman.'[49] Adaptations—of which there have been many, spanning radio dramas, opera, plays, and films—reveal ever-changing conceptions of female coming-of-age. As film critic Jessica Bennett muses, 'people have been adapting, and then critiquing, and then adapting, and then critiquing [*Little Women*] for decades—each iteration a kind of Rorschach test for how the world feels about women at the time.'[50]

Thomas Newman and Alexandre Desplat composed the scores for Gillian Armstrong's 1994 and Greta Gerwig's 2019 film adaptations of *Little Women* respectively. The manner in which Newman and Desplat deploy musical topics—and the Childhood topic in particular—reveals a lot about these shifting mores, particularly vivid in the divergent characterizations of Jo March—a characterization consistent with, and indeed partly constitutive of, their overall films' attitude toward women's progress into adulthood. Briefly: Newman's music captures a neat and clear transition for Jo into adulthood. By contrast, Desplat's score casts Jo as existing in an unstable 'in-between,' on one side the childhood she resists relinquishing and the other maturity she has yet to achieve; this ambivalence is an indicator of the life stage psychologist Jeffrey Jensen Arnett has labeled 'emerging adulthood.'[51] Despite coming only a few decades apart, these different musical constructions reveal quite clearly changed views of growing up in American culture. A brief description of this notion of emerging adulthood will prove useful in grounding the more detailed topical analysis that follows.

The journey to adulthood that 20-somethings in the 2010s make has been described as complicated and uncertain compared to the uniform, unproblematic, and swift journey made by their parents and grandparents. Post-World War II, many 20-somethings within a certain socio-economic class followed a clear path to adulthood: Complete education, land a stable job, and start a family.[52] Yet, around 2000, journalists and academics noticed a trend of 20-somethings postponing traditional benchmarks of adulthood (e.g., marriage, home ownership, children, etc.), seemingly occupying a liminal state between adolescence and adulthood.[53] To account for this change, Arnett proposed 'emerging adulthood' as a new life stage in industrialized societies from the age of 18 to early 30s, distinguished by identity exploration, instability, self-focus, feeling in-between or in-transition with respect to maturity, and entertaining multiple life possibilities.[54] Arnett attributes this feeling of 'in-between' in part to a shift from measuring the achievement of adulthood on the basis of an all-at-once social transition to a more gradual process revolving on incremental criteria, such as accepting responsibility for oneself, making independent decisions, and becoming financially independent.[55] As millennials postpone or disregard traditional benchmarks of adulthood, they use more internal and individualistic criteria for measuring adulthood status.[56] As the 'emerging adult' label peppered the press and entered popular consciousness, critics began noticing themes of deferred maturation in media as well, in formats ranging from film and television to indie rock.[57] Within this 'emerging adult' meta-genre, a character or persona does not *feel* like an adult, despite being one legally and biologically. Their narrative involves overcoming the various obstacles, character flaws, and psychological difficulties that stand in the way of reaching proper adulthood, a status reached by the end—often signified by a commitment to a long-term heterosexual relationship.[58]

In the 1994 adaptation of *Little Women*, music, narrative, and dialog communicate that Jo (Winona Ryder) becomes an adult when she moves away from her family home to New York City [1:10:50]. Once Jo arrives in NYC, audiences hear the film's main theme not as in its accustomed pastorale guise but instead reimagined through a troping of Western Cowboy and Fanfare topics, including features such: Pentatonic pitch structures, major mode, paired horns in similar motion, syncopated chordal accompaniment, and melodic outlining of harmonic series (Example 5.2).[59]

This interpretation is supported by Jo's voiceover as we watch her walk down the street: 'Marmee [mother] helped me find a place in the great city of New York. And so I stepped over the divide between childhood and all that lay beyond.' The fanfaric aspects of this cue signify the arrival of a triumphant hero while the Western cowboy topic signifies adventure and a confident striding into unknown frontiers. These topics emphasize that Jo has embarked on an adventure, successfully crossing over into the wilds of adulthood. She begins to engage in traditionally 'adult' spaces, initiating a sexual relationship with Professor Bhaer and participating in political conversations.[60] Significantly, the Western-influenced fanfare topic returns once Jo receives a copy of her published book from Professor Bhaer, marking another triumphant moment in this new phase of her life.

Absent from this musical characterization of Jo in her post-NYC stage is the Childhood topic. Newman uses the topic in a literal sense, accompanying Jo and her sisters as children as they engage in child-like activities.[61] For instance, the early scene of Jo reading stories to her sisters in

EXAMPLE 5.2   Newman, *Little Women*, 'New York,' 0:04–0:13.

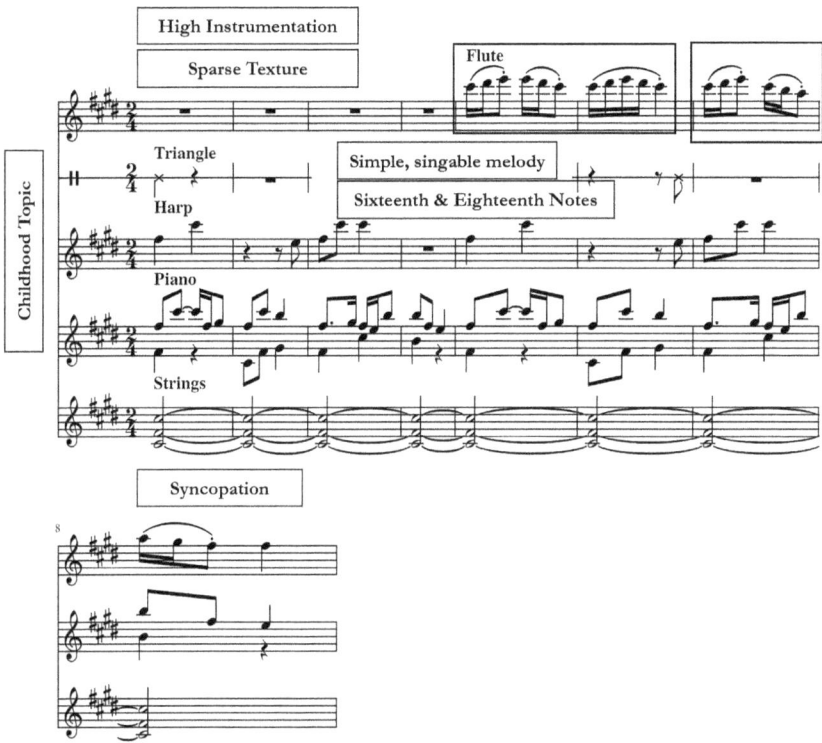

EXAMPLE 5.3   Newman, *Little Women*, 'The Laurence Boy,' 0:00–0:12.

the attic—where the score infuses the children's activities with a sense of playfulness and imagination [0:08:49] (Example 5.3).

Leaving home for a new city, getting a job, engaging in a long-term relationship—these are clear and uncontroversial markers of adulthood, reminiscent of becoming an adult in post-war America, a social ideal still active in the general cultural consciousness of the 1990s family values era. As Linda Grasso has noted, the 1994 adaptation of *Little Women* 'appeals to right-wing ideologues who see these "family values" in the mythical, golden-era past depicted on the screen.'[62] Representing this post-war American ideal of adulthood which was endorsed by politicians of the 'family values' eras, the Childhood topic does not appear accompanying post-NYC, adult Jo.

In vivid contrast with the 1994 adaptation, director and screenwriter Gerwig's more recent take on Alcott's novel challenges the existence of a clear transition from one life stage to another, leaving space for emerging adulthood, this messy in-between of child and adult. In Desplat's score, we hear the Childhood topic far past the point Jo (Saoirse Ronan) has moved to NYC, musically signifying she is still in a child-like space, she is an emerging adult, rather than an adult proper.[63] The film begins with an adult,

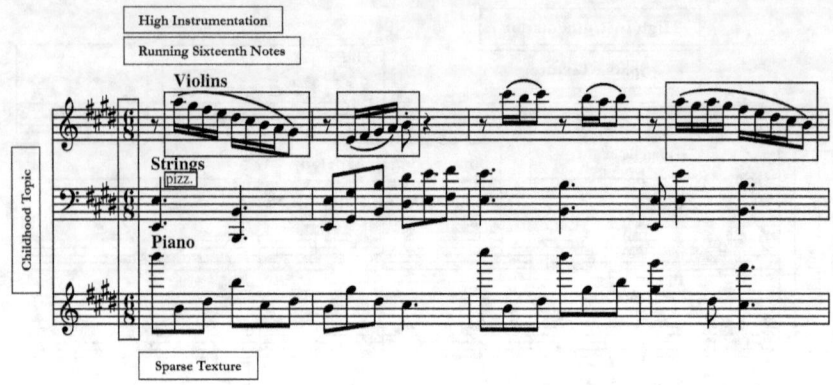

EXAMPLE 5.4   Alexandre Desplat, *Little Women*, 'The Letter,' 0:33–0:42.

post-NYC Jo, writer and director Gerwig having chosen to present the narrative nonlinearly. She crosscuts between scenes of the sisters as their older and younger selves, often to the effect of a kind of cinematic 'rhyming.'[64]

One token of the Childhood topic that accompanies post-NYC Jo actually begins during one of the childhood scenes. Her friend Laurie (Timothée Chalamet), standing outside the March household on a winter night, looks up at the attic window and sees Jo writing [0:17:48]. The scene cuts to Jo, now several years later in NYC, still writing at night in an attic, the Childhood topic cue bridging the editorial flash-forward as a sound link (Example 5.4).

On one level, the film is telling us Jo is an adult: Biologically, of course, and in terms of achieving traditional milestones such as leaving home and having a job. Yet there is a tension between external image and self-image, rendered cleverly in Desplat's score, with still youthful musical topics suggesting she hovers in this liminal space between childhood and adulthood.[65] Jo's move to NYC in the 2019 adaptation signifies an emerging, not established, adulthood. Yet, the goal of any emerging adult film is to become an adult proper.

2019's version of Jo establishes herself as a proper adult at the end of the film with the writing of her book [1:52:13] (see Figure 5.2). This moment is the 2019 version's apotheosis of the character's personal development, especially since she spent most of the film struggling to find her voice as a writer. Desplat scored earlier significant moments in Jo's authorial development with either the Childhood topic, no music at all, or an Elegy topic connected to Beth's (Eliza Scanlen) death, whose memory ultimately inspires her. Significantly, as Jo finally sits to write her book—a novel based on her personal experiences growing up—the audience hears a new musical signifier, the Genius topic (Example 5.5). This topos is

Topic Theory and Film 103

	Jo writes as child	Jo moves to NYC	Beth dies (inspires Jo)	Jo writes book	Jo's book is published
1994	Pastoral topic	Western fanfare topic	Hymn topic	Pastoral (with reprise of "For the Beauty of the Earth" hymn)	Western fanfare topic
	CHILD → ADULT				
2019*	Childhood topic	Childhood topic +	Elegy topic	Genius topic	Learned style topic (counterpoint)→ sustained strings
	CHILD → EMERGING ADULT		ADULT		

* To make comparison easier, scenes for the 2019 adaptation rearranged in plot chronological order, not order the viewer encounters them
+ This scene is not given as much cinematic weight in the 2019 adaptation as the 1994 adaptation

FIGURE 5.2 Topical scoring for some significant moments in Jo's development as an author for the 1994 and 2019 adaptations. Thickness of line correlates to coming of age.

EXAMPLE 5.5 Desplat, *Little Women*, 'Joe Writes,' 1:43–1:52.

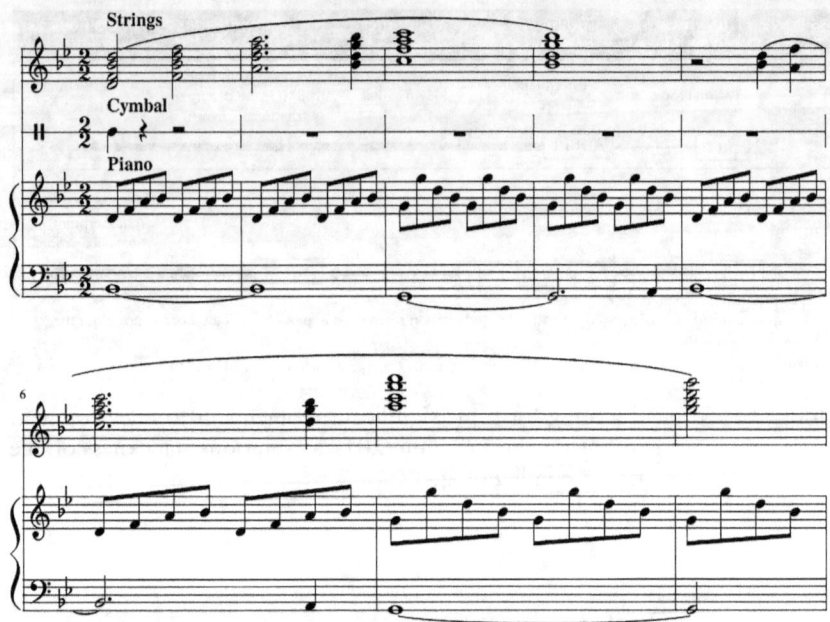

EXAMPLE 5.6 Desplat, *Little Women*, 'It's Romance,' 0:35–0:45.

characterized by minimalistic features, such as thin texture, repetition, and steady pulse.[66] Instead of measuring Jo's attainment of adulthood using a traditional status marker (such as marriage), Gerwig's adaptation employs a distinctly 2010s criterion, internal and individual to the specific character: Jo comes of age when she self-actualizes and finds her voice. Excepting meta-fictional framing scenes of the film—ambiguous as to whether they actually take place in the movie's diegesis—Jo is not scored with the Childhood topic after she writes her book.

In the final shots of the 2019 adaptation, as Jo holds a copy of her book, visual flashbacks of her and her sisters having tea parties appear, reinforcing that the novel symbolizes her transition to adulthood proper—out of the liminal emerging adulthood state. Writing it meant both letting go of and memorializing her childhood. After a screening in New York, Gerwig stated:

> What I was trying to reverse-engineer [in these final shots] was this moment that Jo getting her book would make the audience feel like you usually feel when the heroine is chosen by the hero. I wanted to see if I could create that feeling, but with a girl and her book.[67]

As noted before, marriage is a conventional narrative marker of the attainment of adulthood; we see it in Armstrong's 1994 adaptation, which ends with Jo accepting Bhaer's marriage proposal, a moment underscored by Newman with a pastorale reminiscent of love and romance. In Gerwig's adaptation, however, Jo getting together with Bhaer is suggested to be meta-fiction, taking place in *Jo's novel* as part of her pitch to the publisher, rather than a real event in her biography. Musical topics support this interpretation: Desplat scores the union of Jo and Bhaer with a Romance topic redolent of Max Steiner's scoring practice, giving the scene an over-the-top and out-of-date sensibility (Example 5.6). In her feminist portrayal of female adulthood, Gerwig validates using individual and character-specific markers for adulthood, rather than relying on the cliché of the character committing to a long-term relationship. And Desplat's musical topics are the building blocks for this modern transformation of a 150-year-old piece of American literature, a new Rorschach test for how the 2010s feel about women and adulthood.

Notes

1 Claudia Gorbman, *Unheard Melodies: Narrative Film Music* (Bloomington: Indiana University Press, 1987).
2 Philip Tagg, *Music's Meanings: A Modern Musicology for Non-Musos* (New York: Mass Media Music Scholars' Press, 2012).
3 Raymond Monelle, *The Musical Topic: Hunt, Military and Pastoral*, Musical Meaning and Interpretation (Bloomington: Indiana University Press, 2006), 3; James Buhler, *Theories of the Soundtrack*, The Oxford Music/Media Series (Oxford: Oxford University Press, 2019), 189–190. Some scholars restrict 'topic' to music that alludes to other styles and genres.
4 In traditional semiotics, these go by the name of 'signifiers' and 'signifieds' respectively.
5 Leonard Ratner, *Classic Music: Expression, Form, and Style* (New York: Schirmer Books, 1980), 19; Raymond Monelle, *The Sense of Music: Semiotic Essays* (Princeton: Princeton University Press, 2000); Monelle, *The Musical Topic*; Danuta Mirka (ed.), *Oxford Handbook of Topic Theory* (Oxford: Oxford University Press, 2014). For a review of topic theory scholarship between 1980 and mid-2000s, see Nicholas McKay, 'On Topics Today,' *Zeitschrift Der Gesellschaft Fuer Musiktheorie* 4.1–2 (2007): 159–183.
6 See Buhler, *Theories of the Soundtrack*. For the sake of background, here are examples of topic theory scholarship for Western art music and popular music: Mirka, *Oxford Handbook of Topic Theory*; Janice Dickensheets, 'The Topical Vocabulary of the Nineteenth Century,' *Journal of Musicological Research* 31. 2–3 (2012): 97–137; Johanna Frymoyer, 'Musical Topic in the Twentieth Century: A Case Study of Schoenberg's Ironic Waltzes,' *Music Theory Spectrum* 39.1 (2017): 83–108; William Echard, *Psychedelic Popular Music: A History through Musical Topic Theory* (Bloomington: Indiana University Press, 2017).

7 Quoted in James Buhler, 'Ontological, Formal, and Critical Theories of Film Music and Sound,' in David Neumeyer (ed.), *Oxford Handbook of Film Music Studies* (Oxford: Oxford University Press, 2014), 211.
8 Juan Chattah, *David Shire's The Conversation: A Film Score Guide*, Film Score Guides (Lanham: Rowman & Littlefield Publishers, 2015), 114; Mark Brownrigg, 'Hearing Place: Film Music, Geography and Ethnicity,' *International Journal of Media and Cultural Politics* 3.3 (2007): 307–323.
9 Monelle, *The Musical Topic*, 3.
10 Robert S. Hatten, *Musical Meaning in Beethoven: Markedness, Correlation, and Interpretation* (Bloomington: Indiana University Press, 2004), 45.
11 The analytical levels I describe here are similar to the three levels described by Neumeyer and Buhler: 1) identifying traits of a topic in general, 2) the degree and manner a topic is invoked in a cue, and 3) how topics deploy dramatically in film. See David Neumeyer and James Buhler, 'Analytical and Interpretive Approaches to Film Music (I): Analysing the Music,' in Kevin Donnelly (ed.), *Film Music: Critical Approaches* (Edinburgh: Edinburgh University Press, 2001), 16–37.
12 Hatten, *Musical Meaning in Beethoven*, 45.
13 Neumeyer and Buhler, 'Analytical and Interpretive Approaches to Film Music (I),' 24.
14 Erno Rapée, *Motion Picture Moods for Pianists and Organists* (Schirmer, 1924); Erno Rapée, *Encyclopaedia of Music for Pictures* (Belwin, 1925); Hans Erdmann and Giuseppe Becce, *Allgemeines Handbuch Der Film-Musik* (Berlin-Lichterfelde: Schlesinger, 1927).
15 For topics in silent film, see Tobias Plebuch, 'Mysteriosos Demystified: Topical Strategies within and beyond the Silent Cinema,' *Journal of Film Music* 5.1–2 (2012): 77–92.
16 Neumeyer and Buhler, 'Analytical and Interpretive Approaches to Film Music (I),' 24.
17 Kofi Agawu, *Playing with Signs: A Semiotic Interpretation of Classical Music* (Princeton: Princeton University Press, 1991), 30.
18 Tagg, *Music's Meanings: A Modern Musicology for Non-Musos*, 176.
19 Monelle, *The Musical Topic*, ix–x.
20 Hatten, *Interpreting Musical Gestures, Topics, and Tropes: Mozart, Beethoven, Schubert* (Bloomington: Indiana University Press, 2004), 58; Monelle, *The Musical Topic*, 207–228.
21 Frymoyer, 'Musical Topic in the Twentieth Century: A Case Study of Schoenberg's Ironic Waltzes,' 85.
22 Prototypes come from prototype theory in cognitive psychology. See Eleanor Rosch and Carolyn Mervis, 'Family Resemblances: Studies in the Internal Structure of Categories,' *Cognitive Psychology* 7 (1975): 573–605.
23 Mirka, 'Introduction,' 28.
24 For differences in networks of associations between Western art music Pastorals and film music Pastorals, see Bourne, 'Hearing Film Music Topics Outside the Movie Theatre.'
25 Rapée, *Motion Picture Moods' for Pianists and Organists*.
26 Kerry Robinson and Cristyn Davies, '"She's Kickin' Ass, That's What She's Doing!" Deconstructing Childhood "Innocence" in Media Representations,' *Australian Feminist Studies* 23.57 (2008): 343.
27 I have intentionally not considered the childhood topic in films of the horror genre, although there seems to be expressive potential. On innocent music in different horror films, see Stan Link, 'The Monster and the Music Box:

Children and the Soundtrack of Horror,' in Neil Lerner (ed.), *Music in the Horror Film: Listening to Fear* (New York: Routledge, 2010), 38–54.
28 Neumeyer, *Meaning and Interpretation of Music in Cinema*, 186.
29 McKay, 'On Topics Today,' 162 (italics in original).
30 Kathryn Kalinak, *Settling the Score: Music and the Classical Hollywood Film* (Madison: University of Wisconsin Press, 1992), 30–31 (italics in original).
31 Therefore, topic theory complements the interpretive methods of critical theories. For topic theory and its connection to critical theories and the 'hermeneutics of suspicion,' see Buhler, *Theories of the Soundtrack*, 187–198.
32 See Monelle, *The Sense of Music*, 62–63.
33 In addressing the peculiarly variegated nature of signification in film music, using a broader definition of trope, David Neumeyer suggests a topic-trope continuum. On one side of the continuum are topics—stable, unaltered instances, analogous to Gorbman's cultural codes—and on the other side are tropes—cinematic, unstable and creative uses, analogous to Gorbman's cinematic codes. See Neumeyer, *Meaning and Interpretation of Music in Cinema*, 185.
34 Hatten, *Interpreting Musical Gestures, Topics, and Tropes*, 295.
35 Juan Chattah, 'From Topics to Troping within Film Music,' in *Proceedings of the International Conference on Music Semiotics: In Memory of Raymond Monelle* (University of Edinburgh, 2013), 408.
36 Ronald Rodman, *Tuning In: American Narrative Television Music* (Oxford: Oxford University Press, 2010), 110; Matthew Bribitzer-Stull, *Understanding the Leitmotif: From Wagner to Hollywood Film Music* (Cambridge: Cambridge University Press, 2015), 10.
37 Rodman, *Tuning In: American Narrative Television Music*, 125.
38 Musical example from Bribitzer-Stull, *Understanding the Leitmotif*, 293, though topical interpretation is by the author.
39 Neumeyer and Buhler, 'Analytical and Interpretive Approaches to Film Music (I),' 24.
40 See Timothy Scheurer, *Music and Mythmaking in Film: Genre and the Role of the Composer* (Jefferson: McFarland Publishers, 2008).
41 Michel Chion, *Audio-Vision: Sound on Screen*, trans. Claudia Gorbman (New York: Columbia University Press, 1994), 5.
42 Ibid., 5. Essentially, this is the Kuleshov effect but in the vertical, rather than horizontal filmmaking dimension.
43 Neumeyer, *Meaning and Interpretation of Music in Cinema*, 265.
44 See Buhler, *Theories of the Soundtrack*, 193.
45 Claudia Gorbman, 'Scoring the Indian: Music in the Liberal Western,' in Georgina Born and David Hesmondhalgh (eds.), *Western Music and Its Others: Difference, Representation, and Appropriation in Music* (Berkeley: University of California Press, 2000), 234–253.
46 For feminine coded topics, see Kalinak, 'The Fallen Woman and the Virtuous Wife.'
47 Buhler, *Theories of the Soundtrack*, 198. For a detailed and thoughtful postcolonial critique of topics, see Buhler, 197–198.
48 Deborah Cartmell and Judy Simons, 'Screening Authorship: Little Women on Screen 1933–1994,' in R. Barton Palmer (ed.), *Nineteenth-Century American Fiction on Screen* (Cambridge: Cambridge University Press, 2007), 78.
49 Madelon Bedell, introduction to *Little Women* (New York: Modern Library, 1983), as quoted in Linda Grasso, 'Louisa May Alcott's "Magic Inkstand": Little Women, Feminism, and the Myth of Regeneration,' *Frontiers: A Journal of Women Studies* 19.1 (1998): 190, endnote 2 (italics in original).

50 Jessica Bennett, 'This Is "Little Women" for a New Era,' *The New York Times*, January 2, 2020, sec. Books, www.nytimes.com/2020/01/02/books/little-women-feminism-2019-movie.html.
51 Jeffrey Jensen Arnett, *Emerging Adulthood: The Winding Road from the Late Teens Through the Twenties*, 2nd ed. (Oxford: Oxford University Press, 2014).
52 Mary Waters, Patrick Carr, and Maria Kefalas, 'Introduction,' in Mary Waters et al. (eds.), *Coming of Age in America: The Transition to Adulthood in the Twenty-First Century* (Berkeley: University of California Press, 2011), 1. Of course, this is a generalization and does not necessarily account for nuances of different socio-economic classes, race, and gender.
53 Many newspaper and magazine articles have been written about the stage of emerging adulthood. For a small selection, see Lev Grossman, 'Grow Up? Not So Fast,' *Time*, January 16, 2005, http://content.time.com/time/magazine/article/0,9171,1018089,00.html; Robin Marantz Henig, 'What Is It About 20-Somethings?,' *The New York Times*, August 18, 2010, sec. Magazine, www.nytimes.com/2010/08/22/magazine/22Adulthood-t.html.
54 Arnett, *Emerging Adulthood*, 9.
55 Ibid., 15.
56 Marc Molgat, 'Do Transitions and Social Structures Matter? How "Emerging Adults" Define Themselves as Adult,' *Journal of Youth Studies* 10.5 (2007): 495–516; Semira Tagliabue, Elisabetta Crocetti, and Margherita Lanz, 'Emerging Adulthood Features and Criteria for Adulthood: Variable- and Person-Centered Approaches,' *Journal of Youth Studies* 19.3 (2016): 374–388.
57 For indie rock and emerging adulthood, see Theo Cateforis, '"Time to Pretend": The Emerging Adulthood of Indie Rock,' *Popular Music and Society* 43,5 (2019): 1–20, https://doi.org/10.1080/03007766.2019.1627043. For the emerging adulthood genre in film and television, see Michael Rennett, 'Bros, BFFs, and the New Romantic Foil: Homosocial Relationships in the Emerging-Adult Film,' *Quarterly Review of Film and Video* 32.6 (2015): 568–583; Michael Rennett, 'How Grown-Ups Are Born: The Emerging-Adult Genre and American Film and Television' PhD diss. (The University of Texas at Austin, 2017).
58 Rennett, 'How Grown-Ups Are Born,' 141, 162.
59 For signifiers and signifieds of military fanfare and march topic in Western art music, see Monelle, *The Musical Topic*, 113–184. Cowboy topics usually involve features that stem from typical soundtrack elements in Hollywood Westerns from 1930s and 1960s. For more on Western influenced topics, such as the cowboy topic, see Rodman, '"Coperettas," "Detecterns," and Space Operas,' 43–49.
60 The 1994 adaptation oversexualizes and romanticizes Jo's relationship with Professor Bhaer beyond the novel and any other previous adaptation, see Cartmell and Simons, 'Screening Authorship.'
61 When the sisters are adults, the childhood topic only emerges as a nostalgic signifier accompanying Amy and their childhood friend Laurie initiating a romantic relationship.
62 Grasso, 'Louisa May Alcott's "Magic Inkstand,"' 182.
63 It is important to remember that Desplat and Newman have distinct musical styles. Many of Desplat's scores sound playful, even if not evoking the childhood topic. This default mode of composition makes him well-suited to this particular film.
64 In his review of the 2019 adaptation in *The Atlantic*, Matteson notes that, 'By telling the story out of chronological order, it shows the extent to which the

childhood self is part and parcel of adulthood.' See John Matteson, 'One Way the New "Little Women" Film Is Radical,' The Atlantic, January 1, 2020, www.theatlantic.com/entertainment/archive/2020/01/where-greta-gerwigs-little-women-and-louisa-may-alcott-meet/604294/.

65 The screenplay presents many instances of Jo resisting growing up in the 2019 adaptation. On Meg's wedding day, Jo puts her head in Meg's lap and says, 'I can't believe childhood is over.' There are arguably also many instances of Jo behaving 'childishly' as an adult. For example, running down the street and writing 'childish' stories. This stance is part of Jo's 'in-betweenness.' Ambivalence toward adulthood is a common psychological trait among emerging adults. Arnett's interview subjects mention being 'overwhelmed' with adult responsibilities, instead idealizing childhood in response. See Arnett, *Emerging Adulthood*, 218.

66 As Eaton has argued, the genius topic works because listeners perceive its musical qualities as metaphorically imitating a brain working through a problem. See Eaton, 'Marking Minimalism.'

67 Quoted in Bennett, 'This Is "Little Women" for a New Era.'

6

A MATTER OF TIME

Reality and Fantasy through Metrical Analysis in Contemporary Hollywood Film

Andrew S. Powell

Ponder for a moment the act of putting a small child to bed. The images of sending a sweet cherub off to dreamland may conjure its own soundtrack, with a lullaby seemingly the most musical means for ensuring peaceful dreams. Perhaps the first such song triggered is 'Wiegenlied' from Brahms's *Lieder und Gesänge* Op. 49, a portion of which is presented in Example 6.1.

Lullabies such as this are certainly not foreign territory to film scores, especially in the contemporary fantasy genre. The opening title cue to *Edward Scissorhands* (1990), its iconic four-measure intro presented in Example 6.2a, has become a common source of background music for fantasy trailers, as well as a frequently recruited (and even more regularly imitated) piece of underscore for both winter and dreamlike settings on the silver and small screen.[1] In setting the cobweb-covered artifacts and bizarre machinery of the Inventor's castle with the ethereal sounds of the bells and choir, Danny Elfman's music distinguishes this space and its inhabitant from the normalized, realistic Suburbia below.

A similar technique appears in Javier Navarrete's music for *El laberinto del fauno* (*Pan's Labyrinth*) (2006). The score is primarily structured around a lullaby, 'Hace mucho mucho tiempo' ('A Long, Long Time Ago'), the beginning of which is reproduced in Example 6.2b. Opening with the image of a young child slowly dying, the scene quickly gives way as the film's underlying fairy tale—and its alternate (Under)world—is brought before the viewer, accompanied by this haunting refrain. In both films, the function of the lullaby is identical: A physical, psychological,

DOI: 10.4324/9781003001171-6

EXAMPLE 6.1 Johannes Brahms, *Lieder und Gesänge* Op. 49, no. 4, 'Wiegenlied,' mm. 1–8.

EXAMPLE 6.2 (a) Elfman, *Edward Scissorhands*, 'Main Titles,' mm. 1–4 [0:00:15–0:00:21] (all examples transcribed by author); (b) Navarette, *El laberinto del fauno*, 'Hace mucho, mucho tiempo,' mm. 1–6 [0:00:51–0:01:03].

and temporal disruption of the initial narrative reality, creating a genuine separation between the fantastic and the real in the film's diegesis.

Several different characteristics link these two lullabies—notably qualities in orchestration and texture—and such aural similarities tend to reflect general topoi in film music literature. (For a more extended exploration of cinematic-musical topics, see Janet Bourne's chapter in this volume). The use of a female voice or children's choir, for example, creates a variety of plausible images depending on the narrative, including a sense of maternal love or childlike innocence. And yet, in opposition to this more positive connotation, these higher-pitched vocals may instead *remove* a sense of reality, creating an aura of mystery, supernatural, or Other. Quite often, the textual component we usually associate with sung music—that is, lyrics—is absent, the non-linguistic vocalise being paired with legato strings also in higher registers, adding to its ethereal and otherworldly quality. The use of celesta, bells, or other metallic sounds creates a music-box aesthetic, invoking strains of nostalgia and memory in addition to literal, temporal, and metaphorical distance.[2] The use of a plucked string instrument to mimic the music box striking or tinkering becomes more common when its source is identifiable on-screen, with the guitar overwhelmingly becoming the instrument of choice.

In addition to the previously identified examples from fantasy films, a plethora of songs invoking a lullaby aesthetic incorporate the aforementioned qualities. Mrs. Jumbo's tender 'Baby Mine' (by Frank Churchill and Ned Washington), sung to her infant elephant son in Walt Disney's *Dumbo* (1941), incorporates a textless female choir and high legato strings to add to the dreamy and distant qualities of the mother's song as she sings her newborn to sleep. The lullaby here reflects the metaphorical distance of the dream world as well as the more tangible spatial separation between the child and the caged adult pachyderm. Similarly, 'Mother Earth and Father Time' (Robert and Richard Sherman) from *Charlotte's Web* (1973) uses a legato string countermelody in conjunction with a harp, its plucking sound simulating the tinkling of a music box, to portray elements of pastoral nostalgia as well as temporal disruption. The use of scenes from the past, as well as the incorporation of future images from later in the film, adds to the sense of timelessness of the moment. This parallels the lyrics of 'Moon River' (Henry Mancini and Johnny Mercer) in *Breakfast at Tiffany's* (1961), simultaneously reminiscing on the past while yearning for a freer future. Pastoral nostalgia likewise becomes essential in the 1965 film adaptation of 'Edelweiss' (Richard Rodgers and Oscar Hammerstein) in *The Sound of Music*. Here, the lullaby conveys Captain von Trapp's rekindling of musical fondness and paternal love for his children—as well as foreshadowing a symbolic defiance of the Nazi regime and longing for Austria's past.

While there are indeed orchestral and timbral similarities between all the previously identified excerpts, there is a far more consistent, underlying, *structural* design that is shared as well. Used by each lullaby setting is a triple meter, situating the music in an organizational 'three' at its primary pulse layer, or *tactus*. *El laberinto del fauno* creates an even higher-level organization related to this numeric importance, as its melody is grouped into three-measure sections. This relationship of three with a sense of dissociation from the physical body, comparable to the previous discussions of distance or Otherness, is most certainly not novel in art, and recent scholarship has begun to examine this age-old affiliation. Juan Chattah offers such a description based on the relationship through physical labor, notably citing the lullaby as a paradigmatic example of triple metrical space, intimating the nonphysical, sitting in opposition to the 'duple-physical' complex:

> To the duple organization of sound events during physical labor (**one**-two, **one**-two, etc.), cycles of three (**one**-two-three, **one**-two-three, etc.) present a stark opposition. Coincidentally (or perhaps not), music associated with activities not related to labor (dancing a waltz, singing a lullaby) is characterized by a triple pattern. As a result, bodily engagement with music, for work or dancing, results in a cultural construct that serves to delineate social boundaries.[3]

Chattah's discussion of duple and triple and the identification of representative sources can be seen corroborated in various film scores (and corresponding analyses). For example, Janet Halfyard's analysis of Elfman's score *Batman* (1989), composed one year prior to *Scissorhands*, omits any consideration of metrical hierarchy while simultaneously proposing the existence of a similar affective potential as Chattah for the duple/triple separation in film music analysis:

> The use of 3/4, especially Strauss and 'Beautiful Dreamer' waltzes, effectively codes this meter as an indicator of the irrational through association with the Joker and his actions… Throughout the film, instances of Batman or Bruce's music occurring in triple time usually have some implications in relation to the darker side of his nature, Bruce's secrets, and Batman's potential to be like his enemies. In the internal working of the Bat-theme, the 3/4 meter encodes an idea of Bruce-Batman's own internal duality and battle with the irrational, and this meter becomes one of the principal signifiers of the Secrets and Revelations theme.[4]

Chattah's affective mapping of metrical space to associative distinctions like physical/nonphysical and self/other, and Halfyard's observation of this dichotomy in *Batman* are apt. Yet, like much scholarship on meter, neither addresses a critical point of metric perception: The distinct layers of hierarchical pulses in which such patterns exist. We perceive rhythm at multiple timescales, not just the primary perceived pulse (*tactus*) but also larger groupings of tacti (metric/hypermetric layers), and divisions of tacti into smaller pulses (submetric layers). By equating *all* pulse layers of a given meter, the independence of each layer and their potential expressive and representational qualities are erroneously conflated. (See Rebecca Eaton's essay in this volume for more on this point.) This lacuna arises again and again in analyses where notated meter or meter signatures have served as the primary point of entry in the study of film music.

The above survey, however cursory, reveals striking parallels between triple metric activity and the evocation of fantastic narrative space. But there remains room for both the further delineation of hierarchical layers of meter and the analytical exploration of metrical relationships to narrative. To begin to understand this metrical/affective association, our analytical methodology needs to address these musico-narrative axes of meaning: The aforementioned physical/nonphysical elements of fantasy on one side, and the careful separation of metric layers into their perceived organizational (or divisional) layers on the other.

Using a narrative-centric approach to rhythm and meter can help us move beyond the more limited ways in which musical time has traditionally been discussed in the analysis of music and film, which laid disproportionate emphasis on the audio*visual* nature of the medium. Such analysis typically placed music in a subservient role to the visual components, with musical terminology adapted to focus on the temporal qualities of *mise-en-scène*, the setting and editing of multiple shots, and so on. We frequently see in the film-theoretical literature certain temporal parameters of music—a sense of a beat (or, perhaps more appropriately, a pulse), identifiable relationships of accentuation, and a feeling of tempo—invoked to characterize an overall sense of rhythm that unfolds in cinematic time.[5] Similarly, a sense of meter may be identified in the visual field or the audio track—including dialogue, foley, etc.—based on repetitions of beat groupings, alternations of durational patterns, particular cadences (in the vocal sense) in patterns such as speech and sound effects, fluctuations in tempo, etc.[6] Indeed, as soon as audiovisual synchronization became technologically possible, Michel Chion argues that 'filmic time was no longer a flexible value... time henceforth had a fixed value; sound cinema guaranteed that whatever lasted x seconds in the editing would still have this same exact duration in the screening.'[7] Underlining this point, Chion summarizes: 'Rhythm... is an element of film vocabulary that is neither (spatial) nor (temporal), neither specifically auditory nor visual.'[8]

While this tight synchronization certainly manifested in the process of 'mickey-mousing' prevalent in animation of the 1930s (as well as the scores of Max Steiner), the concept of the 'audiovisual score' in Sergei Eisenstein's experimentations with (and later analysis of) music in *Alexander Nevsky*

(1938) elevated the relationship of sound and screen to considerably new heights. Eisenstein's own analysis strives to draw a meaningful symmetry between individual frames from the film, Sergei Prokofiev's written score, and audience eye movement in tracking the events of the scene; the product, slightly notorious in film music critical circles, has been both lauded and criticized.[9] (Notably, Eisenstein's analysis appeared ten years after the film's debut and relies specifically on the music's notation—a graphical (non-aural) feature.[10])

Other film-musical analyses that do integrate perception of meter tend to remain relatively inconsistent in methodology. Chattah's identification of groupings relies primarily on the cognitive identification of meter through the symmetrical body; while narrative associations can be established in relation to metric patterns, on his account they are formed through cognitive consonance or dissonance with physical patterns and bodily activity.[11] Meanwhile, the conflation of parallel meters through time signature correspondence, seen in the aforementioned analysis of Halfyard, removes the differentiation of metric layers and any potential associations of narrative elements to different facets of meter. Clearly, this is an area ripe for more systematic investigation.

In this chapter, I make a case for the graphic depiction of meter and corresponding metric/meaning mappings within contemporary films. For the majority of the chapter, I shall focus on Navarette's contribution to *El laberinto del fauno* and another score by Danny Elfman, *The Nightmare Before Christmas*. Following these analyses, a handful of smaller case studies, including a look at *Repo! The Genetic Opera*, will be used to probe questions of the relationship between symmetrical and asymmetrical meters. In each film and cue studied, viewing the score through a metrical lens reveals how something as seemingly commonplace as a time signature or beat (sub)division can powerfully enhance narrative, paralleling various states of cinematically constructed and culturally encoded reality and fantasy. Moreover, the transformation of such mappings, either immediate or over the course of a film, can mirror the narrative's development, adding a new and hitherto seldom appreciated dimension of musical depth to the score.

Developing a Methodology

Depicting relationships of different pulse layers necessitates a *Zeitnetz* ('time network'), an analytical device that conveys two essential criteria: 1) Groupings or divisions of pulses in relation to a central, perceived *tactus*; and 2) the specific duple or triple patterns through which groups of these pulses form meters. Introduced by theorist Richard Cohn to modern music analysis, the utility of the *Zeitnetz* is framed thusly:

> [A] graph of 'metric space' allows us to gauge the proximity of states along a finely-calibrated scale of measurement [and] provides an instrument for charting patterns and assessing the syntactic coherence of successions of metric states... [G]raphs of metric space can offer a window onto metric semantics.[12]

The exclusively binary/ternary mindset of this system is in fact an asset: Using only patterns of twos and threes not only follows Richard Cohn's notions of *metric states* (a hierarchical arrangement of pulse layers) and pulse layer consonance but also nicely accords with Chattah's previously identified bodily recognition of such configurations.[13]

The efficacy of *Zeitnetze* in displaying relationships between meter and narrative has been previously demonstrated through the analysis of Romantic music. Cohn uses what he calls 'ski-hill graphs' as a visual metaphor to depict possible individual and simultaneous active pulse layers in a manner analogous to harmonic consonance and dissonance. For instance, Cohn depicts the host of singular, double, and complex hemiolas in Brahms's *Von ewiger Liebe*, Op. 43, No. 1, as a series of switches and shifts down the metaphorical ski hill; Cohn further uses these diagrams to facilitate a narrative reading that enriches and transforms one purely based on a more conventional analysis of Brahms's harmonic syntax.[14]

Scott Murphy expands Cohn's *Zeitnetz* by organizing metric states as a list of numerical factors, partitioning pulses from slower to faster levels (half—quarter—eighth = [222], dotted-half—quarter—eighth = [322], etc.), to create a three-dimensional cube with vertices differing by a single factor.[15] Though not explicitly narratological in nature, Murphy's metric cube emphasizes the significance of proportional relationships of elements by perceived tempo rather than notation, unlocking potential pathways ripe with narratological interrelationships.[16] More dramatically oriented is Daphne Leong's analysis of Engelbert Humperdinck's *Hänsel und Gretel* (1893), which uses path 'shapes' generated from *Zeitnetze* graphings and their transformational relationships to extract novel narrational readings.[17] Despite the success of such analyses within their respective domains, a more flexible model is needed to accommodate the medium of film. Because of the innately multimodal experiential nature of film (music), the typical lack of (or difficulty in acquiring) a written score, and the unreliability of even carefully considered notated meter in capturing actual *perceived* meter, a strictly notation-based graphing methodology is inadequate. Finding an ideal uniform starting point around which such graphs can be generated must first be addressed at a perceptual level. In their foundational study of music cognition, Fred Lerdahl and Ray Jackendoff list three different types of accent that listeners use in parsing relative strength and potential hierarchical layering of pulse:

> By *phenomenal accent* we mean any event at the musical surface that gives emphasis or stress to a moment in the musical flow. Included in this category are attack points of pitch-events, local stresses such as sforzandi, sudden harmonic changes, and so forth. By *structural accent* we mean an accent caused by the melodic/harmonic points of gravity in a phrase or section—especially by the cadence, the goal of tonal motion. By *metrical accent* we mean any beat that is relatively strong in its metrical context… Phenomenal accent functions as a perceptual input to metrical accent—that is, the moments of musical stress in the raw signal serve as 'cues' from which the listener attempts to extrapolate a regular pattern of metrical accents.[18]

Murphy's brief summary of filmic considerations of musical rhythm aligns nicely with elements from Lerdahl and Jackendoff:

> [T]he frequent musical silences in a movie's soundtrack afford good opportunities for the music that enters to easily assert a downbeat. Beginnings of measures are also articulated by the beginnings of fairly stable and often terraced textural blocks, which are distinguished from one another by secondary parameters such as instrumentation, number of lines, volume, and register. Sometimes, beginnings of measures are synchronized with a visual 'hit' or cut to another filmic shot. Both the beginnings of measures and the beginnings of durations in the asymmetrical succession are often articulated through change of pitch, either harmonic or melodic, and recurrence of some pattern. Beginnings of durations in the succession, if not implied through the process of categorization, tend to be accented through contour, dynamics, and so forth, if the onset itself is not sufficient.[19]

Murphy's metric identifiers also suggest a potential pitfall inherent in film music meter analysis: Music is but one strand in the interwoven fabric of a complex audiovisual medium, and metrical considerations may become subordinate to other, less musically inspired parameters. Although formal contingency is a fact beyond the analyst and viewer's control, it should not be deplored but rather always kept in mind when approaching rhythmic aspects of a film score's structure—or any other aspect, for that matter.

Following Cohn and Leong, triple groupings and divisions are organized around an axis that runs diagonally, beginning in the northwest and descending to the southeast to construct the *Zeitnetz* graph; duple divisions begin in the southwest and run diagonally to groupings to the northeast. Rather than exactly preserving Cohn's and Leong's system which uses music-notational symbols, here integers and fractions indicate pulses of different tempi, with any integer >1 representing groupings of tacti, and fractions indicating divisions and subdivisions. The two axes bisect at the central tactus, isolated as the '1' pulse in the center to create an hourglass shape[20] (see Figure 6.1).

The previously discussed example from *El laberinto del fauno* displays the efficacy of the *Zeitnetz* as a metric mapping tool, shown in Figure 6.2. The division of the primary tactus (84 bpm) is clearly established as duple through the eighth notes in the vocal melody. The subdivision is never heard in this cue, so its selection is essentially arbitrary, though the absence of any triple divisions in any divisional layers lends more credence to remaining along the duple axis. Meanwhile, the organization of the melodic grouping structure—a three-measure unit with three beats per measure—resides entirely along the triple axis, necessitating a shift in the graph.

The diagonal axes generating the *Zeitnetz* relate directly to storytelling aspects of *El laberinto*, with duple numbers representing the real world and triple signifying the fantastic or Other. As the hourglass figure

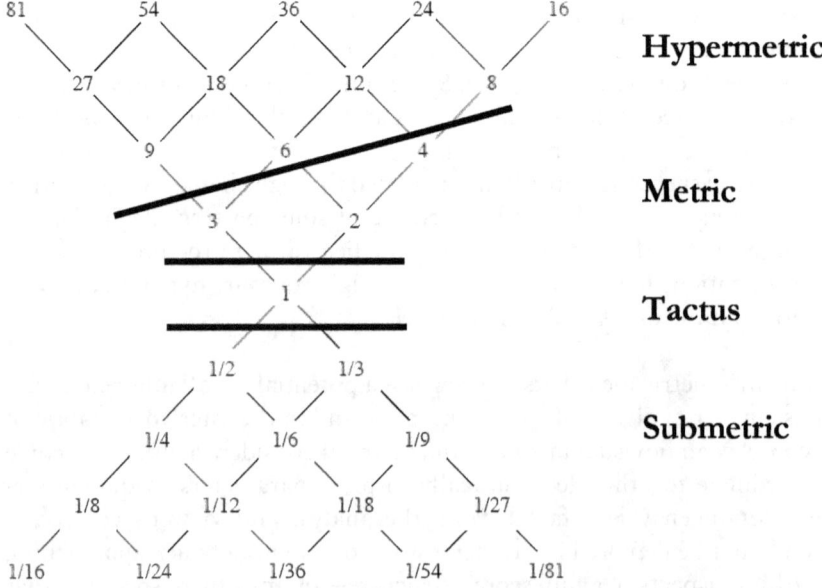

FIGURE 6.1 *Zeitnetz* for film meter analysis, with delineated pulse layers.

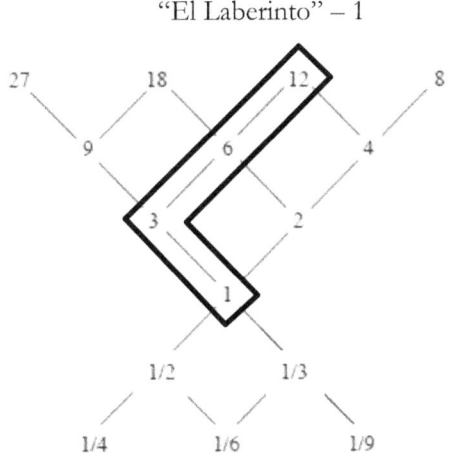

FIGURE 6.2 *Zeitnetz* graph of Navarrete, *El laberinto del fauno*, 'Hace mucho, mucho tiempo,' mm. 1–6.

expands to present both larger-scale groupings and smaller-scale subdivisions, the vertical plane develops its own metrical-narratological significance, entwining with the audience's (or character's) perception. Larger values (toward the 'north' of the graph) which correspond to slower pulses in the metric hierarchy represent the physical diegetic elements that either exist—or *seem* plausible—within a given film's internal world. By contrast, faster pulse values (toward the 'south' of the graph) reflect psychological perception and comprehension of surroundings and situations. This creates a possibility of four quadrants of motion through which dramatic relationships can be identified within the *Zeitnetz*:

- **Fantastic Physical**—A physical representation of a fantastic or Other element of the diegesis;
- **Real Physical**—A physical representation of reality or a non-foreign element of the diegesis;
- **Fantastic Psychological**—A character's (or audience's) perception of the fantastic or Other;
- **Real Psychological**—A character (or audience's) perception of reality or a non-foreign element.

With the quadrants organized based on relevant axes—fantastic/real diagonally and physical/psychological vertically, the resulting relationships along the *Zeitnetz* become evident, as will any modifications to those relationships as pieces unfold in time (Figure 6.3).

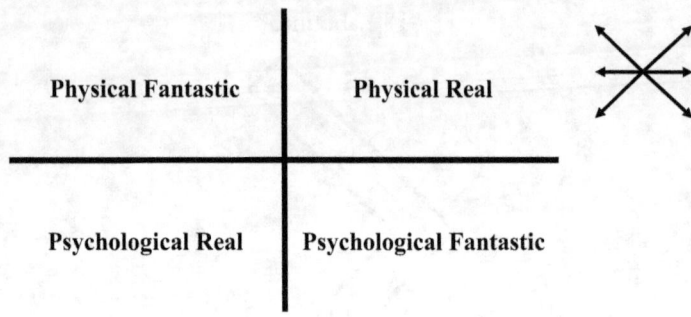

FIGURE 6.3   *Zeitnetz* musico-narrative quadrants.

To apply these terms and concepts to the previous graph from *El laberinto del fauno*, one could identify the two distinct areas occupied within the *Zeitnetz*. The upper half of the space confirms the Underworld's physical separation from 1944 Spain, while the lower portion establishes the child's cognizance of its existence, rendering it psychologically real in the moment. What must be stressed for the consistent application of this methodology is that the central tactus does not serve as an essential dividing line between the physical and the psychological. While numerous examples may shift above or below the tactus as the narratological border, what is fundamental to the associative-metrical network Navarrete establishes is change in the *pulse layer*.

Surveying the Landscape: Two Case Studies

Through tracking relationships of pulse layers rather than notation, the hourglass *Zeitnetz* can provide a visual counterpoint to the aural component of a movie. Applied with care, this tool is useful for revealing several understudied aspects of film music structure: The degree of narrative depth to individual cues or scenes unfolding within small-scale spans; the presence of transformations of important thematic or recurring material; and the long-term development of musico-narrative associations that unfold across the entire duration of a film.

The young protagonist Ofelia's discovery of the physical maze in *El laberinto del fauno* provides an example of expanding musico-narrative space within an individual scene. The sequence is underscored by 'El Laberinto' ('The Labyrinth'), of which only a portion of the original cue remains in the film. An analysis of the full cue reveals a transformation of metrical implications as Ofelia traverses deeper into the woods and closer to the labyrinth, achieved through the addition and supplementation of metric layers in both the filmworld and extended metanarrative world which includes the omitted material from the soundtrack. (See Examples

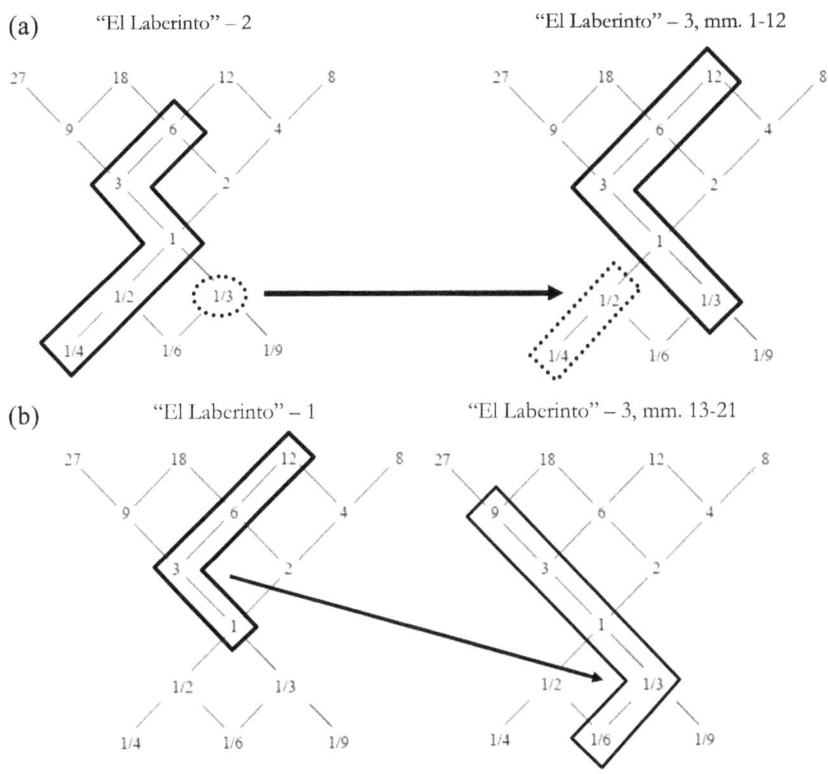

FIGURE 6.4 (a) *Zeitnetze* depictions of Navarrete, *El laberinto*, 'El Laberinto – 2,' and 'El Laberinto – 3,' mm. 1–12; (b) *Zeitnetze* depictions of Navarrete, *El laberinto*, 'El Laberinto – 1,' and 'El Laberinto – 3,' mm. 13–21.

6.3a–d and Figure 6.4a–b.) The first section (Example 6.3a) is devoid of any divisions below the tactus, leaving its lone presence of 'three-ness' at the level of the measure. Despite this passage's absence from the final cut of the film, its implications of the physical labyrinth are achieved through its melodic references to the opening lullaby.

A degree of cognitive dissonance—not just belonging to the theme's narrative referent of the distant maze but also structured deeply into Navarette's music—becomes more apparent in the cue's second section (Example 6.3b). Observe how the addition of triplet divisions in the cello part contributes momentum but is clearly subordinate to the prevailing duple structures projected throughout the rest of the ensemble. The addition of the supplemental yet subsidiary triple division layer initiates the metaphorical dissonance by activating the new pulse layer in conflict with the principal duple division, thereby mapping Ofelia's growing curiosity in the titular fantastical maze.

EXAMPLE 6.3A Navarrete, *El laberinto del fauno*, 'El Laberinto – 1,' mm. 1–11.

EXAMPLE 6.3B Navarrete, *El laberinto*, 'El Laberinto – 2,' mm. 10–14.

EXAMPLE 6.3C Navarrete, *El laberinto*, 'El Laberinto – 3,' mm. 5–8 [0:07:16–0:07:27].

The appearance of an anthropomorphic stick insect [0:07:32] which lures Ofelia toward the labyrinth (and simultaneously initiates Navarrete's cue during the sequence) brings the submetric triplets to the foreground. The onset of this music effectively transposes the graph through its reversal

A Matter of Time **123**

EXAMPLE 6.3D Navarrete, *El laberinto*, 'El Laberinto – 3,' mm. 13–18 [0:07:38–0:07:56].

of melodic and accompaniment layers. (See Example 6.3c.) The elevation of the triple division layer to a more prominent role in the accompaniment similarly emphasizes the labyrinth now coming to the foreground of the narrative, transforming the pulse layer horizontally through 'fantastic physical' motion.

The emergence of the trumpet solo inverts (and slightly extends) the original *Zeitnetz* graph when compared to the original beginning of the cue. Now, triple space has been achieved in both fantastic hyper- and submetric spaces, as shown in Figure 6.4a and b. The end result is two-fold.

First: The in-film score features a gradual unfurling of activation in both directions along the triple axis as Ofelia wanders deeper into the forest and closer to the labyrinth. In this gradual process, the music mirrors the emergence of the established fantastic physical space within the diegesis now appearing before the child, while simultaneously capturing her active imagination, delving into the psychological as well. Second: When expanding the analytical lens to include the entire cue from the soundtrack album, the trumpet's arrival signals an inversion of the graph as the labyrinth becomes reoriented within the narrative, establishing itself as a new 'real' location for character and audience going forward. Aside from allusions to the original lullaby, only one cue ('El Río') makes extensive use of 'fantastic physical' space, and its imagery is connected to a land free from the chief antagonist, Captain Vidal.[21]

∗∗

The line between reality and fantasy is also partially constructed through metrical means in Danny Elfman's score for *Nightmare Before Christmas* (1993). Among the numerous songs he wrote for the soundtrack, all follow a rotational narrative progression through the *Zeitnetz*, mirroring the distinction between holiday worlds both familiar and novel, and the attendant cognitive dissonance that arises from the epistemological shift in holiday paradigms.[22] Protagonist Jack Skellington's arrival in the foreign land of Christmas Town establishes the area as his literal fantasy come to life, for it is the antithesis of his home of Halloween Town and represents all of his desires to break free from the monotony of the macabre. His exuberance alternates between sheer awe at the spectacle of Christmas and darker reflections on his melancholy existence. This sense of Yuletide awe is conveyed through metric and hypermetric articulations of triple time, while expressions of morbid thoughts—Jack's reality—return to duple structures throughout all metric layers. (See Example 6.4.)

EXAMPLE 6.4 Elfman, *The Nightmare Before Christmas*, 'What's This?' [0:14:58–0:15:08].

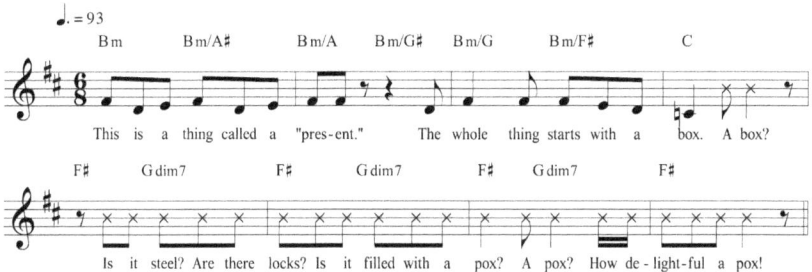

EXAMPLE 6.5 Elfman, *Nightmare*, 'Town Meeting' [0:22:09–0:22:19].

Upon Jack's subsequent return to Halloween Town, he strives to teach his fellow ghoulish denizens of the Yuletide land's existence, calling a town meeting to discuss his grand vision: For Halloween's residents to put on their own, unintentionally grotesque version of this newly discovered holiday in the 'Town Meeting Song' (Example 6.5). The real nature of Christmas remains unknown to the townspeople, and, for that matter, Jack. Triple divisions confirm this misunderstanding, expressed as a kind of rhythmic encapsulation of a psychological image of the festivity, without any sense of its physical actuality.

The physical construction of Halloween Town's twisted take on Christmas sees itself mirrored through Elfman's unique metric distortion of triple space in two forms, both further revealing that Jack and his cohort never fully embody the opposite holiday. As the townsfolk construct their own monstrous versions of presents, decorations, and other assorted accouterments, they join in a warped labor song, 'Making Christmas,' featuring an abridged setting of the *Dies Irae* (Example 6.6). The tripartite organization of the song's main verse contains two separate designs: An initial statement that extends into hypermetric (12 = 4 + 4 + 4) triple space, and the jubilant declaration of 'It's ours this time!' that ultimately connects to the original Christmas Town space with a change in grouping structure (6 = 3 + 3) at the metrical level.

The counterclockwise rotational map shows each song's individual deviations away from Halloween Town's prevailing duple (reality) pulse

EXAMPLE 6.6 Elfman, *Nightmare*, 'Making Christmas' [0:41:44–0:41:57].

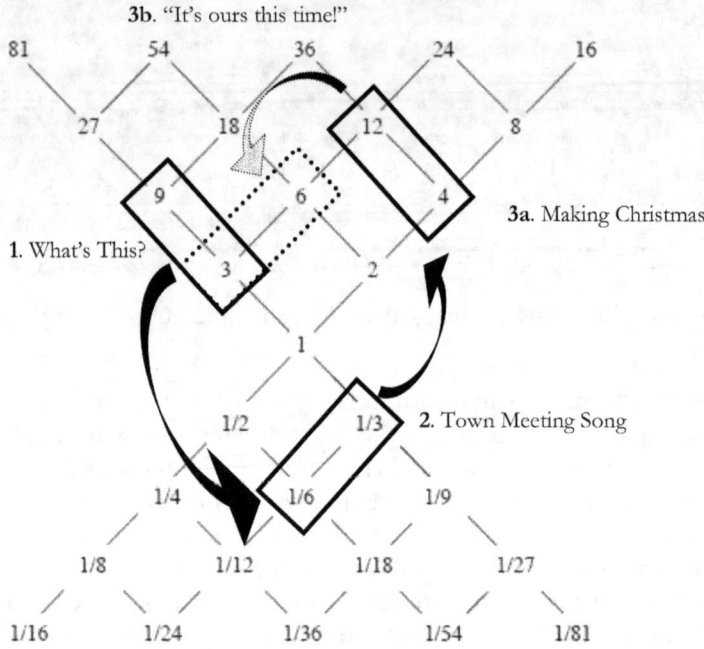

FIGURE 6.5 Rotational *Zeitnetz* of musical narrative in *The Nightmare Before Christmas*.

layer after his discovery of the winter wonderland, the metrical pathway in effect paralleling Jack's physical and psychological journey through the narrative. This trajectory is depicted in the score-spanning *Zeitnetz* in Figure 6.5. The initial discovery of Christmas Town (**Stage A**), capturing the physical essence of the narrative's fantasy, lies purely upon the triple axis in its metric/hypermetric space (3–9). Jack's attempts to bring the fantastic to a mental (psychological) sphere (**Stage B**) inverts the meter's triple locale into only a psychological division (1/3–1/6). An outright denial of a physical metric space by using only divisions confirms that Christmas truly remains just an idea at this point in the narrative. The jolly working song (**Stage C**) which serves as the music's reestablishment in hypermetric space (4–12) displays the musically most salient attempt to manifest the fantasy physically, yet the score is also hinting for us not to trust the spectacle: Jack's efforts are to prop up an illusion, an unreal, perverse idea of the holiday still existing only in the Halloween townspeople's imagination. Hypermeter is achieved through an offshoot of the duple axis, confirming this version of 'Christmas' as a Halloween-based distortion. The final declamation by the ghouls (**Stage D**) claims Christmas as their own, but the holiday is still tinged with the spirit of the macabre (3–6). Jack has clearly realized his fantasy, but his own true nature is inescapable.

Anticipating the Next Beats

While a perceptual-narrative model of meter can offer a more precise depiction of music-dramatic relationships in cinema, it would be folly to assume that this approach can be universal. Such graph- and quadrant-based organization is reliant upon stylistic tendencies and sometimes text-specific networks of meaning, not immutable laws. Indeed, a rather restraining limitation of this methodology is its restriction to 'consonant' rhythmic arrangements, removing asymmetrical patterns (particularly quintuple and septuple) from accurate depiction, which carry their own sorts of semantic and affective significance.[23] Such patterns can reflect varying narrative states, including a direct reference (such as the use of 7/4 with the character 'Septimus' in *Stardust* (2007)), religious context (7/8 and 7/4 for Diana's godlike status in *Wonder Woman* (2017)), or paralleling moments of significant tension (5/4 during the dinosaur chase in 2005's *King Kong*).

The plight of organ repo man Nathan in *Repo! The Genetic Opera* (2008), as expressed in Darren Smith's score, displays the potential for powerful musical meaning to be driven by the metrical consonance/asymmetrical divide. The use of quintuple tactus (expressed as 3 + 2) in the song 'Legal Assassin' is a clear example. Nathan is forced into a compromised position in which he must violently reclaim unpaid organ transplants, hiding this bloody double life from his daughter who believes he is a benevolent doctor. His vocals (Example 6.7a), set in simple quadruple, are offset by the instrumental reflection of his quandary, set in quintuple. These vocal interjections create momentary fluctuations of the prevailing metric structure when cast against the opening eight-measure introduction in

EXAMPLE 6.7A   Smith and Zdunich, *Repo! The Genetic Opera*, 'Legal Assassin' [0:19:49–0:19:55].

EXAMPLE 6.7B   Smith and Zdunich, *Repo!*, 'Legal Assassin' [0:22:28–0:22:32].

quintuple. Nathan's calls to his deceased wife in the following quadruple section create an even stronger dichotomy between the two meters.

Succumbing to the monster within at the close of the song (Example 6.7b), Nathan accepts his life as a lawful murderer, and the soundtrack responds, with the quintuple meter now effectively consuming the entire musical score.

Asymmetrical groupings within prevailing well-formed structures at larger hierarchical levels face similar issues of depiction, primarily with respect to conflicting IOI (inter-onset interval) at the tactus level. As noted by Scott Murphy, the alternating grouping patterns of (33222) found in the *guajira* rhythm (Figure 6.6) find frequent employment at moments of conflict of both a physical and psychological variety and have become a relative staple in the catalog of such composers as Hans Zimmer and his company.[24]

An acute example, nicely portrayed analytically through a *Zeitnetz* undulation, appears in Elfman's score for *Beetlejuice* (1988), where the title character's transformation into a large striped snake parallels both the film's thematized living-dead duality as well as the cognitive dissonance experienced by the (living) Deetz family and their companion Otho. (See Example 6.8.)[25] With the 'Beetle-Snake' freely slithering between

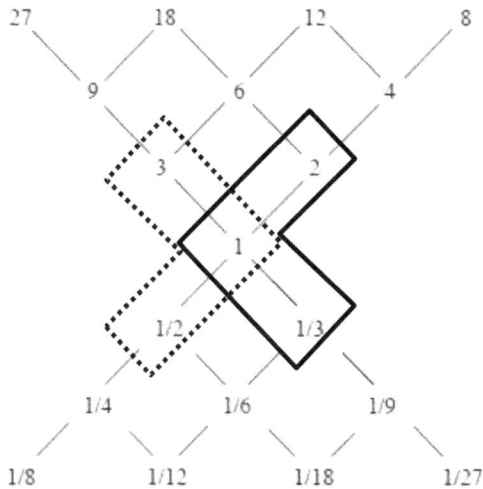

FIGURE 6.6 Guajira rhythm and *Zeitnetz* portioning of metric conflict.

opposing halves, the serpentine design of portions of *Zeitnetze* mappings literally mirrors both Beetlejuice and the narrative as he prepares to strike.

Similarly, a 'double tresillo,' identified by its (333322) underlying pulse pattern, often connotes a duel, drawing from antecedents of Western film music topoi and later action films.[26] Such opposition is inherent in the duality between the real (or the heroic and lawful good) and fantastic (or antagonistic and chaotic Other) in its midst, a natural source of struggle. A noteworthy example is Jack Kelly's brief dance break in 'Santa Fe' from the original production of *Newsies* (1993). Undoubtedly, the choreography and costuming—even Jack's nickname 'Cowboy'—all seem to reinforce the archetypal Western iconography, but these are predominantly superficial compared to the underlying *narrative* duality that motivates Jack: The reality of his troubled life in urban New York City and his fantastic vision of the idyllic Wild West embodied by the town of Santa Fe. The double tresillo's use in film trailers sees a similar unification of action and fantasy.[27] And the pattern's usage is hardly limited to cinema: Both the tresillo and double tresillo see frequent employment in video game battle music as well, uniting the sense of battle boundaries separating the (real) heroes in opposition against the (typically fantastic) antagonists.[28]

Through its perception-centric approach and inherent malleability afforded by its pulse layer hierarchical construction, the hourglass *Zeitnetz* can provide a visual representation of music's narratological role in film. The correlation of narrative significance with distinct shifts

EXAMPLE 6.8 Elfman, *Beetlejuice*, 'Beetle-Snake' [1:00:13–1:00:22], with metric mappings below measures.

along particular rhythmic axes mirrors alterations in character and/or setting, offering a compelling audiovisual metaphor, one no longer reliant on durational values or graph location to tease out meaning. Further explorations using this tool, and the metrical concepts and concerns I have raised more generally in this chapter, can provide insight into genre, composer, and director tendencies. Worth investigating too are musical examples that lie outside both consonant metric layers and (especially) the Western tradition. By circumventing previous methodological oversights, and utilizing an analytical lens more apropos to the filmgoer's perspective, metric analysis indeed brings areas once considered analytical fantasy into reality.

Notes

1 More specifically, material from the opening seventeen measures has appeared in at least seven different trailers. See Soundtrack.net, 'Edward Scissorhands,' retrieved Sept. 19, 2020. Soundtrack.net/trailers/cd=trailer.php?id=154.
2 For a discussion of such techniques directly applied to Elfman's larger scoring methodology, see Janet Halfyard, *Danny Elfman's* Batman: *A Film Score Guide* (Lanham, MD: Scarecrow Press, 2004), 32–34. Allison Wente further explores the connection of music boxes with 'collective nostalgia and lost memories,' suggesting 'the music box topic shows us that this is a past that we long for… we still reach for that past every time we wind a box and listen to its tune.' See Allison Wente, *Mechanizing Nostalgia: The Music Box Topic in Film*, paper presented at *Music and the Moving Image* VII, New York, May 31–June 2, 2013.
3 Juan Chattah, 'Film as Embodiment,' in Marrten Coëgnarts and Peter Kravanja (eds.), *Embodied Cognition and Cinema* (Leuven: Leuven University Press, 2015), 103, emphasis in original.
4 Halfyard, *Batman*, 117.
5 See David Bordwell and Kristin Thompson, *Film Art: An Introduction* (New York: McGraw-Hill, 2001), 182.
6 See James Buhler, David Neumeyer, and Rob Deemer, *Hearing the Movies: Music and Sound in Film History* (New York: Oxford, 2010), 38.
7 Michel Chion, *Audio-Vision: Sound on Screen*, ed. and trans. by Claudia Gorbman (New York: Columbia, 1994), 16–17.
8 Ibid., 136.
9 For the original analysis of *Alexander Nevsky* and representations of audiovisual score, see Sergei Eisenstein, *The Film Sense* (New York: Harcourt, Brace & Co., 1947). Theodor Adorno and Hanns Eisler use Eisenstein's own analysis as a counterexample when discussing aesthetic theory in deference to the visual image, arguing that the sense of 'picture rhythm' and 'musical movement' becomes erroneous through Eisenstein's use of static single shots, rather than the unfolding filmic (and musical) time. Adorno and Eisler summarize, 'What they prove in reality is that there is similarity between *notation* of the music and the sequence. But the notation is already the fixation of the actual musical movement, the static image of a dynamic phenomenon… It cannot be perceived directly, and for that reason cannot fulfill a dramatic function.' See Adorno and Eisler, *Composing for the Films* (New York: Oxford, 2007), 104–107. Claudia Gorbman makes explicit mention of Eisenstein's approach in *Unheard Melodies: Narrative Film Music* (Bloomington: Indiana University Press, 1987), 117 and 127.
10 See Roy M. Prendergast, *A Neglected Art: A Critical Study of Music in Films* (New York: New York University, 1977), 211–213.

11 Chattah, 'Film Music as Embodiment,' 103–105.
12 Richard Cohn, 'Complex Hemiolas, Ski-Hill Graphs and Metric Spaces,' *Music Analysis* 20.3 (2001): 312.
13 Ibid., 296.
14 Cohn argues that '[the] logic of my analogy suggests that Brahms reads the *Bursche's* despair as initially tentative and over-played for dramatic impact. It is only when the poor lad stops singing that he is overtaken by the anxieties that he has just articulated. The increase of the level of metric dissonance in the interlude suggests a disorganised state. The subsequent resolution to a new state of metric consonance, remote from the original, suggests that his despondency threatens to consolidate into a permanent depression,' Ibid., 321.
15 See Scott Murphy, 'Metric Cubes in Some Music of Brahms,' *Journal of Music Theory* 53.1 (2009): 10–11.
16 Ibid., 31–40.
17 See Daphne Leong, 'Humperdinck and Wagner: Metric States, Symmetries, and Systems,' *Journal of Music Theory* 51.2 (2007): 215. Leong further summarizes, '[I]f one defines a ski-path *shape* as a ski-path's particular configuration of left- and right-sloping vertices of those edges, then the subgroup of symmetries as I have described them are operations on such shapes. This way of viewing the symmetries is more general than seeing them as relations on ski paths, because it allows one (via their shapes) to link ski paths that do not even occur on the same ski-graph plane, that is, whose tempi do not relate by factors of 2 or 3 (a distinct advantage when dealing with performed tempi)' (221).
18 Fred Lerdahl and Ray Jackendoff, *A Generative Theory of Tonal Music* (Cambridge: MIT Press, 1983), 17, emphasis in original.
19 Scott Murphy, 'Cohn's Platonic Model and the Regular Irregularities of Recent Popular Multimedia,' *Music Theory Online*, 22.3 (2016), 4. Retrieved July 14, 2020. www.mtosmt.org/issues/mto.16.22.3/mto.16.22.3.murphy.php.
20 A 'maximum pulse salience' for all ranges has shown a lower limit at approximately 100 ms, with 200–250 ms commonly identified as the typical threshold, while the upper limit has shown a potential of 5–8 seconds, with around 1000–1500 ms more commonly identified as the ceiling. The typical tempo of the tactus shows a bias among listeners of approximately 85–100 bpm. The maximum speed has shown a fast limit at approximately 600 bpm at which individual pulses can be discriminated, with 240–300 bpm commonly identified as the typical threshold for tacti. The slower end of the spectrum has shown a potential of 5–8 seconds for complete metric unit identification, with around 40–60 bpm more commonly identified as the ceiling for tactus perception. See Justin London, 'Cognitive Constraints on Metric Systems,' *Music Perception* 19.4 (2002): 536–539, and Rebecca Eaton's contribution to this volume for additional explorations within a film music-analytical context.
21 Elements of the music which are functioning as accompaniment (firmly established as secondary to principal melodic/motivic material) are delineated with a dotted frame for the following two graphs and isolated from the primary mapping structure to express further this separation.
22 The author discussed the relationships of harmony, melody, and meter in *The Nightmare Before Christmas* previously in Andrew S. Powell, 'A Composite Theory of Transformations and Narrativity for the Music of Danny Elfman in the Films of Tim Burton,' Ph.D. diss. (University of Kansas, 2018), as well as 'The Interconnectivity of Elfman's Film Scoring and Burton's Narrative,' in Adam Barkman and Antonio Sanna (eds.), *A Critical Companion to Tim Burton* (New York: Lexington, 2017), 57–70.

23 Recent scholarship has most certainly identified the narrative associations of asymmetrical meters but likewise remain unable to produce graphing solutions. Notable writings include Nicole Biamonte, 'Formal Functions of Metric Dissonance in Rock Music,' *Music Theory Online* 20.2 (2014), www.mtosmt.org/issues/mto.14.20.2/mto.14.20.2.biamontephp; Richard Cohn, 'A Platonic Model of Funky Rhythms,' *Music Theory Online* 22.2 (2016), www.mtosmt.org/issues/mto.16.22.2/mto.16.22.2.cohn.php; and Murphy, 'Cohn's Platonic Model.'
24 See Murphy, 'Cohn's Platonic Model,' 8.
25 The provided example first appeared in Powell, 'A Composite Theory,' 153.
26 Scott Murphy has initiated inroads into analysis of asymmetrical organizations and narrative connotations with respect to overall durations, focusing on sums of 5, 7, and 10; see 'Cohn's Platonic Model,' 6–8. The present author has also explored the use of septuple meter and the expression of the fantastic/real conflict within the mind of Jack Skellington in the song 'Jack's Obsession' in *The Nightmare Before Christmas*; see Powell, 'A Composite Theory,' 213–219.
27 The frequent appearance of the cue 'Ode To Power,' produced by Immediate Music, is tied not simply with action sequences but also fantasy films. Notable trailers which feature this piece include (but are not limited to) *Van Helsing* (2004), *War of the Worlds* (2005), *X-Men Origins: Wolverine* (2009), two *Chronicles of Narnia* films, three Harry Potter films, and *The Hobbit: An Unexpected Journey* (2012). See Soundtrack.net, 'Trailerhead Triumph (2012),' retrieved September 26, 2020. https://soundtrack.net/trailers/cd-trailer.php?id=8946.
28 Video games provide excellent instances of this rhythmic trope. Examples of tresillo can be found in the primary battle music for *Final Fantasy X* (2001), while the double-tresillo can be found in the primary battle theme for *Final Fantasy VII* (1997). Battle music in *Hyrule Warriors: Age of Calamity* (2020) contains multiple examples of the tresillo pattern, as well as significant amounts of triple activity in various metric and submetric layers to enhance further its fantastic elements.

7
FILM MUSIC AND DIALOGIC FORM

Charity Lofthouse

Amidst welcome recent theoretical attention to film music's thematic and harmonic organization, the topic of the *formal* structures within movie scores remains comparatively less explored.[1] The reasons for this may lie in the general circumstances of film composition and production: Unlike with a creator of musical works of comparable scope such as operas, the film composer is perceived to lack agency in the design of the overall text's length, its editorial construction, and ultimately its narrative.[2] Additional complications for straightforward formal analysis include the brief duration of many musical cues, the plot-driven serendipity of much localized musical content (leitmotifs and stingers, for example), and, perhaps most crucially, the discontinuity of cues and variability of space between their appearances.[3]

At the level of discrete theme, the formal structures of film music share many commonalities with predecessors in the late-Romantic repertoire. Most directly, themes in both idioms constantly and consistently make use of internal repetitions, phrase-length alterations, and various deviations and transformations from ordinary formal 'defaults'—devices that interact with various expected, and ever-shifting, formal and genre norms. Still a robust presence in the film-music universe, scores that are strongly in dialogue with the 'classic Hollywood' sound may be viewed as a nexus of influences ranging from late-Romantic tone poems, Wagnerian music dramas, and theme-and-variation sets—influences that themselves trace back to interactions of form, tonality, and theme in the classical tradition.

This chapter will broadly engage formal structure in film music through the lens of what theorists James Hepokoski and Warren Darcy call *dialogic form*. Hepokoski and Darcy define this as the way linear musical processes are always heard in dialogue with an 'intricate web of interrelated norms as an ongoing action in time.'[4] Hepokoski positions dialogic form as a relationship between listener, composer, and genre thus:

> First… perceptions of form are as much a collaborative enterprise of the listener or analyst as they are of the composer. And second, I suggest that grasping the full range of an implicit musical form is most essentially a task of reconstructing a processual dialogue between any individual work (or section thereof) and the charged network of generic norms, guidelines, possibilities, expectations, and limits provided by the implied genre at hand. This is 'dialogic form:' form in dialogue with historically conditioned compositional options.[5]

He continues by outlining the orientation of form as:

> not exclusively a property of the individual piece, an attribute to be uncovered once and for all by the analyst as a substantive thing, nor is it only an abstract shape or *ad hoc* design to be charted or culled from the work's audible surface—a mere set of descriptive data (however accurate), a linear massing of statistics, a graph. Instead, the deeper sense of form with which we are concerned here is something to be produced—an engaged act of understanding—through a dialogue with an intricate and subtle network of piece-appropriate norms and guidelines (rules of the game) both for constructing compositions (the concern of the composer) and then for grasping how the composer was likely to have wished us to construe what he or she accomplished in the individual piece under consideration. Listeners also create dialogic form in their own non-closed dialogues with individual works.[6]

In essence, dialogic form positions thematic and tonal norms and variations in creative dialogue with the expectations of a given work's genre, the ways in which composers play with or against those expectations, and how expectations accumulate over the course of the work. This approach is synergistic with analytical understandings of film genre. In the opening to *Introduction to Film Genres*, film scholar Lester Friedman notes,

> Many of America's best genre films successfully negotiate a passage between the neoclassical and Romantic ideals. Indeed, the productions of mainstream cinema in the United States can be aptly characterized as a continual process of convergence, both in form and content, between repetition and variation, formula and innovation, and commercially

popular conventions and novel deviations... genre films inevitably become amalgamated productions replicating some recognizable structures and conventions from the past while simultaneously incorporating inventiveness and originality that speaks to the present.[7]

Given this framework, dialogic form is well suited to offer an analytical framework for film music. This suitability is especially evident for scores that are highly polystylistic; that interestingly support or thwart genre expectations; that base their formal trajectories on elements other than traditional purely harmonic punctuation (themes, motives, gestures, timbre, etc.); and that create cycles or repetition schemes that are congruent with extramusical narratives in addition to (or in opposition to) traditional formal models. In the following study, dialogic formal analysis is used to draw special attention to thematic rotational and evolutionary processes. Discerning such formal processes at work does not merely illuminate aspects of small- and large-scale structural cohesion in film music—it facilitates hermeneutic and narrative interpretation, making clear how film music structures are in conversation, overtly and tacitly, with received formal traditions and generic practices that range across styles, from classical music and popular music to other film scores and more.

Rotational Form and Teleological Genesis in Film Scores

Dialogic form can be broadly examined by means of two generative, interacting, and interrelated concepts: *Rotational form* and *teleological genesis*. Rotational form results from the presentation and recurrence of thematic, motivic, and textural elements in a regular order. Teleological genesis describes the compositional strategy wherein a thematic/motivic element or excerpt is presented early in a work or movement, then developed over time in pursuit of the theme's *telos*—its most definitive, fully realized statement. While works that feature teleological genesis distribute the process over one or more formal rotations, conventional rotational forms typically present themes in their more-or-less complete or holistic state from the work's outset. Broadly speaking, rotational form is concerned with generic expectations evoked by ordered presentations of a work's material, while teleological genesis outlines the thematic transformation of a partial idea over time, with the realization of the theme's telos serving as the culmination of any co-occurring rotational processes.

Rotational Form

A selection of complete film scores are presented below as instances of Hepokoski and Darcy's rotational form, embodying that large-scale dialogic design principle wherein thematic materials are restated cyclically, 'extending through musical space by recycling one or more times—with appropriate alterations and adjustments—a referential thematic pattern established as an ordered succession at the piece's outset.'[8] Hepokoski and Darcy state that

> tonality is irrelevant to the task of identifying the rotational principle. The central thing is an implied or actualized ordered sweep through a temporal sequence of thematic modules, along with the assumption that the most 'natural' or expected continuation of the layout's last module will be to lead to a relaunching of the initial module of the next, thus producing the characteristic spiral or circular effect.[9]

This architectural principle is commonly used to describe sonata-allegro works (symphony movements, instrumental sonatas, etc.) wherein an exposition section sets up an ordered set of themes, typically a primary theme, a transition, and a secondary theme in a new key. These themes then return in the same order in the sonata's recapitulation section, with the secondary theme restated in the primary theme's global tonic. But while it is most often applied to this well-known procedure from classical instrumental music, rotational form also extends large-scale analytical options in ways both congruent with and more flexible than any one specific formal category. In film music, the establishment of a referential rotation can set up subtle expectations—expectations with powerful generic and narrative implications—which may be subsequently fulfilled or avoided, as through varied repetitions, in accordance or defiance with the filmic narrative being portrayed.

Serving as perhaps an archetypal example of rotational form in film music is the soundtrack to the 1960 film *Psycho*. Bernard Herrmann seemed to display a particular concern for formal structure in his compositions for film and two of his best-known scores for Alfred Hitchcock stand out in this regard: *Psycho* and *Vertigo* (1958).[10] Herrmann's score for *Psycho* brings to life a tale of crime, mistaken conclusions, and the inner life of an Oedipal madman, Norman Bates (Anthony Perkins). The famous 'Prelude' constitutes an impressively concise microcosm for the film as a whole, with an unusual rotational structure and assortment of phrase endings and referential sonorities that may be mapped onto the film's most significant plot events. Indeed, Bernard Herrmann spoke about *Psycho*'s Prelude as presenting the film's climax 'right at the moment the film begins.'[11] He goes on to note, 'After the main titles you know something terrible must happen. The main title sequence tells you so, and that is its function: to set the drama.'

Figure 7.1 displays the Prelude's overall structure and potential plot associations. The formal layout features three full rotations of two thematic

	Rotation 1					Crime #1: complete rotation	
Subrotations:	SR1			SR2			
Measure #:	1	5	21	25	29	37	49
Theme:	Psycho	Menace (semitones/ triplets)	Suspense chords	Psycho	Menace	Marion	Suspense chords
Correspondence to plot narrative:	Setting the stage: Marion is corrupted, skips town, and meets Norman.			Marion flees with money	Marion meets Norman, intrudes by suggesting Norman commit his mother.	Marion is killed	Norman hides Marion in the swamp, takes great care with the clean-up.

	Rotation 2					Crime #2: incomplete rotation	
Subrotations:	SR1			SR2			
Measure #:	53	57	63	67	69	77	
Theme:	Psycho	Menace (semitones/ triplets) (shortened)	Suspense chords	Psycho (only 4)	Menace	Marion	No Suspense chords!
Correspondence to plot narrative:	Setting the stage: Arbogast is looking for Marion and the money.			Arbogast finds the Bates Motel	Arbogast intrudes	Arbogast is Killed	No elaborate clean-up or mystery; the reason for Arbogast's killing is clear.

	Rotation 3					Crime #3: incomplete rotation	
Subrotations:	SR1			SR2			
Measure #:	89	91	103		107	111	
Theme:	Psycho (only 4 chords)	Menace (semitones/ triplets) (altered)	Suspense chords	No Psycho chords!	Menace	Marion + Menace triplets	No last note of Marion or Psycho chord!
Correspondence to plot narrative:	Setting the stage: things do not go according to Norman's plan this time...			Sam and Lila arrive at the Bates Motel.*	Sam and Lila intrude	Norman's secret is found out.	Norman is unable to murder Sam and Lila. Phrase is left incomplete

* Psycho chords also missing from larger rotation, corresponding to Sam's and Lila's arrival at Bates Motel.

	Rotation 4		No crime: shortened rotation	
Subrotations:	SR1		SR2	
Measure #:	121	123	127	
Theme:	Psycho (only 4 chords)	Menace (only triplets) (altered)	Weak Psycho chord plus D natural	
Correspondence to plot narrative:	Norman is captured, an explanation for the killings is supplied.	Norman is supplanted by his "mother"	Norman is gone, but "mother's" D remains.	

FIGURE 7.1 *Psycho* Prelude, formal diagram.

subrotations (consisting of a pair of highly contrasting melodic ideas), plus a fourth truncated rotation. This architecture—three rotations of both main themes and a partial fourth rotation—differs significantly from the more traditional overture and song forms previously common to film-title sequences. The Prelude's rotational design, and cadential events that articulate that design, correspond precisely to the three crimes at the Bates Motel and Norman's eventual capture, with changes to each rotation's ending mirroring the crimes' details. The first of these murders, of Marion Crane (Janet Leigh), is mirrored through a complete rotation of the Prelude's two contrasting thematic ideas, whereas later crimes are reflected in altered

Film Music and Dialogic Form   139

phrase endings, curtailed motives, and omitted sonorities. The final rotation is truncated, as Norman is captured and his crimes are revealed.

These rotational correspondences are maintained throughout the film, as returns and overwrites of Herrmann's referential themes and sonorities correspond to the plot associations listed below their appearances in Figure 7.1. Figure 7.2 displays the overall rotational nesting of the film's cues across four rotations. The Prelude's overt foreshadowing parallels the story and soundtrack's narrative design more globally. Since each crime is openly displayed on screen, tension is created not by obfuscating who committed each crime but by the myth-like cycles of missed opportunities for Marion's arrest and discovery of Norman's 'mother's' murders.

The other prelude from Herrmann's *oeuvre* that most closely resembles *Psycho* is that of *Vertigo*. Consisting of a large-scale rondo-like ABABA structure, the *Vertigo* Prelude's structure, shown in Figure 7.3, presents formal sections that are generally longer than those of *Psycho*'s. The cue features alterations to its two restatements of the A section and a truncation of the final A section while maintaining the proportions of the B section throughout.[12]

The precise mapping of the Prelude's rotational design onto the overall layout of the soundtrack, as seen in *Psycho,* is not precisely replicated in *Vertigo*. While its theme of resurrecting a past love seems an obvious justification for a similar rotational nesting, *Vertigo* not only largely forsakes its Prelude's melodic material in favor of developing Madeleine's (Kim Novak) thematic incarnations but also does not consistently reiterate cues heard earlier in the film in unaltered form. Herrmann instead favors

Large-scale rotation	Rotation 1								
	Marion steals the money, flees to Bates Motel, meets Norman, is killed.								
Smaller-scale rotation	Rot. 1			Rot. 2			Rot. 3		
	Prelude	The City	Temptation	Flight Patrol Car	Car Lot	Package	Rainstorm	Hotel Room	Window Parlor * Bathroom**
Based on:				Prelude	The City	Temptation	Prelude	Temptation	The City

Norman's music [013] emerges:
*after Parlor: Madhouse   (Collectively
                Peephole   variants of
**after Bathroom: Murder   Temptation)

Large-scale rotation	Rotation 2			Rotation 3			Rotation 4	
	Arbogast looks for Marion, is killed.			Sam and Lila look for Marion, discover Norman's secret.			Norman is detained, the murder is explained.	
Smaller-scale rotation	Rot. 1			Rot. 1			Rot. 1	
	Search A	Shadow Phonebooth The Porch The Stairs	Knife	Search B First Floor Cabin 10/1	Cellar Discovery		Finale	
Based on:	Prelude/ City	Madhouse (Temptation)	Murder	The City	Temptation/ Murder		Prelude/The City Madhouse	

FIGURE 7.2   *Psycho* overall nested rotational structure.

Rotation:	Rot. 1		Rot. 2		Rot. 3 (half)
Section:	A	B	A (with double-time accompanimental arpeggios)	B	A (truncated, with double-time arpeggios)
Time index:	0:00	1:10	1:44	2:20	2:44

FIGURE 7.3   *Vertigo* Prelude, formal diagram.

thematic development and transformation. In keeping with *Vertigo*'s focus on reinvention and climactic (and Orphic) loss, the evolution of Madeleine's first theme into the full-fledged 'love theme' occurs well into the film, not long before the dissolution of her regained identity (through Judy) into chaos, madness, and loss. Perhaps by forgoing strictly nested rotational cycles, Herrmann reflects Scottie's (Jimmy Stewart) desperate hope for, and belief in, a different outcome the second time around. This contrasts with the proportions, characters, and narrative design of *Psycho*; in that film, there is no hope of change or of redemption, only a series of inescapable events set in motion by the rotations of Herrmann's Prelude. *Psycho*'s rotational form and nested structures reflect repeated, gruesome crimes and the obsessive nature of Norman's madness. From the soundtrack's opening rotation to its final sonority, Herrmann's formal processes effectively seal each character's fate.[13]

The score to the 2016 Denis Villeneuve film *Arrival* is more loosely organized at the level of internal repetitions within and allusions between cues, but nonetheless features rotational aspects across its soundtrack. Composed by the late Icelandic composer Jóhann Jóhannsson, the score's structure reflects the architecture of the film's plot, which revolves around the visitation of 12 alien ships seeking to communicate their language to humanity as a helpful means of conceptualizing time. *Arrival* follows a cyclical story arc wherein linguist Louise Banks (Amy Adams) makes repeated visits to the alien ship ('the shell') in an attempt to communicate with the aliens, eventually leading her to piece together their language, and with it an expanding awareness of their way of experiencing non-linear time. It is worth noting that, unlike *Psycho* or *Vertigo*, whose composed scores correspond to the film's ultimate soundtrack with only infrequent and minor internal omissions, *Arrival*'s commercial album and the film's actual soundtrack differ quite markedly: Some cues appear in total within the movie, while other are truncated from several minutes to 15 seconds.[14] Discrepancies aside, Jóhannsson's originally composed underscore may nonetheless be viewed as an evocative use of rotational

EXAMPLE 7.1 Richter, *Arrival* opening excerpt ('On the Nature of Daylight') (all examples transcribed by author).

form when coupled with the development of several motives from Max Richter's 'On the Nature of Daylight.' Significantly, the ordering of thematic returns corresponds to the film narrative's cycles of visitation and communication.

Example 7.1 displays the opening of 'On the Nature of Daylight.'[15] Composed for the 2004 album *Blue Notebooks* and used in over a dozen films and TV programs since, its opening four-note melodic motive is split by Jóhannsson into a pair of two-note cells used throughout the score. Table 7.1 outlines the score's rotational structure. The first rotation includes eight cues that first develop motives and chords from Richter, then later highlight symmetrical trichords and tetrachords. The emergence of symmetrical motives corresponds to a major development in

TABLE 7.1 *Arrival* overall rotational layout

CUE IN FILM	TIME	REFERENCE(S)	FORM/TONAL EVENTS
ROTATION ONE			
Richter	1:11		2 rotations of sentence, then B♭ min. pedal coda
Shells Landing	6:35		Low B♭ drone.
Around the Clock News	8:41	Richter	B♭ drone, descending dyad and chords from Richter (two rotations), concluding B♭ minor triad.
Arrival	17:41	Drone (C) from Shells Landing plus semitone dyad and (036), heard in bar 20 of Richter.	D-F-D-B for 5 reps; 6th rep loses F, 7th rep loses D.
Hydraulic Lift	23:45	C drone, F-G ascending dyad from Richter.	
First Encounter		Return of (036) from Arrival.	Series of m3 ascending dyads. B♭-D♭-E (036) adds Drone G for (0369); (036)/(0369) 3 times, then short-short-long rhythm and C-D♭-B♭ blast three times.
Fear of Shells (Xenolinguistics)	34:13	Timbre allusions to Arrival.	C Drone, C/G dyad; B♭/D dyad added.
Logogram Break (Sapir-Whorf)	38:14		E♭/G voices with F/A strings, then F/A voices (0246). C Drone returns.
ROTATION TWO			
Fear of Shells v2	40:58	Arrival	D-F-D-B for one rep
Hazmat	46:08	Hyd. Lift/First Enc./S-W	G/A♭/A tremolo; D-A fifth; E♭/G and F/A, ends with B-D ascending dyad.
Heptopod B	52:35	Rhythm kernel from Arrival, voices singing repetitive C-G, C-G-B motives. Rising dyad motive from Richter.	C major emphasis, with A-B rising dyad. C-G and D-A rising fifths emerge in instruments. D-E rising dyad in lower parts.
ROTATION THREE			
Fear of Shells v3 (Xenoanthropology)	57:19	Arrival, hints of First Encounter & Xenolinguistics	C drone, flutter strings, B-C dyad & C/G fifths.
Hammer/Nails	1:05:05	Shells/Arrival/Hept B	Very brief cue.
Properties of Explosives	1:12:52	Shells/Arrival, Around the Clock, Sapir-Whorf	Drone and rhythm; Richter two-chord motive from Around the Clock; Sapir-Whorf voices plus D-F-G triad.
Ultimatum	1:18:33	Sapir Whorf	E♭/G and F/A (0246) dyads in voices. G drone in dotted triplets. B♭-A-C motive.
Principle of Least Time	1:22:34	Sapir Whorf	Very brief cue.
ROTATION FOUR			
Non-Zero Game	1:24:19	Arrival	G-D-A stacked fifths/ninth. String slides followed by D-F-D-B (036) from Arrival with added vocal G and D/A dyads.
Transmutation	1:27:20	First Encounter	A-C ascending motive from First Encounter.
Escalation	1:31:55 1:35:13	Ultimatum/Sapir-Whorf	A♭-B♭-A♭ over A♭ major, then Ultimatum quote.
Deciphering	1:36:44	Sapir-Whorf	Pedal E♭, then F-E♭ descending dyad with voices/rhythm from Sapir-Whorf.

(Continued)

TABLE 7.1 (Continued)

CUE IN FILM	TIME	REFERENCE(S)	FORM/TONAL EVENTS
ROTATION FIVE (*TELOS*)			
Dvorak	1:38:54	Presumed Diegetic with instrumentation of Richter.	Segues into Dvorak from previous cue.
One of Twelve	1:40:55	First Encounter, Xenolinguistics	C/E dyad. G in horns slides down to E. Emphasizes C major triad. String clusters from First Encounter, then strings and voice figures from Sapir-Whorf. Adds fifths in voices and strings.
Rise	1:43:50	One of Twelve, Xenolinguistics, Around the Clock News.	Voices and strings, C major with F-C, adding minor triads and descending dyad from Richter, all simultaneously.
Richter	1:45:25	Richter, extended	Extended; Third rotation with added descant.

narrative, materializing only as humans and aliens learn to communicate. Following Richter and the cue 'Shell's Landing,' a brief drone-like leitmotif representing fear of the alien ships, 'Around the Clock News,' features the descending two-note opening motive from Richter as its melodic core. Next, the cue 'Arrival' outlines a diminished triad motive, mirroring the chord heard at the conclusion of 'Daylight's' first sentential phrase (m. 20). 'Hydraulic Lift' uses the opening's ascending whole-tone motive over a drone, while 'First Encounter' returns to the diminished triad from 'Arrival,' blooming into a diminished seventh chord. Finally, 'Xenolinguistics' presents a (024) symmetrical motive centered around C, and 'Sapir-Whorf' concludes the rotation with a fast-paced cue highlighting the first breakthrough in communicating with the aliens: Two major-third dyads in the voices and strings are juxtaposed and combined into a symmetrical (0246) tetrachord over a C drone.[16]

Subsequent cues unfold cyclically in alignment with the plot, as each cycle of visits to the alien ship commences and a new discovery ensues. Table 7.1 traces recurrences of material from the film's expositional cues as successive visits to the shell take place. Rotation two represents an ordered reappearance of the cues presented after Louise's initial arrival at the shell, concluding at the montage wherein scientific findings about the aliens are communicated to the public via the media. Rotation three encompasses the miscommunication surrounding the word 'weapon,' a bombing attempt that strains alien-human relations, and the discovery that the information shared before the bomb went off was one of 12 pieces to the extraterrestrials' message. Rotation four traces Louise's direct conversation with the aliens, her discovery of their non-linear experience of time, and the revelation of their ultimate purpose for visiting. Lastly, rotation five begins with a diegetic excerpt from a piece by Dvořák as a kind of Richter substitute; this accompanies a scene in which Louise sees a future conversation with General Chang that allows her to diffuse China's threat to the aliens. Through a cumulative event that presents several of the rotational cues simultaneously, the climactic span of 'Rise' serves as a telos. By combining all of the film's major themes and motifs, the soundtrack affects a parallel experience to Louise's newfound sense of flattened time. Louise observes in *Arrival*'s opening scene that 'we are so bound by time, by its order,' yet Jóhannsson is able, through ordered rotational processes and the cumulative telos of radical simultaneity, to take advantage of music's ability to present a film's worth of experiences in one singular moment.

Teleological Genesis

The convergence of musical strands at *Arrival*'s climax showcases the power of structuring a score around an eventual thematic telos, but it is just one example of a much broader and more versatile technique. Hepokoski describes teleological genesis as 'the concept of a composition as gradually generative toward the revelation of a higher or fuller condition [and] is characteristic of the modern composers, especially Mahler, Strauss, and Sibelius.'[17] Examples abound in these composers' works; Hepokoski originated the term to describe the introduction of motivic seeds in the earlier movements of Sibelius's Fifth Symphony, which then bloom in the theme of the symphony's finale. Darcy notes that this process involves repetitions of an initial short theme or thematic segment that then leads to a fully developed 'telos' during an ultimate presentation. Earlier presentations or snippets become 'a sort of generative matrix within which this telos is engendered, processed, nurtured, and brought to full presence.'[18] Teleological genesis is dependent upon rotational form insofar as successive iterations of thematic presentations are viewed as developments of previous statements, and they partake in the principle of rotational restatements, that according to Hepokoski and Darcy, 'are often subjected to telling variation... not infrequently these varied multiple recyclings build cumulatively toward a larger-range goal.'[19] A theme heard as an incipit at a work's opening is heard in retrospect as the beginning of a process of thematic development, culminating in a fully formed realization, achieved by means of change over time.

John Williams's score for Steven Spielberg's 1977 film *Close Encounters of the Third Kind* employs rotational and teleological strategies in the unfolding of several notable themes over the course of the soundtrack. Tom Schneller outlines appearances of two thematic allusions central to the score, both derived from preexisting themes: The *Dies Irae* and the

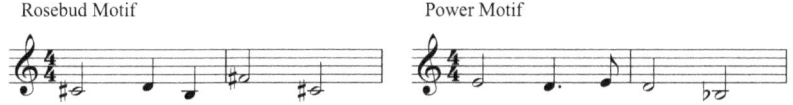

EXAMPLE 7.2   Herrmann, *Citizen Kane*, Rosebud and Power motifs.

B section of 'When You Wish Upon a Star.' Schneller quotes Williams, reflecting on his collaboration with Spielberg in much the same way Herrmann did with respect to *Psycho*: 'Spielberg's subjects and way of directing are very compatible with a sense of musical development' and notes that 'the opportunity to use sophisticated formal strategies like teleological genesis in film music is entirely dependent of the structure of the narrative.'[20]

Schneller compares the teleological development of Williams's 'Fate is Kind' motive and the film's famous five-note 'communications' motive, both reflections of the extraterrestrial's fundamental benevolence as revealed late in the movie. Schneller contrasts these themes with the thematic 'red herring,' the Dies Irae motive. The Dies Irae is a static, largely unaltered presence, at first more ominously salient at the music's surface, and reflects the misinterpretation that the aliens are malevolent. Here I add one more allusion unmentioned in Schneller's account: The 'Rosebud' leitmotif from Orson Welles's 1941 film *Citizen Kane*, presented in the rhythm of *Close Encounter's* 'Power' leitmotif (both are shown in Example 7.2).[21]

Close Encounters features three appearances of the Rosebud/Power leitmotif: First heard at 55:37, it accompanies the emergence of government agents in rose-colored jumpsuits. This statement of the theme most closely resembles its model from *Citizen Kane*: It is presented as a slow horn melody that adds a small turn to Herrmann's leitmotif for Rosebud, and follows it with a three-note concluding gesture, shown in Example 7.3a. After three presentations in its original seven-note slow version, the theme returns as the agents are mobilized to head to Devil's Tower [57:15] in a militarized, more fully developed theme, shown in Example 7.3b.[22]

The theme is finally liquidated during the chapel scene [2:01:02], as Roy (Richard Dreyfuss) himself dons the rose suit in preparation to board the alien ship. Hints of the opening C-D♭-B♭ cell emerge within a thicker texture of harp runs and motives from 'When You Wish Upon a Star,' whose telic statement is soon to emerge. Aside from the shared allusions to Dies Irae, the thematic nods to *Citizen Kane* reflect another connection: Herrmann's score follows a tale of a man, much like *Close Encounter*'s

EXAMPLE 7.3 Williams, *Close Encounters of the Third Kind*, (a) Rosebud/Power motif first presentation; (b) Rosebud/Power expansion.

Roy, whose obsessions and single-minded pursuit of his goals estrange him from his family and friends. Further, the evolution of the Rosebud/Power theme loosely mirrors the Communications motive: The Rosebud/Power theme is expanded in subsequent appearances, corresponding to its evolving role in accompanying the government's growing military mission to cordon off Devil's Tower. Similarly, the Communications motive is extended from its familiar five-note version to a full-fledged contrapuntal dialogue between the alien ship and the government's keyboardist at the film's climactic encounter. In each case, thematic expansions, at the hands of the experts and authorities, add complexity, energy, and length to an earlier straightforward and brief utterance that represented innocence.[23]

Rotational expectations and teleological assembly of themes also take place in compilation scores, including those based on pop music. Among the most well-known songs in film music history, 'Mrs. Robinson,' from Mike Nichol's 1967 film *The Graduate*, offers such an example. The only song Simon & Garfunkel composed specifically for the film, it first appears at 1:30:00 as guitar strums and a whistled introduction and refrain, concluded by a record-scratch moment that cuts off the final chord. The next presentation [1:33:45] adds the iconic vocal 'dee-de-dee-dee' syllables in harmony and ends less abruptly, yet still before the iconic refrain appears. Listeners have now heard two partial statements: The intro and refrain without vocals, and the guitar with its duo of vocalists cut off before the refrain. At 1:36:10, a complete presentation of the intro, dee-de-dees, and refrain with lyrics finally reveals the song's *telos* version as Ben (Dustin Hoffmann) races through the night to stop Elaine's wedding. (In fact, it is the only complete presentation of the intro and refrain during the film.) A lengthy final appearance at 1:38:00 begins with abbreviated strumming and dee-de-dees (now with an extra repetition) and continues to strum along during Ben's phone call to find the wedding's location. As he leaves the gas station, Ben runs out of gas; a comical slowing of guitar as the car runs out of gas vividly illustrates the coordination of narrative and musical forms of nonattainment.

Dialogic Form and Popular-Song Underscoring

The formally constitutive role of 'Mrs. Robinson' in *The Graduate* is certainly at least in part a function of its having been written for that movie, though its structural design is ultimately functional as both underscore and standalone pop song resembling the others used in the film. And yet, as seen with 'On The Nature of Daylight,' preexisting music can have film-formal implications too, when distributed and developed carefully. Naturally, most film scores are read as an accompaniment to the film, and thus through a formal lens that assumes a synergistic relationship between the music and the film for which it was composed. In contrast, popular music—a term used here to encompass a variety of genres that contrast with absolute instrumental music—may be coopted into a film with differing expectations regarding formal synergy with, or semantic allegiance to, the on-screen action. As K.J. Donnelly notes, considerable differences emerge when film music is 'tracked' instead of scored; the former involves 'taking an existent piece of music and editing it to the images, or more commonly editing the images to fit the music.'[24] This distinction between scoring and tracking affects the relationship between film form and musical form deeply. Donnelly continues:

> There is an assumption of equivalence at times between film and popular music. Prevalent musical structure in popular music is highly regulated and not particularly amenable to more fluid film structure, which is why written-to-picture orchestral scoring of precise dynamic developments in film remains prevalent.

Popular music soundtracks introduce distinct formal issues related to Donnelly's points. First, popular music's generic formal configurations are well known by most (if not all) listeners and ubiquitous in a variety of physical and aesthetic situations. Second, the pop song is typically a self-contained structure of approximately three minutes with a highly codified (if not entirely uniform) formal schema. Third, preexisting popular-song soundtracks may more readily invite interpretations of the song both as part of the filmic soundtrack and in comparison between the film's underscore and the song's *Urtext*, a recorded artifact existent outside of the film's structural or artistic meaning. Thus, popular songs may create a kind of double dialogic form: The song's form is in dialogue with both the formal expectations of the original pop song recording and with the song-as-underscore (interacting with the plot and visuals as underscoring).[25]

Because of the potential for specific familiarity with a particular song and generic familiarity with popular-song formal processes, pop song cues are often presented either unaltered or with changes limited to those that least disrupt the perception of thematic ordering. That the film audience member doesn't know the specific pop song from another source does not necessarily lessen the expectations that it will achieve or enact a dialogue with its implied genre's concomitant norms and trajectories. Popular music now spans a wide variety of formal influences (jazz, blues, vaudeville, EDM, etc.) and multiplies the options for formal templates, with each bringing its own expectations.

Formal expectations will vary based on a variety of factors related to the pop song used, including its style, genre, decade of release, texture, timbre, and so forth.[26] One of pop music's most enduring formal features is the rotation of two or more sets of verse-chorus segments (Temperley's verse-chorus unit or VCU), wherein the chorus is emphasized via texture, timbre, and repetitive lyrics. There may then be a contrasting bridge section building anticipation for the final verse/chorus rotational cycle.[27] Generally, popular-song underscoring presents at first the referential verse-chorus rotation, then incorporates structural alterations that tend to confirm the rotational layout in conjunction with general efforts to preserve phrase structure.

The following case studies demonstrate three rotational modifications for popular songs used as underscore: Medial extraction, open-close, and rotational extension.[28] **Medial extractions** feature omissions that preserve the rotational ordering of the original song form while fitting the generic or narrative needs of the underscore. Though double-rotational verse-chorus examples abound in film, medial/sectional excerpting may fit especially well with strophic songs, wherein each verse's rotational structure tends to precisely match the others and where alterations or truncations to any verse's rotation are especially noticeable. Returning to *The Graduate*, Table 7.2 outlines the excerpting of Simon & Garfunkel's 'The Sound of Silence' across the film. First heard as an opening song accompanying Ben as he makes his way through LAX, the opening sequence presents four of the song's five verses, seamlessly edited to sound close to the original while emphasizing the monotony of travel and summer home from college.

This usage of 'The Sounds of Silence' and others preserve the perception of rotational form by editing: Montage sequences are cut to fit the song's rotational structures. Here, a complete statement mirrors the narrative of Ben's being trapped in trysts with Mrs. Robinson (Anne Bancroft). Similarly, 'Scarborough Fair' appears only once in its entirety, while other

TABLE 7.2 *The Graduate,* rotational structures of cues for 'The Sound of Silence' and 'Scarborough Fair.'

TIME	ROTATIONS	TIME	ROTATIONS
"Sounds of Silence"		"Scarborough Fair"	
1:00	Four	1:10:10	Three
37:51	Five (complete)	1:13:10	Five (complete)
1:44:25	Two	1:17:00	Two (flute solo)
		1:20:15	Intro/Outro

appearances are truncated to three or two rotations. In one instance, 'Scarborough Fair' is heard in even more extreme abbreviation: Only the intro/outro is heard as Elaine (Katherine Ross), creeped out by Ben's following her to the zoo, leaves him behind at the monkey cage. But this is an exception. Neither wholly unedited nor drastically transformed, the treatment of pop songs in *The Graduate* generally preserves the underlying strophic or verse-chorus form, while allowing smart editing and montage to enable preexisting music to respond to and comment on the action in the fashion of originally composed underscore.

The second modification, **open-close**, pairs a song's opening with its ending in such a way that a complete VCU or refrain-verse rotation is presented as a truncated yet complete single rotation. Often flanked by intro and outro sections, this formal alteration omits one or more additional verses, as well as the bridge and final chorus. A straightforward example can be found in *Guardians of the Galaxy*'s opening credits, beginning at 6:19 and ending at 7:53. This sequence resembles the opening number of a musical, with Starlord (Chris Pratt) introduced dancing across an alien chamber on his way to steal a powerful orb. As he plays Redbone's 'Come and Get Your Love' on his Walkman, the music moves in a degree of diegetic correspondence from dance number to underscore and back. The song's original and somewhat unusual four-rotational structure, shown in Table 7.3, is shortened in *Guardians* to a summary double-rotation: Verse and chorus, turnaround, bridge, and truncated final chorus.

A more intriguing case is Prince's 'Partyman' from 1989's *Batman*. Composed specifically for the film, this song appears as a diegetic cue at 1:01:47, where it first presents a verse/chorus unit, followed by a bridge that concludes by standing on the dominant, and a final chorus. Prince wrote the song quickly, inspired by his introduction to Jack Nicholson on set. Rather than being edited to the open-close rotational structure, the song was seemingly composed to evoke this structure from the outset: The standalone music video for 'Partyman' initially replicates the music heard in the movie precisely. But once the 'film version' is fully stated,

TABLE 7.3 *Guardians of the Galaxy*, comparison of film cue and commercial single of Redbones 'Come and Get Your Love.'

	"Come and Get Your Love" Commercial Single						"Come..." Film Cue	
ROTATION		1	2	3	4		1	2?
SECTION	Intro	Verse 1/ Chorus/ Turnaround	Verse 2/ Chorus/ Turnaround	Bridge (chorus-based)/ Chorus/ Turnaround	Verse 3!/ Intro!!/ Bridge/ Chorus	Fade out	Intro	Verse 1/ Chorus/ Turn-around	Bridge (chorus-based)/ Chorus

the music video then unexpectedly repeats the bridge. Following this are approximately 90 extra seconds of loosely organized improvisation over the song's funk progression.

A third modification, **rotational extension**, serves as a kind of rotational fermata: After a verse or chorus, interpolations or extensions are worked into the form, preserving the rotational ordering while extending its length. For example, the song 'Girl, You'll Be a Woman Soon' appears as source music in 1994's *Pulp Fiction*, beginning at 50:59. Mia (Uma Thurman) plays the song as Vincent (John Travolta) talks himself out of falling for her seduction. The scene presents the song in its entirety but also with two additional internal repetitions: The second verse is repeated as a whole, and the subsequent statement of the refrain repeats the antecedent phrase. Both expansions are added to the second verse/refrain rotation and are then followed by an unaltered bridge and final refrain.

A final example demonstrates the convergence of several of these song-formal modification schemes in a filmic context. An elegant hybrid of pop song and orchestral underscore, the cue 'Where No One Goes' from 2016's *How to Train Your Dragon 2* provides creative extensions to both rotations of an energetic pop song with a standard two-part verse/pre-chorus/chorus structure (shown in Table 7.4). Composed by Jón Thor (Jónsi) Birgisson and John Powell for the film and performed by Icelandic band Sigur Rós, the cue beginning at 5:20 features a straightforward verse and pre-chorus, combining pop-style percussion and vocals with strings and accompanying Hiccup (Jay Baruchel) and his dragon Toothless as they race over the ocean and through the clouds. The beginning of the chorus initiates an ethereal change in texture as Hiccup takes to flight: The percussion drops out, and Jónsi's voice becomes a high-voiced ambient chorus as the music's floating quality corresponds gracefully to the scene's narrative and visuals. This moment's sublime effect derives in part from this timbral shift and an orchestral extension at the end of the chorus, both of which obscure whether the music has transformed from pop song to orchestral underscore and, consequently, whether the pop song's structural process remains preeminent. With the return of the percussion, the next musical rotation unfolds similarly, presenting an intro vamp, verse, pre-chorus, chorus, and extension. After the

TABLE 7.4 *How to Train Your Dragon 2*, formal layout of 'Where No One Goes.'

ROTATION 1		ROTATION 2		-	
TIME	SECTION	TIME	SECTION	TIME	SECTION
5:20	Intro	6:28	Intro	7:23	Dissolving Bridge -> ...
5:41	Verse 1	6:35	Verse 2	--	... -> Underscore
5:55	Pre-chorus	6:49	Pre-chorus		
6:09	Chorus	7:02	Chorus		

second rotation, pop percussion and vocals begin a seven-second bridge section before dissolving as danger lurks: As a rock emerges from the mist and Hiccup and Toothless try to escape sudden doom, the orchestral transmutation and rotational extension become a full reorientation to traditional dramatic underscore and away from pop-song formal space, by landing (somewhat) safely on an extended bridge-section runway.

Conclusion

Formal elements are often absent from analytical discussions of film music, a notable omission in an otherwise rich landscape filled with considerations of timbre, harmony, melody, orchestration, narrative, semiotics, and more. As Robynn Stilwell notes,

> Film music is perhaps the only predominantly instrumental musical which comes with no formal expectations; to the extent that conventionalized forms are a ramification of absolute music, expecting to find them in the dramatic or narrative context of film is slightly absurd.[29]

In addition to the relative dearth of formal analyses, the word 'form' is often used in a broader sense when discussing film music to refer to the music's semiotic or narrative functionality, substituting these elements for structural considerations and relegating formal design to a subsidiary or invisible realm. Nonetheless, as a temporal art form, musical structures serve as a dynamic, descriptive, and dramatic partner with a film's narrative, and understanding the implications of a film's musical structure allows for a more nuanced read of the interaction between musical content and filmic expression.

Film music has become a location of enormous creativity, received into a generative hermeneutic matrix of composer, filmmaker, and viewer/listener. Dialogic form's overarching emphasis on collaborative analytical enterprise places music-theoretical tools and analytical meaning-making into the center of this matrix. As Hepokoski notes, 'Every work—a sonata, a symphony, an individual movement, and an individual passage—is but a single node within a reticulate, multidimensional network—socially accumulative—of other works within and outside of its genre.'[30] Rotational form and teleological genesis, by emphasizing thematic ordering and reiterative processes, span a multitude of artistic and philosophical approaches to genre and structure while highlighting the place of creative alterations and cumulative cyclical progress as a means of expressing narrative. By engaging with these possibilities, film music scholars will discover that a space thought to be devoid of formal expectations turns out to have been in musical and structural dialogue with its audience all along.

Notes

1 Regarding thematic and phrase structure in film music, see Mark Richards, 'Film Music Themes: Analysis and Corpus Study,' *Music Theory Online* 22.1 (2016). Bernard Herrmann's scores have received particular attention regarding form: See Scott Murphy, 'Three Audiovisual Correspondences in the Main Title for Vertigo,' *Music Theory Online* 28.1 (2022) and 'An Audiovisual Foreshadowing in Psycho,' in Philip Hayward (ed.), *Terror Tracks: Music, Sound and Horror Cinema* (Oakville, CT: Equinox, 2009), 47–59; Dan Blim, 'Musical and Dramatic Design in Bernard Herrmann's Prelude to Vertigo (1958),' *Music and the Moving Image* 6.2 (2013): 21–31; David Cooper, 'Film Form and Musical Form in Bernard Herrmann's Score to Vertigo,' *Journal of Film Music* 1.2–3 (2003): 239–248; Antony John, 'The Moment I Dreaded and Hoped For,' *Musical Quarterly* 85.3 (2001): 516–544; Tom Schneller, 'Easy To Cut: Modular Form in the Film Scores of Bernard Herrmann,' *Journal of Film Music* 5.1–2 (2012): 127–151; and James Wierzbicki, 'Psycho-Analysis: Form and Function in Bernard Herrmann's Music for Hitchcock's Masterpiece,' in Philip Hayward (ed.), *Terror Tracks: Music, Sound and Horror Cinema* (Oakville, CT: Equinox, 2009), 14–46. Connections between musical form, narrative form, and tonality are examined in Brian Jarvis, 'Analyzing Film Music Across the Complete Filmic Structure: Three Coen and Burwell Collaborations,' PhD diss. (Florida State University, 2015). Robynn Stilwell connects sonata form, musical form, and film structure in 'Sense & Sensibility: Form, Genre, and Function in the Film Score,' *Acta Musicologica* 72.2 (2000): 219–240.
2 Robynn Stilwell states, 'While comparisons are often drawn between film music and opera, there are at least as many differences as similarities, not least that music is the driving force of opera while it is rarely considered such in film.' See Stilwell 'Sense & Sensibility,' 222, f10.
3 James Hepokoski and Warren Darcy, *Elements of Sonata Theory: Norms, Types, and Deformations in the Late-Eighteenth-Century Sonata* (New York: Oxford University Press, 2006), 10. Táhirih Motazedian, in discussing discontinuity and tonality in film music, observes that audiences are accustomed to discontinuity and edits 'across disjunctions in filmic form. We can apply this same logic to the musical structure [emphasis original].' See Motazedian, 'To Key or Not to Key: Tonal Design in Film Music,' PhD diss. (Yale University, 2016), 17.
4 James Hepokoski and Warren Darcy, *Elements of Sonata Theory*, 10. For additional examples of the authors' approaches to nineteenth- and

twentieth-century works, see Darcy's 'The Metaphysics of Annihilation: Wagner, Schopenhauer, and the Ending of the Ring,' *Music Theory Spectrum* 16 (1994): 1–40; 'Bruckner's Sonata Deformations,' in Timothy L. Jackson and Paul Hackshaw (eds.), *Bruckner Studies* (Cambridge: Cambridge University Press, 1997), 256–277; 'Rotational Form, Teleological Genesis, and Fantasy-Projection in the Slow Movement of Mahler's Sixth Symphony,' *19th-Century Music* 24 (2001): 115–154; Hepokoski's *Sibelius: Symphony No. 5* (Cambridge: Cambridge University Press, 1993); 'The Essence of Sibelius: Creation Myths and Rotational Cycles in *Luonnotar*,' in Glenda Dawn Goss (ed.), *The Sibelius Companion* (Westport, CT.: Greenwood, 1996), 121–146; 'Rotations, Sketches, and [Sibelius's] Sixth Symphony,' in Timothy L. Jackson and Veijo Murtomäki (eds.), *Sibelius Studies* (Cambridge: Cambridge University Press, 2001), 322–351; and 'Beethoven Reception: The Symphonic Tradition,' in Jim Samson (ed.), *The Cambridge History of Nineteenth-Century Music* (Cambridge: Cambridge University Press, 2002), 424–459.
5 James Hepokoski, 'Sonata Theory and Dialogic Form,' in Pieter Bergé (ed.), *Musical Form, Forms & Formenlehre* (Leuven: Leuven University Press, 2009), 71–72.
6 Ibid., 72.
7 Lester Friedman, 'Introduction,' in *An Introduction to Film Genres* (New York: W. W. Norton, 2014), 4–5.
8 Hepokoski and Darcy, *Elements of Sonata Theory*, 611.
9 Ibid., 612.
10 David Cooper relays a quote from an interview with Herrmann where he states, 'the most important [thing] is the form, the shape of it.' See Cooper, 'Film Form and Musical Form,' 240.
11 Quoted in William Cameron, *Sound and the Cinema: The Coming of Sound to American Film* (New York: Redgrave, 1980), 132.
12 Though *Vertigo*'s final, partial third rotation is truncated like *Psycho*'s, the latter is unique among the examples offered here in its gradual and perpetual tightening of the rotational noose through successive truncations of the referential rotation. This tightening occurs at the level of both cue and whole score. During the *Psycho* Prelude, each rotational cycle shortens restatements from the 41-second referential rotation to the 30-second rotation two, 26-second rotation three, and 16-second final rotation, not even half as long as the first rotation. This contraction also appears, as noted earlier, in the truncations seen in each of the four rotations at the larger level of the entire soundtrack.
13 Dan Blim situates Herrmann's cyclic approach to form in *Vertigo* as reflecting the motif of mirrors and spirals emphasized in the visuals, though he does not discuss rotational form. See Blim, 'Musical and Dramatic Design,' 21–31. David Cooper writes of the film's overall form as being grouped into three presentations via 'a subtle process of variation and transformation of a small group of related ideas, which gives the impression of their being constantly relit or reframed.' See Cooper, 'Film Form and Musical Form,' 240.
14 There are various accounts of cue titles that may have been used to refer to the soundtrack as it appears in the film. For ease of reference, the titles from the official soundtrack release will be used here; despite the at-times sizeable differences between the commercial soundtrack and the film's cues, each cue on the commercial release does appear at least in part in the released version of the film. Consideration of the commercial soundtrack adds substantial amounts of music, along with more subrotations and additional referential allusions to earlier cues.

15 *Arrival*'s score was precluded from eligibility for an Academy Award due to Jóhannsson's recurring use of Richter's work throughout the soundtrack.
16 The interval formed between the tetrachord's lowest member, E♭, and the C drone is identical to that formed between the drone and the tetrachord's highest member, A, forming another symmetry in this cue.
17 Hepokoski, *Sibelius: Symphony No. 5*, 26.
18 Warren Darcy, 'Rotational Form, Teleological Genesis, and Fantasy-Projection,' 52.
19 Hepokoski and Darcy, *Elements of Sonata Theory*, 611.
20 Tom Schneller, 'Sweet Fulfillment: Allusion and Teleological Genesis in "Close Encounters of the Third Kind,"' *Musical Quarterly* 97.1 (2014): 123.
21 *Citizen Kane*, Bernard Herrmann's first film score, makes extensive use of the Dies Irae motif and the 'power' leitmotif is itself an allusion to the theme from Rachmaninoff's tone poem 'Isle of the Dead.' For more details, see William Rosar, 'The *Dies Irae* in *Citizen Kane*: Musical Hermeneutics Applied to Film Music' in K. J. Donnelly (ed.), *Film Music: Critical Approaches* (Edinburgh: Edinburgh University Press, 2001).
22 Fred Karlin refers to this theme as the 'Baroque Action Theme.' See Karlin, *Listening to Movies: The Film Lover's Guide to Film Music* (New York: Schirmer Books, 1994), 133.
23 Williams says he intentionally ends the Communications motive on the second degree of the scale (i.e., 're') to make the theme sounds open ended, 'like a doorbell'; he also ends the added three-note ending for the Rosebud/Power motif on $\hat{2}$.
24 K. J. Donnelly, *Magical Mystery Tour: Rock and Pop in Film Soundtracks* (London: Bloomsbury, 2015), 8.
25 In addition to Donnelly, there are numerous excellent explorations of the use of pop music as underscore. See Jonathan Romney and Adrian Wootton, *Celluloid Jukebox: Popular Music and the Movies since the Fifties* (London: BFI, 1993); Steve Lannin and Matthew Caley (eds.), *Pop Fiction: The Song in Cinema* (Bristol: Intellect, 2005); Ian Inglis, *Popular Music and Film* (London: Wallflower, 2003); Anahid Kassabian, *Hearing Film: Tracking Identifications in Contemporary Hollywood Film Music* (London: Routledge, 2001); Jeff Smith, *The Sounds of Commerce: Marketing Popular Film Music* (New York: Columbia University Press, 1998); and Hilary Lapedis, 'Popping the Question: The Function and Effect of Popular Music in Cinema,' *Popular Music* 18.3 (1999), 367–379, among many others.
26 See, for example, David Temperley, 'The Cadential IV in Rock,' *Music Theory Online* 17.1 (2011); Kyle Adams, 'Harmonic, Syntactic, and Motivic Parameters of Phrase in Hip-Hop,' *Music Theory Online* 26.2 (2020); Nicole Biamonte, 'Formal Functions of Metric Dissonance in Rock Music,' *Music Theory Online* 20.2 (2014); and Trevor DeClercq, 'Interactions Between Harmony and Form in a Corpus of Rock Music,' *Journal of Music Theory* 61.2 (2017).
27 Use of the term 'rotation' to denote a full, ordered presentation of a pop song's constituent parts (verse, pre-chorus, chorus, and post-chorus when applicable) and *rotational form* to indicate multiple rotations in a pop song appears in Osborn 2023 and Adams 2019. Geary 2022 refers to the pop song's VCU as the first and second rotations and the bridge as a non-recurring beginning of a third formal rotation but does not include rotations in formal diagrams. These works do not discuss incomplete, truncated, or expanded rotations. See Brad Osborn, 'Formal Functions and Rotation in Top-40 EDM,' *Intégral* 36 (2023); Kyle Adams, 'Musical Texture and Formal Instability in Post-Millennial Popular Music: Two Case Studies,' *Intégral* 33 (2019); and

David Geary, 'Analyzing the Beat in Metrically Consonant Popular Songs: A Multifaceted Approach,' *Music Theory Online* 28.4 (2022).
28 Pop songs, like other underscore cueing, are also routinely subjected to the so-called 'record scratch,' a quasi-diegetic phenomenon where the music responds to the on-screen action with immediate cessation in sympathy with a character at a moment of interruption, surprise, or shock. This also tends to migrate the music from (seeming) underscore to the diegesis (see Stilwell, 'The Fantastical Gap between Diegetic and Nondiegetic,' in Daniel Goldmark, Lawrence Kramer, and Richard Leppert (eds.), *Beyond the Soundtrack: Representing Music in Cinema* Berkeley: University of California Press, 2007), 187–202. Also unaddressed here is the technique of using a pop song to accompany the start of a scene to add energy, evoke a certain time or place, or create a general mood, then fading the song out as the dialogue begins without presenting an entire phrase, section, or rotation. Such cues are common throughout *American Graffiti* (1973) and begin *Apocalypse Now* (1979) and *Guardians of the Galaxy* (2014), among others.
29 Stilwell goes on to note, 'While formal processes can add dynamism to an action sequence or a montage, the force of a musical structure can also disrupt the flow of a scene by overriding its dramatic or cinematic rhythm. For this reason, the most acerbic commentators on film music, Theodor W. Adorno and Hanns Eisler, described "good motion-picture music" as "fundamentally anti-formalist"' (Stilwell, 'Sense & Sensibility,' 223). Frank Lehman argues that engaging film music as concert music presents the notion that 'the conversion [of film music] into concert music suggests that a "gnostic" (mediated, interpretive, intellectual) perspective such as formalism is, if not automatically valid, then at least available as an analytical stance.' (2018, 12). In advocating for 'cinematic listening,' Lehman notes that 'film-as-concert music helps subvert two facile attitudes in particular: naïve formalism and reflexive anti-formalism.' Frank Lehman, 'Film-as-Concert Music and the Formal Implications of "Cinematic Listening,"' *Music Analysis* 37.1 (2018).
30 Hepokoski, 'Sonata Theory and Dialogic Form,' 87.

8

TONAL ANALYSIS OF THE INTEGRATED SOUNDTRACK

Music, Sound, and Dialogue in *Baby Driver*

Táhirih Motazedian

The first sound we hear in the *Baby Driver* soundtrack is a high-pitched D that rings in on the introduction of the Sony logo, subtly joined a few seconds later by strings, and persisting through the rest of the studio logo sequence. As soon as the logos fade away to reveal a busy city block, this D is matched by the D-pitched squeal of car brakes as a red Subaru pulls into the foreground. Before the driver of the car is even revealed, we see a close-up shot of his iPod as he cues up 'Bellbottoms' by The Jon Spencer Blues Explosion—a song in D minor. As the annotated score excerpt in Example 8.1 shows, the driver, Baby (Ansel Elgort), is revealed on the first downbeat (D pitch, $\hat{1}$) of the song, his three crew members on the second, third, and fourth downbeats (also Ds). And, preserving this musical pattern, they open the doors on the song's fifth downbeat, exiting the car amidst a sea of Ds.

The hero of the 2017 bank heist film *Baby Driver* is a conductor with an odd kind of orchestra: Armed with his iPod, getaway driver Baby entrains everyone and everything in his vicinity as instruments in the soundtrack of his life. With surrounding people and objects incorporated—both rhythmically and harmonically—into the music playing in his earbuds, Baby creates a living symphony out of car horns, gunshots, and passersby alike. In the opening sequence described above—the crew's first bank heist and ensuing getaway car chase—Baby cues up 'Bellbottoms' to set the team in motion, and thereafter all their actions (and associated sound effects) are tightly synchronized to this music. Baby himself becomes animated (from his initially stoic pose) the moment the song's vocals begin, lip-syncing joyfully and enlisting his car's windshield wipers, steering wheel, and doors

EXAMPLE 8.1 Opening 13 measures of 'Bellbottoms' by The Jon Spencer Blues Explosion in *Baby Driver*, with actions annotated (all examples transcribed by author).

as percussion instruments as he watches the crew enter the bank. When a wailing police siren interrupts Baby's reverie, holding unnaturally on $\hat{3}$ (F), the song pauses and then restarts double time. With this new frenetic pace, things ramp up inside the bank, and gunshots are fired on the downbeats of the next four measures (now driven by the lead guitar). All these violent sound effects come to an abrupt halt when the song's instruments drop out for a spoken soliloquy by the lead singer, lip-synced by Baby.

Perfectly timed with the meter of the song and Baby's movements, the bank alarm begins wailing on $\hat{1}$-$\hat{3}$ (D-F), soon joined by another alarm that beeps on $\hat{1}$ (D) as the rest of his crew piles back into the car. As they tear off from the scene of the crime, 'Bellbottoms' veers into a frenzied instrumental interlude, supplemented with numerous brake squeals on $\hat{1}$ (D) and $\hat{1}$-$\hat{5}$ (D-A), a truck back-up beeper on $\hat{1}$ (D), and car horns on $\hat{3}$ (F) and $\hat{3}$-$\hat{5}$ (F-A)—plus countless precisely synchronized traffic sounds too numerous to enumerate.

Collectively, all of these sound effects coordinate with the D-minor tonality of the 'Bellbottoms' song to immerse the audience in the key of D minor for the first six minutes of the film—we'll delve into the significance of this key after we've explored the broader role of music in the film. The car chase ends when Baby pulls into a parking garage, where he and the crew hop out of his red Subaru Impreza WRX and into a green Toyota Corolla. Leaving his Subaru door open, the door chime pings on the quarter-note beat of the song, on a G pitch. The song moves to a G-major chord seconds later, and the door chime continues to ping quarter notes on $\hat{1}$ (G) as the song ends (in G major) and Baby chauffeurs the crew back to headquarters.

This type of tonally curated and meticulously choreographed musical space encompasses Baby wherever he goes; it facilitates his every action and is essential to his existence. Music is the driving force in his life, along with driving itself—he feels happiest when he is behind the wheel with his iPod. Music is Baby's activator (as we saw in the opening bank heist) as well as his soothing mechanism, and he uses music to process his experiences and make sense of the world. He frequently records conversation clips which he later samples and remixes to create song tracks, because music allows him to deal with people on his own terms. For instance, when a crew member ridicules him, Baby records the insult and reappropriates it, converting it into a form of musical expression that *he* controls. Music is the most vital part of Baby's identity, which is why we see his iPod before we even see his face. When he feels comfortable and in control of his life, every surrounding element, animate and inanimate, becomes perfectly pitched and timed to fit his music.

One of the clearest examples of this linkage of musicality with Baby's state of mind is the scene after the opening bank heist when he goes on a coffee run for the crew. Swelling with confidence over the successful bank job, Baby joyfully grooves down the street to the coffee shop, listening to Bob & Earl's 'Harlem Shuffle.' His surrounding environment grooves along with him, as a glorious host of car horns, crosswalk signals, ATM beeps, and construction sounds snap magnetically into the sonic landscape he creates and dances through. Even though 'Harlem Shuffle' is strictly heard only inside Baby's earbuds, the musical collaboration between subjective and environmental sound feels entirely organic, as though the entire city is participating in the song. For example, Baby passes a young woman dancing on roller skates to the rhythm of 'Harlem Shuffle,' even though there is no visible music source near her. Words from the song lyrics are physically incorporated into the urban environment in the form of graffiti and stickers which Baby passes at precisely the moments those words are sung in the song. A barista asks Baby a question at just the right moment to align his response with the 'yeah, yeah, yeah' of the song lyrics. And as 'Harlem Shuffle' approaches a climactic brass riff, Baby pauses in front of a music store, where a trumpet is suspended in the display window, positioned at *just* the right height for him to pose behind it and play air trumpet along with the riff. The fortuity of all the elements involved in Baby's sentient soundscape creates a fantastical realm that defies rational explanation. A series of 'but how did that happen at exactly the right time?' type questions accumulate until they crumble under the suspension of disbelief that facilitates the unspoken contract between filmmaker and film viewer. After the opening car chase and coffee run scenes, the viewer realizes that this is no ordinary bank heist film and that Baby is no ordinary protagonist; he is a quasi-superhero whose superpower consists of turning the world into his own personal opera.

Baby can't function without music, to the point where he sometimes has to stop his human instruments ('Wait wait—I gotta start the song over') and restart them ('Okay go!') in order to correctly choreograph a sequence of events. Or he'll partially rewind a song to account for unexpected complications and get the action back on track. When things aren't going well for Baby, actions and sound effects fall out of sync with his music. And the music in his earbuds becomes heavily muted (or disappears altogether) when he is in a situation that makes him feel trapped and incapacitated.

Baby's enemies know that his well-being is strongly coupled with his musical coordination, and they use this against him. Antagonists attack him by invading his musical space, either by seizing control of sound effects, cutting off his music source, or misappropriating one of his signature songs. Buddy (Jon Hamm) wages psychological warfare on Baby in increasingly aggressive stages. He begins early on by grabbing one of Baby's earbuds in a mock-playful gesture, and then yanking away both earbuds altogether. Later in the film, Buddy usurps the song Baby had specifically named as his favorite power anthem ('Brighton Rock' by Queen), blasting it in his car as he chases Baby down. Finally, Buddy shoots a gun past both of Baby's ears to burst his eardrums, in a cruel attempt to take music away from him permanently. But despite Buddy's vicious attacks, Bats (Jamie Foxx) establishes himself as the *most* odious villain of the movie when he spews a vitriolic tirade against music—which, in the context of *this* narrative (and Baby's place within its construction), serves the sole purpose of conveying how utterly despicable he is. The crew boss, Doc (Kevin Spacey), is far more subtle and nuanced in his villainy, but at the crucial moment when he makes a veiled threat toward Baby, he lifts his hand to authoritatively cue the chime of the elevator Baby awaits, symbolically demonstrating his control over Baby with his control of diegetic sound. This elevator chime cued by Doc is the same pitch (C) as the tension-filled tinnitus that fills Baby's ears when the boss makes his threat, imbuing Doc's sonic strike with an even more tangible impact.

Baby's tinnitus is the most prevalent audio motif of the film. The high-pitched D that opens the film is our first glimpse into the piercing din that plagues Baby—and this opening D literally *sets the tone* for the entire soundtrack (more on this later). Parsing this opening pitch a bit further, we realize that it is preceded by a faint, dull roar (similar to the vacant sound heard when holding a seashell to one's ear), and the D's initial reverberating instrumental timbre subtly transforms into the clinical ringing-in-the-ears sound of tinnitus, before being masked by music with the onset of the strings. As the film progresses, we see that Baby's tinnitus and his need for music are intertwined, and we realize why music is so essential to Baby. A dramatic flashback reveals that Baby received his first iPod from his beloved mother as a child, learning to use it as an escape mechanism whenever his father became violent with them. He was listening to his iPod at the moment his fighting parents were killed in a car crash. The crash marked the onset of Baby's tinnitus, and he has used his iPod to block out this traumatic sound and memory ever since. Without music, the shrill ringing in his ears consumes him, and he feels lost and impotent. His fervent need for music and concomitant impulse to drive thus stems from a desire to rectify this childhood trauma by staging the perfect run-through—striving to coordinate everything perfectly to achieve a successful do-over.

Each time it occurs, Baby's tinnitus is pitched differently to fit the tonality of the situation. The tinnitus sound effect occurs 14 times at eight different pitch levels during the course of the film, serving as $\hat{1}$ of the concurrent music in all instances but one. (See Table 8.1.) In the final instance, the tone acts as $\hat{1}$ of the concurrent cue and $\hat{5}$ of the *ensuing* cue—an important moment that will be discussed later. The pitch fluidity of his tinnitus is another manifestation of Baby's obsessive music

TABLE 8.1 Every occurrence of Baby's tinnitus throughout *Baby Driver*

Timestamp	Pitch	Relationship to concurrent music
0:00:05	D	$\hat{1}$
0:16:34	F	$\hat{1}$
0:21:55	F	$\hat{1}$
0:32:50	A#	$\hat{1}$
0:34:08	G	$\hat{1}$
0:34:15	G#	$\hat{1}$
0:48:10	D#	$\hat{1}$
0:49:13	C	$\hat{1}$
0:52:22	C	$\hat{3}$
1:17:12	D#	$\hat{1}$
1:18:08	G#	$\hat{1}$
1:26:30	C	$\hat{1}$
1:28:48	F#	$\hat{1}$
1:42:31	D	$\hat{1}$

drive since even his hearing disorder is dynamically incorporated into the musical world he creates.[1] The tinnitus may be unbearable to him, but like all other sounds in his environment, Baby finds a way to turn it into music.

Baby's emancipation—both from the trauma of his past and the constraints of his present criminal job—begins when he meets Debora (Lily James), his soulmate in music. They bond instantly through music when Debora breezes into the diner singing Carla Thomas's 'B-A-B-Y,' unknowingly spelling out his name as she walks past him. As they start a conversation about songs featuring their names, Debora and Baby bond over their shared feeling of being personally defined by music. The *source* of the music during their first three scenes together traces the trajectory of the relationship: They begin by listening to their own separate iPods in the diner, then they share earbuds to a single iPod at the laundromat (twirling around each other within earbud wire distance), and finally they create a source-less music between them on their date at the restaurant. This dinner date features the Detroit Emeralds' song 'Baby Let Me Take You,' which begins the moment Baby shows up at Debora's house to pick her up. This song is intriguing in its apparent lack of source. It isn't strictly diegetic, because the foregrounded volume of the song and the complete lack of external sound effects imply that it is not playing over restaurant speakers (nor does Baby have his iPod playing). It isn't nondiegetic either, because of the marked way Baby and Debora interact with the music, both rhythmically and harmonically.[2]

As the annotated score excerpt in Example 8.2 shows, their movements are perfectly synchronized with the musical nuances of 'Baby Let Me Take You.' Baby and Debora each run a finger around the rims of their wine glasses, generating $\hat{1}$ and $\hat{5}$ pitches on beats 1 and 3 (respectively). They clink their glasses together, producing a $\hat{1}$ pitch on the song's beat 2 (which is an accented beat in the funk genre). This type of musical correspondence marks every one of their physical motions and gestures—all while the cameras swirl tightly around them, simulating their earlier laundromat earbud dance. It becomes apparent during this sparkling moment that this music is metadiegetic (heard internally only by them), conjured by their powerful chemistry; their music is immediately backgrounded the moment another person (the waiter) interrupts their space, and it dies away altogether when Doc summons Baby across the restaurant. And it is through Debora's musical collaboration that Baby will find the strength to overcome his troubles and achieve his happy ending, as our examination of musical key will now demonstrate.

As noted earlier, *Baby Driver* begins in the key of D minor, a tonal center firmly if somewhat non-traditionally established by the 'Bellbottoms' song and the plethora of D-minor-centric sound effects during the opening bank heist. The film ends in the key of D major, so the overall tonal arc of the film follows a *tragic-to-triumphant* trajectory—a term coined by Robert Hatten to describe the sense of overcoming adversity exhibited by a work whose initial minor tonic transforms into the parallel major.[3] The key of D major occurs at the end of the film narrative when Baby is released from prison to find Debora waiting for him. The song is Simon & Garfunkel's 'Baby Driver'—the obvious inspiration for the title of the film itself—and it is immediately preceded by original orchestral underscoring by composer Steven Price, also in D major, played when Baby gets a postcard in prison from Debora. This D-major arrival is anticipated by a large-scale $\hat{3}-\hat{2}-\hat{1}$ motion in the preceding showdown scene between Buddy and Baby. In that climactic context, a car door-ajar chime pings insistently on an F♯ pitch ($\hat{3}$), followed by a sustained orchestral E pitch ($\hat{2}$), and finally an orchestral D ($\hat{1}$), matched by Baby's D-pitched tinnitus when Buddy blasts his eardrums.

Tonal Analysis of Integrated Soundtrack 163

EXAMPLE 8.2 Opening 14 measures of 'Baby Let Me Take You' by The Detroit Emeralds in *Baby Driver*, with actions annotated.

EXAMPLE 8.2 Continued

But rather than leading *directly* to the tonally conclusive D-major 'Baby Driver' song, this tonal trajectory is briefly interpolated by a crucial G-major event, hovering atop the sustained D pitch of Baby's tinnitus. The key of G major plays a pivotal role in the narrative, as we will now see. As mentioned earlier, the persistent D—the last sonic manifestation of Baby's tinnitus of the film—functions simultaneously as $\hat{1}$ of the concurrent music and $\hat{5}$ of the ensuing music, bridging the connection between D and G (the two most important tonal centers of the film). Baby and Debora join forces to vanquish Buddy, clearing the path to escape their former lives, and a glowing rendition of 'Easy' in G major shines forth to celebrate their triumph. G major holds special significance for Baby, being the key in which both his beloved mother and his beloved Debora sing. The first time we encountered this key was during Baby's flashback of his mother, in which she is shown singing 'Easy' in G major. The next instance occurs when Baby meets Debora and she sings the Beck song 'Debra' for him, also in G major. When Baby and Debora defeat Buddy, we hear an orchestral version of 'Easy' in G major, and when the couple begins their escape together, Debora plays a tape of Baby's mother singing the song in G major; and thus, the two loves of his life are brought together by the key of G.

Within the film's overarching D minor-to-major tonal envelope, G major provides a large-scale plagal pathway to the achievement of D major. The plagal relationship between these keys evokes the redemptive associations of the so-called 'Amen cadence' (IV–I). The plagal pathway and its suggestions of salvation are especially fitting because the final (and lengthiest) instance of G major accompanies the montage sequence of Baby's court trial and prison sentence, during which Baby—dressed head-to-toe in white, and surrounded by white prison walls—receives absolution from every person affected by his criminal activities. This G-major sequence leads directly to the closing D-major 'Baby Driver' song, granting our protagonist benediction to pursue his happy ending: Debora waiting for him beside a (white) car, with nothing but the open road before them. Thus, the two women in Baby's life, represented by G major, deliver him from evil and help him find his way.

The song 'Easy' was not originally written in G major, and it actually appears at a few different transposition levels in this film, as shown in Table 8.2.

While we first hear 'Easy' in G major (during the flashback of his mother), the original song was written and sung by The Commodores (1977) in A♭ major—which is the version we hear immediately after the G-major flashback version, when Baby cues it up on his iPod and walks away from the job, resolving to quit crime and run away with Debora. Later on, an orchestral version of 'Easy' in C major accompanies Baby's road-trip escape fantasy. An orchestral G-major version plays over the mayhem

TABLE 8.2 Iterations of the song 'Easy' throughout *Baby Driver*

Timestamp	Key	Situation
33:10	G major	Baby's flashback of mom
34:24	A♭ major	Baby walks away from job after flashback
1:14:19	C major	Baby's road-trip fantasy
1:43:23	G major	Debora and Baby defeat Buddy
1:43:35	G major	Baby's court trial and prison montage

when Debora and Baby defeat Buddy. And finally, Debora plays the tape of Baby's mom singing it in G major on their road trip, and throughout Baby's court trial and prison montage. Clearly, 'Easy' is a cathartic piece of music for Baby, but the key of the song does make a difference in its effect on his life. The first, G-based version we hear is what inspires Baby to realize he wants a different life. The A♭ version is powerful in its foregrounded volume level, but it does not actually lead Baby where he hopes—he *tries* to quit his crime job, but he is pulled back in against his will. During the C-major version, Baby gets one step closer by seeing a vision of his new life, but the vision is dispelled and he remains stuck.[4] It is only when 'Easy' is situated back in G major that Baby is finally able to escape. And, in light of its functional role within the overarching tonal progression of the film, G-major salvation is what allows Baby to achieve his D-major happiness.

'Easy' is not the only preexisting piece of music transposed to multiple tonal centers in this film: Two other important songs are shifted into different keys, with meaningful effects on the narrative, as shown in Table 8.3.

The first is 'Harlem Shuffle,' which is first sung in A minor by Bob & Earl (1963) and later transposed up to B♭ minor by The Foundations (1969). Both versions accompany Baby (on his iPod) as he goes on a post-heist coffee run, but to very different effects. The A-minor 'Harlem Shuffle' plays

TABLE 8.3 Transposition of 'Harlem Shuffle' and 'Debora' songs in *Baby Driver*

Timestamp	Song	Key	Situation
6:25	'Harlem Shuffle'	A minor	Baby's coffee run, feeling *good*
31:18	'Harlem Shuffle'	B♭ minor	Baby's coffee run, feeling *bad*
37:41	'Debora'	B♭ major	Baby sings *alone*
39:07	'Debora'	A major	Debora and Baby listen *together*

after the opening bank heist discussed earlier when Baby is feeling great about his life and the successful job. But 'Harlem Shuffle' plays in B♭ minor after a bank heist gone badly awry, when Baby is feeling frustrated and despondent. This B♭-minor version occurs after Baby has met the beguiling Debora and realizes he wants a different life. Right after this B♭ minor, Baby goes into the diner to see his love interest, and he sings the T. Rex song 'Debora' (1968) for her in the parallel major mode, B♭ major, *after* she sang Beck's 'Debra' (1999) for him in G major. Under Debora's restorative influence, Baby transforms his mode from (B♭) minor to major. (And in fact, B♭ is subtly alluded to the first moment Baby lays eyes on Debora: During Bob & Earl's 'Harlem Shuffle' in A minor, while Baby is in the coffee shop, the music temporarily moves to a ♭II chord [B♭ major] when his attention is caught by a young woman—Debora—walking past the coffee shop. The music moves back to a tonic chord as she walks out of sight, and then modulates permanently to B♭ minor when Baby hurries out of the coffee shop to try and follow her. But she is nowhere to be seen, and Baby is mildly agitated as he looks up and down the street to find this mysterious girl, while the song fades out in the key of B♭ minor. Thus, even before he has officially met her, Baby is perturbed from his A-minor tranquility to B♭ minor when Debora first walks into [or past, more accurately] his life.)

Immediately after this B♭ minor-to-major modal transformation involving Beck's 'Debra,' Baby and Debora jubilantly listen to T. Rex's 'Debora' together on his iPod, now in the key of A major (transposed from its original B♭ major).[5] So whereas Baby's initial feel-good song was in the melancholic key of A minor, Debora helps Baby not only return to the A tonic, but transform the overriding mode from minor to major. We can reconstruct a rough narrative trajectory from these transpositions: Baby starts out feeling fine in A minor, but becomes unsettled in B♭ minor; Debora then helps him turn that B♭ minor into B♭ major when he is singing *alone*, and the two of them listening *together* turn B♭ major into A major. There is thus a smaller-scale tragic-to-triumphant trajectory embedded within the larger one (D minor to major). Figure 8.1 captures the important tonal relationships in this film.

It seems likely that the T. Rex 'Debora' song was the inspiration for the Debora character's name, just as Simon & Garfunkel's 'Baby Driver' was the inspiration for the Baby character's name, as well as the name of the film itself. (Director Edgar Wright has discussed his music-driven creative process for this film in interviews, as we will see below.) That the main characters and the film title are built around preexisting songs demonstrates how fundamental music is to this film—at an even deeper level than the obvious role of music in the narrative. As a thought experiment in reconstructing the development of this soundtrack, one can imagine that because the 'Baby Driver' song was pre-selected as the ultimate musical payoff of the film, its key (D major) served as the tonal germ of the

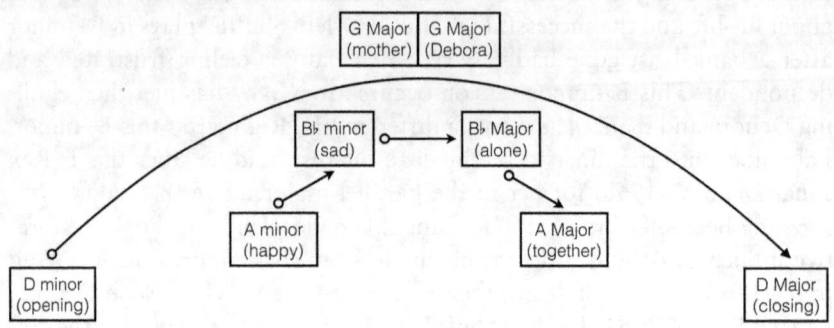

FIGURE 8.1 Large-scale tonal relationships across *Baby Driver*.

soundtrack.⁶ The D-minor starting point ('Bellbottoms') would naturally come next, to create a satisfying tonal arc leading to the D-major ending point. And the D-pitched tinnitus that opens the film plants the seed for the D minor-to-major arc—*setting the tone* for the whole soundtrack, as I punned earlier. G major would be the next step, in order to set up the long-range plagal atonement for Baby's sins, with the G-major version of the 'Easy' song produced specially for the film. Incidentally, the D–G–D relationship features prominently in both the opening 'Bellbottoms' song (which begins in D and ends in G, as mentioned earlier) and the closing 'Baby Driver' song (in which the intro and most of the verse consists mainly of I–IV–I progressions). Finally, the smaller, internal arc of A minor-to-major fits nicely within the overarching D minor-to-major arc. Together, these main keys create a conceptual sort of meta-progression across the film, with the i→I frame filled in with important contributions from V (A major) and IV (G major).

Edgar Wright has stated explicitly that music inspired this film. Long before the film began to take shape in his mind, certain songs suggested imagery and action sequences to him:

> I would literally listen to 'Bellbottoms' by the Jon Spencer Blues Explosion and visualize this car chase and be able to visualize: 'So the first half of this section, they're all pulling up. On these guitar stabs, you cut around the gang and they get out and go inside. And now he's on his own and he starts singing along with the song. And then they come back and it's building up to the song really kicking into gear and then they drive off.'⁷

It wasn't until decades later that Wright began envisioning 'a car chase movie driven by music' and 'started to get the idea of a getaway driver who listens to music the whole time.' In 2002 he 'road test[ed] the idea for the first scene' of *Baby Driver* in a three-minute music video he directed for 'Blue Song' by Mint Royale—likewise featuring a getaway driver waiting for his colleagues to rob a bank but with far less fastidious synchronization than he would incorporate in *Baby Driver* 15 years later. He explains the synchronization in *Baby Driver* as a precisely 'mathematical' process with 'a lot of to-the-millisecond planning,' staging the action both forwards and backwards to work between a multitude of anchor points in every song. Wright describes it as one of many 'happy accidents' that this filming process 'also speaks to the [Baby] character,' since 'when he's rewinding the song, he's trying to get back in control again.'

Music in *Baby Driver* was not tacked on during post-production to fill silences or make chase scenes more exciting—music was the *progenitor* of the narrative, the characters, and the actions—and of the film itself. The film's protagonist uses music to align the world around him and direct his life according to the score of his choosing. But despite his superhero-like power to entrain and conduct everything and everyone as instruments in his life opera, Baby is stuck in a criminal life he cannot escape. Meeting Debora makes him realize he wants a different life, but his criminal colleagues manipulate him, at times musically, to keep him in place. But he 'gets by with a little help from his friends,' as the two women he loves give him the tonal boost he needs to drive off into the sunset in pursuit of his happy ending.

The analytical approach of studying keys and large-scale tonal relationships across a musical composition is known as 'tonal design' (a term coined by David Beach), and it has long been used in the context of instrumental works.[8] Key is one of the most basic building blocks of music, and most musical inquiries begin by identifying a composition's key. But it has not been one of the traditional parameters of film music analysis, mainly due to theoretical restrictions stemming from the traditional model of tonality delineated by the harmonic processes of common-practice, monotonal, functional music. However, this model no longer represents the tonal soundscape in which the Western ear is immersed: Tonality has evolved substantially during the twentieth and twenty-first centuries, as jazz, pop, and rock music (among others) have pushed past the boundaries of eighteenth-century harmonic practice and developed tonality in new directions. (Indeed, even *within* the common-practice period there is no single harmonic logic that neatly codifies hundreds of years of Western music; Mozart's tonality certainly behaves differently than that of Mahler.)

Acknowledging that tonality is continually evolving and transforming entails updating our expectations for how tonality might function in new contexts.[9] For example, in the film music context, we must account for the fact that the musical 'composition' of the soundtrack consists of multiple elements (original scoring, preexisting music, sound effects, and dialogue) crafted by multiple artists rather than a single autocratic 'composer.' The finished end product of a film soundtrack acquires its own gestalt as the *mise-en-bande*, in the same way that the heavily spliced and sutured image track coalesces into the resulting *mise-en-scène* perceived by the film viewer-listener.[10]

The question of intentionality ('Did they do this on purpose?') often arises in the context of filmic tonal design, as people wonder whether the complex tonal machinations of a soundtrack were knowingly planned that way. If we were to apply this type of question to the fractal patterns found in Jackson Pollock's paintings, we would still find Pollock's fractals fascinating regardless of whether he knowingly intended to paint in fractal form.[11] As Ronald Rodman has observed, 'film has become one of the rare American cultural artifacts in which esthesic [analyst-centric] readings have revealed a masterwork greater than the sum of its parts.'[12] The analyst's job is not to uncover the artist's intentions or reveal the one correct interpretation but to create a reading—one of many possible readings—that will be compelling and engaging to other readers. From this perspective, filmmaker commentary (such as the Edgar Wright quotes we considered in the past few pages) can be used to supplement rather than prove or justify one's analytical interpretations.

The validity of long-range tonality in music *in general* (not restricted to film music) has long been questioned on the basis of audibility: Must a listener *hear* tonal relationships in order for them to matter? This concern can seem heightened in the context of a film soundtrack, when long stretches of time may separate musical cues. However, both the visual and narrative structures of film are *also* inherently disjunct; take flashbacks, flashforwards, ellipses, scene changes, and alternating camera shots, for instance. The filmic art form simply demands cooperation from the viewer-listener in seeing and thinking past these inherent disjunctions of the form—and we can train ourselves to hear past the sonic disjunctions as well.

Theoretical concerns such as these have kept scholars from considering the relevance of key in film soundtracks. (Similar objections were raised when scholars began tonally analyzing opera, but proved less of a deterrent because opera was a longer-standing and more overtly music-based art form.[13]) It wasn't until the 1990s that film music scholars actually began attempting to analyze film soundtracks with respect to key—and the results have been compelling.[14] As our tonal exploration of *Baby Driver* in this chapter has demonstrated, the most enticing incentive for tonal analysis is the interpretive power it yields. It provides us with new tools for engaging with the narrative, and for understanding the narrative work music does. Studying a film's tonal design also enables us to perceive the soundtrack as a cohesive entity and explore the gestalt of a film's sonic plane (much as we assess the visual plane in terms of elements like cinematography and set design).

Hailed as a 'car-chase opera,' *Baby Driver* features a truly integrated soundtrack in which music, sound effects, and dialogue are woven together to form a living musical fabric that occupies *the* central role in the narrative.[15] Music and sound in this film do not simply decorate empty space and overdetermine the visuals; turning off the audio and watching this film with closed captioning would strip away crucial information about Baby's character and narrative arc. Key tells a story in this film—whether this tonal story-beneath-the-story was consciously planned or one of the happy accidents of the production process.

Notes

1 In reality, tinnitus sufferers may occasionally experience pitch variations, but not as frequently (or artistically) as Baby does this film.
2 To explore the complex boundaries between diegetic, nondiegetic, and metadiegetic film sound, see Claudia Gorbman, *Unheard Melodies: Narrative Film Music* (Bloomington: Indiana University Press, 1987); Robynn Stilwell, 'The Fantastical Gap Between Diegetic and Nondiegetic,' in Daniel Goldmark, Lawrence Kramer, and Richard Leppert (eds.), *Beyond the Soundtrack* (Berkeley: University of California Press, 2007), 184–202; and Guido Heldt, *Music and Levels of Narration in Film: Steps Across the Border* (Bristol, UK: Intellect, 2013).
3 Robert Hatten, 'On Narrativity in Music: Expressive Genres and Levels of Discourse in Beethoven,' *Indiana Theory Review* 12 (1991): 75–98.
4 Taking the plagal key relationship even further, this C-major rendition of 'Easy' provides plagal preparation for the G-major rendition. In narrative terms, his C-major vision foretells the G-major reality that will follow.
5 The T. Rex recording was transposed down from B♭ to A major for the film, and one might assume that this pitch alteration was simply a byproduct of slowing down the pace of the song to achieve the desired pacing for the scene. However, the pace of this song was actually *sped up* for the film (from 78 bpm to 84 bpm), which means the sound engineers had to alter the pitch (key) separately and purposely.
6 Incidentally, the original 1970 recording of Simon & Garfunkel's 'Baby Driver' is pitched slightly higher (~600 Hz) than the standard modern D pitch (~587 Hz)—sounding somewhere between D and D♯—even though the song was performed in D major (as can be verified from Simon & Garfunkel's live performances). The film, however, adjusts the song down to the standard D pitch, which highlights the significance of the D-major key and makes the tonal framework of the film seem even more deliberate.
7 Jacob Hall, 'Baby Driver: The Edgar Wright Interview,' */Film* (June 28, 2017), www.slashfilm.com/baby-driver-edgar-wright-interview. All the Wright quotes that follow are also from this source.

8 David Beach, 'Schubert's Experiments with Sonata Form: Formal-Tonal Design versus Underlying Structure,' *Music Theory Spectrum* 15.1 (1993): 1–18.
9 For a detailed exploration of these and other theoretical considerations of filmic tonal design, see Táhirih Motazedian, 'To Key or Not to Key: Tonal Design in Film Music,' PhD diss. (Yale University, 2016) and *Key Constellations: Interpreting Tonality in Film* (Berkeley: University of California Press, 2023).
10 The term '*mise-en-bande*' was coined by Altman, Jones, and Tatroe (2000) as a parallel to *mise-en-scène*. See Rick Altman, McGraw Jones, and Sonia Tatroe, 'Inventing the Cinema Soundtrack: Hollywood's Multiplane Sound System,' in James Buhler, Caryl Flinn, and David Neumeyer (eds.), *Music and Cinema* (Hanover: Wesleyan University Press, 2000), 339–359. For more discussion on the concept of *mise-en-bande*, see: David Neumeyer, *Meaning and Interpretation of Music in Cinema* (Bloomington: Indiana University Press, 2015); James Buhler, *Theories of the Soundtrack* (New York: Oxford University Press, 2019); and Motazedian, *Key Constellations*.
11 On this riveting finding, see Richard Taylor, Adam Micolich, and David Jonas, 'Fractal analysis of Pollock's drip paintings,' *Nature* 399.6735 (1999): 422.
12 Ronald Rodman, '"There's No Place Like Home": Tonal Closure and Design in the *Wizard of Oz*,' *Indiana Theory Review* 19 (1998): 128.
13 Motazedian summarizes the history of the debate over operatic tonal design. Motazedian, 'To Key or Not to Key,' 4–10.
14 See David Neumeyer, 'Tonal Design and Narrative in Film Music: Bernard Herrmann's *A Portrait of Hitch* and *The Trouble With Harry*,' *Indiana Theory Review* 19 (1998): 87–123; Ronald Rodman, 'Tonal Design and the Aesthetics of Pastiche in Herbert Stothart's *Maytime*,' in James Buhler, Caryl Flinn, and David Neumeyer (eds.), *Music and Cinema* (Hanover: Wesleyan University Press, 2000), 187–206; Rodman, 'The Operatic Stothart: Leitmotifs and Tonal Organization in Two Versions of "Rose Marie,"' *The Journal of Film Music* 4.1 (2011): 5–19; and Motazedian, 'To Key or Not to Key,' and *Key Constellations*.
15 Terri White, 'Baby Driver Review,' *Empire* (June 19, 2017), www.empireonline.com/movies/reviews/baby-driver-review/.

9
ANALYZING MUSICAL METAMORPHOSES

Thematic Transformation in Shirley Walker's *Batman*

Frank Lehman

> *Alfred:* Am I correct in assuming the metamorphic Mr. Hagen is back in town, sir?
> *Batman:* Back, but not for long, I'd guess. It seems that Clayface is losing his integrity.
> *Alfred:* I wasn't aware that he ever had any to begin with.
> *Batman:* I'm speaking in a physiological sense, Alfred. Based on destructive ultrasonic analysis of the sample, the molecular bonding of his clay flesh is breaking down. He's falling apart, literally.
> *Alfred:* How grotesque… Tea?
> From 'Mudslide,' *Batman: The Animated Series*, Episode 52

Scientific mumbo-jumbo and droll puns notwithstanding, a deep anxiety about the human body is powerfully evident in the above exchange. The thought of human flesh 'falling apart' is terrifying, and so too is the notion of a metamorphic man. This dialogue comes from an episode of the celebrated 1990s television show *Batman: The Animated Series* entitled 'Mudslide' (S2E3, 1993). The character in question, an actor named Matt Hagen—turned into a villainous mass of goo named Clayface (Ron Perlman)—has resurfaced in Gotham City. Hagen is a shape-shifter: His super-power consists of an ability to assume any form at will, human or inanimate. His skill at camouflaging, disguising, and weaponizing his own body makes him one of Batman's most physically dangerous adversaries.

All is not well for the gelatinous felon, however. 'Mudslide' witnesses Hagen's ability to cohere, to keep the orange gunk that composes his body together, on the wane. Throughout the episode, the viewer is treated to

DOI: 10.4324/9781003001171-9

images of Clayface at the extremes of bodily 'integrity:' From a sleek, statuesque parody of the Oscar statuette, through intermediate forms of normal human appearance (though never his own), to a bulging amoeboid, and ultimately, a dissolved mass of sea foam. But Clayface's form of choice (Figure 9.1a) seems to be an orange, muck-spattered hulk, with empty eyes and toothy grin scooped out of his sunken face.[1]

In one 30-second sequence halfway through the episode, Clayface, now disguised as a female scientist, flees from the scene of a crime she/he/it committed (Figure 9.1b, [12:54]). Music enters as she runs toward the camera, smiling, purloined chemical that could help reintegrate her body clutched in hand. Her grin turns into an effortful wince as she notices her hand losing its shape, dripping onto the pavement. We see her struggle to keep together (Figure 9.1c, [13:04]), and we hear the sound of her clenching face, which seems, temporarily, to dispel the gurgle of dripping mud. It is at this point that music begins to assert a controlling role in the narrative, as an evocative cue comes to the fore on the soundtrack. Example 9.1 depicts a reduced transcription of the passage. The music—one of countless exquisitely conceived examples of thematic transformation in the series—was written by *Batman: The Animated Series* composer, conductor, and general music director, the acclaimed Shirley Walker.

Over a nervous, hexatonically disposed string ostinato, a solo flute melody glides into audibility; it too is struggling, here against drooping chromatic intervals in bassoon and bass clarinet.[2] A cut to an aerial shot, and Walker's flute melody is transposed up a fifth, eerier in the higher register, and more ill-at-ease with the dragging force of the lower wind figures. The theme continues through two more iterations, first transposed down a minor third, then a minor second, now with a slight, discomfiting chromatic alteration. The string ostinato loses steam, flute and bass settle on a tonally unhinged major seventh, and the musical cue ends.

a) Monster Form

b) Scientist Form

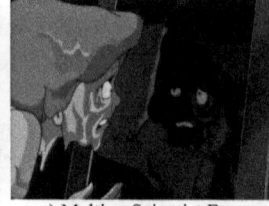
c) Melting Scientist Form

FIGURE 9.1 *Batman: The Animated Series*, season 3 episode 2 'Mudslide' (1993), forms of Clayface.

EXAMPLE 9.1   Walker, *Batman: TAS*, 'Mudslide,' Clayface escapes (all examples transcribed by author).

Clayface-as-scientist descends into a subway, unaware that Batman is in hot pursuit.

The flute melody in this brief cue is a transformed version of one of Clayface's two leitmotifs, what I will refer to as his 'tragic theme.' The sagging bass line is a mutated derivative of Clayface's other motif, his 'horror theme.' (The hexatonic ostinato is also motivic in this and Hagen/Clayface's other episodes, though with less symbolic importance.) The cue is an instance of **thematic transformation**. One can observe the change the creature's thematic material undergoes here by comparing Example 9.1, a reduced transcription of the 'Mudslide' sequence, with Example 9.2, which shows the leitmotifs' definitive forms as heard earlier in the episode.

Compounding this musical alteration of Hagen/Clayface's two themes is a third transformative process: Contrapuntal overlay. While the tragic and horror motifs are often sounded in close succession, this is a rare example of direct combination. The motivic workout they undergo produces a kind of combinatorial meaning, whose emotional and narrative power stems from the built-up associations of those twin motifs over the course of three Matt Hagen-centered *B:TAS* episodes. Thematic construction is, of course, only part of the cue's effectiveness: A full interpretation would need to grapple with a host of other affective qualities—texture, orchestration, timing. Particularly potent is the ostinato-driven tension of the music, against which that dissonantly supported flute melody slides queasily. Soon, any attempt to read the aural-visual-narrative interplay here becomes gooped up, as it were, in a morass of overlapping transformations. What sort of analytical model, then, exists for reading narrative

EXAMPLE 9.2 Walker, Clayface's leitmotifs.

significance into musical metamorphosis, particularly in relation to screen media such as film and television?

This little moment in 'Mudslide' is a throwaway compared to the bravura action and morphing scenes that flank it. Yet it captures a crucial aspect of thematic and audiovisual transformation that will inform the rest of this chapter: Clearly, metamorphosis of the sort Alfred attributes to Clayface is not limited to the domains of sight or plot. In both live-action and animated media, audio is recruited to mingle with other elements of the frame, and through its capacity to change, it reinforces, undercuts, and generates metamorphic meanings in manifold ways. Music, in particular, has been exploited throughout cinema and television for its capacity to convey *change* in a vivid and audience-legible way. This is most apparent in the treatment of referential melodic themes as subjects for continuous variation, a clear (if somewhat more complicated than often acknowledged) technical and aesthetic inheritance of nineteenth-century classical practices, Wagnerian leitmotif above all. The general term that has taken hold for this mutative procedure is *thematic transformation*, what musicologist Hugh McDonald defines as the 'process of modifying a theme so that in a new context it is different but yet manifestly made of the same elements.'[3] This characterization may sound simple, but it entails an attitude toward music composition (and analysis) that is far from simplistic.

If thematic transformation is a boon to standalone texts, it is a musical godsend to multi-entry franchises; indeed, it is hard to name a visual multimedia property that does *not* feature melodic metamorphosis in some meaning-generating capacity, and many of the most musically striking and successful modern film and television properties—*Lord of the Rings, Star Wars, Indiana Jones, Battlestar Galactica, Dr. Who, Game of*

Thrones, Avatar: The Last Airbender, Rings of Power, and so on—boast extraordinarily wide-ranging and sophisticated thematic transformations across their musical scores.[4] And, singular in the superhero genre—even today, after various iterations of the DCU and MCU—is the musical tapestry that formed around *Batman: The Animated Series.*[5]

The task of this chapter will be to explore the myriad means by which music metamorphoses, and to sketch a methodology to aid interpretation of sequences such as Clayface's escape. Manipulation of thematic material has, of course, been of perennial interest to music analysts, both in programmatic repertoires (where the concept of leitmotif is of central importance) and more absolute ones (in which more abstract procedures like developing variation and teleological genesis are celebrated). Matthew Bribitzer-Stull, author of *Understanding the Leitmotif,* notes that 'leitmotivic emotional associations contribute in large part to the sense of drama in multimedia works like opera and film' and goes on to provide numerous examples from modern cinema to illustrate processes such as thematic evolution, thematic fragmentation, thematic irony, and so on.[6] The storytelling capacity for thematic transformation is well-recognized, but few studies have focused on the way in which categories of musical transformation relate to specific *narrative* processes or archetypes—and none to the author's knowledge link the metamorphic potentialities of music on one hand, and the nature of animation as an inherently transformational medium on the other.

In an effort to narrow down the topic matter, only *Batman: The Animated Series* (*B:TAS*) and its filmic counterpart *Batman: Mask of the Phantasm* will be analyzed in any depth here, though it is hoped interpretive principles drawn from these media will have manifest applicability to other texts and franchises with comparably rich thematic scoring. I will first provide an introduction to *B:TAS,* its scoring practice, and its peculiar concern with mutable bodies. This will be followed by a general consideration of 'morphing' as it occurs in animation and sound. A substantial section is dedicated to organizing our intuitions about musical transformation as they occur in *any* context, drawing concepts from a perhaps unexpected source—narrative theory—to construct a working model of multimodal morphs. This admittedly theoretical and fairly abstract undertaking will ease our transition into tackling specific cases of musico-metamorphosis.

A detailed reading of two episodes, involving the villains The Mad Hatter and Clayface respectively, will close out this study. In both these cases, Shirley Walker's usage of leitmotivic transformation goes beyond the standard descriptive [*read: Semiotically redundant*] charge of screen music, approaching an active critique—even a dismantling of—the mythic bases of the show and its inhabitants. Remarkably, Walker's manipulation of villain themes can be seen to reflect insight back onto the Caped Crusader himself. Just as the exaggerated psychoses of Batman's foes may implicate the hero's own questionable psyche, the score's thematic transformations play into certain ironic subtexts in a manner exceedingly subtle and eloquent for a purported children's show.

Dark Deco and Transfigured Knights

Batman: The Animated Series (1992–95), and its subsequent incarnation *The New Batman Adventures* (1997–99), was a popular animated show produced by Bruce Timm and Paul Dini under the aegis of Warner Brothers Studios. Under a perpetually scarlet-hued sky, *B:TAS*'s Gotham City was a heavily stylized universe in which modern technology is capable of engineering a perfect cyborg but whose criminals still speak in 1930s criminal cant and wield Tommy guns. Notable for its eye-catching visuals and noirish atmosphere, the series' modern-cum-gothic tone has been evocatively described as 'dark deco.'[7] This descriptor could well be applied to the musical atmosphere of the show, as it too was a synthesis of throwback and innovation. Each episode hosted its own unique orchestral score—a rarity then and almost unheard of today. While varying in tone and thematic material from episode to episode, the overall musical vocabulary was carefully maintained across the series, drawing primarily from action serials, psychological thrillers, and film noir soundtracks of earlier decades, and always with Danny Elfman's work on Tim Burton's 1989 *Batman* (itself a throwback to those same styles) as a stylistic reference point.

While Elfman was enlisted to write the music for the impressive opening sequence that preceded each episode, the person truly behind the soundscape of *B:TAS* was Shirley Walker. A gifted orchestrator by trade, Walker had worked closely with Elfman in scoring Burton's *Batman*, conducting the score as well as contributing orchestrations and arrangements.[8] When it came time to recruit someone with experience sonifying Gotham to head the musical side of *B:TAS*, Walker was the obvious choice. In addition to writing about one-quarter of the show's scores, Walker served as *B:TAS*'s composing supervisor. This entailed overseeing the production of music from a deep roster of talented composers like Lolita Ritmanis and Carlos Rodriguez, and generally guiding the show's timbral and thematic milieu. Walker typically was handed the reins for the more ambitious episodes—those in which a new villain is introduced or that required special care in the production of a sound world. In addition to the television show, Walker wrote a full-length film score for the direct-to-video feature *Batman: Mask of the Phantasm*, which includes some of her most impressive work.

Walker's most decisive contribution to *B:TAS* may have been her composition of the show's collection of character leitmotifs. These run an expressive gamut from the nobly morose theme for Kevin Conroy's Bruce Wayne/

Batman to a disturbing carousel tune for Mark Hamill's Joker. Developed far beyond mere reminiscence themes or 'calling cards,' most of this melodic material is leitmotivic in a sense Wagner would have recognized—concise ideas with distinct and dynamic associative qualities, strung through the process of variation to create much larger spans of music. The sheer breadth of B:TAS the show—encompassing 85 individual episodes, 25 minutes each, with a huge host of recurrent characters and narrative arcs—lent itself to a degree of motivic exploration unprecedented in the genre. Walker's leitmotif lexicon furnished nearly all of Batman's 20 or so 'Rogue's Gallery' villains (and a few notable heroes too) with their own highly individuated musical material. Clayface, whose music we have already encountered, is a rare case of a character with multiple motifs, a curiosity that will be examined in due course. With the notable exception of The Joker's creepily major tune, all motifs are either in a firmly minor mode or a flirtatious relationship with atonality (such as the themes for Two-Face, Poison Ivy). This oppressive harmonic ambiance contributes as much as anything to the 'dark deco' aesthetic of the show. A handful of motifs are onomatopoetic, such as The Penguin's waddling tune. Most, however, abstract some aspect of the character's *psychology* into musical terms, such as brutality (Bane), fastidiousness (Clock King), or just plain quizzicality (The Mad Hatter).

Walker's musical encapsulations of (super)criminal pathology reflect the broader concerns of the show. The psychological angle on Batman's cast of characters conjoins with a flair for animated transformation to form what may be B:TAS's overriding thematic metaphor: *Human metamorphosis*. The show is preoccupied with plots involving the transformation of the human mind and body. Metamorphosis is thematized most consistently in the origin story, wherein a character is shown to mutate from relative normalcy into an exaggerated, often dangerous state. Physical change inevitably accompanies mental realignment, usually in the form of modifications or disfigurements of the body. Narrative seeds that suggest the nature of this alteration, especially the precursors to insanity, are typically shown before the moment of transformation. In the case of Matt Hagen, the former screen actor and master of disguise is involuntarily morphed into a shape-shifter; his earlier personality quirks—melodramatic personality, propensity for mimicry—are amplified into monstrous dimensions.[9]

Metamorphosis is thus poetic and literalizing: It takes some trait, such as theatrical vacuity (Clayface) or inordinate love of a certain animal (Catwoman, The Penguin), and externalizes it in a bodily exaggerated way. On the deepest level, B:TAS perpetually reenacts a transformational meta-narrative. It posits the ego as frail and vulnerable, so that in the origin story—the fable of 'morphogeny'—a character succumbs or is driven to change. In every case of human metamorphosis in B:TAS, such transformations are one-way affairs. Changed characters cannot go back to their initial state, whether they want to or not; the outlook of the show is thus a fundamentally pessimistic one. Redemption or recovery is not an option. Indeed, for a Saturday morning cartoon, *B:TAS* paints a remarkably hopeless picture of the human condition.

Clayface/Hagen is but an extreme case of a character whose body and mind are radically changed over the course of *B:TAS*. The mere act of putting on a costume is a metamorphosis of sorts, and the most vivid case is of Batman himself. The film-length *The Mask of the Phantasm* (1993) details Bruce Wayne's difficult path to becoming the Caped Crusader. The scene in which Wayne first dons his cowl in the newly discovered Batcave [0:35:50] is emphasized by the filmmakers as the 'moment of metamorphosis.' Sensational cinematography, an absence of dialogue (save Alfred's uncharacteristic expression of shock 'My god!'), and magnificent scoring all conspire to mark this as the *birth* of a superhero. It is a moment of mixed romance and tragedy: Wayne has achieved his new identity and fully owns it, but recognizes that it is a dark identity born of trauma and that by taking hold of the Batman persona, he crosses a point of no return.

Key to the scene's impact is the dramatic rendition of Walker's leitmotif for Batman. A prototypical version, as heard before over the movie's opening credits, is shown in reduction in Example 9.3—note already the harmonic duality, with the theme's second, major phrase liquidating the minor chromatic coloration of the demonic first.

Walker's cue for the mask-donning sequence in which this theme is stated in its definitive form is literally titled 'Birth of Batman.' She transitions from a pained version of the *love theme* (representing the principle obstacle, however positive-seeming, to Wayne's realization of the vigilante persona) to a long-breathed statement of the intensely chromatic *promise theme* (representing the opposing force to Wayne's romantic interests, his obligation to his murdered parents). Walker's expert imposition of the tragedy motif against a harmonically unconsummated rendition of the love theme suggests the culmination, and loss, of the ongoing struggle between these aspects of Wayne's personality; duty wins out over love.

The upshot of this musical development is now inevitable. Wayne's silhouette, all but fully suited up, briefly broods upon the mask in

EXAMPLE 9.3   Walker, *Mask of the Phantasm*, Batman theme during 'Main Title.'

FIGURE 9.2 Batman donning his cowl.

his hands, shown in Figure 9.2. This is accompanied by a chilling annunciation of the *Batman theme* entirely in low brass. He places on the mask and we see only his eyes, transformed into those of a demon. The theme's second phrase rings out in tutti orchestration, replete with gothic choir; this gloriously dark moment is the objective of the scene, the flashback in which it occurs, and to a certain extent the entire show's mythology. An *apotheosis* of Walker's theme for Batman, a Knight, transfigured.[10]

The 'Ani-morph'

As we have seen in *B:TAS*, some characters are prone to spontaneous change, a narrative device that presented the show's animators with many opportunities to show off their craft in impressive and disturbing imagery. Yet this opportunity reflects a more general, indeed inherent proclivity of animation itself. All animation is an art of transformation: An object, be it a running horse or a lump of clay, is drawn (or, if CG, rendered), cel by cel, in different positions to create the illusion of movement. Of course, the transformational nature of animation involves more than a series of slightly differently drawn pictures. Speaking of the tendency for animators to resort to 'tangibly interfering' with objects in their natural, drawn state, Norman Klein claims that this 'effect is essentially the same in hundreds of animated shorts. One substance transmutes into another, from line to protoplasm and back again. And with this transformation, gravity itself, or time, transforms as well.'[11] Klein notes case after case of artistically-imposed physical instability across the history of animation and enlists a neologism, *'ani-morphing,'* to carry the meaning of this phenomenon.

Because of the radical absence of limits placed on what animators can depict, cartoons are in principle free to explore extraordinary changes in familiar—or completely alien—sights. Klein paints animation as adept, almost prone, to constant 'molting, melting, melding, mutation,' an entropic impulse that may well need to be suppressed lest it defeat all other motivations for putting an idea to cel.[12] Animorphosis is an effect so common and capable of such 'realism' in the digital age that what once may have caused an awareness of the animator's virtuosity is now likely to be accepted as a convention, or worse, cliché. Yet for all its familiarity verging on overuse, ani-morphing is still capable of generating a profound feeling of beguilement. In the right contexts, feats of visual alchemy can be implemented so carefully that the spectator feels mesmerized as if they were witnessing magic.

Klein's discussion of animorphosis is exclusively visual, but we can imagine a similar approach for music. It is no stretch to substitute his 'molting, melting, melding, mutation' into a context of musical discourse. Indeed, similar terms often couch talk of thematic transformation. The analogy is possible thanks to the inherently temporal nature of film and music: Without the passage of time, transformation is impossible. In the context of animation, music is terrifically suited to realize Klein's mutagenic tendencies. In the hands of a skilled composer, it can alter the perception of time in its metamorphic image, drawing change out or causing it to seem spontaneous. It can capture the inherent queasy feeling of visual metamorphosis, or soften the blow through musical continuity. It can match each visual shift with corresponding musical gestures, or ignore individual morphs in favor of a more through-composed approach, emphasizing instead a certain affect or gradual trajectory. Collectively, these transmutative compositional strategies all proved ripe for sounding beneath the red-vaulted skies of Gotham City.

Metamorphic Mythoi

The world surrounding Batman—the characters, the technology, the kinds of stories Gotham makes possible—is often referred to as a mythology or *mythos*.[13] As a mode for examining stories and their roles in society, mythic analysis (for literature or otherwise) has waxed and waned in popularity over the past century, its totalizing and cultural-flattening tendencies coming under particular scrutiny in post-structuralist critiques. But, used modestly, and with a grain of skepticism, elements of a mythic-narratival theory prove quite helpful in moving from an informal to a more systematic approach to analyzing and interpreting *thematic change* in metamorphosis-prone multimedia.

Northrop Frye, a twentieth-century literary critic, devised a now well-known system of mythic-narratival analysis in his essay collection *Anatomy of Criticism* (1957), and his ideas, for all their unabashedly formalistic tendencies, have made recent inroads in musicology.[14] In particular, the work of Michael Klein and Byron Almén, both of whom were influenced by the semiotician James Liszka, have demonstrated the utility of Frye-style archetypal analysis to understanding music. However—and not surprisingly given new music-analytic frameworks are generally first utilized on the most sanctioned of musical styles—Klein and Almén's Frye-inspired work has focused exclusively on Western art-musical repertoires, and primarily at the level of the whole piece rather than isolated passages and smaller-scale moments.[15]

To paraphrase Frye's rich theory is obviously to do him a disservice but is necessary in an essay of this scope. The model of narrative codified in *Anatomy of Criticism* is essentially a cyclic one. Regardless of surface story structures or genre conventions, all plots are elaborations upon four basic archetypes (or *mythoi*), universal 'pregeneric' story structures which correspond to stages of life, and, relatedly, the four seasons. In order from spring to winter, they are Romance, Comedy, Tragedy, and Satire/Irony. The top half of this mythic wheel bears analogy with the outlook of innocence, while the bottom with experience.[16] Because Frye conceives the components of his system as intrinsically dynamic, he treats *motion* and *process* within and between these archetypal poles as constitutive of drama. The resulting four 'plot motions' are thus determined both with an associated innocence/experience outlook (*ethos*) with a certain conflict-driven narrative profile.[17]

Comedy, the first turn of the wheel, involves the establishment of a new, better society in which conflicts are not so much overcome as reconciled through a moment of epiphany or recognition—*anagnorisis*, after Aristotle—the same dramatic principle that, more darkly hued, drives the tragedy genre. The comic moment of recognition is paradigmatically reflected by the coming together of a romantic pair through marriage, concomitantly establishing a more idealistic status quo to replace the dangerous or absurd world from which the couple escapes.

The comic movement, like spring, is to move ever closer to the utopic stability of the next rung on the wheel of mythoi. This archetype is the arcadia of **Romance**. It has at its base a conflict of contradictory poles, or in Aristotelian terms *agon* (roughly, struggle). At the nexus of this agonistic tension lies the romantic hero, a member of a pre-established social order, who strives and succeeds against an external threat.

Tragedy, the Autumn of Frye's cycle, involves the hero's struggle with natural law, social prohibition, and/or unflinching fate. The conflict inevitably leads to his or her destruction, evoking a characteristic mixture of pity and fear—*pathos*—that feeling of purgative sympathy and cathartic elevation. With the tragic turn, the disrupted worldly order is rebalanced.

Tragedy may end badly for the protagonist, but the bleakest mythos is **Satire/Irony**, in which no hierarchies, norms, or forms of knowledge are stable and the very possibility of heroism or meaningfully goal-directed action is dubious. Satire is distinguished from irony by its capacity for subversive humor. Irony, on the other hand, possesses an altogether darker outlook. In the words of James Jakób Liszka, a semiotician who took up the mantle of Frye's mytho-narratival criticism, satire 'recounts the failures of norms or hierarchies or values as they break on the wheel of fate or on the rack of an inexorable or supremely powerful cultural force, and end in the *sparagmos* of the hero and the anomie of his values.'[18] Or, in Frye's own dire assessment, irony presents 'human life in terms of a largely unrelieved bondage.'[19]

The potential for Frye's mythoi to describe narratives of metamorphosis, especially in terms of change impacting a character (and, we shall see, leitmotif) is hopefully evident from their cursory description above. A romantic transformation, for example, can be said to alter the protagonist over the course of their quest in a goal-directed way, through struggle with and negation of some opposing contradictory force. Its characteristic form of change thus might be called *Evolutionary*. A comedic transformation is more dialectical: Opposing forces are reconciled, changing them through reconciliation of difference—thus *Combinatorial*. Tragic transformation, contrasted with both the romantic and comedic, involves divisive change in which stability is restored by the separation or dissolution of the individual; it can therefore be designated *Destructive*. The duality of Frye's Satire/Irony category is reflected in two varieties of transformation, either a negation in principle (change is impossible) or an unavoidably disorderly affirmation (change is ever-present). This inherent duality is captured in the transformative binary *Permanent/Anarchic* transformation.

These four metamorphic categories can easily be mapped onto tales of the Dark Knight and his enemies. Two-Face, who suffers a tragic fall from grace and with it a dramatic split of personality, is a neat example of a negatively-colored *destructive* transformation. Catwoman, on the other hand, fuses opposing forces of her psyche—human materialism and feline cunning— into a persona who is among the best-adjusted (if still off-kilter) of the *B:TAS* Rogue's Gallery. Batman embodies an archetypal hybrid that Frye, who dismissed the blending of opposed mythoi, might have balked at: An *evolutionary-destructive* transformation. His maturation clearly involves a striving for change, evident especially in the nigh-Wagnerian 'Birth of Batman' scene. But this metamorphosis is predicated on trauma, a quest for vengeance that effectively and irretrievably fractures his personality in two, the Bat and the

Wayne. This transformational profile reflects the mixed romantic and tragic aspects of Batman's career and shows that *destructive* change may well be desired by a character as a means of fulfilling some overarching romantic goal.

Table 9.1 presents a master table of metamorphic categories drawn from Frye and translated into musical terms. For an additional aid in conceptualizing these transformational archetypes—and a means of further analogizing visual and sonic metamorphosis—an (*extremely schematic*!) geometric representation of the four categories is also provided.[20]

The musical categories in Table 9.1 include recognized processes of thematic transformation which are active in *Batman*'s scoring style. Examples from some of the best-known classical practitioners of thematic transformation are provided, with the intent that recognizing their compositional strategies in a few models will obviate in-depth exposition of how musical metamorphosis can happen on a fine-grained level. The sense of evolution

TABLE 9.1 Metamorphic categories in narrative and music

Frye's Mythoi	Romance	Comedy	Tragedy	Satire/Irony
Transformational Trajectory	Evolution	Combination	Destruction	Permanence/Anarchy
Nature of Character Change	Character strives for goal	Character reconciles opposing forces	Opposing forces effect divisive change on character	Character unable to achieve change or relinquishes control
Visual Analogue				
THEMATIC TRANSFORMATION ARCHETYPES	APOTHEOSIS	FUSION	FRAGMENTATION	VARIATION
Nature of Musical Change	Theme strives for, achieves completion or actualization	Themes combined in musically rational or productive way	Theme dissected, split into parts, loses or has liquidated a characteristic aspect	Theme refuses change/theme passes through kaleidoscopic transformations without hierarchy
Examples in Wagner, Liszt, and Strauss	*Die Walküre* (Wotan's Spear --> Brunhilde's Love) *Les Preludes* *Death and Transfiguration*	*Die Meistersinger* (Overture: Combination of 3 Leitmotifs) Sonata in B-Minor (3rd Movement Fugue) *Also Sprach Zarathustra* (Nature Motif in Tanzlied)	*Parsifal* (Prelude Grundthema") *Faust Symphony* (Mephistopheles Movement) *Die Frau Ohne Schatten* (Trial Scene)	*Ring Cycle* (Nature, Ring Motifs) *Totentanz* Variations *Don Quixote*
Examples in *Batman: The Animated Series*	Batman; Batgirl Leitmotifs	Harley Quinn + Poison Ivy's Leitmotifs	Two-Face; Mad-Hatter; Clayface Leitmotifs	Joker; Penguin Leitmotifs

and goal-directedness of the Romantic paradigm is translated to the notion of thematic apotheosis. This occurs when an initially unstable or ill-defined theme moves from an embryonic state to a fully realized statement, often at the climax of a work in blazing tutti orchestration; the Greek 'Telos' (purpose) or German 'Verklärung' (transfiguration) might also have been used. *Fusion*, the comedic approach to thematic transformation, involves synthesizing themes in musically harmonious ways, such as carefully coordinated counterpoint or the production of a third theme from elements of two formerly independent ones. The 'harmonious' condition is important: The fusion of musical elements—even if associated with negative affects on their own—should not sound incongruous or forced, else we are likely hearing another transformational archetype. *Fragmentation*, a technique perhaps most archetypically displayed at the end of the slow movement of Beethoven's Third Symphony (*Eroica*), splits a once-whole theme into constituent parts. It fractures, corrupts, dissolves, disintegrates.

The spirit of Satire is a little more complicated to translate into thematic transformational terms. The familiar process of *Variation*, in its constant working over of the same material in different lights, does suggest the genre's emphasis on the breakdown of stable norms or consistent identities, or alternatively its ability to present multiple, potentially unreconciled perspectives on the same idea. Variation implies infinite mutability—think of the endless permutations across centuries of the 'BACH' motif (B♭-A-C-B♮), a melodic pattern whose 'essence' is so slight that it permits mutation in any texture, or indeed, any musical idiom, from Bach himself to Brahms to Schnittke.

By virtue of its lack of goal orientation, variation as a thematic transformational strategy is set apart from the romantic apotheosis model. In the apotheotic paradigm, we might think of working backwards, from a summational statement of a theme to its more inchoate predecessors. This kind of temporal dependency is besides the point in a pure variation form. That is, there is no intrinsic concept of hierarchy or directionality in musical variation, while that is the very quintessence of transformative apotheosis. However, this distinction applies only to the purest conceptual formulation of these two transformational archetypes. In actual practice, most pieces in variation form do have an intentional trajectory, and most works that build to an apotheotic iteration are not *completely* based on a single-minded telic process, in which no single musical detail fails to contribute to an evolutionary trajectory in some way. Variation + Apotheosis is a viable thematic transformational strategy, in other words, as is any other combination. This model does not bar the mixing of archetypes, but rather admits and encourages it. I leave it to the reader to dream up combinations of two (or more!) of these models and locate examples in any repertoire they wish![21]

Fragmentation and Reintegration in 'Perchance to Dream'

The episode 'Perchance to Dream' (1992, S1E21) features some of Walker's most clever and sustained leitmotivic development, the analysis of which will nicely demonstrate the usefulness of thinking in terms of Frye-inspired archetypes. In particular, her score is based on a mixture of the qualities of *pathos* and *anagnorisis*—in musical terms following a fragmentation-to-reintegration trajectory. The episode follows a 'concocted paradise' trope in which Batman is trapped within an idyllic but illusory dream state. The action revolves around the hero's growing awareness of this fabricated perfect world and his eventual break out back into the series' veridical diegesis. The agent behind Batman's entrapment is *B:TAS*'s resident mind-control specialist, Jervis Tetch, a.k.a. The Mad Hatter (Roddy McDowall). Tetch is revealed as the orchestrator of this illusion only late in the episode; correspondingly, the true conflict takes place between various aspects of Batman/Bruce Wayne's ego, not with some external antagonist.

Walker does not hide the fact that this is a Mad Hatter episode; the title card bears a straightforward rendition of his quizzical leitmotif, and much of the score consists of his material in varying degrees of disguise, which an attentive viewer will notice with little trouble. Accordingly, musical interest is not aimed at a moment of a big reveal, an unambiguous disclosure of The Mad Hatter leitmotif. Rather it is Walker's ingenious *fragmentation* of Hatter's theme that drives the episode's score, supercharging the dramatic tension surrounding how/when Batman properly understands his situation. By the time the theme properly *reintegrates*, the music has commented more on Bruce Wayne's psychology than it ever did Jervis Tetch's.

Example 9.4 displays The Mad Hatter leitmotif in undisguised form as it appears at the episode's beginning. The theme in this fully-fledged guise does not return until the last seconds of the episode: Wayne's dream state is illustrated instead by a collection of motivic splinters drawn from this odd little *grundthema*. Walker extracts four components and allows them to split, fuse, and develop independently before their final re-synthesis. The first derived motif is the head of the Hatter's tune itself (**Component 1** in Example 9.4). One of the many striking transformations of this melody is in a tense cue near the episode's climax [15:32], where we hear its natural whimsy violated as stretto entries in the brass crawl over each other in panic. The leitmotif's second detachable aspect (**Component 2**) is its arpeggiated chromatic bass. The way this figure is left loping on its own during one key scene when Wayne's situation is beginning to dawn on him [11:45] is an elegant expression of the character's confused suspicion. The tenor line as played by horns in the Main Title forms yet another separable building block (**Component 3**); it becomes a malleable third-filling motif of vague unease, heard

EXAMPLE 9.4 Walker, 'Perchance to Dream,' title cue.

prominently when Wayne confronts an impostor Batman on the roof of a *Vertigo*-esque clock tower [16:38]. Finally, Walker extracts a harmonic idea from the alto voice of the third and fourth measures (**Component 4**), shrouded behind parallel harmonization and octave displacements. This serves as a granule of musical aporia for moments when the Hatter's dream façade shows hints of cracking. An early instance [5:58] sees the pattern voiced in queasy, overlapping clarinet dyads, with Wayne tapping his pen on a desk in an office he doesn't quite understand how he arrived in.

These thematic splinters, once detached from the stable Hatter theme, participate in motivic free play, sometimes coalescing, more often spun out rhapsodically. We are in the world of satirical *Variation*, where no (musical) value is more stable than any other, and strange resemblances and anarchic juxtapositions are the norm. It is interesting that, save for the last, post-reveal rendition of the theme, all the Hatter's material is firmly attached to *Bruce Wayne's* subject position, not Tetch's. These disintegrated musical ideas are used to characterize Wayne's own psychological dissociation, a state rendered literally once he does battle with faux-Batman at the episode's climax, Hatter motifs blasting away at each other as the hero struggles to reassemble his broken persona.

At times in 'Perchance to Dream,' Walker allows the Hatter's influence to infect Batman's own musical identity. Aspects of the Hatter's motif are shown to betray uncanny linkages with the Dark Knight's *own* leitmotivic material. For instance, when Wayne's parents are revealed, living and breathing [3:56], Walker responds with music shown in Example 9.5. The material here is derived from the Hatter's tenor line (Component 3) but manifestly affined with Batman's own timbral, affective, even rhythmic domain, such as we encountered earlier in Example 9.3.

Even more telling is the scene in which Wayne's hallucination really begins to fray, the first 33 measures of which are offered in Example 9.6. As he thrashes around a bookcase in confusion, Walker's cue skillfully exhibits numerous thematic fragmentational procedures, each particle of the Hatter theme phasing in and out of the soundtrack at unpredictable moments and with eerie metrical displacements. Again, the impact of a swarm of entangled Hatter motives is enabled largely by the ramifications they bear on the Batman leitmotivic complex—observe the way in which a disconcertingly sunnified Batman theme dovetails *all too naturally* with particles of the Hatter tune at the cue's onset. This is thematic transformation of truly superlative musical sophistication and psychological insight.

By associating the fragmentary Hatter motifs with Bruce Wayne's gradual *anagnorisis*, Walker accomplishes three feats. On the surface, she offers clues as to the villain materially responsible for the episode's hallucinatory trap: This is thematic disguise in service of literal plot. Secondly, she illustrates a state of dream-induced identity confusion through leitmotivic disintegration and recombination: This is thematic fragmentation and variation in service of psychological shading. Thirdly, she renders in purely musical terms the instability of Wayne's personality, showing just how tenuous the sublimation of his all-too-human desires can ever be with

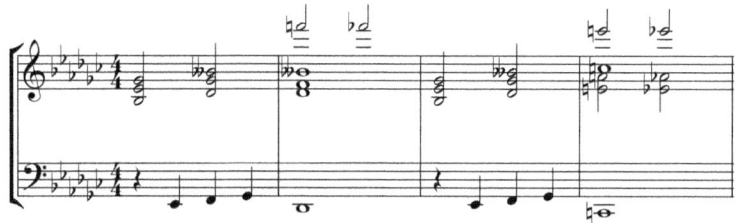

EXAMPLE 9.5   Walker, 'Perchance to Dream,' parents revealed.

EXAMPLE 9.6 Walker, 'Perchance to Dream,' illusion dissolving.

respect to his more proper persona as mythic angel of vengeance: This is thematic mismatching, interpenetration, and fusion in service of a character critique. It is only with the purging of Hatter's motivic material that Wayne-contra-Batman can reconsolidate his identity into a singular whole, Wayne-as-Batman. And so we hear definitive and reconstructed versions of the Hatter followed by Batman themes at the episode's conclusion [21:15], each unambiguously attached to the correct character. Yet even after this thematic rectification, a feeling of vague unease lingers: If music can hint at an undercurrent of similarity between Batman and the villains he battles, what's to say anything about the (musical) superheroic persona is coherent?

Molding/Modeling Clay

Figure 9.3 displays the title card to Clayface's two main episodes: 'Mudslide' (which we have already encountered), as well as the image for his introductory two-parter, 'Feat of Clay' (S1 E3–4). The music Walker provides for the 'Mudslide' title is a barely recognizable transformation of his tragic motif (pictured earlier in Example 9.2), now evoked merely by a chord progression and an implied melodic line that shares, more than it recreates, the theme's piteous affect. The picture ironizes the well-known trope of grinning and frowning masks as symbols for comic and tragic drama respectively. (An un-ironized version was recruited as the title card for the two-part origin story.) Where tragedy was counterbalanced by the possibility of a redemptive ending earlier in Clayface's villainous career, by 'Mudslide' the grinning mask must be replaced by something less optimistic. Instead, we see a shadow of Clayface's repellent physiognomy, implying either a generic distortion of comedy or some new, sinister outgrowth of tragedy: Tragi-*something*? Now that we have a model of metamorphic archetypes in place for narrative and musical domains, we are in a better place to inspect what this something is, and how it relates to the musical depiction of Batman's most protean adversary.

In 'Feat of Clay,' we witness Matt Hagen's initial descent into formlessness. The journey from famous character actor and 'man of a million faces' to amorphous blob has trappings of Frye's *tragic* archetype. The man Hagen is annihilated by the episode's end, in an intensely pathetic scene where

FIGURE 9.3 'Feat of Clay' and 'Mudslide,' title cards.

he appears to self-destruct through wild, uncontrolled shape-shifting. The immutable (comic-book) law Hagen runs up against may well be the cosmic injunction against the accumulation of too much power: No character seems fit to control such an excess of possibility. Certainly, Hagen's personal flaws, his narcissism and venality, are also at work in bringing about catastrophe. However, the limitedness of his consciousness—Hagen is allowed no opportunities for self-reflection, and it's doubtful whether he has the capacity—bars him from achieving a truly tragic *pathos*.

Rather than adhering to a tragic narrative archetype, Clayface's plight is better understood in terms of the *Satire/Irony* paradigm. A critical aspect of satire is its undercutting of values and stability. Hagen's degeneration is a satire on the idea of acting, and on the stability of personal identity in general, and in dramatic actors in particular. For what is a character actor but a person who can assume many exaggerated roles but has no type, no consistent on-screen persona? This observation on the soulless nature of acting is carried over, in typically B:TAS literalizing fashion, into a monster who exemplifies that very lack. Hagen's devolution, accompanied by his mutable leitmotifs, implies that whatever stable personality the actor once had has been lost in a sticky mass of orange.

Clayface embodies an *anarchy* of substance: His ability to shape-shift, and the diminishing presence of his former ego (at one point, he exclaims to Batman, 'There is no Hagen—it's only me now, Clayface!') mark him as a kind of wandering blob of malevolent disorder. Discussing figures in popular entertainment who can change shape, Terrie Waddell links the shape-shifter with the Jungian archetype of the *trickster*. Tricksters inevitably serve to expose holes in an apparently stable order, a transgressive force obviously affined with Satire and its derivatives. In the case of Clayface, that order is personal identity itself. Waddell claims that 'when the trickster function kicks in to address the unstable, erroneous and splintered identities of the chief protagonists… the brittle nature of the persona, "semblance," or "two-dimensional reality," as Jung called it, is made patently clear.'[22]

We have noted the unusual duality of Clayface's motivic material earlier. Now we are in a better position to account for his bithematic personality. The tragic and horrific leitmotifs capture the mixed-generic aspects of his story respectively. The former, capable at turns of tender pity and over-the-top grandeur, evokes a kind of theatrical pathos, bordering on and sometimes lapsing into sentimentality. The construction of this leitmotif out of a four-fold repetition of a single melodic cell ($\hat{6}-\hat{4}-\hat{5}$) implies something already *fragmented*. It is as if Walker, resisting the urge to create a fully lyrical melody for Hagen, opted for a pre-digested sequence fused from one single idea. The metamorphosis has been already achieved, frozen in this little melody. There is a miniature narrative embedded in the theme, a trajectory of intensification from the minor tonic (iv–i) to the minor dominant (i–v), followed by a reversal (VI–III) and collapse (iv–V). The insistence upon that $\hat{6}-\hat{4}-\hat{5}$ motif generates a strong sense of inevitability for the tragic (i.e.; minor tonic-confirming) character of the final authentic cadence. Yet the phrase is open-ended, inherently unstable, always terminating on the dominant chord and its attendant fifth scale degree. Hagen's dark fate is suggested, but not sealed. The return to that initial motif at the cadence also hints at cyclicality, though not necessarily of the identity-purgative variety, for which Clayface's second theme seems tailor-made.

Clayface's horror motif contrasts with its tragic counterpart in readily audible ways: Jagged and unsympathetic as opposed to the latter's lyrical sentimentality. The motif occupies a different mode of harmonic construction from the diatonic tragic theme as well, its blunt triadic parallelism growling over a dissonant chromatic bass line—easier to detach as an independent polyphonic line for its relative harmonic autonomy. Here, too, is an element of obsessive cyclicality, now in the form of an incessant return to the same pitch (for example, B♭–A–B♭–D♭–C–B♭–A–B♭). The compact, anti-lyrical quality lends itself well to *variation* (and its mytho-narrative archetype); indeed, no two versions of the horror motif ever sound the same.

The melodic sequence's similarity to the famous BACH motif (B♭–A–C–B♮) is hard to miss once one is aware of it. The major- rather than minor-third interval at the motif's core prevents a perfect equivalency of the two four-note cells, but the aural impact of tightly constrained chromaticism is similar. Both are 'germs'—the negative connotation is appropriate for Clayface!—able to transform and mutate endlessly to suit new environs. The chromatic makeup of the two mottos, preventing as it does a standard diatonic habitation, means there exists no prototypical harmonization or arrangement, no musical ideal behind those four, free-floating notes. The horror motif differs from the BACH germ not so much by dint of pitch dissimilarity as it does connotation. In principle, the well-known classical idea can be employed in any affective context, yet even with its gnarled chromaticism, it tends to connote elite, polished, *learned* extramusical matters. Clayface's second motif by contrast finds itself spun out in variations that invariably maintain a sense of unease or tension; the motif could have easily come from a horror movie. This resistant sameness, compounded with the motif's potential for (and, via the BACH connection, associative link with) variation, places the horror motif and its narratival tendencies squarely in the *Satiric/Irony* quadrant of our thematic transformational space. Whenever we hear the motif, we are assuredly hearing a variation of it, but a variant with a suspiciously limited emotional range. The dichotomy of mutability and stasis that characterizes Frye's Satire/Irony category and its multimedia analogs is powerfully reflected here.

Like Batman, Clayface is treated to a dramatic birth scene. At the end of the first half of 'Feat of Clay: Part One' (scored, under the supervision of Walker, by Jeff Atmajian and Carl Johnson), Hagen's friend discovers him slouched in a car. The actor has been doused with near-fatal amounts of a substance he used to cosmetically resculpt his disfigured face [20:04]. A tentative, embryonic version of the horror motif is heard, gently, and only with the first three notes, devoid of the lumbering dotted rhythm of the fully formed theme. Or is it a perverted, chromatic variant of Hagen's tragic motif, grasping onto its familiar minor third range and down-up contour? The friend places his hand on what he takes to be the actor's shoulder, only to see it leave a squishy imprint. Sympathy kicks in for a moment, with the friend's question 'Matt is that you? What in heaven's name did they do to ya?,' accompanied by a short rendition of the tragic motif in its bittersweet diatonic clothing.

The former-Hagen opens his eyes and sees himself in the rear-view mirror. It is a moment of recognition, one that provokes instant disgust in both the friend and the nascent villain. Clayface lets out a tremendous moan, and the soundtrack quickly responds with an abrupt transition to the horror theme, now in fully mature form. The screen goes black, and 'To Be Continued' appears, accompanied by the horror theme, almost triumphant in its sheer assertiveness. That brief intimation of musical empathy, the more 'human(e)' origin of the horror motif in the tragic theme, has been sinisterly tainted. If the horror motif were indeed derived from the tragic motif, this on-screen birth implies there will be no return to Hagen's once-human state.[23] It is a case of the potentially pessimistic shadow of the romantic ethos, where the dramatic *telos* is aimed at disaster rather than self-fulfillment, and musical motifs grope not toward some life-affirming climax but a new state of polymorphic perversity.

As in 'Perchance to Dream,' this mixture of narrative trajectories engulfs the Dark Knight and his music as well. Indeed, Hagen's degeneration seems to put quotation marks around the notion of 'personal identity' for any and all Gothamites. As the man becomes nothing but a series of empty masks, it is inevitable his heroic secret sharer should be sucked into the destabilizing goo as well. Unable to best Clayface physically, Batman lays a clever trap at the end of 'Feat of Clay: Part 2': Hagen is drawn into a room and subjected to images of his past life—or, rather, his past *roles* [17:01]. Batman hopes for a redemptive solution to the clay menace. But instead of the expected response of pacified remorse, a wild, uncontrolled bout of virtuosic shape-shifting follows. (See Figure 9.4.) Unable to contain the multitude of masks that 'make up' his outward identity, Hagen appears to self-destruct.

Satire is key to understanding the strangely ineffectual nature of Batman's rescue of Clayface at the conclusion of 'Feat of Clay: Part Two.' The hero's ploy actually pushes Hagen over the edge by presenting him with this visual collage, overwhelming him with overabundance rather than reminding the creature of its humanity. Batman's implication in the demise of Hagen is mitigated, however, by another ironic twist. We learn at the end of the two-parter that the expiration was an act, a fantastically over-the-top staging of a death scene, and the real villain is still at large. This endows Gotham with yet another cyclical villain-hero game that ensures the city remains perpetually unstable.

Clayface, as an anarchic trickster, is able to cast doubt on the ego-stability of Batman. The last specific morph he assumes before expiring is the appearance of Bruce Wayne, shown in an uncomfortable close-up, face visibly screwed up in agony and terror. (See Figure 9.4c.) As we saw already with The Mad Hatter, villains often are made to reflect some insight back on Batman during the course of a *B:TAS* episode. Rarely are those revelatory moments as eloquent—or grotesque—as this, however. The shape-shift is not motivated by the plot and serves entirely as a disturbing reminder of the mutability of Wayne/Batman's own persona. He, too, is a damaged trickster, a 'clay-face' who sculpts his image no less arbitrarily as a justice-obsessed urban vampire. Norman Klein observes that 'in the world governed by animorphs, [this is essentially Clayface's world, and more broadly speaking, the world of Gotham] brute matter comes to life but has forgotten why. Instead, it languishes somewhere between discovery and annihilation, fails to connect.'[24] A facet of Bruce Wayne, it

FIGURE 9.4 'Feat of Clay: Part Two,' uncontrolled transformations.

seems, languishes in the muddy soup. The threat of Clayface, his satirical barb so to speak, is to unsettle that which may have gained uncritical acceptance at this point in the show: The stability and very coherency of the Batman persona.

Multimodal Morphing

Previously, I noted that metamorphic music can interact with animation in a variety of ways—matching each morph, bringing out feelings of unease, or altering the perception of morphic time, for instance. It has been taken for granted so far that the music in *B:TAS* acts in a fundamentally collaborative way. That is, it was assumed that Walker and the rest of the composing team were asked to write music appropriate for the scene in some general sense, rather than music that contradicts or undercuts the teleplay's desired effect. However, taking into account a multi-layered notion of multimedia interaction, where different levels of meaning—both surface and subtextual—need not replicate each other, it becomes possible to read scenes as instantiating these narratival-transformational relationships in more complex ways than one-to-one relationships demand. To conclude this chapter, we now consider the ways in which morphic music *and* sound interact to produce meaning, without resting on the crutch of presumed semiotic reinforcement or redundancy.

Examples of precise coordination between layers of sound, visuals, and narrative are not difficult to locate in *B:TAS*: We would expect as much from any mainstream form of entertainment. Batman's first encounter with Clayface ('Feat of Clay: Part Two,' [9:30]) offers an exemplar of just such close audiovisual synchrony. In this sequence, a series of variations on the horror motif closely mimic the various forms (and implied degrees of peril) Hagen assumes. The rapidity of change makes Clayface's animorphic antics positively balletic, bringing out the virtuosic spontaneity of his abilities. The cue veers toward mickey-mousing when Hagen involuntarily assumes Batman's face—another opportunity for one of those villains-reflect-back-on-Batman moments, here with a darkly satirical twist. The soundtrack responds to the visual mutation with a rapid mutation of the recently heard Batman leitmotif into a twisted 'clayful' version [9:50]. Hagen is a *tabula rasa* here, able to absorb and pervert the identities of others.[25] Clayface's birth pangs during his earlier origin scene, on the other hand, seem to synchronize with image at a slightly more abstract level. The score follows Hagen's state of mind, without matching precisely with the cuts and actions of the two characters on screen, and it sculpts the emotional trajectory through a careful transformation of Clayface's twin motifs.

Most revealing are cases in which musical and visual modes of metamorphosis do *not* line up. Consider again Clayface's big finish at the end of 'Feat of Clay: Part Two.' Walker chooses not to accompany his rapid cycling through faces with individually appropriate changes in the score. This would be technically daunting but certainly accomplishable task. She opts instead for an ultimately more effective approach: A deviously muddied version of the horror theme's bass line—or is it a misshapen cousin of the tragic theme's scooping melody?—that quietly rumbles under the sound effects as a low, chromatic ostinato. Example 9.7 portrays the basis for this marvelous feat of dramatic underscoring.

Despite a certain family resemblance to both horror and tragic themes, Walker's material for this sequence forgoes straightforward renditions of Clayface's familiar leitmotifs. The character has so exceeded the limits of his bodily integrity that it is hard to imagine any theme adhering to him any longer. The atmospheric scoring effectively focuses attention squarely on the stupendous feat of animated transfiguration that occupies the frame, while simultaneously contributing a degree of tonal unease at the border of audibility, a classic means of insinuating insanity through music. The cue's sluggish tempo also effectively slows down the metamorphic *coup de théâtre*, freeing the viewer to draw connections between the dispersed and dissolved ego of Matt Hagen and the inefficacious figure of Batman in the background. The avoidance of mickey-mousing siphons emphasis away from each specific visage Hagen assumes, heightening instead the underlying tragi-satiric flux of identity enacted before our eyes and ears. If the sublime comingles awe and dread, Walker's more 'sticky sublime' transmutes that dread into outright revulsion. The monster's descent into formlessness needs no theme—for in the world of Gotham, where maintaining a stable ego seems a Sisyphean ordeal, a leitmotif is, in the end, just another mask, unable to stay attached forever.

Returning to this essay's initial scene will help draw all these analytical and narratological strands together. Recall from the chapter's beginning that the escape scene from 'Mudslide' posed a problem of how to interpret musical and visual information together. The musical

EXAMPLE 9.7   Walker, 'Feat of Clay: Part Two,' ground bass for Hagen's big finish.

metamorphoses featured seem oddly emphasized for a scene with no real animorphic interest (besides the dripping hand). But the apparent lack of visual motivation for musical transformations presents a challenge only if we limit ourselves to the episode's narratival foreground. The motivic play here is an indicator that the escaping female scientist is currently *in* a metamorphosed state, not that the audience should expect her to be changing in synchrony with the soundtrack. As such, the music is operating at more of a subtextual level, requiring an implicit understanding of Clayface's general condition.

What Walker has latched onto in her scoring of this scene is a certain affective stance with which the audience is meant to relate to Clayface as he makes his getaway. Consider the guise of the tragic theme here: Elongated and fragmented, strewn out over the cue like the puddles of glop trailing Hagen (refer back to Example 9.1). The flute, usually an instrument of consolation, here sounds mildly demented. Gone is the unmixed, plaintive harmony that typically supports the theme, replaced by dissonant shudders in string and winds. The horror theme is less recognizable as such, being a distilled and detached result of the lurching bass accompaniment that typically undergirds the motto. Still, the line is manifestly the product of thematic transformation, in keeping with the flexible reshaping of the horror material at all other points in the episode's score. These two motifs, played against each other thus, represent a negatively-inflected instance of the *fusion* variety of musical transformation: The reconciliation is dangerous and obscene, but nevertheless rational given the narrative of the scene. Clayface's getaway suggests the character's tragic dependency on chemicals—an allegory throughout for the agonies of drug use. But the prospect of his successful reintegration by this substance, not just the sight of his runny flesh, is horrific. After all, he's a sadistic personage, well-deserving of his place in Batman's villainous Rouges' Gallery. As such, turbid rivulets of visual, musical, and narrative metamorphosis converge to offer a distinctly emergent dramatic mythos to the cue and scene at large: *Tragisatirico-comedy*—pity mixed with doubt, disgust, and perverse enjoyment.

This chapter has concerned itself with analogs between various aspects of musical-multimedia storytelling that all involve the idea of transformation. By spinning out variations on Frye's mythic archetypes for both narrative and compositional metamorphoses, I hope to have illuminated the rich variety of ways in which change can be thematized in the arts, particularly in the realm of screen music. The model sketched out here hopefully goes some way to adding systematicity to the analysis of thematic transformation, a frequently observed yet rarely methodically investigated phenomenon in music. Not every multimedia text will host musical transformations as technically sophisticated or dramatically suggestive as Shirley Walker's masterly contribution to *Batman: The Animated Series*, of course. But, as I hope to have shown, even the most modest of thematic manipulations can sometimes hold the key to unlocking the deepest—and darkest—of narrative meanings.

Notes

1 All images and timestamps are derived from the official DVD releases of these shows (*Batman: The Animated Series*, Volumes One, Two, Three, and Four, [DVD], Dir. Various. [Warner Brothers Studio, 1992 (2004)]. Transcriptions have been rendered exclusively by ear by the author from the above DVD releases and expanded soundtrack recordings from the La-La Land label (*Batman The Animated Series: Limited Edition*, Volumes One, Two, Three, and Four [CD set], Comp. Various. (La-La Land Records Inc., 2008, 2012, 2014, 2016).
2 Hexatonic refers to the pitch collection, well-mined by screen media composers for its strange properties, that is derived from alternating semitones and minor thirds (e.g.,: B-C-E♭-E-G-A♭).
3 Hugh Macdonald, 'Transformation, thematic,' *Grove Music Online*, 2001, accessed 20 July 2022, https://doi.org/10.1093/gmo/9781561592630.article.28269.
4 The motivic materials and transformations thereof in these respective franchises have been analyzed in various studies. These include Doug Adams, *The Music of the Lord of the Rings Films* (South Korea: Carpentier, 2010); David Butler, 'The Work of Music in the Age of Steel: Themes, Leitmotifs and Stock Music in the *New Doctor Who*' in Kevin Donnelly and Philip Hayward (eds.), *Music in Science Fiction Television* (New York and London: Routledge, 2013): 163–178; Melinda Eschenfelder, 'Musical Narratives: Thematic Combination and Alignment in Fantasy and Superhero Films,' MA Thesis (University of Oregon, 2019); Megan Francisco, '"The Shape of Things to Come": Identity and Destiny in the Music of *Battlestar Galactica*,' PhD diss. (University of Washington, 2020); and Frank Lehman, 'The Themes of *Star Wars*: Catalogue and Commentary,' in Emilio Audissino (ed.), *John Williams: Music for Films, Television and the Concert Stage* (Turnhout: Brepols, 2018), 153–189, and Lehman, 'A Guide to the Musical Themes of *Indiana Jones*' (2021), http://franklehman.com/indiana-jones-themes/.
5 Prior musicological research into Batman has focused primarily on live-action iterations. See, for example Janet K. Halfyard, *Danny Elfman's Batman: A Film Score Guide* (Lanham: Scarecrow Press, 2004) and Vasco Hexel, *Hans Zimmer and James Newton Howard's The Dark Knight: A Film Score Guide* (Lanham: Rowman and Littlefield, 2016).
6 Matthew Bribitzer-Stull, *Understanding the Leitmotif: From Wagner to Hollywood Film Music* (Cambridge: Cambridge University Press, 2015), 6.
7 Audio commentary on *Batman: The Animated Series*, DVD Volume 1 Disc One, Episode 'On Leather Wings.'
8 Halfyard, *Danny Elfman's Batman*, 12–13.
9 Hagen becomes such a non-character that in 'Mudslide' he is unable to express thoughts beyond quoting himself from old movie roles. By the time Clayface is reintroduced in *The New Batman Adventures*, Batman no longer recognizes him as Hagen (and therefore offers him no opportunity for redemption).
10 For more in-depth analysis of Walker's 'Birth of Batman' cue, its remarkable harmonic make-up in particular, see Frank Lehman, *Hollywood Harmony:*

Musical Wonder and the Sound of Cinema (New York and Oxford: Oxford University Press, 2018), 108–110.
11 Norman Klein, 'Animation and Animorphs: Brief Disappearing Act,' in Vivian Sobchack (ed.), *Meta-morphing: Visual Transformation and the Culture of Quick Change* (Minneapolis: University of Minnesota Press, 2000), 21.
12 Ibid., 25.
13 See, for example, Halfyard, *Danny Elfman's Batman*, 50, and Bill Boichel, 'Batman: Commodity as Myth,' in Roberta Pearson and William Uricchio (eds.), *The Many Lives of the Batman: Critical Approaches to a Superhero and His Media* (New York: Routledge, 1991), 2.
14 Northrop Frye, *Anatomy of Criticism: Four Essays* (Princeton: Princeton University Press, 1971).
15 A thorough summary of the nuances of these particular adaptations of Frye-style narrative analysis to musicology is well beyond the scope of this chapter, but readers interested in a representative sampling should consult Byron Almén, *A Theory of Musical Narrative* (Bloomington: University of Indiana Press, 2008); Michael Klein, 'Ironic Narrative, Ironic Reading,' *Journal of Music Theory* 53.1 (2009): 95–136; and Yayoi Uno Everett, *Reconfiguring Myth and Narrative in Contemporary Opera* (Bloomington: University of Indiana Press, 2015). A tentative endorsement of narratological priorities (though not explicitly Frye-derived ones) to film may be found in Nicholas Reyland, 'The Beginnings of a Beautiful Friendship: Music, Narratology and Screen Music Studies,' *Music, Sound, and the Moving Image* 6.1 (2012): 55–71. Also relevant, though not influenced by Frye, is the groundbreaking music-semiological work of Jean-Jacques Nattiez, as in *Music and Discourse: Towards a Semiology of Music* (Princeton: Princeton University Press, 1990).
16 Frye, *Anatomy*, 162.
17 For Frye and Liszka, each mythos has a definite positive or negative valence, mapping loosely onto archetypes with victorious endings vs. defeated endings. For the purposes of music-thematic analysis, it is advantageous to divest these metamorphic categories of their positive/negative requirements. An *Evolutionary/Romantic* metamorphosis, for example, could easily be pitiful and frightening if the result of a character (or character leitmotif) striving is to become an arch-villain. Similarly, an *Anarchic/Satiric* metamorphosis may be joyous if a character's eyes are opened to the inherent instability of the world, leading to a transformation that accords positively with this freedom, *sparagmos* is coupled with *anagnorisis*.
18 James Jakób Liszka, *The Semiotic of Myth* (Bloomington & Indianapolis: Indiana University Press, 1989), 132.
19 Frye, *Anatomy*, 238.
20 The association of various archetypes with visual change should be evident from the diagram. In a *Telic*-morph, an object becomes something else in essence (a square becomes a circle). *Synthetic* and *Analytical* morphs involve a multiplicity of objects, in which essence isn't questioned so much as integrity or constitution—the objects are either conjoined or split apart (a circle and square combine and come apart). The *Solidity/Flux* morph repudiates *telos* by insisting absolutely on either object-permanence or its impossibility. In the case of *flux*, the change might be one of perspective rather than essence, which may very well not exist. The amoeboid shape is straightforward, but the seemingly solid three-dimensional cube was chosen cheekily, for it demonstrates both the *Solidity* and *Flux* category; the top of the box depends entirely on our point of view, rather than an essential 'top-ness,' and thus is an intrinsically unstable (or multistable) image. Alternatively, one could imagine the category analogized

with the four-dimensional hypercube, whose complete form is ungraspable to lower-dimensional viewers, who can only observe shifting its 3-D projections. A discussion of precisely this morpho-mathematical idea comes up in Kevin Fischer, 'Tracing the Tesseract: A Conceptual Prehistory of the Morph,' in Vivian Sobchack (ed.), *Meta-morphing: Visual Transformation and the Culture of Quick Change* (Minneapolis: University of Minnesota Press, 2000), 103–129.
21 One might object that such gleeful interbreeding of categories undercuts the very distinctions we aim to make in the first place. Yet in all examples of mixed musical-transformations, the processes which are combined remain distinct. For example, contrapuntal-fragmentation, a ubiquitous technique in symphonic development sections, does not invalidate the opposed categories but rather shows them at work and might even draw their muto-archetypical distinctions into higher relief.
22 Terrie Waddell, *Mis/takes: Archetypes, Myth and Identity in Screen Fiction* (New York: Routledge, 2006), 36–46.
23 Hagen's tragic motif in this more acerbic setting recalls the treatment of the chaconne-theme of Malcolm Arnold's Third Symphony, Second Movement, a set of queasy *tragico* variations on at times identically-structured (and comparably protean) intervallic germ [B♭–G–A].
24 Norman Klein, 'Animation and Animorphs,' 34. An even more spectacular illustration of this sentiment comes from the episode of *The New Batman Adventures* in which an ailing Clayface splits off a 'scout' to reconnoiter the surround before he attains full strength. The scout, in the form of a little girl, begins to gain sentience of her own, but is a total amnesiac. In one of the darkest scenes in the show, Clayface-father swallows this budding-consciousness alive, reintegrating her/it in a truly disturbing murder scene.
25 This is not so unlike the Mephistopheles of Liszt's *Faust Symphony*, a force who has no theme of his own but who twists and blasphemes those of Faust and Gretchen. Indeed, in much the same manner as 'Perchance to Dream,' one almost cannot but begin to hear Walker's Batman leitmotif through the dark mirror of Clayface's. (And certain motivic features facilitate this linkage; it is left to the reader to tease them out.)

10

POST-TONAL THEORY AND HOLLYWOOD SCORES

Three Analytical Vignettes

Erik Heine

Post-tonal music, rightly or wrongly, tends to be associated with horror films. As Neil Lerner writes in the Preface to *Music in the Horror Film*, music in this genre is often more disturbing to the audience than the visual elements:

> It may be regarded as a commonplace of twentieth-century music history that film music absorbed some practices of aesthetic modernism from the concert hall, and that in particular the genre of the horror film turned to unresolved dissonance, atonality, and timbral experimentation as part of its characteristic stylistic qualities. Frightening images and ideas can be made even more intense when accompanied with frightening musical sounds.[1]

Lerner makes the case that a tonal language can function as a generic marker and a way of provoking anxiety in the audience. But it would be hasty to assume music involving 'unresolved dissonance, atonality, and timbral experimentation' has one single meaning in film. If we accept that these matters of pitch design act as cultural codes in film music for 'the disturbing,' and they do so specifically by virtue of their opposition to consonance and functional tonality, then should we, as an audience, be disturbed *any* time we hear atonal, serial, or even non-functional passages? How should triadic harmony that does not clearly adhere to the norms of the tonal Common Practice be interpreted? And what are we to make of films such as *The Exorcist* and *The Shining* which make use of pre-existing music from Béla Bartók, György Ligeti, and Krzysztof

DOI: 10.4324/9781003001171-10

Penderecki, despite these concert composers not necessarily intending to represent anything horrific through their music?

One need not look far for examples of a post-tonal musical language being used for purposes other than to disturb or frighten filmgoers. One of the earliest serial scores for a Hollywood film came from Leonard Rosenman. He opted to score *The Cobweb* (1955) with serialist procedures, not because the film took place within a mental institution but because of the sense of psychological depth the idiom afforded. 'I felt it was important to write a serial score,' Rosenman claimed, noting 'it was my intention not to "ape" or mimic the physical aspect of the screen *mise-en-scène* but to show what was going on inside characters' heads.'[2] Rosenman had previously studied composition with Arnold Schoenberg, the first and foremost purveyor of atonality and serialism, so it might come as no surprise that Rosenman's own work would be influenced by the father of the Second Viennese School. Yet, regardless of Rosenman's personal experiences or background, *The Cobweb* clearly demonstrates that not all atonal or serial film music was, or need be, specifically designed to support horror. (Juan Chattah's chapter in this volume, on three scores by David Shire with dodecaphonic elements—none of which are straight horror movies—makes this point as well.)

As concert composers develop new post-tonal compositional techniques, those devices slowly find their way to Hollywood composers, where they are filtered and assimilated into an amalgam of existing musical styles, with more musical choices available to composers (and directors) today than ever before. This essay examines cues in three films, *It*, *Signs*, and *The Matrix*, where **post-tonal** musical elements are used within the larger construct of predominantly *tonal* film scores. To match the eclecticism of compositional techniques, this chapter adopts a range of analytical devices, including neo-Riemannian theory, pitch-class set theory, serial analysis, and polychordal analysis. Each case study presents an issue for which a hybrid approach is ultimately the most useful means of understanding matters of post-tonal pitch design. In the opening cue of *It*, the music is purely triadic, yet attempting to tether it to a specific tonal center is problematic, so the most practical analytical tool is neo-Riemannian theory. Meanwhile, the primary gesture heard throughout *Signs* is a three-note motive that often defies tonal grounding. Here, the tools of set theory—including concepts of normal order, prime form, and ordered pitch intervals—can be used to show relationships between statements of the motive. *The Matrix* employs several post-tonal techniques, including sound masses and timeline notation, as well as an occasional moment of functional harmony, but the most significant post-tonal elements in the score are polychords and 12-tone serialism. The resulting effect of incorporating such diverse techniques in this score is one of polystylism, creating a sense of a (post)modernist soundworld, while still being tethered to the long tonal tradition of Common Practice tonality in important ways. In this sense, *The Matrix* is the most instructive case study, as it highlights in vivid terms a general principle of film music study: One single analytical methodology is often not enough to create a comprehensive or musically faithful reading of any given score.

Neo-Riemannian Theory and Horrific Juxtapositions in Benjamin Wallfisch's *It*

The film *It* (2017) is based on the Stephen King novel of the same title, so it comes as no surprise that the book's genre is horror. An inter-dimensional being, the movie's titular 'It' often takes the form of Pennywise the Dancing Clown while terrorizing the small town of Derry, Maine, which it has done for centuries. After feeding on children, It hibernates for 27 years before returning to dine on the next generation. A group of kids calling themselves 'The Losers Club,' must overcome their fears and battle It in order to save themselves and their town. Composer Benjamin Wallfisch's opening cue for the score, 'Every 27 Years,' is neither horrific nor scored in the manner of a traditional horror scene, instead sounding childlike and innocent, despite a subtle undercurrent of ambiguity. This scene [0:00:35–0:02:30] occurs at the film's outset, as a rainstorm occurs outside the Denbrough family house, where Bill (Jaden Lieberhehr) crafts a paper boat for his younger six-year-old brother Georgie (Jackson Robert Scott).[3] Nothing about the onscreen action is ominous or frightening.

While many film scores that rely on the consonant triad as their foundational harmony follow Common Practice tonal norms—take Rachel Portman's score for *The Cider House Rules* or Jerome Moross's *The Big Country*—others use alternative, less functional or centric approaches to chord-to-chord progressions. One such procedure is to have chord roots primarily move by chromatic thirds, rather than the more familiar intervals of the diatonic fifths and seconds. When non-diatonic intervals occur between triads in abundance, a distinctive idiom called 'pantriadic chromaticism' can arise. An effective way to analyze this style is through neo-Riemannian theory (NRT). This methodology, which focuses on musical relationships and transformations rather than functional routines, has witnessed a rapid and thorough adoption into film music studies in recent years, with significant contributions from theorists Frank Lehman and Scott Murphy.[4] In the book *Hollywood Harmony*, Lehman writes,

Though developed largely in an effort to understand the refractory sorts of chromaticism that run through nineteenth-century art music, in many ways, NRT's priorities render it *more* suitable for certain genres of film music than its originally intended repertoire of Schubert and Wagner.[5]

Later, he provides a detailed primer for those unfamiliar with the system's terminology and approach.[6]

Wallfisch's *It* contains pantriadicism that would make Schubert and Wagner envious. The first 15 measures of 'Every 27 Years' feature a constantly shifting tonal center and, relatedly, a lack of root motion by the fifth—all successive chords are arrived at either by root motion of a second or a third. I will provide three different analytical readings of these measures, employing the methodological resources of NRT, as well as a taxonomic system for categorizing and assigning meaning to chromatic mediants, and the traditional and still versatile system of Roman numerals. As will be shown, while individually all of these approaches contain limitations, together they give a compelling picture of how Wallfisch's distinct style of triadic post-tonality works and, importantly, why music like this serves the dramatic ends of a film like *It*.

The cue is in the style of a quadruple-meter dance with a bass-afterbeat accompaniment, with the chordal root appearing on the downbeat of each measure and the full triad lightly articulated on beats 2 and 4. Despite the square meter, the cue feels like a waltz that contains an extra beat. The regular harmonic shifts and textural consistency in the left-hand pattern make the music sound like a spiritual relative of Erik Satie's *Gymnopédies*, short pieces that also challenge the listener to find a traditional tonal grounding.[7] Example 10.1 depicts the passage, with annotations indicating chord names and qualities, plus neo-Riemannian descriptions for each triadic transformation. Examples 10.2 and 10.3 render the same passage in harmonic reduction while showing alternative layers of analytical information: Chromatic mediant relationships and Roman numeral designations, respectively.

The opening two measures of melody imply a tonic of G major, and although the bass note is G, neither chord above is a literal G major triad; rather we hear C major followed by E minor. By m. 3, a borrowed chord from the minor mode, C minor, has been introduced, and in m. 4, all sense of G major is subverted by the A♭ minor triad. The harmonies in mm. 2–7 move through two major third cycles—E–C–A♭ and F–A–D♭—with the first descending and the second ascending. Following these third cycles, Wallfisch's roving chord begins to progress via the **SLIDE** motion (**S**): This is the chordal relationship that links two triads that share the same third and differ by root and quality. In mm. 7–8, the harmonies move from D♭m to Dm. While this looks like a **SLIDE**, the D♭m triad has to also move

EXAMPLE 10.1 Wallfisch, *It*, 'Every 27 Years,' neo-Riemannian analysis (all examples transcribed by author).

through a mode-shifting **PARALLEL** motion (**P**) to D♭M before sliding up to Dm. The effect of this relationship is that the chords are separated by more than one triadic transformation, with the effort of moving from the D♭m to Dm chord sounding that much more laborious and strange.

Starting in measure 8, the melody sounds as though a new phrase is beginning. Ordinarily, eight-measure subdivisions are expected of conventional themes, but the initial part of the cue only presents seven measures. The effort in moving from m. 7 to m. 8 could serve as a sort of ending to the opening melodic thought in mm. 1–7—not a cadence but perhaps instilling a sense of closing one portion and moving to another. The start of the phrase in m. 8 then oscillates between Dm and D♭M. The section concludes with another ascending **SLIDE**, this time from G♭M to Am—a harmonic motion nowhere close to achieving a cadence in the functional, Common Practice sense of the term.[8]

The motion between chords that takes the most effort, in terms of the number of sub-transformations within the algebra of neo-Riemannian analysis, is found in mm. 10–11, from Dm to BM. As shown in Example 10.1, the simplest NRT analysis is **PRP**—whereby these two triads are connected by an implied relative transformation flanked by two modal shifts, or Dm–(DM–Bm)–BM. An alternative explanation might be **LSP**—that is, Dm–(B♭M–Bm)–BM. In both analyses, the penultimate passing chord must be Bm in order to perform the parallel operation to move to BM. Indeed, because of the presence of the ascending **S** operation in other locations in this excerpt, it may be more appropriate to use the **LSP** analysis here, as it integrates a distinctive triadic transformation already established and marked for attention moments earlier in the cue.

The visual representation of the harmonic pathway given as charted through the Tonnetz in Figure 10.1 illustrates how far afield the music travels from its point of origin. Over half of the chords only share a single note with the following chord, rather than the more expected two notes, and the moves from D♭m to Dm and Dm to Bm share no common tones. While connected, at least on the surface, by close movements of the fingers on a keyboard, the chords in 'Every 27 Years' often require multiple NRT operations to get from one chord to the next. The effect is to take what might otherwise be interpreted as an innocent scene of building a paper boat and, by underscoring it with strange and complicated tonal motions, instead prepare the audience for the constantly shifting, centerless evil of Pennywise.

Not only does Wallfisch's music implant a sense of vague unease in this opening sequence by grafting such a roving harmonic make-up to an otherwise pleasant, lilting dance: The specific qualities of certain of those triad-to-triad progressions encode certain well-established sinister connotations.

'Chromatic mediants' refer to a pairing of harmonies where the chord roots are a third apart and the triads do not belong to the same diatonic scale. Chromatic mediants have been frequently employed in film music as shorthands for certain narrative connotations, which arise from the type of third they sit apart (m3 vs. M3, or interval-class 3 vs. 4) and the triadic quality (major or minor triad, or [037] vs. [047]). The chromatic mediant analysis in Example 10.2 suggests the presence of evil lurking within the dance, particularly in its usage of the major third (M3) and minor third (m3)-driven progressions between minor triads.[9]

208 Erik Heine

FIGURE 10.1 Wallfisch, 'Every 27 Years,' Tonnetz representation.

While the M3 relationship between minor triads is quite common—think 'The Imperial March' from *The Empire Strikes Back*—the m3 relationship occurs with far less frequency, semiotically suggesting a kind of hierarchy of evil and foreboding progressions: Hence the names given to the two types as Vader (m4) and Palpatine (m3), the big-bad and even-bigger-bad of the *Star Wars* saga, whose respective themes provide perhaps the most iconic instances of these two, semantically freighted chromatic mediants.

The opening tonal center in 'Every 27 Years' of G major, implied by the melody, is never confirmed through a standard authentic cadence, or even a root-position tonic chord, and the fluctuating tonal centers are an apt musical metaphor for the otherworldly shape-shifting titular monster, taking the form of whatever is most unexpected and frightening. Despite the fact

EXAMPLE 10.2 Wallfisch, 'Every 27 Years,' chromatic mediant analysis.

EXAMPLE 10.3 Wallfisch, 'Every 27 Years,' Roman numeral analysis.

that clowns are supposed to be funny and benign, Pennywise is an avatar of evil in a physical form, an upsetting perversion of a friendly and familiar entity. And so Wallfisch finds ways to upset a friendly genre (a simple piano dance) through irregular phrases and unexpected formal twists, and familiar sonority (the consonant triad) through grotesquely undermined functional progressions and ominously associated chromatic swerves. Example 10.3 provides the last ingredient for a proper harmonic understanding of the cue: A Roman numeral analysis, which strives to account for those fleeting tonal centers, and, through its inability to do so unequivocally, demonstrate the productive awkwardness of ideas of functional progression, cadence, and pivot-chord modulation native to Common Practice tonality (and studiously avoided in pantriadic chromaticism).

In a way, this Roman numeral analysis models the default, naive approach with which an average listener might first approach this cue. As seen in Example 10.3, no dominant chords are present. The majority of the modulations between key centers, such as they are, consist of chromatic rather than diatonic pivots. Little surprise, of course, as modulations imply a clear sense of functional tonality, which this cue lacks. In many ways, the analysis presented in Example 10.3 is grasping for any sense of tonic, local or global. Even the initial tonality of G major is only supported by melodic motion. Although modal readings, such as C Lydian or E Aeolian are possible, the melody strongly emphasizes the tendency tones of G major—F♯ and C—and both resolve exactly as expected. Certainly, any Roman numeral analysis was going to be problematic, as Wallfisch's cue lacks the one thing—goal orientation—that powers traditional functional diatonic harmony. Cadences, a crucial ingredient in that goal orientation, are absent, without which tonics can only be established by duration rather than the conventional contrapuntal/prolongational means of Common Practice tonality. There is a poetic quality to this. The cue's shifting tonal centers, like the evil character that often takes the shape of Pennywise the Clown, cause problems with discerning what is truly a tonal center and what is not, while a sinister lack of harmonic function operates beneath the seemingly innocuous faux-waltz.

Through these three analytical tactics—neo-Riemannian theory, chromatic mediant theory, and Roman numerical theory—we can see ways in which *It*'s music, albeit hardly atonal or dodecaphonic, nevertheless defies a clear analysis through any single methodology. Chromatic mediants highlight the connotative presence of evil in the music, while NRT shows the effort in moving from one chord to the next, analogizing with the constant motion of Pennywise. The Roman numeric reading is dependent upon clear tonal centers, of which there are none in this cue. Instead, tonal centers are implied and vague, with an absence of both dominant harmonies and cadences, foregrounding the shifting nature of the music and its denial of conclusivity. On its face, 'Every 27 Years' presents the pastoral nature of the town of Derry, but under the surface, like Pennywise inhabiting the sewer system, the music has a dark and sinister undercurrent.

Set Theory and Alien Sonorities in James Newton Howard's *Signs*

Signs (2002) was the third collaboration between director M. Night Shyamalan and composer James Newton Howard. Howard's score is unlike anything that he had composed before or indeed since. The primary source of the entire score's melodic material is a three-note motive that is repeated in various ways throughout the film. Because the motive does not outline a diatonically available pattern—consonant triad or otherwise—the best methodology to analyze *Signs* is through the tools of set theory, initially codified by theorist Allen Forte and applied to the free atonal music of the Second Viennese School. Unlike Common Practice music, atonal music avoids articulating tonal centers or pitch-reference points and, both as a consequence of this aesthetic and a strategy to enforce it, generally eschews consonant triadic harmony. Analytically, this means that less tonally-determined elements should become analytical focal points: These include ordered and unordered interval classes, abstract motivic collections, and especially groupings of distinct pitch classes (pcs) into vertical sonorities and horizontal melodic cells collectively known as 'sets.' Together, set theory identifies and relates these elements to show connections between gestures that might not be readily apparent on the music's surface.

On its surface, *Signs* appears to be a horror film—a family is terrorized by an alien invasion, isolated in their farmhouse. Indeed, comparisons to films such as *Night of the Living Dead* and *The Birds* are not inapt. However, the primary horror element is not the alien invasion *per se*; it is that the protagonist, Graham Hess (Mel Gibson), a former Episcopalian minister, has lost his faith following his wife's death. Once his faith returns at the film's climax, the aliens are defeated, and the movie ends with him returning to his church.

Every cue in *Signs* uses the 'three-note motive' (TNM)—the first music composed for the film, in fact. Howard, speaking about the TNM said,

> The 'Main Title' that you see over the opening of the movie was written before the movie was ever shot. And it's based on a three-note motif. Dee-dee-dee, dee-dee-dee... [Howard sings the motive] and that motif is reprised throughout the movie in all kinds of benevolent, hostile, threatening, mysterious kinds of ways.[10]

Much of the score for *Signs* can be analyzed using the tools of set theory, as the TNM, while sometimes harmonized with tertian chords, typically defies attachment to any one tonal center. The TNM takes multiple forms in the film, with slightly but impactfully different intervallic structures, the sorts of which set theory is well equipped to describe and differentiate.

As noted above, the three-note motif is initially presented in the 'Main Titles' as A4–D5–E♭5.[11] Example 10.4 shows two characteristic guises of this film-spanning cell. Using set theoretical nomenclature, the normal order is (923), and the prime form is 3–6 (016). The normal order represents the most closely packed collection of the three notes, from bottom to top, regardless of how the notes appear in the score, while the prime form, in this instance 3–6 (016), designates the sixth of 12 inversionally and transpositionally unique trichords. If C is taken to be pitch 0, then

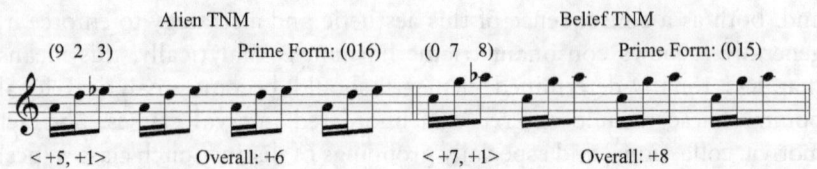

EXAMPLE 10.4 Newton Howard, *Signs*, three-note motive (Alien and Belief Forms).

(016) spells out what could be considered its simplest form, C (0), C♯ (1), and F♯ (6). The Ordered Pitch Intervals (OPIs) are <+5, +1>, and the Interval Class Vector (ICV) is [100011], indicating a relatively high level of dissonance within the trichord's tight frame. Both the ascending semitone and the distance of the tritone being covered from bottom to top are indicative of the prevailing dissonance that defines the sound of the score. This version of the motive is what I call the *Alien TNM*. In contrast, the less dissonant *Belief TNM*, which I have also named, is initially presented in the cue 'First Crop Circles' as C5–G5–A♭5. The normal order of this collection is (780), and the prime form is 3–5 (015). The OPIs are <+7, +1>, and the ICV is [100110]. Compared with the Alien TNM, the span of the tritone here has been replaced in this version by the span of a comparatively less dissonant minor sixth, as is the initial ascending perfect fifth leap.

Although the normal order for the Alien TNM is (016) and the normal order for the Belief TNM is (015), the Belief TNM has a wider span from bottom to top, demonstrating that normal order, while useful, is not always the way that the music is heard. The intervallic expansion from +5 semitones to +7 in the Belief TNM allows for both the leap between the first and second notes and the overall distance from bottom to top to both be consonant intervals—a perfect fifth and a minor sixth, in contrast to the Alien TNM, which features dissonant intervals in the parallel places—a perfect fourth and diminished fifth.

One of the cues that features a prominent development of the TNM is 'Asthma Attack,' an excerpt of which is shown in Example 10.5. Beginning in m. 19 of the cue [1:23:30], the TNM appears, but in an apparently unexpected metric position and with different durations and contours than have been heard elsewhere in the film. At m. 20, Graham says, 'We don't have [his son Morgan's] medicine,' a significant line, implying that Morgan (Kieran Culkin) could very easily die from the incident that caused his asthma attack.

In this case, the TNM can be seen and heard in two different ways. The first way is by shifting the short-short-long pattern to the downbeat,

EXAMPLE 10.5 Newton Howard, *Signs*, three-note motive in 'Asthma Attack,' mm. 19–20.

where the pattern would become short-long-short. In this way, the ascending contour of the TNM remains the same, but the OPI of <+1, +4> is inverted, the smaller of the two intervals lying on the bottom rather than the top. The harp doubles the piccolo and supports this reading. In the strings, only the viola and cello are playing sustained notes on F♯ and C♯, so no motion or metric change is present in those instruments. The change in pattern is a significant transformation in musical meaning, as the family is in the basement of the house, repelling the aliens attempting to abduct them. Graham is below ground; he is figuratively and literally in Hell, and the TNM's OPI is inverted to illustrate this.

It is also possible to interpret the TNM here as remaining in its short-short-long pattern, but to do so requires a metric displacement and a contour change, which can be done due to the accent in the highest sounding pitch, the F♯6, which can sound like the initiating pitch of the varied TNM. Throughout this part of the cue, Graham talks to his son, Morgan, trying to help him breathe through his asthma attack. In this instance, the TNM neither represents aliens nor belief in a higher power. (Indeed, at the end of the cue, Graham rhetorically says, 'I hate you,' twice, as though God is listening.) Instead, it is representative of a father's love for his child, and the will to help him overcome a physical limitation. Both interpretations are aurally valid, and a listener could hear one form or the other—or both—on a single hearing, or might hear it one way, and then the other way on a successive listening. The ambiguity present is due to the inversion of the TNM itself, as well as its metric location.

Signs' final musical sequence, titled 'The Hand of Fate,' falls in two parts. The sections are split between action inside and outside of the house. Inside the house, at the film's climax, the TNM is expanded out to an OPI of <+7, +5,> a perfect fifth and an octave, a (05) dyad in prime form. The TNM has been enlarged so as to exceed its previous dissonance over the course of this score. This is operative both in terms of the initial leap and in the total distance spanned in its originary form (the Alien TNM <+5, +1> for a total of +6 semitones), progressing to consonance in both the leap and overall distance in its modified form (the Belief TNM

<+7, +1> for a total of +8), and finally in 'Hand of Fate' to perfect consonance in both the leap and overall distance <+7, +5> for a total of +12, a perfect fifth and a perfect octave). The aliens have been defeated, and Graham's faith is about to be restored.

Outside the house, the TNM reflects Graham's resumption of his faith, and the Belief TNM is accompanied by triadic harmonies, with one pair related by chromatic mediant as Morgan begins breathing normally again, a miraculous occurrence. In this second segment of 'The Hand of Fate,' Newton Howard finally progresses past the first 15 measures of the Belief TNM—which have been heard in multiple cues—to support Morgan's awakening from a second asthma attack and a shot of epinephrine [1:38:38–1:39:35]. Example 10.6 highlights how music accomplishes this dramatic breakthrough.

As shown in the example, the harmonies in this cue are exclusively triadic. And while tonal centers are momentarily alluded to, they are fleeting and never confirmed; a Roman numeral analysis is not particularly useful here. A neo-Riemannian reading doesn't emphasize any patterns, and nearly every chord connection must go through two or more operations, so, again, of limited analytical use. The TNM itself is constantly changing, and its second constitutive interval is rarely +1. The motif appears to be changing in order to support the underlying harmonies, rather than the TNM being the driving musical force. Notably, a chromatic mediant—the 'Hero' progression (a minor third span between major triads)—is heard between mm. 22–23, just after Morgan awakens and the family sees his recovery, after thinking he was dead. It is this miraculous recovery, both of Morgan's body and of Graham's faith, that allows the music to truly change, the passage ending on the (05) dyad, much like in Part 1 of the cue. As shown, the TNM had been the musical driver of the horror of the absence of faith, manifested in physical form by aliens, and once that faith is restored, the TNM becomes subject to consonance and dissonance rules, supported by triadic harmonies, not a driver but harmoniously integrated component of a larger consonant idiom.

Polychordal Mind-Bending in Don Davis's *The Matrix*

When Morpheus (Laurence Fishburne) meets Neo (Keanu Reeves) for the first time, he asks, 'Have you ever had a dream, Neo, that you were so sure was real?' At this point in *The Matrix* (1999), the audience begins to understand that the world that has been depicted on screen is not actually the 'real world.' Instead, it is the machine-generated dream world

EXAMPLE 10.6 Newton Howard, *Signs*, three-note motive in 'The Hand of Fate 2,' mm. 8–28.

of The Matrix. We have seen signs that things are amiss in The Matrix, with inhabitants performing impossible physical acts and bodily manipulations. The false world that had been presented to the audience is one of false consciousness, illusion, the irrational.

The Matrix was Davis's second film directed by the Wachowski siblings, following 1996's *Bound*. The directors asked for a score that would be acoustically- and orchestrally-based, rather than reliant on synthesizers, a blend of elements of film and concert music.[12] The end result is a hybrid of various nineteenth- and twentieth-century compositional techniques, invoking at turns polychords, polyrhythm, stratification, serialism, atonality, aleatoric/indeterminate music, minimalism, and even functional harmony. Davis's use of these various techniques is not surprising considering his avowed influences: He named Lutoslawski, Boulez, and Berio as composers who shaped his voice as a young composer, and Roger Reynolds, John Adams, Steve Reich, David Lang, and Aaron Jay Kernis as composers who inspired him at the time of composing *The Matrix*. The use of these various compositional techniques reveals an aural pastiche, a score that is post-modern but still retains certain hallmarks of the 'Hollywood sound.'

One of the most striking, if subtle, modernistic elements in *The Matrix* score is the use of 12-tone serialism. Davis recruits this procedure for musical passages where the emotionless, purely logical machines are in focus. This connection of the machine antagonists with dodecaphonic music is apt, as serialism uses all 12 chromatic pitches equally, much as a computer or machine might do. The initial use occurs in 'Trinity Infinity,' in mm. 78–90, part of which is shown in Example 10.7. The passage occurs as Trinity attacks the police officers in the room of the hotel, defeating all of them while breaking the laws of physics, the first time this plot device is shown. Sixteenth notes in the piano are continuously sounded during these measures, and at first listen their tonal content might appear arbitrary. But the question of why so much effort would be placed into writing so many notes without some level of organization must be answered.

The first 12 notes of the 'Trinity Infinity' piano run are, in pitch-class nomenclature: 460T5713E928. Nothing here is repeated, and the order seems to emphasize the notes in a whole-tone 0 scale (i.e., the collection containing C♮) before shifting to whole-tone 1 (i.e., the collection containing C♯) and returning to whole-tone 0. When this ordered pitch sequence is depicted as a serial matrix, what emerges is a repeating pattern, much like what a machine might create. Every three beats of music create a complete row. The cue's row succession is, in order of occurrence and grouping: 1) Three iterations of a pattern of P_4, RI_3, I_0, and R_5 row forms; 2) P_4 and variations thereof; and 3) I_4, all concluding as the last officer hits the floor on the downbeat of m. 91. Davis truly uses a matrix within *The Matrix*.

EXAMPLE 10.7 Davis, *The Matrix*, 'Trinity Infinity,' mm. 78–80.

While Davis's employment of strict dodecaphonic organization within the (limited span of) 'Trinity Infinity' cue demonstrates the expressive utility of the technique in film, serial procedures are not the primary motivator of melody or harmony in the score. (Indeed, based on the range and timbre of its use in 'Trinity Infinity,' as well as being very low in the audio mix under the sound effects, it is unlikely that anyone without a score would even hear the particular pitch make-up of the music, let alone recognize a serial pattern.) Much more representative are polychords, a sound that dominates the aural texture of *The Matrix*. A polychord is a combination of two discrete sonorities—often but not necessarily consonant triads or sevenths—played simultaneously, creating a more complex and dissonant vertical harmony. Famous examples from the Classical repertoire include the 'Petrushka Chord' [C major and F♯ major] from Stravinsky's *Petrushka* (1911) and the opening of the 'Augurs of Spring' [F♭ major triad and E♭ dominant seventh] from the same composer's *The Rite of Spring* (1913). Film composers were quick to adopt polychords as a coloristic and expressive musical resource, where they served as a signal for 'the Irrational' for many decades, with particularly memorable deployments in scores by Bernard Herrmann such as *Psycho*, *The Seventh Voyage of Sinbad*, and *North by Northwest*.[13]

Unlike Herrmann's typical usages, which tend to be frozen in place and dramatic situation, the internal composition of Davis's polychords changes based on the diegetic situation. Two textural types can be discerned in *The Matrix*. The first is what would become the chief sonic signature of Davis's score: The 'Swell' polychord, in which one consonant triad fades in while the other fades out, alternating back and forth in a dynamic play of volume and tonal complexity. The other textural type is similar to

EXAMPLE 10.8   Action polychords, (a) Adams, *Harmonielehre*, Movement 1, m. 473; (b) Davis, *The Matrix*, 'Trinity Infinity,' m. 151.

what is used by John Adams in the first movement of his orchestral work *Harmonielehre* (1985), beginning at m. 472 and continuing to the end of the movement. In *Harmonielehre*, the polychord is a combination of E♭M and Em triads. Rhythmically, it is somewhat syncopated, and the polychord is constantly articulated. The parallel location in *The Matrix* is in the cue 'Trinity Infinity,' mm. 151–154, where the polychords are GM and C^{aug}. These action polychords are shown in Examples 10.8a and 10.8b.

Polychords are not just used for superficial color in *The Matrix*: They serve a crucial structural function, driving the music and the narrative, from the very beginning of the studio logos to the end of the film. The polychord that sounds as the Warner Brothers logo is displayed—initially ambiguous in its referent, and ultimately revealed to be 'Neo's Polychord'—is an Em triad in the horns combined with a CM triad in the trumpets. Registrally, this polychord is as compact as possible, with the complete polychord only spanning the interval of a minor tenth, as seen in Example 10.9. Davis's polychords can be described by adapting music theorist Scott Murphy's **MnM** nomenclature for inter-triadic relationships (see Murphy's chapter in this volume for a thorough explanation of this system).[14] Every polychord can be categorized in terms of the modes of its respective component sonorities and the interval that separates the chord roots; the first letter representing the mode of the registrally lower of the two triads via capital (**M**ajor) or lowercase (**m**inor) letter, the second the higher of the two, and the numeral the span in semitones. Thus, 'Neo's Polychord,' shown in Example 10.9, would be categorized as an instance of **m8M**, meaning a fusion of a minor triad and the major one rooted eight semitones (a minor sixth) above.[15]

Regarding this gesture, Andy Hill writes, '[Davis] lays [the triads] out, in bold counterpoint: The two worlds, the red pill and the blue pill, the form and its mirror image,' and later refers to the shared common tones between the triads—E and G—as 'close enough for one to be the dark mirror of the other.'[16] Hill's mirror metaphor is aided by the relative lack of dissonance between the two triads, in fact related by a **LEADING-TONE** (**L**) transformation, the triads only being a semitone different, and that semitone providing the sense of the 'dark mirror,' an imperfect reflection.

EXAMPLE 10.9 Davis, *The Matrix*, 'Logos/Main Titles,' mm. 2–5 (Neo's Polychord).

In his article 'Concepts of Harmony and Prolongation in Schoenberg's Op. 19/2,' Olli Väisälä uses the idea of *registrally ordered interval* (ro-interval) to describe the spacing between constituent pitches within complex harmonies.[17] This is in distinction to the metric of interval class, which ignores voicing and registration: For example, an ic-based analysis treats a minor second the same as a major seventh. Väisälä uses ro-intervals instead to maintain intervallic distance within an octave. This is similar to how set theory uses the difference between ordered pitch-class intervals (from 0 to 11) and unordered pitch-class intervals (from 0 to 6). Väisälä suggests that ro-intervals closer to 1 and 2 are more dissonant, while ro-intervals closer to 10 and 11 are less dissonant.[18] In the instance of this opening Em/CM polychord, only one instance of a ro-interval occurs in that range, from B4 to C5, a ro-interval of 1; the polychord itself is largely consonant. All other ro-intervals in 'Neo's Polychord' are 3, 4, 5, 7, 8, 9, 12, and 15. Following Väisälä's ascription of expressive content to consonance and dissonance in complex sonorities, it is reasonable to claim that the polychords that contain more dissonant intervals are likely to emphasize tension and present a higher degree of difficulty for the protagonists to succeed. Conversely, polychords that contain more consonant intervals are likely to predict or affirm the success of the protagonists. However, since the focus of all of these intervals is on seconds and sevenths—intervals that are inherently dissonant—none of these polychords present a clear aural sense of victory, only degrees of relative potential success.

Following the inaugural 'Neo' Em+CM over *The Matrix*'s opening studio card, polychords are reinforced as an essential aspect of the film's soundscape in the film's opening action cue, 'Trinity Infinity.' Polychords are used throughout the sequence, but three instances stand out, shown in Examples 10.10 and 10.11. The first occurs as Trinity (Carrie-Anne Moss) runs across the rooftops, with an agent and police in hot pursuit (Example 10.10a). This 'Chase' polychord is constructed of a combination of Dm and BM chords: An **m9M** polychord, in other words, voiced such to have two instances of ro-interval 1, one instance of ro-interval 2, and one instance of ro-interval 10. The ro1 intervals are present between D4–D♯5 and F4–F♯5, while the ro2 is located between A4 and B4, and the ro10 between F4 and D♯5. Trinity looks to be in a bad situation, and the high level of ro-dissonance reflects this.

As the 'Chase' polychord ends, a 'Leap' polychord begins (Example 10.10b), a combination of FM and EM triads (**M11M**) and with three different ro-interval 11 values. Based on its internal structure and the textual associations with polychordal dissonance Davis is establishing, the 'Leap' sonority suggests a much higher degree of narrative success than 'Chase,' this musical prediction is indeed validated as the audience sees her defy physics by leaping across buildings in bullet-time. If the polychordal ordering was reversed, the constituent triads would present three ro1 intervals, and we might surmise Trinity would be less likely to reach the other side safely. The specific spacing of the two triads thus signals—and in a way even enables—Trinity's successful leap.

Trinity has not yet escaped, her safety still in question at this point. She is followed by Agent Jones, who also leaps across the same gulf. Agent Jones's jump is accompanied not by a polychord but by a single interval of a minor second, B4/C5, an elegant musical means of differentiating human from machine. In a final attempt to escape Agent Jones, Trinity makes a dash to leap through a window. As she runs to make the jump, yet another polychord, 'Flight,' is introduced, composed of a fusion of GM and EM (**M9M**), shown in Example 10.10c.

Crucially, this last polychordal pairing instantiates a minor-third chromatic mediant relationship, one that indicates the 'Hero' topic. With this action occurring so early in the film, it is difficult to know who we should be rooting for: Trinity or the police. Davis's use of the 'Hero' relationship allows the audience to get a hint that she is on the side of the good guys, even if it is disguised through a dissonant simultaneity rather than being clearly stated through oscillation between the two triads. The 'Flight' polychord contains one ro1 and one ro2, with no ro10 or ro11 values—the tensions inherent in the triadic juxtaposition matching the lingering fear that Agent Jones might catch her. Indeed, both Trinity and the audience wait for Agent Jones to appear through the window, and surprisingly, he doesn't. Her safety is momentarily confirmed, her status as a protagonist clearly established musically.

Early instances of polychords associated with Neo (Keanu Reeves) are somewhat curious. The first time a pairing of triads is heard clearly in association with the character of Neo is in the cue 'Neo on the Ledge,' although at this stage in the film, he is still more identified as office worker Thomas A. Anderson, not his eventual messianic hero role. Near the end of the cue, Neo attempts to escape from a trio of agents, led by a phone call from Morpheus (Laurence Fishburne). He looks out from the ledge outside of the building where he works, and the polychord F♯m–Cm (**m6m**) is sounded, as seen in Example 10.11. According to Murphy, **m6m** is generally representative of antagonism and danger in film music—and

EXAMPLE 10.10 Davis, *The Matrix*, 'Trinity Infinity'; (a) mm 132–136 (Chase); (b) mm 137–140 (Leap); (c) mm 155–159 (Flight).

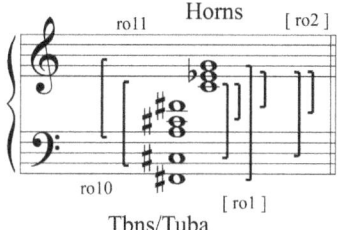

EXAMPLE 10.11   Davis, *The Matrix*, 'Neo on the Ledge,' mm. 87–94.

much else, in accordance with its minor, tritonal pairing. And the threat of danger is realized: Neo is captured by those three agents.

Because of the registral overlap in the voicing of this polychord, four instances of ro1 are present. This is essentially the worst-case scenario for Neo—trapped in an office job, about to be in the custody of agents, and seemingly with no way out. The relative level of dissonance here encapsulates all of that danger and antagonism in Tom Anderson's life, a far cry from the triumph to come in 'Neo's Polychord.'

Polychords are regularly present throughout the film's later acts, dominating in particular the final four cues. As Morpheus breaks his physical (and mental) bonds, he takes a leap of faith out of the window of a building, hoping Neo will catch him. The film moves into bullet-time, much as it did with Trinity's leap at the start of the film. Example 10.12 illustrates the relevant passage in 'Ontological Shock,' featuring a Dm–F♯M (**m4M**) polychord, constructed to highlight three ro1 values. Things are not looking good for the protagonists—Morpheus is shot during his escape attempt—but despite the musical dissonance, Neo does indeed catch his mentor, just as the polychordal swell ends.

As the film moves toward its climax, Neo and Agent Smith (Hugo Weaving) begin the first part of their final showdown, accompanied by the cue 'That's Gotta Hurt.' As they fire their guns at each other, an AM–FM (**M8M**) polychord is sounded. This polychord contains two ro1 and one ro11 values, signaling that Neo is not likely to hit his target. Matters deteriorate, and Smith nearly beats Neo to death. After Smith thinks the fight is over, Neo rises, accompanied by the very same Em–CM polychord

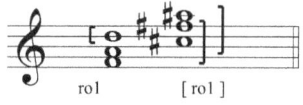

EXAMPLE 10.12   Davis, *The Matrix*, 'Ontological Shock,' mm. 28–32.

heard at the very beginning of the movie—'Neo's Polychord'—seen in Example 10.9. Smith cannot believe his adversary's refusal to accept death. Neo's belief in himself, conversely, is completely affirmed; he now fully understands and accepts that he is 'The One.'

Round 2 of the showdown finds Neo looking for an exit, chased by the team of three agents. As Neo leaps out of an apartment building, the camera switches to bullet-time, and an Em–E♭M (**m11M**) polychord is used, with one ro1 and one ro11. The situation doesn't sound as dire as before but still doesn't appear as though Neo has a path out. Just when it looks like he will escape, he is shot and killed by Smith; at the end of the cue 'Surprise!' all appears lost, as shown in Example 10.13.

The film's final cue, 'He's the One Alright,' begins with Neo's apparent death. Trinity, confessing her love for the dead hero, kisses Neo in the real world, and he magically begins breathing again, accompanied by a B♭M–G♭M (**M8M**) polychord—a transposition and revoicing of the sonority heard earlier in 'That's Gotta Hurt.' Because of the revoicing, only one ro1 and one ro11 interval are present, meaning the sonority is less dissonant than in its prior iteration. Later in the same cue, after Neo has escaped the Matrix and returned to the real world, a final swelling polychord is heard. While the instrumentation remains the same as the film's initial statement of the motif, the order in which the triads are used is reversed, with the higher-register trumpets sounding before the horns. This is not an alteration reflected in the chord's transformational/registral nomenclature, which would still present it as AM–FM (**M8M**). The change in timbral order is rather due to the change in Neo, who knows now he can do anything in the Matrix, including flying into the air, *á la* Superman, for the film's final image.

***

The three vignettes presented in this chapter all contain elements of the horror genre, ranging from straight horror (*It*) to science-fiction/horror hybrid (*Signs*) to science-fiction with horror tropes (*The Matrix*). And in each, post-tonal principles of pitch organization are used for expressive and formal purposes. More than their generic or tonal qualities, however, what really unites these case studies is the fact that for none does a single

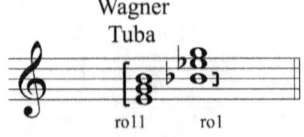

EXAMPLE 10.13 Davis, *The Matrix*, 'Surprise,' mm. 95–100.

analytical methodology sufficiently describe or explain its musical construction. As shown, post-tonal film music can be triadic, atonal, serial, or anything in between, which is why a number of methodologies must often be employed to gain a better understanding of the music and its role within the film. Neo-Riemannian theory and an affective taxonomy of chromatic mediants can be used to gauge how far, or, in a metaphorical sense, how *difficult* is it to move from one chord to the next in a non-functional, post-tonal context. The tools of set and serial often work in an atonal context but can also be used in tandem with triadic harmony, and polychords benefit from triadic-transformational and registral/intervallic analytical approaches. Post-tonal music in Hollywood has much to offer both listeners and analysts alike. The tools employed here are hardly the only ones available, nor the ideal fit for every musical situation. This chapter is just a beginning. As ever for Hollywood, sequels are always a possibility.

Notes

1 Neil Lerner, *Music in the Horror Film: Listening to Fear* (New York: Routledge, 2010), ix.
2 Rosenman is quoted in Roy Prendergast's *Film Music: A Neglected Art*, 2nd edition (New York: W. W. Norton, and Co., 1977), 119. Sabine Feisst, 'Serving Two Masters: Leonard Rosenman's Music for Film and for the Concert Hall,' *21st Century Music* 7.5 (May 2000): 19–25, and Joseph Straus, *Twelve-Tone Music in America* (New York: Cambridge University Press, 2009), 150–153, both briefly mention Rosenman's score for *The Cobweb*, but any level of detailed analytical discussion is absent.
3 At 0:02:10, we see a woman playing piano inside the house. The music has shifted from non-diegetic to (perhaps?) diegetic, an example of what Robynn Stilwell calls 'The Fantastical Gap.' See Stilwell, 'The Fantastical Gap Between Diegetic and Nondiegetic' in Daniel Goldmark, Lawrence Kramer, and Richard Leppert (eds.), *Beyond the Soundtrack: Representing Music in Cinema* (Berkeley: University of California Press, 2007), 184–204.
4 Frank Lehman, 'Transformational Analysis and the Representation of Genius in Film Music,' *Music Theory Spectrum* 35.1 (Spring 2013): 1–22 and *Hollywood Harmony: Musical Wonder and the Sound of Cinema* (New York: Oxford University Press, 2018). Scott Murphy, 'Transformational Theory and the Analysis of Film Music,' in David Neumeyer (ed.), *The Oxford Handbook of Film Music Studies* (New York: Oxford University Press, 2014), 471–499.
5 Lehman, *Hollywood Harmony*, 12.
6 Ibid., *Hollywood Harmony*, 85–125.
7 Wallfisch was interviewed by the online magazine *Collider* in September 2017. While he did not make any overt comments regarding Satie's music, he did note iconic 1980s music for *Back to the Future* and *The Goonies*, and to composers Alan Silvestri, Jerry Goldsmith, and John Williams, particularly

through their respective melodic themes. See https://collider.com/benjamin-wallfisch-interview-it-movie/ (Accessed September 22, 2020).

8 But not that dissimilar from the sorts of pseudo-cadential procedures in certain neotonal works like Alan Hovhaness's *Mysterious Mountain (Symphony No. 2)*, where the first movement ends with F#M and GM, a root motion also of an ascending half-step.

9 The chromatic mediant analysis and terms come from the author's article: Erik Heine, 'Chromatic Mediants and Narrative Context in Film,' *Music Analysis* 37.1 (March 2018): 103–132.

10 Interview from the featurette 'Last Voices: The Music of *Signs*' on the *Signs* DVD.

11 For a more detailed examination of all of the music in *Signs*, see Erik Heine's *James Newton Howard's Signs: A Film Score Guide* (Lanham, MD: Scarecrow Press, 2016).

12 Interview with Don Davis from *The Matrix Reloaded* (2003), www.matrix-fans.net/interview-with-don-davis-composer-from-the-matrix-reloaded-2003/. Accessed January 14, 2020.

13 In his article 'Herrmann, Hitchcock, and the Music of the Irrational,' *Cinema Journal* 21.2 (Spring 1982): 39, Royal S. Brown isolates a 'highly dissonant bitonal chord first heard in *Vertigo* during the subjective shot as Scottie, hanging on to a gutter, looks down many stories to the street below.' The polychord in question—E♭m and DM—has come to be known as the 'Vertigo Chord.'

14 In Murphy's original usage, the **MnM** labeling system illustrates triads in succession, where the first has clear tonal precedence over the second. See Murphy 'Transformational Analysis and the Analysis of Film Music,' 483–496. Edward Gollin applies Riemann's concept of *Doppelklänge* as a way of mediating tonal and post-tonal analysis, 'to describe how collections and events progress in a work, particularly in post-tonal contexts.' (389). See Gollin, 'On a Transformational Curiosity in Riemann's *Schematisirung der Dissonanzen*,' in Edward Gollin and Alexander Rehding (eds.), *The Oxford Handbook of Neo-Riemannian Theories* (New York: Oxford University Press, 2011), 382–399.

15 In all following examples concerning polychords, the horn triad will appear first, and is always the registrally lower of the two triads, unless otherwise indicated.

16 Andy Hill, *Scoring the Screen: The Secret Language of Film Music* (Milwaukee: Hal Leonard Books, 2017), 166.

17 Olli Väisälä, 'Concepts of Harmony and Prolongation in Schoenberg's Op. 19/2,' *Music Theory Spectrum* 21.2 (Autumn 1999): 232.

18 Ibid., 237.

11
ATTUNING SERIALISM

David Shire's Scores for *The Taking of Pelham One Two Three*, *2010: The Year We Made Contact*, and *Zodiac*

Juan Chattah

Twelve-tone serialism—a compositional technique spearheaded by Arnold Schoenberg during the early decades of the twentieth century—ensures the systematic organization of all 12 notes of the chromatic scale, bestowing them with equal importance and avoiding automatic emphasis on any single pitch. By suppressing tonality, one of music's most conventional elements, the twelve-tone system emerged as a means for redefining (or evading) traditional forms of beauty in music. The sounds of dodecaphony (another term for twelve-tone music) were found to be particularly adept at imbuing a score with hostile, distressing, even shocking sentiments. Again and again, composers resorted to this system to render a musical equivalent to Munch's *The Scream*.

Such expressionist aesthetics, it turned out, fit seamlessly within modernist film-scoring styles.[1] The correspondence of a systematic compositional technique and a ready-made anxious affect was of particular appeal within the heightened genres of horror and science-fiction, becoming 'an associative unit... within mainstream American film music.'[2] This prompted a handful of film composers to introduce twelve-tone serialism into their work in the movies, a list that includes prominent and prolific figures such as Hanns Eisler, Benjamin Frankel, Ernest Gold, Jerry Goldsmith, Leonard Rosenman, Miklós Rózsa, and Franz Waxman.[3]

Songwriter and composer for stage and screen David Shire's compositional proclivities did not align with the twelve-tone language's original sensibilities. He refused to write music that conformed to contrived, overly restrictive norms, preferring to explore more familiar—and simultaneously less hidebound—popular and jazz styles. However,

DOI: 10.4324/9781003001171-11

while making initial strides in the film industry, Shire recognized the need to expand his creative strategies and cultivate a more versatile and expressive set of compositional tools. In 1974 and 1975, he attended seminars led by film composers Paul Glass and Hugo Friedhofer, both of whom explored various means for constructing dodecaphonic rows with tonal implications, shaping them into accessible and memorable motifs or melodies.[4] Shire realized he could harness the twelve-tone language's expressive potential by constructing and manipulating rows in ways that allowed him to attune the musical to the extramusical dimensions of a film.

Shire embraced the foundations of twelve-tone composition while distancing himself from its putative atonal imperative. Doing so required deviation from the rules of orthodox twelve-tone practice. He would find ways to contort the principles that define precompositional pitch structures and their realization in dodecaphonic music, developing methods to fuse the twelve-tone language with aspects of other musical genres and styles, arriving at a uniquely suitable musical milieu for any given scoring assignment.

In this chapter, I offer analytical vignettes of three film soundtracks—*The Taking of Pelham One Two Three*, *2010: The Year We Make Contact*, and *Zodiac*—each informed by analysis of the composer's sketches and manuscripts. Collectively, these case studies illustrate that Shire's use of the twelve-tone system originated as a practical approach to controlling dissonance, yet evolved into a refined mode of representation, one capable of contributing entire new layers of expressive meaning to a film's narrative.[5] More broadly, within the context of film musicology, the following case studies offer a glimpse at the fruitful prospects for the analytical exploration of twelve-tone music in film.

The Taking of Pelham One Two Three

Ransoms, heists, and hostages are common themes in crime thrillers. *The Taking of Pelham One Two Three* (1974, dir. Joseph Sargent) ingeniously combines these plot devices with an added dose of urban paranoia. Four mustachioed, identically clothed armed men hijack a New York City subway car leaving Pelham Station at 1:23 PM. The criminals do not know one another and avoid disclosing their identities by assuming color-coded names: Mr. Green, Mr. Blue, Mr. Brown, and Mr. Grey. Plotting and eventually executing their heist as the film unfolds, the colorful characters take control of the subway, hold the commuters hostage, demand a million-dollar ransom, and threaten to execute one passenger a minute if the money is not delivered within the hour.

The film's story plays out in the New York City of the 1970s. New York has always thrived on the everyday interaction between strangers, on the inherent synergy stemming from individuals of widely diverse backgrounds sharing a common space. The movie presents this synergy through the interaction of the unlikely team of hijackers—an English mercenary, a former train operator, a mafia reject, and an accomplice whose reluctance is marked by a stutter—and through the unanticipated encounters of subway passengers, credited as the Hooker, the Pimp, the Mother, the Maid, the Delivery Boy, the Old Man, the Alcoholic, the Salesman, the Homosexual, the Spanish Woman, the Hippie, and the WASP. Shire sought to capture through music this spirit of abrasive interaction of unrelated individuals caught in a chaotic yet confined situation. He accomplished this by fusing two unrelated musical styles—dodecaphony and progressive big band jazz—and by shaping the relations of an otherwise unrelated set of pitches, forcing all 12 tones of the chromatic scale to share a common musical space.[6]

Shire recalls that, in college, he 'was deeply immersed in progressive jazz… and learned that certain intervals give its harmonies their characteristic flavor—the major seventh and minor third, and their inversions, the minor second and major sixth.'[7] In the *Pelham* score, Shire's reliance on these intervals translates into the emphasis of two *interval classes* (an efficient way of reducing enharmonically, inversionally, and registral equivalent intervals into a single category, abbreviated 'ic'). The interval classes Shire privileges are **ic1**—a semitone, capturing the minor second, major seventh, and compounds thereof; and **ic3**—three semitones, capturing the minor third, major sixth, and compounds thereof. These two interval classes play a vital role in the score at various levels. Shire constructs the score's primary row—the source of almost all its tonal materials—by drawing exclusively on these characteristic interval classes, thereby infusing the entire musical soundtrack with a progressive jazz-funk feel. This row is shown in Example 11.1, with annotations for melodic intervals as well as resultant trichordal and hexachordal sets. Throughout the score, Shire further juxtaposes row permutations both within and between cues, systematically connecting them via common tone or melodically by **ic1**.[8] And lastly, he superimposes **ic1** and **ic3** to generate the primary musical tension to be resolved at the end of the film.

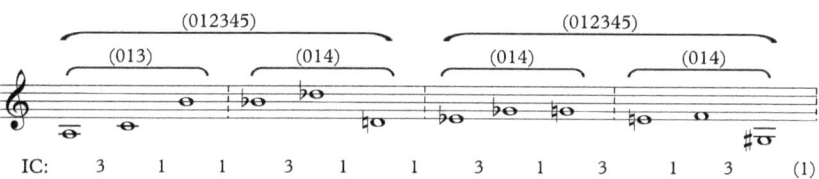

EXAMPLE 11.1 Shire, *The Taking of Pelham One Two Three*, tone row (all transcriptions by author unless otherwise noted).

EXAMPLE 11.2 *Pelham*, Main Titles opening.

The film's Main Titles, whose opening vamp and subsequent primary theme are shown in Example 11.2, act as an overture that establishes *Pelham*'s atmosphere and summarizes all upcoming musical materials. As a way of introduction, a pounding B♭–D♭–ostinato (ic3) initiates the cue, an embryonic gesture suggesting **RI$_9$** of the score's source tone row.[9] The theme proper, however, begins as trumpets and horns combine forces to make a bold statement of **P$_9$**, the primary row. By selecting P$_9$ as the primary row, where the first dyad (A–C) sits at a remove of one semitone (ic1) from the continuing B♭–D♭–ostinato, Shire right away starts setting up the fundamental musical-narrative tension explored across the film.

The melodic figures and harmonic stacks in the Main Titles theme reveal Shire's intention to partition the row into four trichords. Arguably, Shire intended for trichords to serve a quasi-leitmotivic function, with each representing a different criminal. For example, in the manuscript score, a distinctive trichord is used to introduce each of the hijackers, one by one—these cues, labeled 'Enter Mr. Grey,' 'Enter Mr. Brown,' and so on, isolate these trichords and present them verbatim as they appeared in the Main Titles. In addition to this abstract form of musical identification, various other motivic and rhythmic elements strengthen the link between each trichord and the corresponding hijacker. For example, the wedged repetition initiating the third trichord (E♭–F♯–G) in the Main Titles theme, shown on measure 7 in Example 11.2, suggests an onomatopoeic rendition that can be heard as prefiguring Mr. Brown's stutter. Although the film's final cut does not include these cues, they offer insight into the composer's intentions and should enrich our interpretation of the film.

EXAMPLE 11.3 *Pelham*, all-combinatorial figure in Main Titles theme.

Just as in the film's narrative, where the distinct and seemingly incompatible personalities of the hijackers complement one another, these trichords pair well into two all-combinatorial (012345) hexachords.[10] The all-combinatorial properties of the *Pelham* row would, in theory, allow Shire to introduce musical figures that, although deviating from the row's original contour, fill out the missing notes of the first or second hexachord, so as to render a complete chromatic scale (or 'aggregate,' in serial analysis lingo). Shire does occasionally introduce such figures, as exemplified in Example 11.3. However, instead of fully exploiting narratival and expressive potential of the vertical/harmonic, all-combinatorial presentation of these complementary hexachords, Shire generally presents the *Pelham* row in its horizontal/melodic form.[11] Far from being an arbitrary compositional choice, this marked preference for linear presentations has extramusical implications. Instead of conveying the high-aspiring verticality of the city's landscape through stacked sonorities and simultaneities, Shire instead mirrors the film's cinematography, focusing instead on subway trains, endless tunnels, and low-ceilinged rooms. In this way, a specific mode of dodecaphonic writing comes to underline the horizontal, underground, oppressive flatness of New York's subterraneous world.

Figure 11.1 presents two ways to visualize the row and its permutations. Although the matrix on the right, which uses simple pitch-class notation, offers the analyst significant benefits in terms of clarity, the earlier system of using musical notation, as shown on the left, offers additional insights into the row's potential renditions in a composition. For *Pelham*, Shire's charting of the 48 permutations according to the music-notation system influenced his compositional decisions in two realms. First, when presented as a melody with explicit registral and enharmonic

	I_0	I_3	I_2	I_1	I_4	I_5	I_6	I_9	I_T	I_7	I_8	I_E	
P_0	0	3	2	1	4	5	6	9	T	7	8	E	R_0
P_9	9	0	E	T	1	2	3	6	7	4	5	8	R_9
P_T	T	1	0	E	2	3	4	7	8	5	6	9	R_T
P_E	E	2	1	0	3	4	5	8	9	6	7	T	R_E
P_8	8	E	T	9	0	1	2	5	6	3	4	7	R_8
P_7	7	T	9	8	E	0	1	4	5	2	3	6	R_7
P_6	6	9	8	7	T	E	0	3	4	1	2	5	R_6
P_3	3	6	5	4	7	8	9	0	1	T	E	2	R_3
P_2	2	5	4	3	6	7	8	E	0	9	T	1	R_2
P_5	5	8	7	6	9	T	E	2	3	0	1	4	R_5
P_4	4	7	6	5	8	9	T	1	2	E	0	3	R_4
P_1	1	4	3	2	5	6	7	T	E	8	9	0	R_1
	RI_0	RI_3	RI_2	RI_1	RI_4	RI_5	RI_6	RI_9	RI_T	RI_7	RI_8	RI_E	

FIGURE 11.1 Shire's precompositional chart for *Pelham* and corresponding pc-matrix. Reprinted with permission of composer.

EXAMPLE 11.4 *Pelham*, 'Blue and Green Talk,' (top) cue and (bottom) trajectory in precompositional chart. Reprinted with permission of composer.

information, the series exhibits a distinctive contour traceable to the music's surface—not merely a contour-less set of pitch classes as in the numerical matrix. And second, the precompositional chart of 48 permutations can serve as a literal musical space within which it is possible to map the dramatic trajectory of single scenes or the entire film.[12]

In a scene where Mr. Blue and Mr. Green talk [0:44:45], the music slowly unfolds P_9, R_T, I_E, and RI_0 forms of the *Pelham* row. As shown in Example 11.4, the music follows—and in a sense even constructs—the dialogue's trajectory. Here, the two criminals first discuss the potential outcomes of the hijacking, yet they soon digress to reminisce about their pasts. The northwest-to-southeast musical pathway, the score shown in Example 11.4, maps this digression in the conversation. Conversely, at the end of the scene, a fleeting gesture outlining the first hexachord of P_9 signals a return of the narrative focus to the presently unfolding situation and the adverse realities of the hijacking.

EXAMPLE 11.5 *Pelham*, End Titles.

In *Pelham*'s End Titles, after the derailing of the hijackers' plans, Shire resolves the pitch-class tension introduced all the way back in the Main Titles, and in effect, musically transports us to a distinctive, semi-utopian vision of the city. Shire presents a final rendition of P_9, retaining its pitch-class profile but stripping it of its angular contour. As shown in Example 11.5, Shire adds strings and woodwinds to the texture, now supporting a new reharmonization that infuses the music with a cocktail, smooth jazz sound. P_9 culminates in the ic1 transposition of the original B♭–D♭ bass ostinato—now, the A–C dyad in the bass figure seamlessly aligns with P_9's introductory gesture. By radically transforming the musical texture and resolving the initial tension between the ostinato and the primary row, Shire rejects the abrasive and the chaotic, and seeks instead to evoke the 'New York that we all loved,' a hearkening back to 'the glamorous and sophisticated city of years past.'[13]

2010: The Year We Make Contact

Peter Hyams's *2010: The Year We Make Contact* (1984), the sequel to Stanley Kubrick's *2001: A Space Odyssey* (1968), is set amidst a backdrop of growing tensions between the USA and the USSR, tensions that portend nuclear war. Despite the conflict, the two nations must join forces and launch a space expedition to learn the fate of the Discovery One mission to Jupiter from 2001. Through this joint space mission, humanity receives

EXAMPLE 11.6 *2010: The Year We Make Contact*, Main Titles.

a profound message of hope and reconciliation, one that averts nuclear annihilation and bends the course of history.

For his Main Titles theme, shown in Example 11.6, Shire pays homage to one of the original film's most memorable classical pieces, the opening section of Richard Strauss's tone poem *Also Sprach Zarathustra*. Shire's allusion is unmistakable. Both pieces begin with a deep-sounding drone that establishes a strong gravitational pull toward 'C,' and in formal terms, both outline a large-scale sentence structure, gradually adding orchestral forces that build to a powerful climax.[14] Most significant is the *2010* title's adaptation of *Zarathustra*'s modal dichotomy, in which Strauss creates a stark musical conflict—juxtaposing C-major and C-minor triads without immediately resolving the tension between them. By similarly foregrounding the clash between opposing modes, Shire's music parallels the conflict between two nations that permeates the film's narrative.[15]

Despite the evident triadic nature common to both works, Shire did not choose the chords for *2010* in a purely intuitive fashion. As in *Pelham*, serialism provided Shire with an ingenious and systematic solution for creating a consistent sound world for this film. Careful observation of the Main Titles' score reveals serial techniques at play: Four mutually exclusive triads that form twelve-tone aggregates—see measures 5–6, 10–11, 15–16, and 17–18.[16] Here, Shire embeds structural complexity within surface-level simplicity, harkening back to Kubrick's *2001* and its almost Kantian exploration of the humanly unknowable and the veils surrounding the true nature of phenomena.[17]

Throughout his score to *2010*, Shire manipulates the twelve-tone system in three distinct yet interrelated ways. First, his precompositional chart,

#	Triad	PLP	T6	RLR
1	C	A♭m	F♯	Dm
2	D♭	Am	G	E♭m
3	D	B♭m	A♭	Em
4	E♭	Bm	A	Fm
5	E	Cm	B♭	F♯m
6	F	D♭m	B	Gm
7	F♯	Dm	C	A♭m
8	G	E♭m	D♭	Am
9	A♭	Em	D	B♭m
10	A	Fm	E♭	Bm
11	B♭	F♯m	E	Cm
12	B	Gm	F	D♭m

FIGURE 11.2 Shire's precompositional chart for *2010*. Reprinted with permission of composer.

shown in Figure 11.2, suggests that he did not seek to serialize pitches to form a melodic row (as in *Pelham*). To vary and expand on *Zarathustra*'s characteristic major-minor effect, he instead conceived of the twelve-tone aggregate in terms of a quartet of (037) trichords, rendered in the music as alternating major and minor triads.[18] Second, his precompositional chart omits **R**, **I**, and **RI** permutations; this omission stems, in part, from the row's symmetrical design, with hexachords repeating verbatim under T_6. And third, Shire's manipulation of trichords can be understood as an exclusive set of three *triadic* operations (in neo-Riemannian nomenclature, **PLP**, T_6, and **RLR**) applied on a given source triad to render a derived row. Applying any of these operations to any of the row's four triads results in another triad contained in the row.[19]

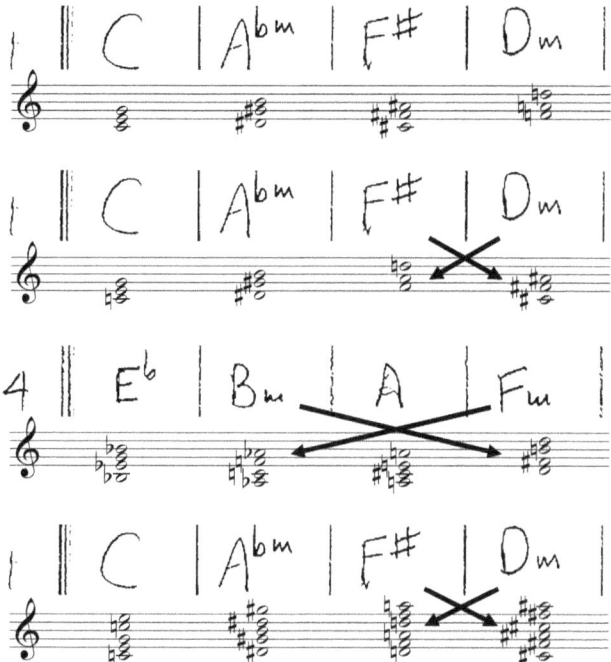

FIGURE 11.3 *2010*, Systematic arrangement of trichords in Main Titles. Reprinted with permission of composer.

Upon closer inspection of the Main Titles' theme, it becomes clear that Shire uses rows #1 and #4 from his precompositional chart, but, as shown in Figure 11.3, he alters the trichords' order in three of the sub-phrases.[20] The seemingly arbitrary arrangement of trichords on the music's surface supports the notion that Shire applies an exclusive set of operations to an initial trichord to obtain a twelve-tone aggregate.[21] Such a circumscribing property of the row, wherein trichords cannot escape the row's boundaries via the available operations, resonates with themes pivotal to both the original *2001* and its sequel—our inability to access knowledge and our technology's limitations.

Shire's design of the *2010* row as deploying **PLP**, **T$_6$**, and **RLR** triadic operations bestows the entire score with archetypical musical gestures reminiscent of other science-fiction scores. In particular, two of these operations carry associations with the 'supernatural'—Richard Cohn characterizes the effect of **PLP**-type harmonic pairings in classical music as 'paradoxical, supernatural, magical, weird, dark… uncanny,' and both Scott Murphy and Frank Lehman note that in the film-scoring repertoire 'progressions between triads of the same mode whose roots are related by tritone (**T$_6$**) are frequently associated with encounters of an alien or

EXAMPLE 11.7 *2010*, **PLP** harmonic stabs in 'Countdown.'

inhuman nature.'[22] The **PLP**, T_6, and triadic operations extend beyond the Main Titles' theme, saturating the entire score with their signifying power.

In the 'Countdown' cue [1:38:48], the longest in the entire film, Shire introduces sporadic harmonic stabs, shown in Example 11.7. These sonorities, formed by pairing doubly chromatic mediants via **PLP** operations—such as F major and D♭ minor or C major and A♭ minor—result in the augmented (or often called 'hexatonic') collection, itself a reliable signifier of both science-fictional and supernatural events.

Elsewhere, Shire juxtaposes T_6 transformations of a triad—C major to F major—to leitmotivically underscore all 'Voice-Over' segments, messages from Dr. Floyd (Roy Scheider) to his wife on Earth:

> 'Dear Caroline, I miss you terribly. The time has come to put ourselves in an orbit around Io, which is where the *Discovery* is.'
>
> 'Dear Caroline, this is finally it. After nine years and hundreds of millions of miles, we are about to come face to face with the Monolith.'

Because it outlines the greatest distance possible for a triadic transformation in terms of distance along the circle of fifths, such a tritonal harmonic gesture, shown in Example 11.8 as part of the 'Voice Over I' cue [0:41:40], seems particularly fitting for highlighting the great distance (in time and space) between the crew and their loved ones on Earth.

PLP triadic operations are also central to Shire's theme for HAL 9000, the supercomputer whose 'malfunction' in the first film is presented here in more human terms as 'paranoia.' We now learn that during the events of the

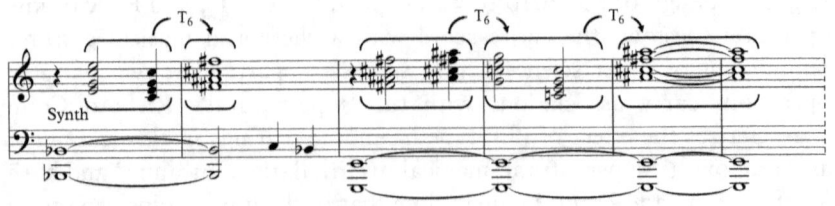

EXAMPLE 11.8 *2010*, T_6 transformations in 'Voice-Over I.'

EXAMPLE 11.9 *2010*, Incipient version of HAL's theme in 'TV Message.'

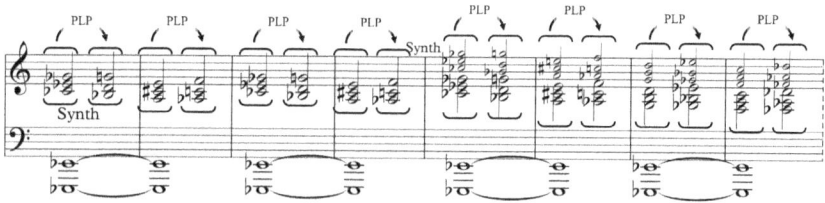

EXAMPLE 11.10 *2010*, Fully realized version of HAL's theme in 'Countdown.'

original movie, HAL received contradictory orders that caused it to engage in an 'H-Moebius loop,' generating an inner conflict it needed to resolve, even if that resolution required eliminating the crew. Shire designs a dodecaphonic theme for HAL that echoes the film's primary musical dichotomy via a harmonic sequence that juxtaposes **PLP**-related major and minor triads, suggesting the looping pattern from which the machine will again be unable to escape. As a video message updates the crew with an official reassuring them that 'HAL appears to be reactivated' and will help them complete the mission [1:20:05], the music introduces an incipient version of HAL's theme, pictured in Example 11.9. Later in the film, during the 'Countdown' cue, as HAL again falls into the 'H-Moebius loop' [1:37:35], the music fully realizes its dodecaphonic sequential theme, shown in Example 11.10. HAL's theme thus resonates with its nature as an automaton and suggests the limits of using machine logic to understand human conflict.

Throughout the score, Shire's music gradually eclipses its initially set associations with *Also Sprach Zarathustra* by drawing on electronic textures and dissolving the original modal dichotomy.[23] Besides contributing to a generically appropriate futuristic timbre, the use of electronic instruments allows Shire to progressively detune the C triad's third to approximate the middle point between C major and C minor. He notates this in the score with the indication 'neutral third' and an accidental resembling a flat sign with a slash, as shown in Example 11.11. The first instance of this sonority in the film takes place in the 'Bowman/Betty' cue [1:07:52], as the

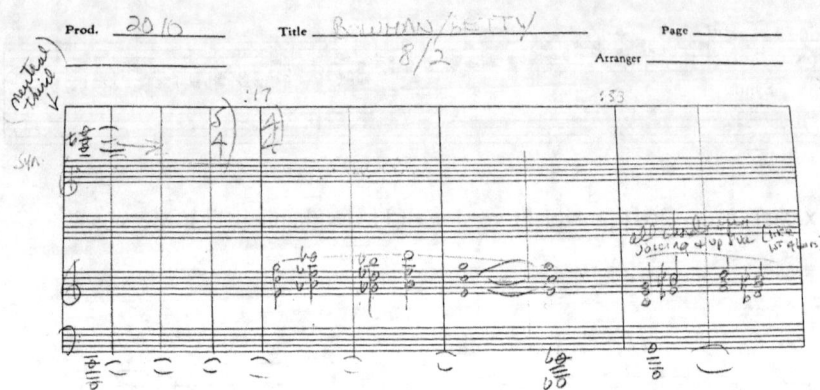

EXAMPLE 11.11   *2010*, Detuned third in 'Bowman/Betty.' Reprinted with permission of composer.

incorporeal essence of Bowman (who had been lost in space in the original film) manifests itself through a television set to express his fond farewells to Betty, his widow. As the film unfolds, Shire systematically interweaves this sonority, musically resolving the major/minor duality with a mollifying-sounding triad—not C major, not C minor, but 'C neutral'—echoing the sequel's final message of reconciliation, one that pertains to interpersonal, international, and even interdimensional relationships:

> ALL THESE WORLDS
> ARE YOURS [...]
> USE THEM TOGETHER
> USE THEM IN PEACE

Zodiac

Crime stories are a staple of realist cinema, but few films depict historical events with the calculated accuracy of David Fincher's *Zodiac* (2007). This true crime film draws on Robert Graysmith's recollections of the search for Zodiac, a never-identified serial killer who terrorized San Francisco in the 1960s and 70s. The movie's narrative is organized around three large-scale arcs, beginning with the horrifying, inexplicable killings, then circling around the tension between the public's toxic collective infatuation with Zodiac and the police's inability to solve the case, and ultimately fixating on a character's personal obsession with discovering the killer's identity. Shire's score for the film keenly follows this narrative trajectory.

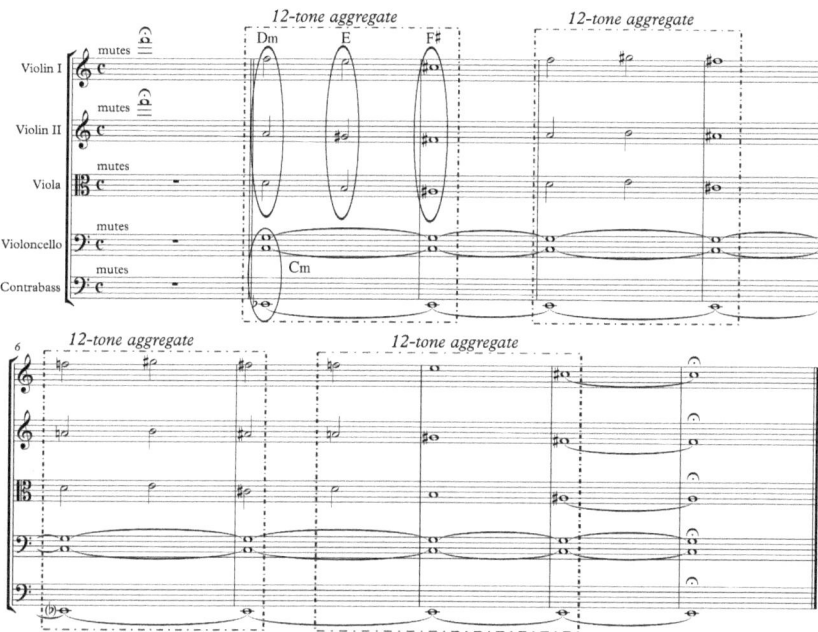

EXAMPLE 11.12 *Zodiac*, string chorale in the 'Blue Rock Aftermath.'

The film and its score work together to bring to life the elusive shadows of the killer's persona, as divulged historically only through cryptic correspondences containing crossword puzzles, Greek letters, words in Morse code, and Zodiac symbols. Because there are 12 Zodiac signs, Shire took the opportunity to embed a layer of symbolism into the soundtrack by constructing a twelve-tone row. As the film opens with the Zodiac killer calling 911 to report a brutal murder, the first non-diegetic cue reveals his musical signature, shown in Example 11.12, a harmonically driven string chorale that produces the twelve-tone aggregate through static vertical harmonies, rather than a melodic series or theme [0:05:40]. As in *2010*, Shire segments the aggregate into four consonant triads (C minor, D minor, E major, and F♯ major), which can create dissonant polychords when superimposed. While the celli and contrabass perform the Cm triad throughout this sequence, the upper strings alternate the other three triads; the trichordal succession atop the pedal chord gives rise to three unique sonorities: The hexachord {0,2,4,6,7,9} resulting from Cm + Dm; {0,1,4,5,8,9} resulting from Cm + E; {0,1,4,6,7,9} resulting from Cm + F♯. Through its accumulated consonant thirds, the music suggests Zodiac's contented state of mind while also embodying his deceptive identity: Consonant triads combine to produce dissonant polychords.[24]

EXAMPLE 11.13 *Zodiac*, twelve-tone aggregate in 'He Gave Himself a Name.'

Whereas in *2010* Shire manipulates his dodecaphonic series with trichordal permutations, in *Zodiac*, he presents the row primarily in its original form, with only sporadic transposed rotations. For example, in a scene in which multiple individuals claim, falsely, to be Zodiac, each providing alternative stories related to the killings, Shire composed a cue featuring multiple transposed rotations of the triadic row: <Cm, Dm, E, F#>, <Cm, D, E, B♭m>, <C, D, G#m, B♭m>, <C, F#m, G#m, B♭>. The music in this scene nicely reflects Shire's overall rationale for using twelve-tone syntax and manipulation techniques—not to suppress tonal effects but to provide a vital link into the confusing narrative, with its presentation of multiple (fabricated) permutations of Zodiac's identity.[25]

In the first section of the film, Shire also offers a contrasting, highly dissonant musical style that becomes associated with the press and the police's perspective on the disturbing events. In his spotting notes, the composer wrote that he sought a musical idea 'that leads us to believe something terrible is going to happen.' He expands the score's expressive palette by introducing a second derived series built on transpositions or inversions of the (0167) tetrachord. As the letter in which Zodiac claims his infamous moniker arrives at the San Francisco Chronicle [0:17:35], the music, shown in Example 11.13, stacks (0167) tetrachords atop one another to form a disquieting twelve-tone aggregate. Just as the tonal and consonant resonances suggested by Zodiac's chorale reveal his warped sense of happiness, the music featuring the (0167) tetrachord allows viewers' insight into the dread felt by the police and press.

As panic grows in the Bay Area, the San Francisco Police Department brings Inspector David Toschi (Mark Ruffalo) onto the case. Bewildering labyrinths of false leads and inconclusive findings consistently undermine his investigation. To represent Toschi's extended, unresolved quest for Zodiac, Shire embeds non-serial references and allusions to Charles Ives's orchestral piece *The Unanswered Question*, situating it within the established twelve-tone fabric. In the foreword to the famously cryptic work, Ives comments, 'The trumpet intones "The Perennial Question of Existence," and states it in the same tone of voice each time.' Shire channeled not only the texture and plaintive character of Ives's piece but also the way in which a solo instrument (the trumpet) is singled out against the ensemble, a haunting representation of Toschi and his frustrated hunt for the truth. The detective is brought onto the case following the killing of a taxicab driver near the intersection of Washington and Cherry Streets. As Toschi ponders Zodiac's true identity [0:29:40], the music, shown in Example 11.14, presents a trumpet melody based on a B♭°7 chord—an 'unresolved' sonority—unfurled over a thickly scored dodecaphonic cluster in the strings—itself a transposed rotation of the original row. In this and subsequent scenes, the musical texture continues to allude to *The Unanswered Question*, representing an 'undisturbed solitude' that fails to provide concrete answers to the trumpet's call.

In the third section of the film, editorial cartoonist Robert Graysmith (Jake Gyllenhaal), who had previously remained on the periphery of the screenplay, develops a years-long obsession with solving the case. The unresolved B♭°7 sonority embedded in Toschi's trumpet melody, originally superimposed over dodecaphonic clusters, comes to link these two characters, united in their obsessive quest—Toschi 'voiced' by the trumpet, and Graysmith by piano. Shire recalled, 'the idea of "irresolution" kept coming to mind as I explored musical materials from which to develop the score... in particular to underscore Graysmith's endless

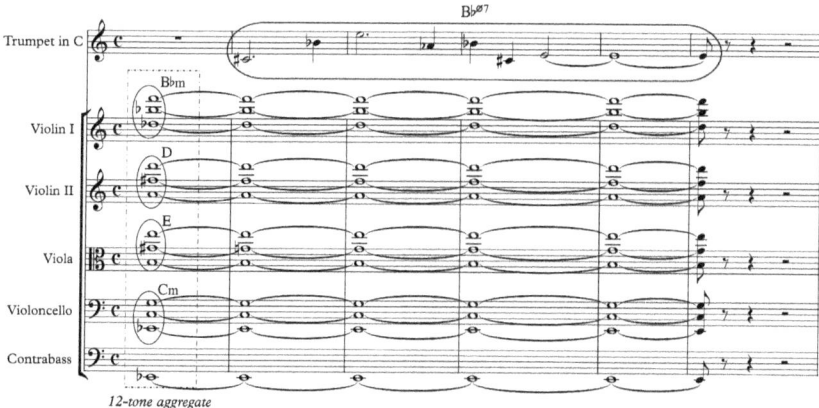

EXAMPLE 11.14 *Zodiac*, trumpet melody representing Inspector Toschi in the 'Washington & Cherry.'

EXAMPLE 11.15 *Zodiac*, prolongation of an E^{ø}7 sonority in 'Zodiac Has Come to San Francisco.'

search for an answer.'[26] Shire singles out the half-diminished-seventh sonority and expands it—complementing it with the ninth, eleventh, and flat-thirteenth—to form an 'unresolved-sounding' scale, the E-half-diminished mode.[27] The 'Zodiac Has Come to San Francisco' cue, in Example 11.15, draws on this mode to underscore the moment when Graysmith's interest in Zodiac transforms into an obsession [0:35:55] as he learns that Zodiac, like Graysmith himself, has moved to San Francisco.

With Graysmith's ever-deepening pursuit of Zodiac's identity, his theme develops to reflect his obsessive desire. Graysmith's fully developed leitmotif as heard late in the movie [2:36:15] is reproduced in Example 11.16, shown intertwining the half-diminished and the mixolydian modes, never providing a sense of resolution by exploiting these scales' inherent tonal ambivalences. The vital link between music and narrative—and the source of its intertextual inspiration—becomes clear from Shire's spotting notes, which allude to a direct, yet simplified quotation of the harmonic underpinnings of the 'Desire' leitmotif from Wagner's *Tristan und Isolde*.[28] Here, Shire adds a level of rhetorical power to the use of dodecaphonic music by highlighting its *absence*. Just as this harmonic gesture has become a marked signifier of unresolved longing and agony suffered by Tristan and Isolde in the opera, in the film's narrative,

EXAMPLE 11.16 *Zodiac*, 'Desire' leitmotif from *Tristan und Isolde* embedded within harmonic progression of Graysmith's theme [02:36:15].

the Tristan progression foreshadows Graysmith's unquenched, lingering quest to uncover the truth about the Zodiac killer. Lost in his own desire, Graysmith longs for a resolution he will never attain. The music's multiphase transformation—from strict dodecaphony to Ivesian ambiance to Wagnerian supercharged romanticism—suggests in music-stylistic terms just how far away Graysmith is from the truth he seeks.

Conclusion

Shire's adoption of the twelve-tone method as a film compositional resource was at first motivated by a need to control dissonance. Yet, over the course of his filmography, it evolved into a refined source of symbolic meaning and representation. Although the aggregate is a constant presence in Shire's twelve-tone works, his tonal references, trichordal permutations, and especially integration and juxtaposition of twelve-tone techniques with disparate styles allow him to transcend the orthodox use of this compositional method. For *The Taking of Pelham One Two Three*, Shire captures the distinctively chaotic, urban feel of New York by scaffolding the twelve-tone method within a progressive jazz-funk style. For *2010: The Year We Made Contact*, he establishes an explicit reference to Strauss's *Also Sprach Zarathustra*—and Kubrick's original film—by constructing a tonal row that embeds the piece's characteristic major-minor modal dichotomy. And for *Zodiac*, he interweaves references to Ives's *The Unanswered Question* and Wagner's *Tristan und Isolde* within a twelve-tone musical fabric to map the story's narrative arc.

These analytical vignettes prompt a nuanced reconsideration of the expressive potential of twelve-tone techniques within film music and remind us that this method ought not to be bound to only films or scenes that demand a modernist, Munch-esque 'Scream' aesthetic. Rather, serialist procedures and sonorities can be deployed to add layers of psychological complexity and aesthetic—even philosophical—depth to a film. Therefore, to film composers, dodecaphony offers a high degree of systematization and compositional control while also providing, through its very constraints, an abundant source of creativity. For the music analyst in turn, this method offers a rich set of formalized tools to inform, frame, and support our close readings, while opening new interpretative windows that allow us to see a film in a new light.

Notes

1 In the words of David Schiff, the use of twelve-tone music in cinema triggers associations of 'unfriendly alien encounters, and psychotic flashes.' David Schiff, 'Fit Only for the Filmgoer,' *Times Literary Supplement* (July 2, 1999): 18–19. Leonard Rosenman, who studied with Schoenberg and Dallapiccola, arguably contributed to establishing this limited conception of twelve-tone music's expressive potential. For instance, his use of twelve-tone techniques in the film *The Cobweb* (1955), the first known instance of twelve-tone in film music, helps depict the idiosyncratic emotional world of disturbed patients at a psychiatric institution. Occasionally, however, film composers strayed away from using dodecaphony for unpleasant effects. For instance, Scott Bradley used the system to underscore comedic moments in the cartoon *The Cat That Hated People* (1948).
2 Frank Lehman, 'Serial Killings and Dodecaphonic Dread in *Zodiac*,' Presentation given at *Voicing the Soundtrack: A Conference in Honor of David Neumeyer*, The University of Texas at Austin (April 16, 2016).
3 Joseph Straus (2009) notes that 'most histories of American music have ignored the presence of twelve-tone music... even though so many major composers continued (and continue) to compose serially.' See Straus, *Twelve-Tone Music in America* (Cambridge: Cambridge University Press, 2009: Cover summary). This chapter addresses this gap, focusing on an American composer whose unique approach to the twelve-tone system, integrated with other compositional strategies, aims to craft a musical language specifically designed to support the narratives of films. Aside from a few studies with an in-depth treatment of twelve-tone serialism in film, published scholarship touches upon the topic only tangentially. For relevant sources, see David Neumeyer, 'Schoenberg at the Movies: Dodecaphony and Film,' *Music Theory Online* 0.1 (1993); Sabine Feisst, 'Arnold Schoenberg and the Cinematic Art,' *The Musical Quarterly* 83.1 (1999): 93–113; Melissa Ursula Dawn Goldsmith, 'Alban Berg's Filmic Music: Intentions and Extensions of the Film Music Interlude in the Opera "*Lulu*,"' PhD diss. (Louisiana State University and Agricultural & Mechanical College, 2002); Vincent Gassi, 'The Forbidden Zone, Escaping Earth and Tonality: An Examination of Jerry Goldsmith's Twelve-Tone Score for *Planet of the Apes*,' PhD diss. (York University, 2019); and Orit Hilewicz, 'Schoenberg's Cinematographic Blueprint: A Programmatic Analysis of Begleitungsmusik zu einer Lichtspielscene (1929–1930),' *Music Theory Online* 21.1 (2021).

4 Although both Glass and Friedhofer taught the twelve-tone technique, they seldom fully fleshed out the system within their own movie scores. The closest approximation may be found in Glass's *Lady in a Cage* (1964).
5 A film is a multiparametric artistic expression, a synthesis of the aesthetic, philosophical, practical, and technical visions of the director, composer, sound engineer, and many others. As a result, the musical score's final rendition often differs from the composer's original creation. Thus, while composers may construct a coherent and self-contained musical narrative through a sequence of cues, these cues are sometimes omitted or rearranged. This presents a challenge for the analyst, who must consider both the composer's manuscript and the final cut soundtrack as alternative 'texts.' In this chapter, I engage with the former because doing so allows insight into the composer's vision and their chosen means for revealing that vision through (in this case) manipulation of the twelve-tone language.
6 In his choice of a progressive jazz-funk feel, Shire was also taking inspiration from the funk soundtracks of blaxploitation films. But his choice of idiom is also attributable to practical reasons. Shire anticipated a formidable opposition of loud diegetic subway sounds to the non-diegetic score and thus envisioned a big band ensemble that would keep the music out of the mid-range, thereby avoiding a conflict between the music and other layers of the soundtrack.
7 David Shire, Personal Interview with Author (June 1, 2015).
8 Example 1 includes 'ic1' in parentheses at the end of the row to reflect the fact that Shire methodically juxtaposes row permutations connected by ic1. Because the interval between the first and last pitches of any row is **ic1** (for example, A3 and G♯3 here), the repetition of any row permutation would not disrupt the sequence of ic1 intervals.
9 The version of the Main Titles included in the soundtrack album presents RI_9 as two fleeting runs, first in the trumpets and then in the saxophones.
10 First defined in Babbitt (1955), an all-combinatorial hexachord is one that, when transformed by any or all four canonical serial operations at certain levels and recombined with the original, completes the aggregate. Those four basic operations are the Retrograde (**R**), Inversion (**I**), and Retrograde-Inversion (**RI**) transformations, plus transposition of prime form by n semitones (P_n).
11 The tendency to construct rows based on all-combinatorial hexachords, however, will become a trademark of Shire's twelve-tone compositional practice.
12 Both the earlier system using musical notation and the PC matrix may serve equally well as a dramatic space. Knowing that Shire resorted to the earlier system, however, allows us to more efficiently and truthfully trace transformational trajectories.
13 Shire, Personal Interview.
14 A sentence structure is a common melodic form, in which a) the first melodic 'presentation' phrase is constructed by a motivic idea and its (modified or exact) restatement, and b) the following 'continuation' phrase—twice the length of the initial musical idea—is characterized by melodic fragmentation, harmonic-rhythm acceleration, and eventually a cadence.
15 Although Shire composed this work for the Main Titles, the film's final cut introduces it later.
16 Annotations in Shire's manuscripts and drafts for all three films discussed here suggest he was familiar with Slonimsky's (1975) *Thesaurus of Scales and Melodic Patterns*. In his notes for *Pelham*, Shire specifies the intention to introduce a musical figure that contains only one of each interval, resulting in a twelve-tone aggregate; such a figure becomes part of *2010*'s cue M42 'Dolowitz Killed.' In his notes for *2010*, Shire jots down possible rows constructed by

four mutually exclusive triads; one of these becomes the film's primary row. In *Zodiac*, the transposed rotations of the row in 5M14 'Informant Montage' replicate verbatim Slonimsky's first four sets of four mutually exclusive triads that result in twelve-tone aggregates. See Nicholas Slonimsky, *Thesaurus of Scales and Melodic Patterns* (New York: Charles Scribner's Sons, 1947).

17 Some listeners may note additional resemblances between *2010* and *Zarathustra*, particularly to *Zarathustra*'s proto-twelve-tone 'Von der Wissenschaft' fugue theme.

18 Although the procedure of generating a row from operations on an initial trichord is akin to Webern's derived rows, redistributing trichords while maintaining all-combinatorial hexachords presents shades of Milton Babbitt's serial practices using trichordal arrays. Addressing Babbitt's music, Mead describes this principle of exhausting permutations of elements resulting in a specific structure as 'maximal diversity.' This generative process facilitates increased combinatoriality, but unlike Babbitt, Shire does not explore the multiple dimensions of aggregate formation; i.e., Shire only achieves aggregates via 'lynes' (i.e., horizontal aggregates) rather than 'lyne pairs' or 'lyne columns.' See Andrew Mead, *An Introduction to the Music of Milton Babbitt* (Princeton: Princeton University Press, 2014).

19 I resort here to a combination of neo-Riemannian and set-theoretical labeling because this allows for uniformly labeling trichordal relationships across row transpositions, and because scholars have singled out these particular relationships as carrying well-defined extramusical associations. On applications of neo-Riemannian theories to film music, see also Erik Heine's contribution in this volume. For formal definitions of **PLP**, **RLR**, and T_6, see Frank Lehman, *Hollywood Harmony: Musical Wonder and the Sound of Cinema* (Oxford and New York: Oxford University Press, 2016).

20 In selecting these rows #1 and #4, Shire may have been drawn by the associative power of the octatonic scale, outlined by the roots of all triads contained in these rows.

21 In the music, nevertheless, Shire recombines trichords to produce all-combinatorial hexachords—the first, second, and last aggregates feature the (014589) hexachord, while the third aggregate features the (024579) hexachord, thereby exhausting the possible all-combinatorial hexachords achievable by combining two inversionally-related (037) trichords.

22 Richard Cohn, 'Uncanny Resemblances: Tonal Signification in the Freudian Age,' *Journal of the American Musicological Society* 57.2 (2004): 285, and Lehman, *Hollywood Harmony*, 102. Cohn further argues that, in addition to the conventionalized uses of these harmonic gestures, their associations stem from their affective power as 'the ear is caught in a liminal space, where the binary distinction between consonance and dissonance is eroded. Such breakdowns in the division between otherwise securely demarcated categories, prototypically the boundary between reality and illusion, or life and death, are a mark of the psychological uncanny.' Richard Cohn, *Audacious Euphony: Chromatic Harmony and the Triad's Second Nature* (Oxford and New York: Oxford University Press, 2012), 22. See also Richard Cohn, 'Uncanny Resemblances: Tonal Signification in the Freudian Age,' *Journal of the American Musicological Society* 57.2 (2004): 285–324; Scott Murphy, 'The Major Tritone Progression in Recent Hollywood Science Fiction Films,' *Music Theory Online* 12.2 (2006).

23 For this soundtrack, Shire uses a Synclavier II, a Yamaha DX-1, and a Roland Jupiter-8.

24 In a personal interview, Shire mentioned he sought to emulate the descending vocal contour of Zodiac's 'Good-Bye?' at the end of his phone call with the

'E-to-C♯' descending melodic motion that concludes the cue. Shire, Personal Interview.
25 The film's final cut does not include this cue. Instead, Isaac Hayes's 'Hyperbolicsyllabicsesquedalymistic' plays under the informant montage, bringing a lighter comedic tone to the various informants' absurd claims.
26 Shire, Personal Interview.
27 Other names for this mode (or scale) are aeolian-♭5, locrian-♯2, and semi-locrian.
28 For the remainder of the film, Shire's compositional attention focuses on the structural possibilities implied by the 'Desire' harmonic progression, particularly on its distinctive movement from a half-diminished-seventh chord to a dominant-seventh chord a minor second below.

12

ROMANCE AND THE TWO POLES OF UNDERSCORE

James Buhler

Aaron Copland credited Max Steiner with the innovation of neutral music for cinema. Neutral music, according to Copland, was

> atmospheric music almost without melodic content of any kind. A melody is by its nature distracting, since it calls attention to itself. For certain types of neutral music, a kind of melody-less music is needed. Steiner does not supply mere chords but superimposes a certain amount of melodic motion, just enough to make the music sound normal and yet not enough to compel attention.[1]

Such music, Copland adds, 'is really the music one isn't supposed to hear, the sort that helps to fill the empty spots between pauses in a conversation.'[2] More generally, neutral music was any music that did not have a strong emotional or affective character and so could accompany a wide range of scenes without distracting from the dialogue. 'To write music that must be inexpressive is not easy for composers who normally tend to be as expressive as possible.'[3]

Copland understands neutral music principally in terms of the absence of sharply drawn musical materials, which he links to its signifying and affective domains. Neutral here means 'neutralized'; that is, its musical properties have been tempered and attenuated, partly from an avoidance of cadence and other means of articulating materials, and partly from techniques of motivic reduction and semantic coolness—scales, turns, arpeggios, and other standard patterns of passage work often used in transitions and bridging material. For Copland, this is useful for scoring because it allows music to be present in a scene and available when needed for dramatic emphasis but without otherwise drawing attention to itself.

When he wrote about Steiner's use of neutral music, Copland likely had in mind music of the sort that underscored the Reunion Scene in *Casablanca* (1942) [33:20]. Hearing Sam (Dooley Wilson) play the song 'As Time Goes By' (ATGB), Rick (Humphrey Bogart) comes over and admonishes him. Sam stops playing and glances toward Ilsa (Ingrid Bergman). Rick follows his glance, and on the cut to Ilsa, the non-diegetic score starts with a musical stinger. This stinger becomes a long-held dissonant chord, and the main ATGB motive emerges from it played slowly by a plaintive oboe. The passage is shown in Example 12.1. Rick's Café Américain is a place suffused with music. Up to this moment, few scenes are without music in some capacity, and many, like the sequence between Ilsa and Sam that opens the Reunion Scene, have featured diegetic performances. But the chord that sounds when Rick sees Ilsa is the first time since the opening prologue—almost 20 minutes—that non-diegetic music has appeared, and its prominent appearance here has the force of establishing a prior attachment between Rick and Ilsa, while also coloring the recognition as shocking. The music here almost single-handedly makes us believe in the history of this relationship, and it will continue to serve this function for the remainder of the scene, indeed for much of the middle portion of the film.

The main motive of ATGB appears initially while Sam scrambles to clear away the piano, and a second statement (m. 3 of Example 12.1) sounds when Louis and Victor appear. The placement of the motive with action that interrupts the cuts between Rick and Ilsa helps cement the sense that the two share a strong bond that unites them amidst these interruptions that would divide them. Indeed, even the introduction of Victor (Paul Henreid)—Ilsa's husband—is made while the tune is clearly sounding. As the group sits down at the table, the first phrase of ATGB cadences (m. 8). A polite conversation begins accompanied by a waltz version of ATGB, shown in Example 12.2, until the mention of Paris, when the music turns ominous. Ilsa recalls the Nazis marching in, and the German national anthem is played in minor with a highly dissonant counterpoint of ATGB sounding above it. The music then dissolves into a rather indistinct, if still affectively laden, musical wash.

When Victor notes that it is getting late, the music grows more animated, finally coalescing back into a statement of the main motive from ATGB when Ilsa refers to Sam. This is where Example 12.3 starts. In m. 31, the music mimics Rick with deflating descending chords as he collapses into the chair, and the main motive of ATGB returns when Ilsa and Victor are outside. But the tune now sounds somewhat disjointed, as though it is not quite in the right key. It cadences on a D♭ major chord, and when the camera passes over Louis, it darkens ominously to minor.

250 James Buhler

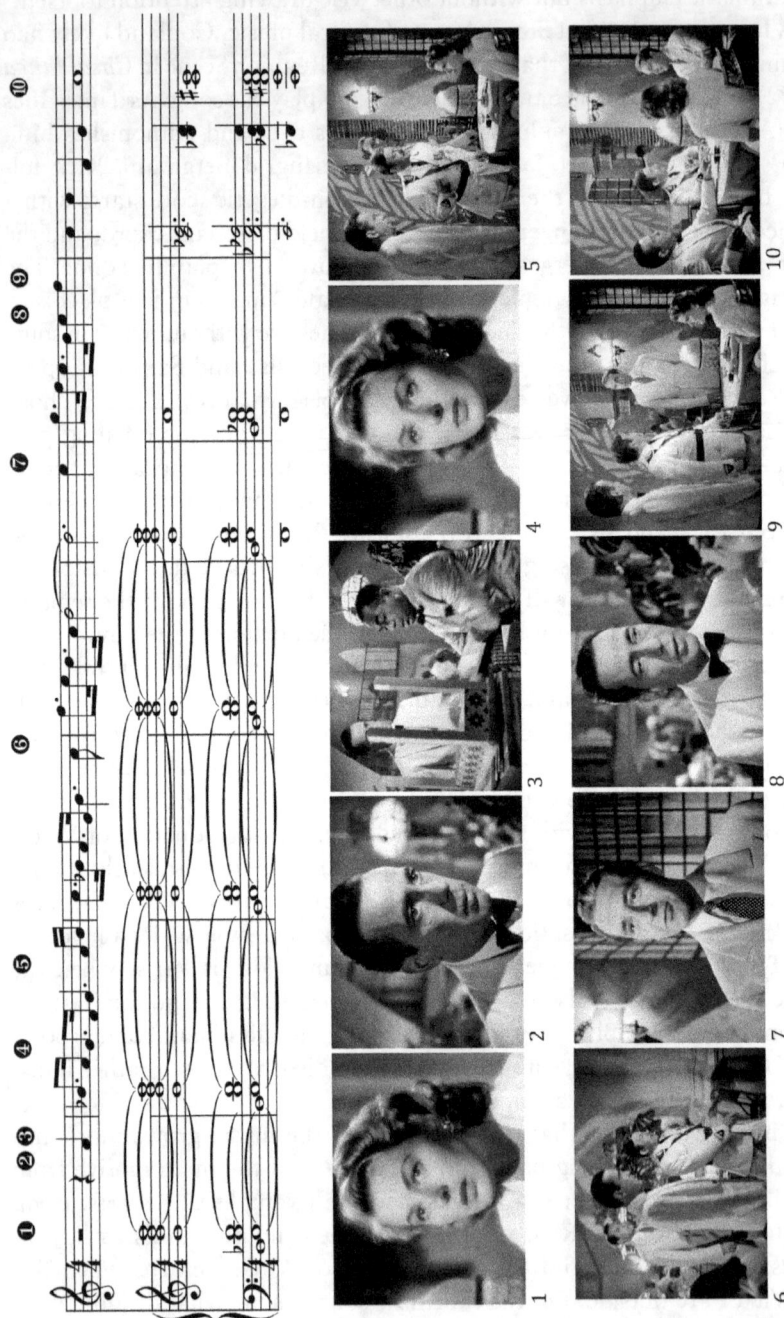

EXAMPLE 12.1 Steiner, Reunion Scene, *Casablanca*: mm. 1–8 (all examples transcribed by author unless otherwise noted).

Romance and the Two Poles of Underscore 251

EXAMPLE 12.2 Steiner, Reunion Scene, *Casablanca*: mm. 10–17.

David Neumeyer and I have argued that the structure of the music for this scene follows something like the outline of a chorus of ATGB.[4] But the departures from the original in this outline are significant, and their collective effect is to wear away the distinctive shapes of the tune through a process of reduction, allowing the presentation of dialogue with a minimum of distraction. The AABA song structure of ATGB can be recovered through analysis of the sort Neumeyer and I performed on the cue.[5] But the formal shape of the melody, or even its motivic particulars, is not especially evident for long stretches of the cue, which retains an affective charge and a certain musical flow; its substance has been dissolved, the boundary between motives and units rendered indistinct. This neutralization moves music into background, but while its affective dimension is perhaps muted, it never wholly disappears. This is a blurry, inarticulate music more than it is inexpressive. Or to put it differently, Copland's analysis posits an identity between articulateness and affective expression that is perhaps not warranted. Indeed, the distinction is one of the things that underscore frequently traffics in, especially in emotionally charged scenes like this one.

The dissolved character of the underscore, its inarticulateness, allows the music to sit under the dialogue and direct its flow, emphasizing less what's being said in the conversation than responding to the surging emotions that distend the discourse under the surface, rendering much of the dialogue cryptic while also cuing the audience that the words do not say what they mean. That is, music here distends the discourse in order to reshape meaning. This is not music as counterpoint in the sense that Sergei Eisenstein or Siegfried Kracauer meant it—that is, where music plays against the dominant narrative line to forge another in contradistinction. Nor is it anempathetic music of the sort Steiner himself talked about, where a banal dance tune sounds as a character learns that a loved one has died (though much of the music of Rick's Café has that

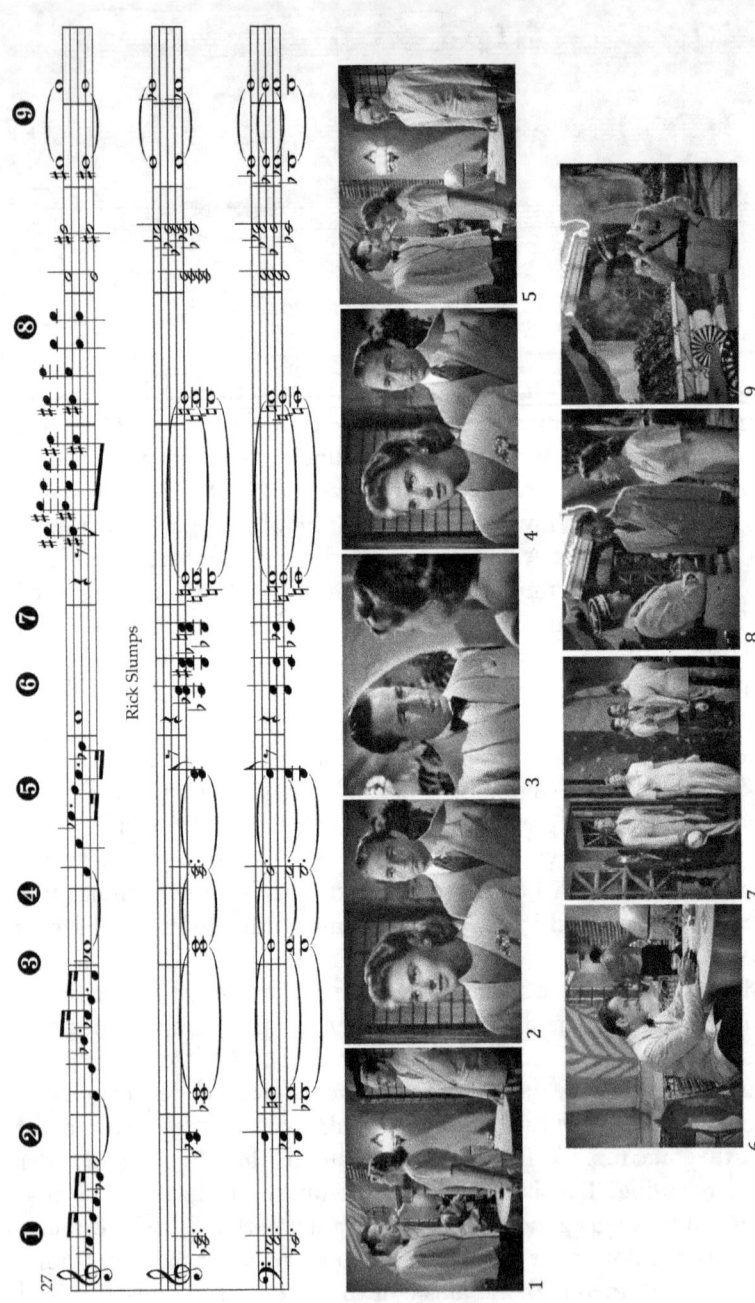

EXAMPLE 12.3 Steiner, Reunion Scene, *Casablanca*: mm. 27–36.

kind of anempathetic relation to the plight of the refugees who flock to it).[6] Instead, the underscore of the Reunion Scene offers a line of affective resonance to the shock of recognition, where surface-level conversational pleasantries carry hidden barbs, registered smartly by the music. The dissolution of ATGB across the cue represents a fundamental organizing lack, seeming to lose again what had just been found, and yet ATGB also furnishes in dissolved form the basic materials for the mushy affective tone, perhaps illustrated nowhere better than when the deflating music accompanies Rick's collapse in the chair as Ilsa leaves with Victor (m. 31 of Example 12.3). The tune regains its motivic shape for the close of the cue as Ilsa leaves the table and mentions Sam. The consequential dialogue has ended, and music coalesces again into an articulate statement. Once Rick and Ilsa have separated, and the scene follows Ilsa and Victor outside, the tune continues, but the harmonization of the final statement is now at odds with itself, the theme in E major while the harmony that supports it is a Cmaj7 chord. And the final cadence harmonizes the rising E major melodic segment in D♭ major, which falls back to D♭ minor for the final chord. Even after the neutralization is overcome, the music remains tonally adrift. It reflects the historical state of the relationship. If the cue is organized around lack and desire, it also forms an intensive series—a series organized around intensities of musical material rather than, say, motivic concerns—as the musical particulars seem to bounce back and forth between scoring now Rick and now Ilsa.

This fluctuating character of underscore, though not uncommon in practice—and Steiner, as Copland recognizes, was something of a master at it—has not been much discussed in the literature on film music, and where it has the focus has generally fallen on marks of coherence: The use of leitmotifs for reference; the identification of melodramatic topics or word painting; figures such as stingers that seek the status of what I have called 'emotion-as-we-hear-it'; and so forth.[7] In this Reunion Scene, an audience committed to coherence would concentrate on the stinger chord that initiates the cue, on the fragments of ATGB that are woven throughout it, on the intrusion of 'Deutschland über Alles,' on Rick slumping into his chair to a series of mickey-mousing chords, on the affective drop from D♭ major to minor passing like a shadow over the scene at the end, and so forth. And much of my analysis of the scene so far has focused on just such marks of coherence. Under this approach, on the one hand, the important shaping force of dialogue is acknowledged: Dialogue supplies the form, and music is reactive, responding to speech somewhat like accompanied recitative. Ilsa mentions Germans marching in, and the music dutifully responds with 'Deutschland über Alles.' On the other hand, music is presumed to be in a subdued 'neutral' state whose main concern is to avoid interfering with the intelligibility of dialogue, so what this kind of analysis highlights are the places music finds a way to assert itself in a positive way, to rise up against its neutralization. The neutralization also allows the music to be present so when Ilsa mentions the Germans marching into Paris, the music can respond immediately and melodramatically (and not at all neutrally) with the distorted rendition of 'Deutschland über Alles'; but the appearance of this melodramatic marking would not be possible without music already sounding almost unnoticed in the background. So neutral music in this sense is music that is designed to fade into the background, retaining its character as continuous music but without forming cogent patterns that would draw the audience to pay attention to the music other than when the drama warranted. This is essentially a summary of Copland's understanding of underscore as neutral music.

The technical means of underscore have only been vaguely presented, by Copland or anyone else, notwithstanding some general comments about avoiding instruments in the same range as the voices and refraining from using busy or sharp figures that call too much attention to the music and distract from the dialogue. This negative definition, cataloging musical practices to avoid, rather than deliver, a sense of how underscore actually ought to be organized or what it should do while waiting in the background, means that little notice has been given to the poles that structure underscoring—one pole in fact not dissolving at all but rather using a melodically based cue to entirely encompass the scene, the other pole presenting neutral music in Copland's sense as a kind of affective mush. The Reunion Scene in essence shifts from one pole to the other, starting with the melody of ATGB to establish a connection and then dissolving into an affective wash when the dialogue assumes importance, only to surge back when the dialogue is over. Such movement between poles that establishes a line of dissolution is also common, no doubt because it conforms to the idea that the drama of the scene has yielded a changed situation. This is not quite what happens in Rick and Ilsa's reunion, however, where the situation does not really 'contract into action,' as Gilles Deleuze would put it, yielding a changed situation; instead, shock reverberates across it.

Rather than contracting into action, the scene is organized around uncertainty and desire, and Steiner's music neatly captures this play. The arrival of Louis and Victor [33:34], which is documented in the screengrabs in Example 12.1, breaks off the intimate reunion of Ilsa and Rick and turns it into a public affair, such that they cannot say what they mean. There remains, despite it all, an intensity that comes from desire. The music detaches from the shock of recognition and becomes more diffuse. And if there is some ambiguity about whose shock the music represents, it is even more difficult to assign the music to Rick or to Ilsa once the music loses its clear connection to ATGB.[8] Instead, the cue devolves into an emblem of desire, inchoate affective responses that seethe and surge below the dialogue and connect to the relationship, not the immediate dramatic action. The music here is dispersive and disconnected. It creates a broken line that turns inward as it forms an intensive series, leaping from quality to quality.[9]

The Two Poles of Underscore

Underscoring, I have claimed, has two poles, and *Casablanca*'s Reunion Scene is striking for how it passes from one to the other, from the presentation of the tune of ATGB to its dispersion into inarticulate figures under dialogue and back, without thereby dramatizing action or responding directly to it. I will call these the **reflective** and **intensive** poles of underscoring.[10] But not all underscoring follows such a circuitous path. Sometimes, underscore remains at the reflective pole, presenting an outline of the whole—melodies, musical unities that express thought, or the romance of a couple. In romantic scenes, these tend to occur when a couple is present, formed, and stable. Other times, underscore works more through features that are restless and dispersed, fragmentary motives or chords that break with the melodic line. The music moves but without extension. Here, the underscore follows an intensive series, relating to the quality or power of the feeling or idea, the possibility and potential, not to the feeling or idea itself, which is always delimited by a situation or context. What the intensive mode captures in the Reunion Scene is not so much the feelings of the characters, of Rick or Ilsa, but the way the words they utter do not mean what they say.

These poles are especially apparent in romantic scenes—or rather romantic scenes generally have to choose between them and determine whether the scene follows an affect of admiration or of desire. Melody is committed to a reflective unity, a presentation of wholeness, and it gathers its elements into reflective, pensive movements that relate to thought or feeling. In such cases, the melody presents the quality of the relationship, the mutual love, that remains fixed in a scene, and it attaches to the quality that is common to each member of the couple, and indeed to most everything that appears in that setting that helps cement that bond, that becomes thereby further signs of that bond. In the musical *Yankee Doodle Dandy* (1942), Mary plays and sings the song 'Mary' that George has diegetically written for her as he dictates the lyrics. Once Mary finishes the performance, they begin to talk and the song moves to the underscore, presented without significant alteration behind the couple's conversation. The reflective pole, the long, uninterrupted flow of what Mark Richards calls a grammatical melody, here encompasses the loving status of the relationship.[11]

In *Casablanca*, ATGB also serves this kind of musical object, associated with a reflecting unity of romance. Note how Ilsa listens to ATGB [32:53], her face fixed in thought, in memory, just before Rick arrives (See

FIGURE 12.1 Ilsa listening to Sam sing 'As Time Goes By.'

Figure 12.1). But after that moment, ATGB is displaced and presented as something no longer obtainable. Rick attempts to replicate Ilsa's reflective listening in the next scene [38:20], but unlike Ilsa's immobile face, Rick grimaces as he listens, and falls into the long flashback that tells the story of their affair. And with respect to the notion that ATGB is the musical signifier of the romance, it is significant that the song never appears whole in the film, from start to middle to beginning, belonging, as it were, to Paris, irretrievably lost to the past.[12]

The restless style of underscore by contrast dissolves melody and relates to desire. Its broken character follows an intensive series, which traces an arc of feeling that is not fixed but fluctuating. The intensive series presents itself as the primary pole each time some facet of the musical materials escapes the kind of formal determination of the musical structure that would corral its quality into the unity of something like a cogent melody. The middle section of the Reunion Scene from *Casablanca*, shown in Example 12.4,

EXAMPLE 12.4 Steiner, Reunion Scene, *Casablanca*: mm. 19–25.

illustrates this restless character. Breaking free of musical structure and the quality the structure forms as a unity, intensive underscore forges a new series that creates a new shape, a line of anger or jealousy, for instance, or a passionate embrace. The music flits, as it were, from one emotion to another, and traces a broken line on its path to a new quality.

Scoring Romance

Love themes have been a favorite object of analysis among film music scholars. Rebecca Fülöp has noted in the conventional Love Theme of a film a systematic semiotic confusion between signifier of the heroine and signifier of the relationship. It is a purposefully overdetermined (and ideological) confusion that serves to present the heroine as narratively subordinate to the hero but also as framed through him: In a love theme we hear the heroine as the hero, in a sense, feels her. The love theme typically presents the hero's image of the heroine, then, and as such the structure belongs to the implicit male gaze that has dominated Hollywood cinema in general. Fülöp calls this conventional complex of Hollywood cinema the Feminine Romantic Cliché (FRC), and she notes 'the FRC works to strip the female character of any identity or value apart from her romantic potential, making her a love *object* rather than an autonomous *subject*.'[13]

The focus of Fülöp's analysis is on the way the themes characterize the heroine as the object of the hero's affections rather than how music, thematic or not, underscores romantic scenes *per se*. But this double connection with the heroine as both character and love object of the hero tends to reinforce its unity as a recurring musical idea. That is, the narrative might place deformational pressure on the love theme to indicate stresses on the heroine or the relationship, but the melody will appear in full form, especially any leitmotivic incipit that is extracted from it, when the relationship is narratively secure, as in the example from *Yankee Doodle Dandy* presented above.[14]

The basic modality of the love theme is admiration, not desire, a point that Fülöp emphasizes with the claim that 'a character accompanied by the FRC typically exudes a femininity that is devoid of sexuality.'[15] Love themes are also an especially effective means of presenting a reflective unity, the presentation of the couple as sharing a quality, love and affection, common to both even when the dramatic purpose of this unity serves to make the hero whole but the heroine partial. And in the adventure film, Brian Taves notes, 'Love forms a subplot that parallels the main themes, placing the woman in a perilous situation that provides the hero with the opportunity he seeks to prove his nobility, chivalry, courage, and altruism.'[16] The hero simply ceases to be without the reflective unity of the couple, which is a central aspect of his identity, a point hit on in *Casablanca* when it is noted that Victor, the nominal adventure hero of the film, would cease to be the leader he needs to be without Ilsa.

In one scene in *Captain Blood* (1935), Peter (Errol Flynn) and Arabella (Olivia de Havilland) ride together on horses and talk [39:12]. Peter has been sentenced to work as a slave at a plantation in the Caribbean but Arabella bought him at auction to annoy her uncle, Colonel Bishop, one of the villains of the film. This is the second time in the film that the couple has a scene alone. The first had been a brief encounter on the Governor's lawn when Arabella had forgotten she had bought Peter. In the second scene with the romantic pair, the music that accompanies the ride largely represents Peter's feelings for Arabella. Scored by Erich Korngold, the music for the first part of the exchange is shown in Example 12.5. The basic form is a pair of nominal 16-measure sentences syntactically connected to suggest a large period.[17] The second sentence is expanded and elongated to lead to a statement of a novel, minor-seventh leaping motif that will assume the role of Arabella's Theme (also the Love Theme) proper. This motif will be further detached, both from its initial appearance as an extension of the sentential period of the Horse-Riding Theme and later assumption of the role of an independent love theme, and ultimately, through a somewhat different harmonization, come to serve as the continuation of Peter's Doctor Theme.[18] But in this early riding scene, the melodic line, however extended and distended, never breaks away from the governing syntactical musical form, nor does it construct an alternative series of intensities to reveal a new quality, aside from not reaching the tonic at the end, dissolving under dialogue on an incomplete plagal cadence. And when Arabella's motive takes over, it grows out of the previous material and retains the basic quality of adoration and affection. So even when detached from its original context, the theme remains a theme and does so without projecting a sense of dissolution. At any rate during the scene, it manifests as a love theme—Fülöp classifies it as an FRC—with its romantic quality being ascribed to both members of the couple, or rather as the expression of the encounter marking its possibility.

This quality of adoration is broken only twice during the riding sequence: First, right after the initial statement of Arabella's motive as it coalesces into her theme, for the cutaway to the slave camp, where a man is being punished by Colonel Bishop and the music underscores the violence; and second, after the scene between Peter and Arabella resumes. The music for this second part of the scene is at first somewhat indistinct, no longer as well formed motivically as the first section, and so something of an affective wash. Yet the tone, if subdued, also remains committed toward adoration, even as Arabella questions Peter about being at the

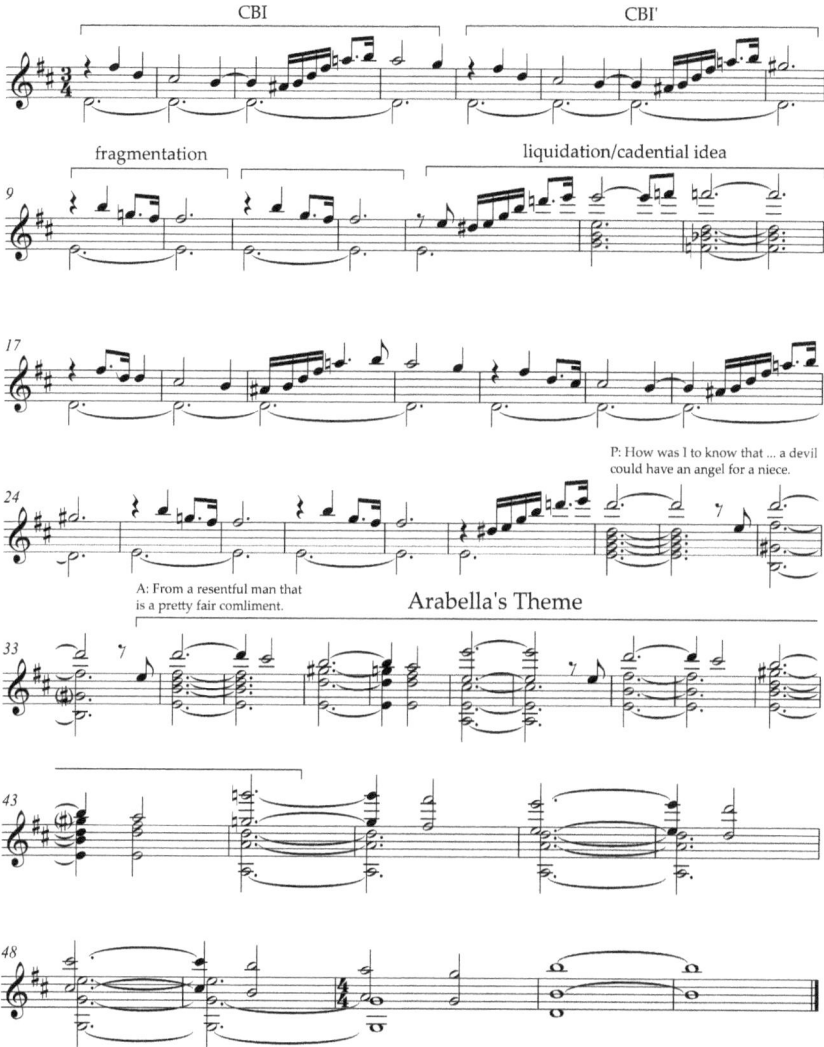

EXAMPLE 12.5 Korngold, *Captain Blood*, Peter and Arabella (example transcribed by author after draft by Jinghong Zhang).

docks. The music grows more distinct when Arabella asks Peter how he feels toward her, the underscore now taking up Arabella's motive, making its appearance here rather more sudden and amorous compared to its first appearance. But Peter's answer says otherwise; Arabella's countenance drops disappointedly when he responds that he thinks of her as the woman who owns him, even as her motive continues in the underscore, belying his words. She becomes more cheerful when he adds that a man can count himself lucky to call her his friend. Arabella offers her hand as she says 'I think you know you can,' and the music surges, commencing another ecstatic statement of Arabella's motive. Rather than take her hand, Peter kisses her, but she reacts angrily to the advance. The music collapses as the crossover to action shifts the poles—not to an action image of dramatic confrontation but to a new element of an intensive series, underscored now by a recollection of another theme, music that had accompanied Peter's voyage on the slave ship.

One thing to consider in this scene is whose perspective is being presented by the music. Is this primarily music of Peter, or of Arabella, or indeed of the couple as a unit? Sometimes it is hard to say, and perhaps for much of the sequence it doesn't matter much, since it is the reflective unity of love that is the basis of adoration, and music serves to establish that the couple is destined to be together. It unites the couple under a figure of romance. This changes suddenly when Peter kisses Arabella. At this point, the romance—the reflecting unity—collapses, and the appearance of the Voyage Theme seems to underscore Peter's recognition that his identity remains that of a slave. But the refusal of romance belongs to Arabella, so the collapse of the theme might also be representing her perspective. The breakdown of Arabella's Theme here might also be Peter's recognition that love is not yet on offer. In any event, music sweetens Arabella's slap with a stinger, perhaps siding with her anger (or his pain) before turning to the Voyage Theme, which itself seems to concentrate and register Peter's emotional perspective alone.

Notice that the Voyage Theme accompanies a close-up of Peter. This shot, especially given its extended duration, helps us understand this music as representing his emotional perspective. Challenged by Arabella's claim that he has forgotten his position, Peter parries with a joke of sorts, comparing the Irish to elephants in terms of not forgetting. And with that, the music seems to shift perspectives, much like the image changes from a two-shot to a close-up of Arabella; now, the remnant of her motive that sounds seems to represent Arabella's perspective, registering both her own commitment to the reflective unity of romance that seems to be dissipating and her emotional disappointment at Peter's departure. It is in this way that Arabella's motive undergoes a symbolic transformation into the Love Theme, representing a reflective unity of romance.

Romance and Power

Now, Voyager (1942) appeared the same year as *Casablanca* and featured another score by Steiner. The films share a narrative situation—in each case, one member of the romantic couple is married—that dooms the central romance on the altar of the Hollywood Production Code. The Production Code makes a final coupling impossible and that impossibility in turn inflects the romance of both films from admiration and reflective unity and toward power and desire.

Presented in an elaborate flashback similar to Rick's flashback in *Casablanca*, the early romance of Charlotte (Bette Davis) and Leslie (Charles Drake)—a crew member of a ship Charlotte is traveling on with her mother (Gladys Cooper)—is scored with a theme associated with the young heroine, and it is treated much like an FRC, though the film is such that it seems to score the romance from Charlotte's perspective rather than from Leslie's. The approach, however, emphasizes a reflective unity, the feeling of romance as a quality, and as a quality distinct from the music associated with the overbearing presence of the mother, who belongs to the domain of power and the intensive series. If the music in this flashback sequence frequently breaks off from the Young Charlotte Theme, this is not distending under the pressure of desire but relates to the mother's control over Charlotte and the secrecy this imposes.[19] Thus, Leslie is introduced kissing Charlotte [11:35], and as Example 12.6 shows, the Young Charlotte Theme plays freely and passionately. Its presence in the score during this flashback is more or less an index to the reflective unity that is presumably

EXAMPLE 12.6   Steiner, Flashback, *Now, Voyager*: mm. 1–13 (example transcribed by author after draft by Jinghong Zhang).

the couple's seafaring affair, but, more than just an amorous relationship, the romance also represents for Charlotte freedom from her mother.

A subdued variant first continues under the couple's dialogue (m. 9), and the passionate form seems poised to play again, only to be interrupted when Leslie notes that the first officer is on deck. This helps establish their relationship as a secret, even as it testifies to Charlotte's fulfillment of self through this romance: It is what the young Charlotte aspires to, perhaps, but more importantly what her mother will ultimately deny her. The connection to aspiration ties back to the lead-in to the flashback, a scene in the present day in which a distressed and broken variant of the Young Charlotte Theme plays as she grows agitated in her conversation with Doctor Jaquith (Claude Rains). Frank Lehman neatly summarizes the musical treatment of this lead-in to the flashback, noting that the music is highly unstable, with fluctuating tonal levels and leitmotivic modules that lack 'cadential reinforcement.'[20] Another variant of the theme continues when Charlotte asks if Leslie would go ashore without her, and it becomes somewhat distended when they again kiss briefly.

Remnants of this leitmotif continue against Charlotte's voiceover as she leaves the deck to find her mother and become progressively distorted as her mother refuses to allow her to go ashore. When in voiceover Charlotte talks about deceiving her mother, her youthful theme momentarily disappears entirely, displaced by a fast version of the oscillating motif associated with the protagonist's interactions with her mother, what I will call 'Mother's Power.' (Example 12.7 presents the theme in its original form as it is used to accompany Charlotte's descent of the stairs at the character's introduction [4:25].) When Charlotte's mother and the ship's captain look for Charlotte among the cars in the cargo hold, brooding fragments of her daughter's theme return, only to disappear again during the subsequent confrontation scene, where Leslie states his intention of marrying Charlotte. When her mother insists that her daughter goes to her cabin, the Young Charlotte Theme appears in a passionate, almost triumphant form as she walks off, the theme dissolving, and with it the flashback. Steiner's underscore doesn't disappear upon the return to the conversation with Dr. Jaquith, however, but dissipates into a long-held, vaguely dissonant chord as Charlotte complains about her

EXAMPLE 12.7 Steiner, introducing Charlotte (Mother's Power Theme), *Now, Voyager*.

lack of desirability, and then crescendos—without thematic content—to accompany her outburst about her mother. The outburst signals a qualitative change—her final psychological collapse—and the change relates to the power Charlotte's mother has over her, here distilled to the void of the crescendo chord and the frantic repetition, 'My mother, my mother, my mother...'

We might be tempted to read a specific and dynamic dramatic arc conveyed within this musical span, one of confrontation followed by tragic collapse. But that is to misread the affective and formal structure of the sequence and its music. The action is encapsulated in a flashback, so we start from a current situation—an *already* defeated state and young Charlotte's Theme in tatters for the conversation with Dr. Jaquith—and the flashback fills in the context that explains the agitation of the scene before the flashback and final collapse after it. The flashback in other words explicates a situation we already know—Charlotte's breakdown—much as a detective story starts from the fact of the murder. And the flashback proceeds through a series of intensities that relate above all to Charlotte's proximity to her mother and index the latter's power of control. We progress through Charlotte's reflective reverie in vivid musical terms: The ecstatic versions of the Young Charlotte Theme that frame the flashback; the dispute with the mother about going ashore that distorts it; Charlotte's subterfuge that brings the Mother's Power Theme to a quicker tempo; the return to brooding developmental fragments of the Young Charlotte Theme as the mother and captain search for Charlotte, as though her blossoming identity has been dispersed; and the strange bare chord that sounds when Charlotte and Leslie are discovered in the car, registering trauma perhaps, but as much through negation—a motivic void—as through affirmative expressive gesture. The flashback traces a series of intensities that then carry into the resumption of the present-day conversation with Dr. Jaquith, accompanied by vague chords. And what changes between the situation before the flashback and after it is registered by the music. The traumatized form of the Young Charlotte Theme that had permeated the underscoring of the conversation with Jaquith before the flashback and had been elevated into a reverie of love with Leslie as a mark of Charlotte's autonomy from her mother during the memory, disappears on the return, and the music repeats, in its way, the trauma of the discovery in the car: Bare chords and a motivic void that renders the traumatic force of the mother's power over Charlotte as a loss of (musical) identity.

Romance—the status of the Young Charlotte Theme as a love theme for Charlotte and Leslie—is an important figure in *Now, Voyager* for the way it identifies and organizes Charlotte's autonomy. As such, Charlotte is drawn to romance because it is the principal site of opposition to her

EXAMPLE 12.8 Steiner, conversation on deck, Jerry Love Theme, *Now, Voyager*.

mother's power, and it is through romance that Charlotte first learns to project a sense of self. After her breakdown and trip to Dr. Jaquith's sanitarium, Charlotte goes on another cruise, this time alone, where she again finds romance. The new romance is marked by a new theme, vaguely related in mood and motivic shape to the one previously established for young Charlotte, when she and her new love interest, Jerry (Paul Henreid), talk on deck after a day sightseeing (the scene on deck starts at 33:37). Charlotte shows Jerry a picture of her family, and the Mother's Power Theme plays as they discuss the image. The music grows increasingly leaden, especially when they talk about 'the fat lady with the heavy brows and all the hair,' as Charlotte admits she is the figure, leading her to reveal her illness through tears. When Jerry asks Charlotte if she is feeling better, a reverse shot of the couple brings the first appearance of the new theme associated with Jerry, played twice in different keys, G and then B♭ (see Example 12.8).

This Jerry Love Theme is presented initially as a waltz, and the phrases develop in two more-or-less regular 12-measure sentences, the half cadence of the first statement moving directly to B♭ for the beginning of the second. The phrase is expanded to 12 measures due to the three-measure basic idea, a compressed continuation phrase, and an extension of the dominant. The tonal shift to B♭ emphasizes that the romance remains tentative but the repetition of the theme in the new key suggests as well the general reflective unity of the romance, its ability to maintain shape and character across the key change establishing it much more securely than the earlier affair with Leslie, which began to dissolve musically almost as soon as it began. The parting of Charlotte and Jerry leads to a somewhat strange cut to a shot of the ship's horn and then engine room, with dissonant scoring for the machines—a figure of power and drive—confirmed by a cut to Charlotte fitfully sleeping while a highly agitated version of the new theme plays. This is followed by Mother's Power sounding over a shot of a tranquil ocean through a porthole, and then a cut to Jerry as a variant of Mother's Power continues to play. He is writing a letter to his daughter, Tina, who Charlotte has suggested is a lonely unwanted child. Mother's Power may seem a symbolically odd choice, lying outside the reflective unity of the couple, usually reserved for Charlotte's feelings of inadequacy; but here it draws a further connection between the couple, thereby expanding

EXAMPLE 12.9   Steiner, Balcony Scene, Jerry Love Theme variant, *Now, Voyager*.

the circle of reflective unity of their romance by means of incorporating this otherwise alien element. (Recall that a reflective unity, according to Deleuze, expresses 'a quality common to several different things.'[21])

A later scene at a hotel where Charlotte is staying in Rio de Janeiro [48:05] emphasizes even more how the Love Theme underscores this reflective unity of romance. The scene opens with Jerry approaching Charlotte on the balcony. The Jerry Love Theme sounds as he walks and continues as dialogue starts, with the level of the music lowered appreciably to duck behind dialogue. The melody repeats, this time with no change of key for the second statement. It then moves to other music after he mentions 'primitive instincts'—a reference to the night they spent together in the mountains—and notes the beauty of the view. When they start talking about immortality, bells sound. This ushers in a return to the Jerry Love Theme, shown in Example 12.9, this time with a more expansive harmonic treatment. When their conversation moves to their shared experience of being burned by happiness, the score becomes thematically less distinct before coming back to the Jerry Love Theme for the end of the scene and a full cadence in C major.[22]

The tune recurs several more times in the film, and each time it underscores a reflective unity, presenting what is common to each member of the couple. The threats to the melody come not as with the Young Charlotte Theme, from the mother and her domineering leitmotif. They are now posed from within, expressed as impassioned versions of the theme, with bold harmonic motions that threaten to dissolve the admiration of love and replace it with desire (represented above all by musical transgression and dissolution). If Charlotte finds a certain independence in the reflective unity of romance, a slide toward desire would unseat that.

Now, Voyager's final scene hangs on the edge between admiration and desire, whether the tune retains its integrity or dissolves. It begins with Jerry visiting Charlotte and his daughter, Tina, whom Charlotte has taken on as a ward. Charlotte and Jerry [1:51:30] retreat to the library to talk, where Jerry announces that he is taking Tina home. Initially, there is no music, then a very fragmented, agitated version of the Jerry Love Theme enters when Jerry gets upset. The fragmentation here presents the sign of desire as a lure. A variant of the Mother's Power appears on the clarinet when Charlotte talks about them being in sympathy. At this point Charlotte's mother is dead and so no longer a threat to her daughter's autonomy. The presence of the theme recalls the collapse of identity that precipitated the initial breakdown, but it also points to the shared feeling of Jerry and Charlotte from when Jerry wrote to Tina from the ship accompanied by this music. After hearing Charlotte talk about his daughter, an ethereal version of the Jerry Love Theme plays as Jerry says he heard no note of pity in Charlotte's words. The tune continues as she pushes away, representing perhaps Charlotte's recognition that physical separation is the mark of the reflective unity on which she has staked her identity. There is a parallel here to the love scene on the balcony, except the finale does not end in a kiss. The impassioned, harmonically rich variant sounds as they consider the situation in silence.

Music grows more vague when Charlotte talks about them being tested, and the Jerry Love Theme returns when they agree to have a cigarette on it. The theme detaches from the couple, associates with their shared love for Tina, reaches for the stars as the final shot tracks out the window and into the sky, and continues for the end card, where it is modified for the cadence. This sequence of music and image into the end card, the dissociation of the theme from the bodies of the couple marking its impossibility (and also placing the reflective unity under the sign of desire) is an elegant recapitulation of the final narrative situation.

The Desire of Romance

A comparison of *Now, Voyager* to *Casablanca* draws out a number of commonalities with respect to the poles of underscoring, but each film winds its own path between the poles and so illuminates different aspects of the dynamic between admiration and desire. These are two films that were made at Warner Bros. Pictures in close proximity, and they share many actors and personnel, including Steiner as composer. In each, it is not just the presence of a recurring tune that places scoring on the reflective line of admiration, but the *integrity* of the tune. *Now, Voyager* retains a commitment to the reflective unity of romance in its second half, and, once introduced, its primary love theme is maintained to the end. In essence, the intensive series of desire serves as a temptation that would bring ruin to the reflective unity of romance, and so destroy Charlotte's hard-won independence that sits precariously between the intensive series associated with the power of the mother and the intensive series associated with the desire of and for Jerry. The reflective unity of romance is the figure that shields that independence, but in doing so, a new quality is articulated, suggesting a shadow of desire.

Casablanca presents a similar musical situation but draws different consequences from it. 'As Time Goes By' belongs to the reflective unity of the romance, and it is presented throughout as already broken up, its variants sequenced along an intensive series that more explicitly expresses desire than is the case of the musical treatment in *Now, Voyager*. There is also a parallel to the treatment of the Marseillaise, which is first heard similarly as part of an intensive series of variants inflected to underscore the gravity of the situation—initially in the main title but also marking several important turning points of the narrative that touch on the nebulous political situation in Casablanca. After its diegetic appearance in the 'Battle of the Anthems,' however, the treatment of the Marseillaise becomes increasingly reflective. And in the end, it binds Rick and Louis as a reflective pair around a common ethereal musical theme, and to some extent Ilsa and Victor as well, since Ilsa's admiration is instilled in Victor's Theme, but also in her gaze as she watches him lead the singing of the anthem.

Like *Now, Voyager, Casablanca* also features a flashback—even lengthier—that presents the story of the now broken romance between Rick and Ilsa, parallel to the broken romance of Charlotte and Leslie, though *Casablanca* presents the reasons for the breakup as an enigma. ATGB serves to launch the flashback, as Sam plays the tune for Rick, the reverie of the tune motivating the flashback, and the song features extensively in the sequence both diegetically and non-diegetically. At the end of flashback, Rick is at the train station with a note Ilsa has left him saying she can't go with him. An impassioned *valse lento* variant of ATGB plays, leading to the dissolve back to Rick's. Sam is still playing ATGB, and he stops only when Rick knocks over his drink. It is at this point that Ilsa returns [48:09], announced with a stinger reminiscent of the one when Rick first sees her, albeit a comparatively subdued one, and quickly pushed aside by a descending motif that forms the first appearance of a musical series of communicating anger.

Example 12.10 presents the music for the opening of the scene, showing how the shots align with the music. The Anger Motif, a descending string line, starts with a close-up of Rick, suggesting that the music here renders his feelings, a kind of seething anger that moves only downward into a musical abyss. The editing and the Anger Motif are loosely synchronized: First note, close-up of Rick; second and third notes, close-up of Ilsa; fourth, fifth, and sixth notes, close-up of Rick, with the accented sixth note underscoring a grimace on Rick's face; seventh and subsequent notes as the musical line dissolves under dialogue: A long shot of Ilsa. This last shot begins as described, as a long shot, but Ilsa moves toward Rick in it and as she sits down, the camera dollies in to reframe for a much closer shot for the conversation proper.

As Ilsa moves toward Rick in this shot, the mixing decreases the score's volume to prepare space for the dialogue. Throughout this segment, the sync points described are somewhat loose—only the second note matches

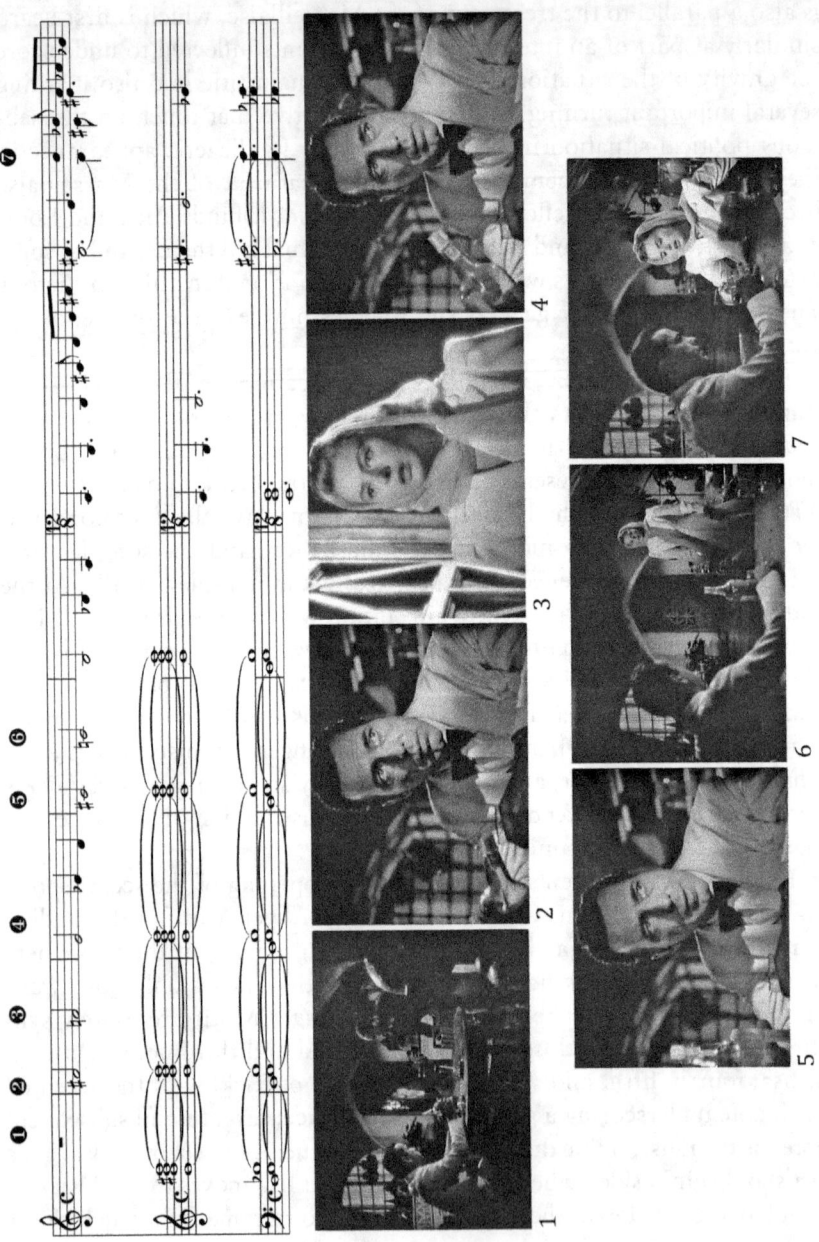

EXAMPLE 12.10 Steiner, After Hours Scene (opening), *Casablanca*, mm. 1–7.

Romance and the Two Poles of Underscore   269

a cut precisely—but the effect is a dramatic coordination of music with these shots, an audiovisual phrasing that both reinforces the sense that there remains a strong connection between the couple, but also that Rick is experiencing a traumatic wound that is pulling them—and the reflective unity of their romance—apart.

The music takes a somewhat different tack, shifting across the scene from Rick's dejected perspective to Ilsa's more hopeful tones and back. Starting with the seething music of the opening and continuing until the beginning of Ilsa's story, a full phrase of 'As Time Goes By' is played, softening to some extent Rick's sarcasm and seeming to recall the old tenderness of the romance. When Ilsa begins her story about Victor, the music makes its first shift in perspective, from Rick to Ilsa. This almost hymn-like music is shown in Figure 12.11 (mm. 23–27), and it will become associated with Victor for the rest of the film; here it presents something like

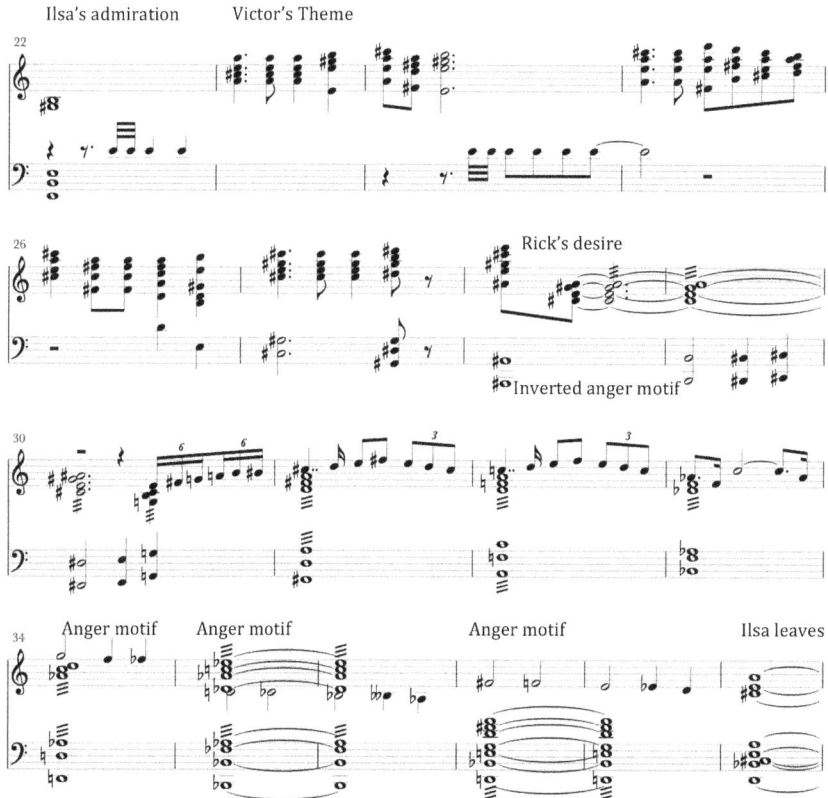

EXAMPLE 12.11   Steiner, After Hours Scene (Victor's Theme and Rick's Brooding: Admiration versus Desire), *Casablanca*, mm. 22–39.

Ilsa's admiration as she tries to explain her feelings toward her husband. When Rick cuts off Ilsa's story and insults her (mm. 28ff.), the music shifts perspectives back to Rick, becoming again fragmented and brooding, the descending motive appearing once more when Rick demands Ilsa tell him who she had left him for in Paris. When Ilsa leaves, the camera settles on Rick alone, and an impassioned fragment of 'As Time Goes By' sounds. This fragment—Rick's musical response to Ilsa's departure—is also essentially Rick's answer to Ilsa's musical portrait of Victor, and much like *Now, Voyager* suggests an opposition between two poles of love, admiration, and desire.

In a later scene [1:19:35], Ilsa returns to get the letters of transit from Rick. The scene is divided, the first portion melodramatic and romantic, the second expository and restrained. Rick climbs the stairs and opens the door. When he turns on the light the stinger chord from the After Hours scene sounds, and the camera wheels to show Ilsa. A cut back to Rick closing the door prompts the appearance of the descending anger motive from the After Hours Scene. This motive is an obsession of the first part of the scene and now seems to encompass Ilsa's perspective as well.

The descending motive ends, and the music devolves into a low rumble when Rick says he's not fighting for any cause anymore. After Rick moves to the window, the music, as shown in Figure 12.12, starts up with a flurry as if to compel Ilsa to follow. Ilsa speaks of them loving each other, and it is again a two-shot, and while in m. 13 the music grows passionate (a descending sequence distantly related to ATGB but without much distinctive motivic material). Rick leaves the shot (m. 17) as the nondescript passionate music continues. Ilsa again pursues Rick (m. 18). This time however there is not a proper two-shot to establish the couple but a set of shot-reverse shots to emphasize their separation. When Ilsa calls Rick 'a coward,' the descending anger motive appears again in m. 21, and this time the motive seems to have gravitated to Ilsa, the reversal binding their anger musically.

Rick turns his back to Ilsa and when he turns back, Ilsa has drawn a gun (m. 29), marked musically by a tremolo stinger that pushes the music in a completely different direction, seeming to register Rick's surprise more than Ilsa's anger. Fragments of ATGB sound as Ilsa demands the letters of transit. The underscore grows frantic when Rick refuses Ilsa's demand, even though Rick remains calm. When he mentions Victor and the cause, a distorted version of the Victor Theme plays. The descending anger motive sounds when Rick tells Ilsa to shoot him, and the gesture continues as she puts down the gun. The music for this incident is given in Figure 12.13. Steiner's score breaks off into a generic romantic sweep (mm. 45–46) that is actually drawn from the After Hours underscore

Romance and the Two Poles of Underscore 271

EXAMPLE 12.12   Steiner, Ilsa's second visit, *Casablanca*, mm. 12–29.

EXAMPLE 12.13   Ilsa's second visit, *Casablanca*, mm. 41–50.

(compare Example 10) and then transforms into the impassioned *valse lento* version of ATGB that is reserved throughout the film for emotional highlights; here it leads to an embrace (mm. 47ff.). The couple kisses as the music plays the cadential pattern from ATGB, but the cue ends on a dissonant chord that motivates a cut away from the couple and to the watchtower, where the music goes silent.

The three scenes I analyzed from *Casablanca*—the Reunion Scene, the After Hours Scene, and the Second Visit—chart a clear progression of the relationship between Rick and Ilsa: Traumatic recognition; broken relationship; restored relationship. The Recognition Stinger Chord initiates all three scenes, and ATGB, as a sign of the reflective unity that is no longer intact, plays an important role in each, the integrity of its statements being a good index to the state of the relationship. A descending Anger Motif appears first in the After Hours Scene but dominates much of the Second Visit when the relationship is at the breaking point. A statement of ATGB ends each of these scenes, and the handling of the melody reflects clear narrative development. In the Reunion Scene, ATGB returns in a more-or-less consonant and complete statement, but the theme and its underlying harmonization are in different keys. In the After Hours Scene, it appears after Ilsa walks out in an incomplete statement that ends dissonantly, and then makes a musical transition to the next scene (featuring a distorted version of the Marseillaise). In Ilsa's Second Visit, an impassioned variant of the tune accompanies the couple's embrace. The melody follows the distinctive cadential pattern of the tune, but its normally consonant final chord is replaced with a dominant minor ninth chord, disturbing the settled image of the reflective unity of romance.

The relationship presents a microcosm of the film's larger theme of rejecting cynicism and embracing the idealism of the cause. Rick's cynicism erodes the relationship as quickly as the prices of the linens in the market plummet for 'Friends of Rick's' and threatens to dissolve the relationship completely, just as remaining cynically detached from the war threatens to plunge the world into the abyss. Rick quietly rejoins the fight by authorizing the café's band to join Victor in the Marseillaise. And after Ilsa breaks down following drawing the gun, Rick recognizes that her love is indeed divided, and divided along the lines of idealism: Admiration for Victor (which at some level he shares) versus desire for Rick. With this recognition, Rick comes to accept Ilsa's present terms for romance, but also that she was correct to have abandoned their prior affair for the idealism of Victor and the cause. This culminates in the final scene with Rick and Louis departing to the strains of the Marseillaise, as though the tune were binding them in a new reflective unity of the war effort (romance transmutes into solidarity).

Conclusion

I have argued that underscore is structured by two poles, one representing a reflective unity, the other an intensive series. Underscore is not generally neutral in the sense that Copland defined it, though when broken down under the pressure of an intensive series into thematic fragments and athematic gestures and textures, it can sometimes give that impression; indeed, a lack of articulateness of thematic structure is one mark that an intensive series is at work. I did not address more recent scoring practices in this essay, but arguably one reason today's films have more or less abandoned the grammaticality of cogent thematic structure in favor of gesture and affect is because character motivation is increasingly organized by the intensive series that moves from one quality to another, that is a correlate of ruminations on the power of becoming.[23] I have further suggested that *Now, Voyager* and *Casablanca* make effective dramatic use of the play between these two poles, in a manner that is prescient for how cinema will develop in the postwar period. Both films animate the two poles, and both pit the reflective unity of romance against the intensive series of desire, and this conflict affects the musical score in profound ways.

In *Now, Voyager* the romance survives, the Love Theme sings us into the end card, but only after the final scene makes clear that romance retains a reflective unity where the formal unit of the couple is present but the actual bodies of Charlotte and Jerry will not occupy the customary romantic positions. The new quality suggests the intensity has reworked the reflective unity of romance into its own series. In *Casablanca*, 'As Time Goes By' serves to recall the reflective unity, the romance of Paris, and here too romance is incorporated into an intensive series even more volatile than the one featured in *Now, Voyager*. Yet over the course of the film, ATGB is dismantled and displaced, and the reflective unity of the romance associated with it dissolves. But desire does not prevail in its place. In the end, Ilsa goes off with Victor, restoring that romance on the basis of admiration, and Rick goes off with Louis, finding a reflective unity of his own—the solidarity and homosocial bond of soldiering—under the sign of rejoining the fight, serenaded by the ethereal strains of the Marseillaise. Yet though the romantic couple of Rick and Ilsa is mismatched at the end, each with a different partner, the overall romance of the fight (romance here as the mark of binding difference into a unity) is now common to all and so yields an expanding reflective unity. Yet the quality has changed, the desperate tone of the opening prologue replaced by the ethereal Marseillaise, and the Marseillaise itself has undergone a transformation from the distortions of the opening credits and early part of the film through the triumphant diegetic 'Battle of the Anthems' to its apotheosis at the end. As befits transformation, all of this makes the reflective unity of the fight a new quality and so the end product of an intensive series.

Attending to the poles of underscoring and the play between reflective unity and intensive series yields important insights into how music can shape the dramatic dynamics of a scene in ways other than by the direct supplemental reinforcement that the term 'underscore' (as emphasis) seems to imply. Moreover, underscoring even in its mushiest, most dissolved form is rarely neutral in the sense that Copland claimed, and it is rarer still for it to be inexpressive even when it is motivically inarticulate. Instead, underscore offers something like an opening into the sequence it accompanies that creates 'a line of flight,' potentially linking most distant relations. Like Deleuze's affection-image, underscoring can give 'an affective reading of the whole film.'[24] It can express quality and power. It is charged with potential that exceeds being defined by the immediate action of the narrative, the usual hermeneutic limit applied to interpreting underscore. In cases like *Now, Voyager* and *Casablanca*, underscore activates its poles to articulate musically the film's thematic concerns so that we come to feel them.

Acknowledgement

I would like to thank Jinghong Zhang, who provided me with draft transcriptions of the scenes from *Captain Blood* and *Now, Voyager*, and the Center for American Music at the University of Texas, which funded this work.

Notes

1 Aaron Copland, 'Our New Music (1941),' in Mervyn Cooke (ed.), *The Hollywood Film Music Reader* (New York: Oxford University Press, 2010), 91.
2 Aaron Copland, 'Aaron Copland in the Film Studio (1949),' in Mervyn Cooke (ed.), *The Hollywood Film Music Reader* (New York: Oxford University Press, 2010), 323.
3 Copland, 'Aaron Copland in the Film Studio,' 323.
4 David Neumeyer and James Buhler, 'Music in the Mix: *Casablanca*,' in David Neumeyer (ed.), *Meaning and Interpretation of Music in Cinema* (Indiana University Press, 2015), 99–180.
5 The research that forms the basis for this analysis of the Reunion Scene is some of the earliest work I did on film music, and it was first presented at *Cinema and Popular Song*, a conference sponsored by the Sound Research Seminar and the Institute for Cinema and Culture at the University of Iowa, April 3, 1999.
6 Max Steiner, 'Scoring the Film,' in Nancy Naumburg (ed.), *We Make the Movies* (New York: Norton, 1937), 224–225.
7 Buhler, *Theories of the Soundtrack* (New York: Oxford University Press, 2019), 181.
8 Ibid, 182–84.
9 Deleuze connects such 'broken lines' to the intensive series of the affection-image and the related small form action-image. See Gilles Deleuze *Cinema 1:*

The Movement-Image (Minneapolis: University of Minnesota Press, 1983), 88–91 and 160–77.

10 These terms derive from Deleuze's analysis of the affection-image in *Cinema 1*, and I am implicitly developing underscore as an analogue to his treatment of the affection-image. But I do not have space in this chapter to present the details of the analogy. Though the theory of underscoring I am developing here is based on the practice of the classic Hollywood sound film, its application does not need to be limited to it so long as the organization of the film is along classical lines, that is, is organized around the repertory of movement-images in Deleuze's terms. Contemporary underscoring practice adds affectively charged sound design that has significant musical properties, and this will affect the particulars of the analysis but less the general framework (or the reflective and intensive poles might occasionally be marked out by music and ambient sound design, respectively). Whether films organized otherwise—say with what Deleuze calls time-images—is more difficult to say, though the close relation of the time-images to the affection-image and small form action-image suggest to me that the theory will need to be extended in similar ways rather than requiring a complete reformulation.

11 Mark Richards, 'Film Music Themes: Analysis and Corpus Study,' *Music Theory Online* 22.1 (2016), www.mtosmt.org/issues/mto.16.22.1/mto.16.22.1.richards.html (consulted August 10, 2022). A full theme is not always stated, and indeed in this scene from *Yankee Doodle Dandy* the ABAC form of the original song is changed to eliminate the repetition of the second A and reworks C into the conclusion of the scene. But the new arrangement presents the theme as a grammatical unit. It does not sound broken or cut off even if the form is in a sense incomplete (being grammatical does not, for instance, require a cadence, if for instance the music covers a transition into the next scene).

12 Martin Marks, 'Music, Drama, Warner Brothers: The Cases of *Casablanca* and *The Maltese Falcon*,' in James Buhler, Caryl Flinn, and David Neumeyer (eds.), *Music and Cinema* (Hannover, NH: Wesleyan University Press, 2000), 161–186, esp. 174–177.

13 Rebecca Fülöp, 'Heroes, Dames, and Damsels in Distress: Constructing Gender Types in Classical Hollywood Film Music,' PhD diss. (University of Michigan, 2012), 31 and 34–35.

14 This is to say that when leitmotivic incipits are used, they tend to appear in definitive form or one tilted through orchestration toward romance (i.e., string dominated scoring) if the romantic form is not also the definitive form of leitmotif.

15 Fülöp, 'Heroes, Dames, and Damsels in Distress,' 38.

16 Brian Taves, *The Romance of Adventure: The Genre of Historical Adventure Movies* (Jackson: University Press of Mississippi, 1993), 123.

17 I say nominal, because though its structuring extent is 16 measures, the actual length has been considerably altered.

18 Kathryn Kalinak, *Settling the Score: Music and the Classical Hollywood Film* (Madison: University of Wisconsin Press, 1992), 66–110; Buhler, *Theories of the Soundtrack*, 127–136.

19 The names of the themes for *Now, Voyager* are quite unsettled with scholars identifying at least three different themes as 'Charlotte's theme.' Kate Daubney, *Max Steiner's* Now, Voyager: *A Film Score Guide* (Westport, CT: Greenwood Press, 2000); Charles Leinberger, 'Thematic Variation and Key Relationships: Charlotte's Theme in Max Steiner's Score for *Now, Voyager*,' *Journal of Film Music* 1.1 (2002): 5–17; Heather Laing, *The Gendered Score: Music in 1940s Melodrama and the Woman's Film* (Aldershot: Ashgate Press, 2007), 31–65.

In a situation of such difference in scholarly opinion, I see no reason that I should not go with names that make sense with the narrative as I understand it.
20 Frank Lehman, *Hollywood Harmony: Musical Wonder and the Sound of Cinema* (New York: Oxford University Press, 2018), 35–37, esp. Fig. 1.5).
21 Deleuze, *Cinema 1*, 91.
22 Leinberger, 'Thematic Variation and Key Relationships,' 11.
23 Buhler and Neumeyer, *Hearing the Movies*.
24 Deleuze, *Cinema 1*, 87, 101. See also Deleuze, *Cinema 2: The Time-Image*, trans. Hugh Tomlinson and Robert Galeta (Minneapolis: University of Minnesota Press, 1989), 238. Deleuze, *Cinema 1*, 87.

CONTRIBUTORS

Janet Bourne is Assistant Professor of Music at University of California, Santa Barbara. She received a PhD in music theory and cognition from Northwestern University, Illinois, and was a Mellon postdoctoral fellow at Bates College, Maine. She combines traditional music-theoretic tools with concepts and methodologies from cognitive science and cognitive linguistics. She has a co-authored article with Robert Gjerdingen 'Schema Theory as a Construction Grammar' and a single-authored article 'Perceiving Irony in Music: The Problem in Beethoven's String Quartets,' both published in *Music Theory Online*. Her work on music cognition and theory pedagogy appears in the *Norton Guide to Teaching Music Theory*, *Frontiers in Neuroscience*, and *Music in the Social and Behavioral Sciences*.

James Buhler teaches music and film sound at the University of Texas, Austin. He is the author of *Theories of the Soundtrack*, co-author of *Hearing the Movies*, and an editor of *Music and Cinema, Music in Action Film: Sounds Like Action!*, and *Voicing the Cinema*.

Juan Chattah is Associate Professor of Music at the Frost School of Music, University of Miami. His research delves into music's impact on cognitive capacities and explores musical multimedia through the lenses of semiotics and neuropsychology. In his book, *Film Music: Cognition to Interpretation*, he draws on models from the humanities and the sciences to explore the dynamic counterpoint between a film's soundtrack, its visuals and narrative, and the audience's perception and construction of meaning, unveiling the thrilling interplay that breathes life into our cinematic experiences.

Rebecca M. Doran Eaton is Senior Lecturer in Music Theory at Texas State University. Her research on minimalism, tempo, gender, and film has been presented at conferences including SMT and AMS, and is published in *The Ashgate Research Companion to Minimalist and Postminimalist Music*, *Music and the Moving Image*, and is forthcoming in the *Oxford Handbook on Music and Television*. A theorist-composer, her works have been performed by groups including the University of Louisville Symphony Orchestra and Vox Musica.

Erik Heine is Professor of Music at Oklahoma City University, specializing in film music and music theory pedagogy. He is the author of the books *James Newton Howard's Signs: A Film Score Guide* and *The Music of the How to Train Your Dragon Trilogy: A Guide to the Scores of John Powell*, along with several book chapters, articles, and liner notes concerning film music. He also regularly contributes to *Film Score Monthly Online* and is a member of the International Film Music Critics Association (IFMCA).

Frank Lehman is Associate Professor of Music at Tufts University, Massachusetts. His publications include *Hollywood Harmony: Musical Wonder and the Sound of Cinema*, the 'Complete Catalogue of the Musical Themes of Star Wars,' and articles in *Music Theory Spectrum*, *Music Analysis*, *Music Theory Online*, and more. He is active in the public musicology community and has had work featured in the *Chronicle of Higher Education*, NPR, *The Boston Globe*, *The Washington Post*, and *The New York Times*.

Charity Lofthouse is Associate Professor of Music at Hobart and William Smith Colleges, New York. She received degrees in vocal performance and music theory from Oberlin Conservatory and a PhD in music theory from the CUNY Graduate Center. Her publications include work on Shostakovich and on the film compositions of Clint Eastwood. Before joining the faculty of Hobart and William Smith Colleges, Charity taught at Baruch and Hunter Colleges and at Oberlin Conservatory. In addition to activities as a music theorist, Lofthouse continues to perform as a composer, singer, and keyboardist, most recently giving vocal recitals at the Graduate Center, CUNY, and performing as a soloist at Union Temple Brooklyn, Holy Trinity Lutheran Church, and Trinity Wall Street, in New York City.

Táhirih Motazedian is Assistant Professor of Music at Vassar College, New York. Her book, *Key Constellations: Interpreting Tonality in Film* (2023), was published by the University of California Press. She has published (and has forthcoming) articles and chapters on a range of topics, including Sergei Eisenstein's production of *Die Walküre*, the 'heartstring schema' in film and nineteenth-century music, Holst's *The Planets*, Shostakovich's second violin concerto, and Tchaikovsky's *Swan Lake* in the film *Black Swan*. She holds a PhD in music theory from Yale University. Before her career in music theory, Táhirih was a planetary scientist at NAS and a mission operations specialist.

Scott Murphy is Professor of Music Theory at the University of Kansas. His contributions to screen music theory appear in the *Journal of Music Theory*, *Music Theory Spectrum*, and other journals and books. He has received two publication awards from the Society of Music Theory for his work on the music of Brahms, and the classical composers on which his other published analyses focus range from J.S. Bach and Clara Schumann to Myaskovsky and Penderecki.

Chelsea Oden is an instructor of music theory at Adams State University, Colorado. She earned her PhD in music theory from the University of Oregon in 2021. Her work on timbre in film music is part of a broader research interest in the role of music in cinematic moments that toy with physics. She has presented her research nationally and internationally at conferences in film music, music theory, and musicology.

Andrew S. Powell is Lecturer of Theory and Aural Skills at Auburn University, Alabama. His research specializes in the relationship between music and narrative in multimedia through the lens of transformational processes, with particular emphasis on interactive dramas and branching narrative media. His writings and presentations have explored the relationship of music, viewer/player, and diegesis in film and video games, and he is currently serving as a co-editor of a forthcoming collection that explores the intersection of film and video game music.

Mark Richards is an independent researcher who received his PhD in Music Theory from the University of Toronto, Ontario, and taught at Florida State University and the University of Lethbridge, Alberta. Richards' research has been widely presented and published in book chapters and in journals such as *Music Theory Spectrum*, *Music Analysis*, and *Music Theory Online*. While his previous work focused on Beethoven, classical form, and harmony in popular music, he now specializes in the analysis of film music. He currently teaches online courses on the theory and composition of film music at his *Film Music Notes* website.

INDEX

Films are indexed in full under the title; entries for composers and directors indicate discussion of the person rather than only the work, with cross-references to film titles as appropriate. Tables (bold) and figures/examples (italics) are indexed only when they provide substantive information about a topic not otherwise discussed on that page.

2001: A Space Odyssey (1968) 232–233, 235, 236–238
2010: The Year We Make Contact (1984) 232–238, 243, 245–246n16, 246nn17–18, 246nn20–21

Abrams, J.J. 83; see also *Star Wars: Episode VII – The Force Awakens* (2015); *Star Wars: Episode IX – The Rise of Skywalker* (2019)
Adams, Brett 40
Adams, John 216, *217*, 218
added value (Chion) 97
Adorno, Theodor V. x, xiii–xivn3, 131n9, 155n29
aFCG progression 58, *59*, **60–61**
Agawu, Kofi 88, 89
Agent Carter (2015–2016) 56
Alexander Nevsky (1938) xiii–xivn3, 40, 114–115, 131n9
Almén, Byron 183
Also Sprach Zarathustra (Strauss) 233, 237, 243, 246n17
amplified agitato 27–28
animation 181–182; see also *Batman: The Animated Series* (1992–1995)

Ant-Man (2015) 56
Arnold, David 52–53
Arrival (2016) 140–144, 153n14
Avengers, The (2012) 46–47, 52, 53, 62n10

Babbitt, Milton 245n10, 246n18
Baby Driver (2017): centrality of music in 156, *157*, 158–162, 163–164, 168–169, 171; key in 156, 158, 160–162, 165–168, 171
'Baby Driver' (Simon & Garfunkel) 162, 167–168, 171n6
'Baby Let Me Take You' (The Detroit Emeralds) 162, *163–164*
Barry, John 52
Batman (1989) 113, 149, 178
Batman films (Nolan) 28
Batman: Mask of the Phantasm (1993) 177, 178, 180
Batman: The Animated Series (1992–1995) 173–198, 199n9, 201n25
Batman vs. Superman: Dawn of Justice (2016) 54
Beach, David 169

beats per minute (BPM) 20, 22–24, 132n20; *see also* tempo
Beautiful Mind, A (2001) 22, 29, **30**, 31–33, **34–35**, 36–38, 39, 40–41
Beetlejuice (1988) 128–129, *130*
'Bellbottoms' (The Jon Spencer Blues Explosion) 156, *157*, 158, 162, 168
Bombshell (2019) 59
Bourne, Janet xii, 20, 112
Bowen, José Antonio 40
Brahms, Johannes 110, *111*, 116, 132n14
Breakfast at Tiffany's (1961) 112
Bribitzer-Stull, Matthew 177
Buhler, James xiii, 24–25, 98, 106n11
Burton, Tim 178; *see also Batman* (1989); *Beetlejuice* (1988); *Edward Scissorhands* (1990); *Nightmare Before Christmas, The* (1993)
Burwell, Carter 97

Captain Blood (1935) 258–260
Casablanca (1942): Reunion Scene 249, *250*, 251, *252*, 253–257, 272; After Hours Scene 266–267, *268*, 269–270, 272; Second Visit Scene 270, *271*, 272; compared to *Now, Voyager* xiii, 266–267, 273–274
Casino Royale (2006) 52–53
cathartic ostinato 27–28
Charlotte's Web (1973) 112
Chattah, Juan xiii, 5, 25–26, 32, 96, 113, 115, 203
Childhood topic 92, *93*, 94–95, 96, 100–104
Chion, Michel 97, 114
chromatic mediants 46–50, 205, 207–209, 210, 214, 223, 236; *see also* $M_8 9M_\emptyset$ progression; 'MnM' labeling (harmonic analysis)
Chuck (2007) 53
Citizen Kane (1941) 145, 154n21
Close Encounters of the Third Kind (1977) 144–146, 154n23
Cobweb, The (1955) 203, 244n1
Cohn, Richard 57–58, 116, 118, 235, 246n22
'Come and Get Your Love' (Redbone) 149
compilation scores 146–150; *see also Baby Driver* (2017)
Copland, Aaron 248–249, 251, 253, 254, 273, 274
Cox, Arnie 4

Darcy, Warren 134–135, 136–137, 144
Davis, Don 215–216; *see also Matrix, The* (1999)
Davis, Richard 21
DAWs (digital audio workstations) 21, 23–24
Day the Earth Stood Still, The (1951) 17
DC Extended Universe (DCEU) 53–55, 58; *see also specific films*
'Debora' (T. Rex) **166**, 167, 171n5
Deleuze, Gilles 254, 265, 274, 275n10
Desplat, Alexandre 99, 105, 108n63; *see also Harry Potter and the Deathly Hallows, Part 2* (2011); *Little Women* (2019)
diachrony 57–59, **60–61**
dialogic form: as analytical framework for film music 136, 150–151; defined 135–136; and popular song underscoring 147–151; rotational form 136–144, 148–150, 151; teleological genesis 136, 14–147, 151
diegetic boundary 8–11, 149, 155n28, 161–162, 249, 267
discursive themes 64, *65–66*, 67, **70–71**, 75, 78
Doctor Strange (2016) 56
Donnelly, K. J. 10–11, 146
double tresillo 129, 133nn27–28
Dumbo (1941) 112

'Easy' (The Commodores) 165–166, 168, 171n4
Eaton, Rebecca M. Doran xii, 13, 114
Edward Scissorhands (1990) 110, *111*
Eisenstein, Sergei xiii–xivn3, 40, 114–115, 131n9, 251
Eisler, Hanns x, xiii–xivn3, 131n9, 155n29
Elferen, Isabella van 11
Elfman, Danny 178; *see also Batman* (1989); *Beetlejuice* (1988); *Edward Scissorhands* (1990); *Justice League* (2017); *Nightmare Before Christmas, The* (1993)
embodiment 4–5, 11, 13, 25

Fales, Cornelia 2
Fantastic Four (2015) 56
fantastical gap (Stilwell) 10–11, 223n3; *see also* diegetic boundary

Fastest Consistent Pulse Per Minute (FCPPM) 24, 31–33, 36–38, 40–41; see also tempo
Feige, Kevin 54
Feminine Romantic Cliché (FRC) 257–258, 261; see also love themes
film music analysis, history of ix–xi; see also Copland, Aaron; Eisenstein, Sergei
filmmaking processes 21–22, 38–42, 169–171, 245n5
Fincher, David see *Zodiac* (2007)
Fink, Robert 24
Flash, The (TV series, 2014–2023) 54
form xii, 64–66, 134–136, 150–151; see also dialogic form; leitmotifs; thematic transformation
Formenlehre xi, xii
Forte, Allen 210
franchises, music in 176–177; see also specific franchises
Friedhofer, Hugo 226, 245n4
Friedman, Lester 135–136
Frye, Northrop 183–186, 191–192, 198, 200n17; see also mythoi (Frye)
Frymoyer, Johanna 90
Fülöp, Rebecca 257–258

Giacchino, Michael 56–57; see also *Inside Out* (2015); *Ratatouille* (2007)
Glass, Paul 226, 245n4
Glass, Philip 25, 26–27, 56
Good, the Bad, and the Ugly, The (1966) 17, 20
Göransson, Ludwig 97
Gorbman, Claudia 87, 98, 107n33
grammatical themes: examples of 69, 70–71, 73–74, 76, 79–80, 81–82; function of 64–65, 67–68
Guardians of the Galaxy (2014) 55, 149
Guardians of the Galaxy Vol. 2 (2017) 56

Halfyard, Janet 113, 115
'Harlem Shuffle' (Bob & Earl) 159, 166–167
harmonic analysis see chromatic mediants; key; 'MnM' labeling (harmonic analysis); neo-Riemannian theory; post-tonal music; Roman numeral analysis

Harry Potter films xii, 5–6, 11, **12**, 13–17; see also specific films
Harry Potter and the Sorcerer's Stone (2001) 7
Harry Potter and the Chamber of Secrets (2002) 5, 9, 10
Harry Potter and the Prisoner of Azkaban (2004) 5, 7, 8, **12**, 13–15
Harry Potter and the Order of the Phoenix (2007) **12**, 15–16
Harry Potter and the Half-Blood Prince (2009) 17
Harry Potter and the Deathly Hallows, Part 2 (2011) 1, **12**, 16–17
Hatten, Robert 88, 90, 96, 162
Heine, Erik xiii, 46–47, 246n19
Henry Danger (2014–2020) 57
Hepokoski, James 134–135, 136–137, 144, 151
hermeneutics 28–29, 95, 151
'heroic' chord progressions xii, 46–47, 51–57, 58–59, **60–61**, 214, 220; see also chromatic mediants; $M_8 9 M_\emptyset$ progression
Herrmann, Bernard ix, 63, 137–140, 145, 153n10, 153n13, 217
Hill, Andy 218
Hook (1991) 95
Horner, James 29, 40–41; see also *Beautiful Mind, A* (2001)
horror film 106n27, 202–203, 222; see also *It* (2017); *Signs* (2002)
Hours, The (2002) 26–27
How to Train Your Dragon 2 (2016) 150
Howard, James Newton 28, 210, 211; see also *Signs* (2002)
Howard, Ron see *Beautiful Mind, A* (2001)
Hyams, Peter see *2010: The Year We Make Contact* (1984)

icon (semiotics) 7–8, 17–18
Inception (2010) 28
index (semiotics) 7–8, 17–18
Inside Out (2015) 92, *93*
instrumentation see timbre
integrated soundtracks 156, 158–161, 171; see also *Baby Driver* (2017)
Iron Man films 53, 54
It (2017) 203, 204–210, 223n3
Ives, Charles 241, 243

Jackendoff, Ray 117
James Bond films 52–53
Jeff Who Lives at Home (2011) 95, 96
Jóhannsson, Jóhann 140–141; see also *Arrival* (2016)
Johnson, Mark 23
Johnson, Rian 85n17; see also *Star Wars: Episode VIII – The Last Jedi* (2017)
Jónsi (Jón Thor Birgisson) 150
Justice League (2017) 54–55

Kalinak, Kathryn 95
Keller, Hans ix
Kendall, Roger 3, 13
key: in *Baby Driver* 156, 158, 160–162, 165–168, 171; in film music analysis xii, 169–171
King Kong (2005) 127
Kingsman trilogy (2014–2021) 53
Klein, Michael 183
Klein, Norman 181–182, 195
Korngold, Erich see *Captain Blood* (1935)
Kracauer, Siegfried 251

Laberinto del fauno, El (2006) 110, 111, 113, 118–124
Lakoff, George 23
Lavengood, Megan 2
Lehman, Frank: on cinematic listening 155n29; harmonic analysis by 29–33, 52, 204–205, 235–236; thematic analysis by 27–33, 40, 44n28, 68, 262
leitmotifs: in *Batman: The Animated Series* 174–175, 177–181, 187–192, 196–198; categories of 63–66; definition of 68; as element of franchises 176–177; for good and evil 66–68, 69, **70–71**, 72–83, 177–178, 179–180; in the *Star Wars* films xii, 63–69, **70–71**, 72–83; and topics 96–97; see also discursive themes; grammatical themes; motto themes; thematic structure; thematic transformation; theme
leit-timbre 8
Leong, Daphne 116, 118
Lerdahl, Fred 117
Lerner, Neil 202
Lidov, David 31
Liszka, James Jakób 183, 184, 200n17

Little Women (1994) 99, 100–101, 103, 104–105, 108n60
Little Women (2019) 96, 99, 101–104, 105, 109n65
Liu, Anan 40
Lofthouse, Charity xii
Lord of the Rings films (2001–2003) 3–4, 5, 56, 58, 97
love themes 257–260, 263–266, 273; see also Feminine Romantic Cliché (FRC)
lullabies 110–113

M3 progression 46–50, 207–208; see also chromatic mediants
$M_89M_{\emptyset}$ progression 50, 51–57, 58–59, **60–61**
McClelland, Clive 24
McDonald, Hugh 176
Man of Steel (2013) 53–54, 58
Mancini, Henry 21, 40, 41
Mandalorian, The (2019–) 97
Marianelli, Dario 52
Martens, Peter 23, 24
Marvel Cinematic Universe (MCU) 46, 53–54, 55–57; see also specific films
Matrix, The (1999) 203–204, 214–222
medial extraction (rotational form) 148
metamorphosis 173–178, 180–182, 184–186, 191–195, 196–199, 200–201n20, 200n17; see also thematic transformation
meter: analytical methodologies for 113–120, 129–131; and musical topics xii, 113, 129; and narrative 115–120, 121–126, 127–131; perception of 113–115, 116–117, 119–120; pulse layers of 113–114, 115–120, 132n20; see also *Zeitnetz*
mickey-mousing 8, 44n23, 114, 253
minimalism 24, 25–28, 31, 104
minimalist mathematical genius topic (MGT) 25–28, **30**, 40–41, 44n28
Mirka, Danuta 88, 90
mise-en-bande 170, 172n10
'MnM' labeling (harmonic analysis) 49–50, 51–57, 58–59, **60–61**, 218, 224n14
Monelle, Raymond 88, 89, 90, 95

Morricone, Ennio see *Good, the Bad, and the Ugly, The* (1966)
Morton, Lawrence ix
Motazedian, Táhirih xii
motto themes: examples of 69, **70–71**, 72, 74–75, 76, 77, 78, 79, 81–82; function of 64, 65, 67–68
'Mrs. Robinson' (Simon & Garfunkel) 147
Ms. Marvel (2022) 56
Murphy, Scott xii, 116–117, 128, 204, 219, 220–221, 224n14, 235–236
music theory, history of ix–xi
mythoi (Frye) 183–186, 191–192, 193, 195, 198, 200n17

Navarrete, Javier see *Laberinto del fauno, El* (2006)
Neely, Blake 54
neo-Riemannian theory: and *2010: The Year We Make Contact* 234–237; as analytical method for film music 57–58, 61n4, 204–205, 214, 223, 246n19; and *A Beautiful Mind* 29, 31, 32–33, 36–37, 45n36; and *It* (2017) 203, 204–207, 208, 210; and tempo analysis 29, 31, 32–33, 36–37
Neumeyer, David 24–25, 97–98, 106n11, 107n33, 251
neutral music 248–249, 251, 253–254; see also underscore, poles of
Newman, Thomas 99; see also *James Bond films*; *Little Women* (1994); *Shawshank Redemption, The* (1994)
Newsies (1993) 129
Newton Howard, James see Howard, James Newton
Nightmare Before Christmas, The (1993) 124–127
No Time to Die (2021) 53
Nolan, Christopher see *Batman* films (Nolan); *Inception* (2010)
Norman, Monty 52
Now, Voyager (1942) xiii, 260–266, 267, 273–274

Oden, Chelsea xii, 20
open-close (rotational form) 148–149

Pan's Labyrinth (2006) see *Laberinto del fauno, El* (2006)
pantriadicism 204–210
'Partyman' (Prince) 149

Peirce, Charles Sanders 6–7; see also semiotics
perception: of form 135, 147; of meter 113–115, 116–117, 119–120; of tempo 20–22, 25, 116, 132n20; of timbre 2–5; of topics 87–88, 92, 95–98, 109n66
polychords 203, 216, 217–222, 223, 239
polystylism 203–204, 215–218
pop music soundtracks 147–151, 154nn27–28; see also *Baby Driver* (2017)
post-tonal music: analytical methodologies for xiii, 203–204, 222–223; association with horror films 202–203, 222, 225; in *It* (2017) 204–210; in *The Matrix* 215–222; in *Signs* 204–210; see also neo-Riemannian theory; serialism
Powell, Andrew S. xii
Prokofiev, Sergei see *Alexander Nevsky* (1938)
Psycho (1960) 137–139, 140, 153n12
Pulp Fiction (1994) 150
Puschak, Evan 11, 13

Ratatouille (2007) 52
Ratner, Leonard 88
Remote Control Productions 23–24
Repo! The Genetic Opera (2008) 127–128
Richards, Mark xii, 255
Richter, Max 141–142, 154n15
Rodman, Ronald 96, 170
Roman numeral analysis 48–49, 205, 209–210, 214
Rosenman, Leonard 203, 244n1
rotational extension 148, 150
rotational form 136–144, 148–150, 151; see also dialogic form

Sargent, Joseph see *Taking of Pelham One Two Three, The* (1974)
Saussure, Ferdinand de 57–58
'Scarborough Fair' (Simon & Garfunkel) 148–149
Schneller, Tom 144–145
Schoenberg, Arnold 203, 225, 244n1
semiotics xii, 6–8, 17–18, 90, 92, 151, 257; see also topics
serialism: in *2010: The Year We Make Contact* 233–238,

245–246n16; in *The Cobweb* 203; as film music technique xiii, 225–226, 243–244; in *The Matrix* 216–217; in *The Taking of Pelham One Two Three* 227–229, 230, 231–232, 245n8, 245n16; in *Zodiac* 239–241, 243, 246n16; see also post-tonal music
set theory 203, 210–214, *215*, 219, 223, 233–235, 246n19, 246n21
Shawshank Redemption, The (1994) 52
Shazam! (2019) 55
Shire, David: *2010: The Year We Make Contact* 232–238, 243, 245–246n16, 246n18, 246nn20–21; musical language of xiii, 225–226, 227, 233, 243, 245–246n16; *The Taking of Pelham One Two Three* 227–228, 229, 232, 243, 245n6, 245n16; *Zodiac* 239–240, 241–243, 246–247n24, 246n16; see also *2010: The Year We Make Contact* (1984); *Taking of Pelham One Two Three, The* (1974); *Zodiac* (2007)
Shore, Howard see *Lord of the Rings* films (2001–2003)
Shyamalan, M. Night see *Signs* (2002)
Signs (2002) 46, 203, 210–214, *215*
Silvestri, Alan see *Avengers, The* (2012)
Simon & Garfunkel 146, 148, 162, 167–168, 171n6
Skyfall (2012) 53
Slonimsky, Nicolas 245–246n16
Smith, Darren 127–128
Sobchack, Vivian 5
Society for Music Theory xi
Sonic Visualizer 23–24, 38–39
Sound of Music, The (1965) 112
'Sound of Silence, The' (Simon & Garfunkel) 148
Spectre (2015) 53
Spider-Man: Homecoming (2017) 56–57
Spider-Man: Into the Spider-Verse (2018) 57
Spielberg, Steven 144; see also *Close Encounters of the Third Kind* (1977)
Star Trek: The Original Series (1966–1969) 96
Star Trek: Discovery (2017–) 59
Star Wars films: good and evil in 66–68, 69, **70–71**, 72–83, 84n3,

208; leitmotifs across xii, 20, 63–69, **70–71**, 72–83, 86n26; see also specific films
Star Wars: Episode I – The Phantom Menace (1999) 7, 70, 74–76
Star Wars: Episode II – Attack of the Clones (2002) 70, 76–77
Star Wars: Episode III – Revenge of the Sith (2005) **70–71**, 77–78
Star Wars: Episode IV – A New Hope (1977) 46, 69, 70, 72
Star Wars: Episode V – The Empire Strikes Back (1980) 70, 78–80
Star Wars: Episode VI – Return of the Jedi (1983) 70, 80–81
Star Wars: Episode VII – The Force Awakens (2015) 71, 72–73
Star Wars: Episode VIII – The Last Jedi (2017) 71, 73–74, 85n17
Star Wars: Episode IX – The Rise of Skywalker (2019) 71, 81–83
Stardust (2007) 127
Steiner, Max 105, 114, 248–249, 251, 253, 266; see also *Casablanca* (1942); *Now, Voyager* (1942)
stereotypes 98
Stilwell, Robynn 10, 151, 155n29, 223n3
Strauss, Richard 233, 237, 243, 246n17
Stravinsky, Igor 217
Suicide Squad (2016) 54
superhero films see *Batman: The Animated Series* (1992–1995); DC Extended Universe (DCEU); Marvel Cinematic Universe (MCU)
symbol (semiotics) 7–8, 17–18
synchresis (Chion) 97
synchronization 21–22, 38–42, 114–115, 156, 158–162, 168–169, 196–197, 267, 269

Tagg, Philip 87, 89–90
Taking of Pelham One Two Three, The (1974) 226–229, 230, 231–232, 243, 245n6, 245nn8–9, 245n16
Taves, Brian 257
Teenage Mutant Ninja Turtles (2014) 57
teleological genesis 136, 144–147, 151; see also dialogic form
Temperley, David 23
tempo: in *A Beautiful Mind* (2001) 30, 31–33, 36, 37–38, 39–41; and the filmmaking process 21–22,

38–42; and harmonic analysis 29, 31–33, 36–37; hermeneutic analysis of 28–29; measurements of 22–24, 38–40, 43n12, 43n14, 132n20; perception of 20–22, 25, 116, 132n20; as starting point for analysis xii, 23, 33; and topics 22, 24–28; *see also* meter
The Graduate (1967) 146, 148
thematic structure 64–66; *see also* discursive themes; grammatical themes; motto themes
thematic transformation xii, 174–181, 185–186, 187–195, 196–199, 201n25; *see also* metamorphosis
theme xii, 257–260, 261–266, 267, 269–270, 272, 273; *see also* dialogic form; leitmotifs; thematic transformation
timbre: definition of 1–2; and the diegetic boundary 8–9; in the *Harry Potter* films 1, 5–10, 11, **12**, 13–17; meaning conveyed by xii, 1, 3–6, 13–18, 151, 160; perceptions of 2–5; semiotic approach to 6–8, 11, 17–18; and topics 20, 28, 90, 112; vocabulary for 1–2, 13; of voices 4, 5, 7, 13, 112
Tiomkin, Dimitri 88
Tomorrow Never Dies (1997) 52
tonal design 169–171; *see also* key
tonality *see* key
tone color *see* timbre
topics: analysis of 88–90, 92, 95–98; categories of 89–90, **91–92**, 92, 97–98; definition of 87–88; and leitmotifs 96–97; in *Little Women* (1994 and 2019) 96, 99, 100–105; and meter xii, 113, 129; perceptions of 87–88, 92, 95, 97–98; semiotic approach to xii; and stereotypes 98; and tempo 22, 24–28; and timbre 20, 28, 90, 112; *see also* Childhood topic; minimalist mathematical genius topic (MGT)
topoi *see* topics
transposition (tonal) 165–167, 171n5; *see also* key
Tristan und Isolde (Wagner) 242–243
troping 96; *see also* topics
True Grit (2010) 97
twelve-tone music *see* serialism
Tyler, Brian 54

Unanswered Question, The (Ives) 241, 243
underscore, poles of xiii, 248–249, 251, 253–257, 273–274
United 93 (2006) 52

V for Vendetta (2005) 52
Väisälä, Olli 219
Vertigo (1958) 63, 139–140, 153n13
voices, timbre of 4, 5, 7, 13, 112

Wachowski, Lana and Lilly 215; *see also Matrix, The* (1999)
Waddell, Terrie 192
Wagner, Richard 242–243
Walker, Shirley 174, 178–179, 187–191, 196–198; *see also Batman: The Animated Series* (1992–1995)
Wallfisch, Benjamin 55, 205, 209, 223–224n7; *see also It* (2017)
Wallmark, Zachary 3, 13
Webern, Anton 246n18
Webster, Jamie Lynn 5
Williams, John: *Close Encounters of the Third Kind* 144, 154n23; conducting style of 42n7; *Harry Potter* films 5, 7; *Star Wars* films 63–67, 73, 82–83, 85n17, 86n26; *see also Close Encounters of the Third Kind* (1977); *Harry Potter and the Chamber of Secrets* (2002); *Harry Potter and the Prisoner of Azkaban* (2004); *Star Wars* films
Wonder Woman (2017) 55, 127
Wonder Woman 1984 (2020) 58
Wright, Edgar 167, 168–169; *see also Baby Driver* (2017)

X-Men films 57

Yankee Doodle Dandy (1942) 255, 257, 275n11

Zeitnetz 115–120, 121, 123, 126, 128–129; *see also* meter
Zimmer, Hans 25, 27–28, 41–42, 45n46, 53–54, 58, 128
Zodiac (2007) 238–243, 246–247n24, 246n16